RACING CRAZY

THE BEST OF DAVID ASHFORTH

RACING POST

This book is dedicated

To the wonderfully strange bunch of characters, human and equine,
who make horseracing so much fun. Thank you for all your help,
over many years.

Bookmakers might like to thank me for all my help.

Published in 2012 by Racing Post Books
Axis House, Compton, Newbury, Berkshire, RG20 6NL

10 9 8 7 6 5 4 3 2 1

A catalogue record for this book is available from the British Library.

ISBN 978-1-908216-21-2

Cover designed by Jay Vincent and Sarah Chubb
Designed by Fiona Pike

Printed and bound in Great Britain by the MPG Books Group

www.racingpost.com/shop

CONTENTS

IN THE BEGINNING

Poised to knock over my cup of tea.

In the beginning was the word, and the word was 'Ashworth'. *The Sporting Life*, 10 August 1988: 'David Ashworth takes a look at some equine enigmas and eccentrics.' Ashworth, Ashford, Ashcroft. It's always been like that.

Two years later, I joined *The Sporting Life* full-time and, in 1992, began a weekly column. Shortly afterwards, I received a postcard from a reader. It featured a gorilla with the gorilla's head replaced by mine. The caption read, 'Some people think David Ashworth should keep his fucking mouth shut.' When I showed it to some friends, they thought it was fair comment, and not a bad likeness.

Later, when I went to Louisville to cover the Kentucky Derby, I was sitting in the press room tapping away at my laptop when I knocked my carton of coffee over the keyboard. I could tell that it didn't like it because it hissed and steamed alarmingly, then died, which was what I wanted to do.

My advice to aspiring journalists is always to put your drink behind your computer, and don't drink too much while you're writing. Sometimes, I used to work in the evening, in company with a bottle of wine. The resulting articles were wonderfully amusing. Unfortunately, on reading them again the next morning, it was necessary to put them straight into the waste paper bin, with the rest of the rubbish.

What follows is a selection of articles from *The Sporting Life* (1988 to 1998) and *Racing Post* (1998 to 2011). In my book *Hitting the Turf* (1996), I drew on my early work for *The Sporting Life* and have tried to avoid repeating myself, sometimes successfully. If you want to check, copies are probably available from Amazon, for about 1p.

Although I have written many serious articles about the racing industry they do not appear here because it would be nice if readers survived beyond the first paragraph. I hope you manage to. After all, it was you who decided to buy the thing. There must be something worth reading in it somewhere (see betting systems, law of averages).

AN AFFAIR FULL OF LOVE BYTES AND MICRO SOFT WORDS *Racing Post*, 1 March 2007

I'm thinking of proposing to my computer. After all, we spend an enormous amount of time together, and hardly exchange a cross word. The sex isn't brilliant, but then the computer's young, and I'm 58. It's a bit like Anna Nicole Smith and J. Howard Marshall, with the silicon but without the money.

I had a stormy relationship with my previous computer, which broke down irretrievably after flashing incredibly irritating error messages at me. The computer had some articles of mine that I needed, and wouldn't give them back. I tried begging, I tried counselling through AOL, and I tried shouting abuse, but nothing worked. In the end I gave the computer a final warning and then took it to a rubbish tip near Slough.

I think the (Microsoft) word got around because its successor has behaved impeccably. Most of the time it just hums quietly, occasionally making noises that mean it's either reinforcing its defences against fatal viruses, or has just succumbed to one.

It's a terrific partner, endlessly supportive. It's doing this for me now. I've no idea how, but then I don't understand telephones, either, or electricity, or why people go shopping.

It's not perfect. For instance, it has an annoying habit of slyly taking a word that is spelt correctly, and misspelling it, without telling me. Also, if you type 'racegoer' – there, it's done it again – it insists that it's two words when I want to present it as one. Hang on, while I show it who's boss.

The computer also has some strange ideas about apostrophes. If I type 'there is nothing that fits the bill' it puts an apostrophe in fit's, which is ridiculous. I expect it's the computer's idea of a joke, but I wish it wouldn't do it. I've told it not to, but it won't be told.

What's more worrying is that, despite lots of practice, the computer is still hopeless at betting. Actually, that's not quite true. It does quite well on Betfair but is a dead loss at spread betting.

I had hoped that, if the computer and I were to have a future together, it would show that it cared. It could show that it cared by refusing access to Sporting Index and displaying a message reading, 'It's for your own good' or 'You're chasing again, aren't you?' or 'Please ring GamCare on 0845 6000 133. Now.'

But it doesn't. What it does do is protect me from e-mails that it thinks aren't worthy of my attention, by filing them in a folder called 'Spam.' Every now and again, I notice this folder and, when I open it, half the messages are from racing organisations. I think my computer must be a puritan. It doesn't seem to like the Association of British Bookmakers at all.

It keeps a list of my favourite websites, which reveals that my main interests in life are the world clock, used books, and court hearings. I particularly like hmcourtsservice.gov.uk, which is indispensable for keeping in touch with people in horseracing.

It's a quiet day on the racing front today. Harry Findlay [a huge punter] is applying for a trial date to be set for his action against Cantor Index Ltd [a spread betting firm] & ors, while the Earl of Cadogan [a wealthy racehorse owner] is in action against 26 Cadogan Square Limited. I hope Cadogan doesn't have to sell his horses to pay for it. There is also 'the matter of Inertia Partnership,' which is bound to drag on.

Maybe it's best if we just live together.

1
COURT 13

Kieren Fallon and Lynda Ramsden take to the Court.

Horseracing has a lot to offer as a spectator sport, especially in court, where it spends an enormous amount of time, and money. Some of the happiest days of my working life have been spent in the High Court and the Old Bailey, enjoying the legal theatre, and the congenial company of barristers.

When you have been in court every day for weeks, or months, a camaraderie develops. Racing tends to indulge in long hearings, for which I am grateful as, I feel sure, are the lawyers, if not the juries. One thing I have learnt is that, in court, it is much better to observe than to participate.

In 1998, racing society gathered at the Royal Courts of Justice in the Strand for a libel action brought against Mirror Group Newspapers, the publishers of *The Sporting Life*, by reigning champion jockey Kieren Fallon and Lynda and Jack Ramsden, a trainer and her gambler husband. The action was prompted by an article dated 11 May 1995, written by Alastair Down, in which he accused them of cheating. The previous day, Top Cees, trained by Ramsden and ridden by Fallon, had won the Chester Cup in impressive fashion, in sharp contrast to his performance when finishing fifth in the Swaffham Handicap at Newmarket on 18 April. Down alleged that, on the latter occasion, Top Cees was a 'non-trier.'

THE FIRST DAY *The Sporting Life*, 4 February 1998

Court 13. Unlucky for someone. 'They're under orders and they're off,' but not quite yet, as a technician grapples with the video player, the first grapple in a day of grappling. The video player and its four satellite screens are going to figure more prominently in Court 13 than a television in an addict's living room.

Justice Morland appears from a secret door behind the bench and the court rises. The court is small and less well packed than the *Titanic*, which is just as well because, if many spectators arrived, there would be nowhere for them to sit. It is a nervous mixture of tradition and technology. Wood-panelled walls, shelves of law reports, stone colonnades, microphones and monitors.

The judge, in black, with white collar and cuffs, red sash, grey wig, sits down and Court 13 sits down with, but beneath, him. To his right is the jury, five women and seven men.

Patrick Milmo QC, for the plaintiffs, bespectacled, doubly grey hair and wig, begins. 'Keeayeron FalON,' he says, as if introducing someone exotic from Brazil, 'who rides racehorses. He rides racehorses rather well.' Milmo mentions Top Cees for the first of countless times. 'Top, T-O-P, Cees, C-E-E-S,' he spells, for the benefit of the jury. There are going to be many explanations for the benefit of the jury, as the mysterious world of horseracing meets 12 normal human beings.

'Don't hesitate to ask if you don't understand the evidence,' chimes in the judge, helpfully. 'I'm sure I won't understand parts of it.' It may be that His Lordship is not one of Victor Chandler's regulars.

There are regular contributions to the glossary – 'stewards, rather like referees,' 'apprentice race, a race for learner jockeys,' 'two out, two furlongs out. There are eight furlongs in a mile.'

The jury is introduced to the mysteries of Rule 151 and to the law of libel. Those who believed that guilt was something that had to be proven beyond reasonable doubt discover that, in a civil case such as libel, they are mistaken. A lesser burden of proof is required, on the balance of probabilities.

'Right, away we go,' says Milmo chirpily, with premature confidence in the audio-visual system. The first of many indistinct images of the Swaffham Handicap, run at Newmarket on 18 April 1995, appears on the screens. A juror reports that the lights are reflecting on the television. The lights are switched off. Justice Morland peers at his own screen. 'It looks as if it's been run in fog or mist. Is this the best you can do?'

Top Cees devotes the race to hiding, first behind an embankment and then behind the horses in front of him, although Milmo does his best to help the jury pick out the right horse. 'Have you picked out the horse?' he asks. 'About one, two, three, four, five, six, seven, eighth off the rails, behind a wall of horses. There's a chap waving his arm.' I think it may be a jockey. Whatever the outcome, the trial will be a triumph for the sheepskin-noseband.

The jury looks variously intent, concerned, bemused. I try to imagine them gathered together in a betting shop, but fail. I wonder if any of them had a thumping great bet on Top Cees in the Chester Cup. At 10.55am, when Mr Fallon walks in, no one sticks their thumb up and says, 'All right, Kieren?'

Lynda Ramsden enters the witness box and takes the oath, on a very small Bible. I cannot believe they would have allowed such a small Bible in the old days. I bet the Victorians had huge courtroom Bibles.

Mrs Ramsden, soon, like Jack, to be bespectacled, addresses her answers to the jury. Not a bad idea, since they are, as it were, the stewards in this case, albeit unpaid amateurs.

Mrs Ramsden is bright lemon in a sea of grey, broken only by one juror's red dress. She is the 'animal person' in her partnership with Jack Ramsden. They had bought Top Cees at a 'second-hand sale' in Newmarket and discovered that he was 'a bit of a monkey.'

We watch the Chester Cup, again. 'Channel 4 took a different view to the stewards,' says Milmo, 'led, it would seem, by a Mr McCririck. Does Mr McCririck have some role on Channel 4?' Mrs Ramsden is asked. 'Yes,' she replies. 'Namely?' 'Well, he talks a lot on it.'

It is a rare moment of humour in a serious, curious day. Curious to see members of racing society, bound by a common love for the sport, opposing each other in a London courtroom. You imagine them, afterwards, chatting to each other about the latest racing news. That figured, too. The jury was instructed not to be influenced by recent news stories of jockeys arrested, and of race-fixing.

The case, as they say, continues. By the time it is over, I don't think the jury will be very keen to see the Swaffham Handicap again.

DAY SIX *The Sporting Life*, 11 February 1998

This is a day full of gaps; split-second gaps, seven-second gaps, gaps opening and closing. Gaps to the left of Kieren Fallon, gaps to the right of Kieren Fallon. On, on, into the seven-second gap he rode. At least, that's what Mr Fallon says; Mr Richard Hartley QC begs to differ.

They differ for most of the day, which starts with a member of the Ramsdens' legal team tucking a copy of *Private Eye* under a pile of papers. Instead of begging leave to introduce an extract from Pseuds' Corner, the opposing side asks permission to introduce a video of the 1995 Cesarewitch. Permission granted.

Mr Hartley gets off to an encouragingly lively start. 'Has Mr Ramsden ever told you, don't be too busy or don't be too close?' 'Never,' replies Mr Fallon, declining to get the day off with a bang.

On this day of gaps, few are larger than the ones between Mr Hartley's questions and Mr Fallon's answers. The champion jockey sets the pace, and it is a slow one. He has a curious manner; dreamy, wide-eyed, as if bemused. There are long, idiosyncratic pauses, even after innocuous questions.

'We know that Major Ker was the stewards' secretary?' Fallon is asked by his own counsel. Time ticks by, as if Fallon is examining a particularly confusing delivery from Shane Warne. Finally, 'Yessir.' All is well. Patrick Milmo QC does not follow up with, 'Liar – it was Patrick Hibbert-Foy!'

Milmo and Hartley both wear spectacles, as does Mr Justice Morland, who wields his quiet authority with benign effectiveness. His interventions are to the point, concise, concluded with a distinctive, engaging smile, devoted mainly to the jurors, who I discover have to bring their own packed lunch.

Mr Hartley seizes on Fallon's witness statement, in which Fallon refers to having his 'first ride in public' on Top Cees. The implication, Hartley maintains, is that he had already ridden Top Cees on the gallops. 'Regardless of the way it's worded,' Fallon retorts, 'I had never sat on the horse before the Swaffham.'

'Is a lot to be gained by this analysis of Mr Fallon's statement?' the judge finally enquires, pointedly. Mr Hartley believes that there is. Mr Justice Morland agrees that that part of the witness statement be put to the jury, and then promptly advises the jury to be careful about witness statements and to concentrate on witness box testimony.

Mr Fallon's pause-ridden testimony perhaps provokes Mr Hartley into speaking for longer than he intends, as questions are repeated, rephrased. He battles on, into the gaps. The gaps, and the vexed question of Mr Fallon's vigour.

At 11.30am we watch our first video of the day. Man cannot live by the Swaffham Handicap alone, unless he is in Court 13, where they speak of little else. Later, Mr Hartley becomes apologetic. 'I hardly dare suggest we see another video,' he says, getting in his apology before Mr Milmo. 'I fear I won't be the most popular man in court if I say I would like us to see the Swaffham Handicap again.' But it doesn't stop him.

I have learnt something else about court procedure. Beware the barrister who proposes to speak 'briefly.' Few briefs are larger than a barrister's.

'You have now started mentioning all these horses names,' says the judge. 'I'm sure the jury have very good memories but ...' Dreams End, Trans Siberia, Polo

Kit, Tudor Island, Well Beloved. All have their part to play, mainly as the sandwich around a gap behind which lurks Top Cees.

Hartley and Fallon debate the gaps endlessly, finally coming to rest on what becomes known as 'the seven-second gap,' the one that Fallon and Top Cees enter.

We move on, fitfully, to the equally contentious issue of the vigour displayed by Fallon in addressing the gap. 'As soon as a gap appeared, I ask my horse to quicken,' says Fallon. 'I'm down behind my horse, I'm lower than most of the other jockeys, I'm asking.'

'No you're not,' insists Mr Hartley. 'The other jockeys have their arms fully outstretched.' He demonstrates what he means, without persuading seasoned racewatchers that he is a champion jockey in waiting.

'I'm under oath,' says Fallon, 'I'm telling the truth. As soon as the gap opened, I've picked him up and asked him to go for home. It's blatant how I've asked. You push and ask a horse to stretch.'

Mr Hartley is not persuaded. 'You're sitting there. You're not urging the horse.'

'Well, if you can't see it, you shouldn't be watching the video.'

Mr Justice Morland suggests a short break, to provide an interval between disagreements. We return to disagree about the Cesarewitch. Mr Hartley insists that Fallon was much more vigorous in the Cesarewitch than in the Swaffham. 'You are riding like the champion you are. Really going for it. Your whole body language is different. There is a sense of urgency.'

Mr Fallon, you will not be surprised to read, disagrees, slowly, quietly, but vigorously.

They finally find common ground on Fallon's disciplinary record. No stricture applied by Mr Hartley seems sufficient to satisfy Mr Fallon's contempt for his own behaviour. 'I have a terrible record,' says Fallon, 'appalling.'

'The worst of any jockey?' Hartley asks, hopefully. 'Probably,' replies Fallon.

Hartley reminds him of the low spots. Hitting horses around the head, hitting K. Rutter around the body, removing S. Webster's body from his horse. 'Awful, disgraceful, terrible.' That was just Fallon's opinion, expressed in his own, unique way. 'I regret all that. I am ashamed of it. I was younger.'

They move on to Captain Carat, and the explanation for his improved performance at Doncaster. 'Do you agree with Mr Ramsden?' 'Definitely, I've never known him to be wrong.'

And, soon, Fallon is out of the witness box and Mr Ramsden, briefly, is back in it. The contrast is striking. The crisp, concise 'yes,' combative, assertive, assured.

Mrs Ramsden and her pink outfit leave Court 13 for the day. I make my way to the Underground. 'Please mind the gap.'

DAY SEVEN *The Sporting Life*, **12 February 1998**

Joyce and Sheila arrived in London yesterday for a spot of shopping, theatre, and High Court libel. Spirits in Court 13 rise sharply. Joyce and Sheila are neither trainers nor jockeys. They will not be asked to look at a video of the Swaffham Handicap. We like them already.

Joyce goes first, a respectable looking grey-haired lady in a smart black tunic and skirt. Where others have sat, Joyce stands, transparently truthful, if inclined to smile more sweetly upon Mr Patrick Milmo QC, for the plaintiffs, than upon Mr Richard Hartley QC, for the defence.

'Joyce Ellis?' 'That's right.' We wait for Mr Milmo to ask, 'Any relation of Ruth Ellis, the last woman to be hanged?' but he doesn't ask.

Joyce reveals that she has worked at Chester racecourse since 1960, and never seen a Chester Cup. Too busy answering the telephone. I get the impression that it would be no use asking Mrs Ellis if she knows one in the first.

Mr Milmo invites Mrs Ellis to consult a blue file. Joyce consults it, but is not impressed. 'It is not a very good filing system,' she testifies, under oath, but she finds the copy of a report in *The Sporting Life* suggesting that the phone lines to the racecourse had been jammed with aggrieved punters following Top Cees' victory.

Does she, Mr Milmo inquires, recall receiving any telephone calls about the Chester Cup? 'Maybe one or two calls,' she concedes, 'nothing abusive.' 'Angry punters jammed the racecourse switchboard?' 'No way.'

Mr Hartley sympathises with the inevitable fallibility of Mrs Ellis's memory. Mrs Ellis gives the distinct impression that his sympathy is not required. 'I can remember what happened in 1969,' she says.

Mr Hartley chooses to ask about 1995, instead, and discovers that Mrs Ellis has perfect recall of the racecourse's telephone numbers; 323170 for the main switchboard, 323938 for the clerk of the course, 324880 for the stables. They do not try them to see if she is right.

Sheila Whittingham, a bit taller, a bit thinner, a bit bespectacled, good clear voice, shares the racecourse switchboard with Mrs Ellis. As to telephone calls on Chester Cup Day 1995, 'I recall only one. That was from a gentleman who said, "Luv, that horse shouldn't have won that race." So, I didn't argue with the gentleman.'

Mr Hartley probes gently, but unavailingly, provoking Mrs Whittingham into revealing that abusive telephone calls are not uncommmon, but generally confined to matters of a non-horse nature.

Video fatigue has overtaken Court 13. It has seeped into the jury, wormed its way along the public benches, infected Counsel. 'There is no need to watch the whole race, unless the jury would like to watch it again,' says Milmo. The jury returns a unanimous verdict, conveyed in the form of 12 smiles. But the video, like the garish yellow and pink highlighter pens to be found even on the judge's bench, cannot be denied. 'Shall we see the video?'

One of Mr Milmo's assistants rummages in the court's extensive collection and pushes a tape into the machine. I cling to the hope that Groucho Marx will appear on the screen in *A Day at the Races*, but he doesn't. It's the Swaffham again, followed by another debate about whether or not Mr Fallon was 'flat to the boards.'

Messrs Hartley and Adrian Maxwell, former jockey and trainer, now a witness, discuss the state of Mr Fallon's bottom. 'He drops his bottom,' insists Maxwell. 'He doesn't drop his bottom,' retorts Hartley. We stare at Mr Fallon's rapidly receding bottom, dropped or not.

I stare around the courtroom and count one bald head in the jury and two and a half in the rest of the court, all men. Mrs Ramsden, who is not bald, is wearing ultramarine. The top of Mr Milmo's wig has a yellowish tinge. Milmo, who is tall and slim, while Mr Hartley is shorter and stouter, without being stout, asks Maxwell, 'The December Sales. What time of the year is that?'

Maxwell chews the end of his spectacles while Mr Hartley makes a valiant attempt to pronounce the Prix Noailles, which he confesses 'has flummoxed me.' It's a nice word, flummoxed. I think it deserves to make a comeback.

Maxwell and Hartley argue about the comparative vigour of Fallon's riding in the Swaffham Handicap and in the Cesarewitch. Mr Hartley has a slightly aggrieved tone to his voice, as if all is not quite well, if not with the world, then with the witness's responses.

When Mr Hartley has stoppped arguing with Mr Maxwell, he starts arguing with Mr Stephen Williams about his riding of Captain Carat at Leicester. Williams seizes a Biro and hits the air in both backhand and forehand position. Like his use of the whip at Leicester, they are 'air shots.' 'I've tried my best to describe it as best as I can but obviously I'm not getting anywhere,' says Mr Williams.

We plod through the subsequent stewards' inquiries. Beware the barrister who says, 'I'll take you through this as quickly as I can,' a phrase that strikes fear into the hearts of those with a limited life expectancy.

'Thank you, Mr Williams,' says Mr Milmo, finally. 'You're welcome,' replies Mr Williams, breathing an audible sigh of relief.

Russ John Garritty is bolder in the box, firm of answer, short of hair, prone to frowning. He introduces an addition to the court's expanding racing dictionary, 'squaring one up'. This seems to be what you do to Top Cees when he has just dumped you. 'I squared him up with a kick in the belly but that didn't go according to plan. He resented that.' Yes, I suppose he would.

I wonder if they are going to show One Man's race at Ascot, but no one says anything, and soon Mr Hartley and Mr Garritty are disagreeing about the vigour with which he rode Top Cees at Edinburgh.

'Your head is bobbing but you are not riding a finish,' alleges Hartley, who compounds the charge by suggesting that the jockey was not squeezing, either. 'If I don't squeeze the horse with my legs, I fall off,' says Garritty.

Mr Hartley pauses for a giggle and returns to the attack. 'How hard are you squeezing?' 'Hard enough to stay on.'

When the clock reaches 4.30pm we are discussing the difference between 'niggling,' 'coaxing,' and 'pushing.' We are all agreed that we must push on, squeezing quite hard. 10.15am tomorrow morning.

DAY TEN *The Sporting Life*, 17 February 1998

There are 48 light bulbs in Court 13, and all of them are working. They were working when the jury first set its puzzled eyes on the case of Ramsden & ors v MGN Ltd, and they are still working. I think this reflects well on our judicial system. As much light as possible is being cast on the evidence.

'Call Mr Alan Amies, please,' calls Mr Richard Hartley QC.

Luckily, Mr Amies has anticipated him, and is already on his way to the witness box, wearing a check jacket, possibly designed by his brother, Hardy. But today's best-turned-out award goes to the lady juror in the violet tunic and white blouse. Unlike Mr Amies, she is not bald.

Occupying the witness box is an experience generally considered to be 'not much fun.' The jurors stare at you, the judge stares at you, the teams of lawyers and members of the press stare at you. Those who want you to do well stare at you, as do those who want you to burst out crying and admit that it is all a pack of lies.

And the QCs question you. The first QC, Mr Friendly, sets to work with his kindly pump. When you are fully inflated, the second QC stands up, presents a smile like the brass plate on a coffin, and sticks a stiletto into you. 'Nothing personal, just business.' For Mr Amies, the pump is Mr Hartley and the stiletto Mr Milmo.

Mr Hartley asks Amies to tell the court about the occasions on which his expertise has been sought out by stewards' secretaries, while Mr Milmo invites Amies to agree that he doesn't know what he is talking about.

I can reveal that Mr Amies lives in Sheriff Hutton, has been a professional race-reader for over 30 years, goes to about 24 race meetings a month, usually bets in £20s or £30s and is *Raceform*'s senior race-reader.

First he stands, then he sits; at first in spectacles, then without them. He is 'in the box' all day, except at lunchtime, which he spends in solitary confinement in

Ye Olde Cock Tavern. During brief intervals, Amies paces the corridors of the High Court, alone with his testimony, which he gives with his elbows on the ledges of the witness-box, bowed, in a soft, Yorkshire-accented voice. He is a quiet, gentle-sounding man, not given to theatrical displays. I don't suppose he's enjoying it very much but, like cleaning the bath, it's got to be done.

We have moved beyond being bored with the videos. Now we are getting bored with the apologies. 'I'm afraid it's necessary to look at the Swaffham once more,' Mr Hartley regrets. 'I've seen so many videos, I'm as bored with them as you and the jury are,' testifies Mr Amies.

Hartley asks Amies what he thinks about Top Cees' stamina, and the ride Fallon gave him in the 1995 Swaffham, the Chester Cup and the Cesarewitch, and about Top Cees' powers of acceleration, if he had any, and Top Cees' reaction to the whip, if there was one. Then there is Russ Garritty's riding of Top Cees over hurdles at Edinburgh and Doncaster to consider, again, not forgetting the affair of Captain Carat and the day when Rafferty's Rules ran at Nottingham.

Amies testifies that Fallon is 'not thick, he's a bright lad,' and 'some jockey,' but 'he's found trouble at various stages [in the Swaffham], all through his own making. He knows if he stays to the inside he's going to find trouble. He just does not ride like that when he's on a horse that's fancied.'

Amies stands next to the jury's television set and tells them what he thinks is happening. 'He's going well enough to take any gap he wants. He can move to the outside, which would be the sensible thing, but he goes inside. There's a gap there you can drive a bus through, but he's still sitting and waiting. He was going far better than anything but the winner. He seemed not to want to win the race.'

At Chester, Fallon's 'whole body language is different and he moves to the outside, completely different.' In the Cesarewitch, too, 'you see a completely different attitude. He's looking for gaps all the time. This is him at his strongest.'

The time comes (11.10am) when Mr Nice sits down and Mr Nasty, alias Mr Milmo, stands up. 'Did you back Top Cees in the Swaffham?' he stabs, without further pleasantries. Amies raises his eyebrows. 'No.'

'Have you ever ridden a horse?' Mr Amies states that he has, a long time ago.

'But not in a race?' 'Absolutely.'

'Absolutely' is common currency in Court 13. Personally, I have my doubts about it.

Mr Milmo has a habit of pausing for a long time between 'Mr' and 'Amies,' as if the witness is so inconsequential that he has difficulty remembering his name. I counted a seven-second gap, possibly longer. After Milmo has established that Amies has never been a jockey, trainer, official or handicapper, he then sets to work on Mr Amies, the race-reader. 'There are thousands of other race-readers,' he suggests. Lots of race-readers, lots of opinions, and lots of people better placed to judge the matters that are being judged than Mr Amies; people like Mr Adrian Maxwell, Mr Kieren Fallon, Mr Russ Garritty, Mr Peter Harris, Mr 'Uncle' Tom Cobbleigh.

Amies manages to get in the fact that, in 1968, he had a horse with Herbert Jones, and it won, at Ripon. Mr Milmo does not seem impressed. Instead, he homes in on an expression used by *Raceform* in connection with Top Cees – 'Never placed to challenge.'

'That,' Amies explains, 'is the phrase I use when I think something didn't try.'

'So it's *Raceform*'s shorthand for non-trier?' 'It's mine.'

Milmo searches the Form Book, which he has by his side, for further examples of 'never placed to challenge,' beginning with Fairy Wind.

'That's a non-trier, is it?' he asks.

'I obviously thought so.'

'Ridden by Mr Cochrane.'

'Was it?'

'That means he wasn't trying. In breach of Rule 151?'

'Possibly.'

Milmo, honing his stiletto, mentions other horses' names, in company with their riders, such as John Reid and Pat Eddery. 'You are pretty liberal in your criticisms,' he remarks.

'They have what you call sympathetic runs,' replies Amies.

Eventually, Mr Milmo sits down and, like the man at the other end of the see-saw, Mr Hartley rises, to offer his assistance.

'We move to a different class of evidence tomorrow,' Mr Justice Morland finally observes, 'the journalists.' Some of them are busy working their way through the Form Book, seeking out those 'never placed to challenge'.

DAY FOURTEEN *The Sporting Life*, 21 February 1998

It's as simple as that. Oh, Tommo, if only saying it could make it true.

Mr Patrick Milmo QC stands up and applies to Mr Justice Morland for an injunction to prevent Mr Derek Thompson, late of Dubai, currently of Court 13, from ending any more sentences with, 'It's as simple as that.' Mr Justice Morland unhesitatingly grants the application, turns to Mr Thompson and says, 'Mr Thompson, I am going to issue you with a set of full stops, which you are to use at the end of each sentence. In return, you must submit your entire collection of "It's as simple as thats" for disposal.'

To be honest, I was lying about the injunction, it was just wishful thinking, it's as simple as that.

Lying lies at the heart of Day 14, for the truth and lies are brought bluntly face to face. Mr Thompson and Mr Fallon have both sworn under oath to tell the truth, but one of them is lying.

In courtroom dramas, there is the familiar shock of the unexpected. Derek Thompson is an unlikely figure to provide it, and a reluctant one. He did not want to come. He was subpoenaed by the defence because of an evening spent at the Old Plough near Newmarket almost three years ago, and what he said about it afterwards.

Court 13 is at its fullest. People line the wall, their backs to the shelves of law reports.

'You have been compelled to give evidence?' asks Mr Richard Hartley QC.

'Yes', replies Thompson. 'I didn't want to.'

Regularly, through two and three-quarter hours, Thompson repeats his reluctance, his sadness, his discomfort at being obliged to sit in the witness box. And he looks all of those things. Hangdog, shoulders bowed, head bowed, frowning, in an almost constant state of open-mouthed surprise. He talks slowly and very quietly. Tommo is not suddenly going to beam with enthusiasm – 'Tell you what!'

'I gain absolutely nothing out of this. Believe you and me, it's the worst feeling in the world sitting here.'

It was the evening of 18 April 1995, the day etched in the court's mind as the day of the Swaffham. Thompson was having dinner at the Old Plough at Ashley, near Newmarket. Fallon was having a drink with a friend. Fallon set off from the bar in search of the toilet and, on the way, exchanged words with Thompson. There, agreement ends.

According to Thompson, 'I was asking what happened with Top Cees because I thought it would win and Kieren Fallon said "I thought it would win as well, but when I got into the paddock Jack told me to stop it."'

In fourteen long days, there has not been a line to match the hushing impact of Thompson's low, slow, explosive revelation, 'Jack told me to stop it.'

The next morning, at Channel 4 Racing's production meeting, Thompson mentioned the conversation. Later that day, he interviewed Fallon on television. He reassured him. 'I said what was said in the Plough would not come out.' He told Fallon he would look after him. Thompson seizes one final chance to say, 'The last thing I wanted was for it to come out in public court.'

Then it is the turn of Mr Milmo QC. He wastes no time on niceties. The fierceness of his assault is a measure of the potential damage Thompson's allegation could wreak.

'What you have just said about Kieren Fallon is an outrageous lie.'

'That is incorrect.'

'And we will examine why you have come to tell an outrageous lie.'

According to Milmo, Thompson has come because Channel 4 have told him to, because he is fearful of losing his job. 'I have come here,' replies Thompson, 'because I have been subpoenaed. I tried to keep it out of court. I am not perjuring myself and I am telling the truth.'

I have learnt something else about the witnesses in Court 13. While one barrister invites the jury to regard the figure in the box as awash with knowledge and integrity, the opposing barrister is inclined to approach the hapless witness with a tub of black paint. Milmo presents a cutting from the *News of the World* headlined 'TV star rips off punters.' Thompson is that TV star.

Thompson vigorously denies the accusations and Milmo then produces a transcript of 'Tommo's' telephone tipping line for last Saturday. He refers to a reference to Graphic Equaliser. 'You know Arthur Moore [an Irish trainer] no better than you know the Pope, do you? Just tell us where you were when all this was recorded?'

'I was in Dubai.'

It may not have been a good idea for Tommo to tell his clients, 'Well, there you are. Four horses for you. I fully expect all four to win.' I leave you to guess the outcome.

Thompson salvages a diary from his jacket and with it some of his reputation as a tipster. Eight winners during the first week in February, nine the next.

'This is a deception, is it not?' suggests Milmo.

'I don't think so.'

Soon, we are back to the conversation in the Old Plough, but the tension has seeped away. It will soon be recaptured. When lunchtime ends, seats are at a premium. People sit on the steps and stand by the walls. The judge rests his chin on his hand, Mr Milmo leans his left elbow on the lectern, Mr Thompson talks even more quietly than before.

Milmo presses him to take the logical step from being told that Top Cees was stopped to acknowledging that, in his 19 April interview, Fallon must have been telling 'a load of rubbish.' Thompson resolutely declines to advance from the first proposition to the second, preferring to confine himself to repeating that 'what he told me the night before was what he told me.'

Milmo produces some photographs of the Old Plough. The first one is number 70A. 'That's the one with a couple of wine glasses and the tulips?' asks Mr Justice Morland.

Thompson is invited to study a gap. 'I think it's a wider gap than it seems there,' he says. Perhaps the infamous seven-second gap has moved on, during the course of the evening, and is now to be found between the bar and the table. Fallon has again found his way impeded.

Briefly, we move on to McCoy's restaurant in Yorkshire, where Thompson had dinner with Mr and Mrs Ramsden, possibly for the last time. At 3.30pm, Thompson stands down and Fallon stands up, prior to sitting down in the witness box. He does not say, 'Yes, sir, that is all true.' On the contrary, he says, 'No sir, it's a lie.'

Fallon is the same as he was before. Long pauses, leaning forward and saying, 'Sorry, sir.' Mr Hartley repeating the question, the court straining to hear his answer. This time, Fallon fiddles with a pen.

Mr Hartley encourages Fallon to say something other than, 'Mr Thompson has invented it and is a liar,' but he won't, and we are all back again on Monday. Early start, 9.00am. Better set the alarm.

THE FINAL DAY *The Sporting Life*, 26 February 1998

Last day today. I don't know, though, that's what we said yesterday. I'm going to miss the buttered scones in Messrs C, over the road from the High Court. Next time you're on trial, you must try them.

Today, they opened the public gallery. Personally, I don't think anyone should be allowed in who didn't come yesterday. It's like turning up late for dinner and expecting to get the cherry on the Knickerbocker Glory. But they are all here, even Emma Ramsden [the Ramsdens' daughter], wearing violet trousers with roses on. I expect they were a Valentine's Day present. And eating sweets. Eating sweets when she's supposed to be in training for my next winning punt in an amateur riders' race.

Yesterday, Mrs Ramsden was wearing a tremendous outfit that could have been created by Matisse. Today, it's a navy blue job with white trim. I think it goes rather well with Mr Justice Morland's red robes. They could get together and turn themselves into a Union Jack.

Today, Mr Justice Morland sums up. It feels like a summary of *War and Peace*, with most of it left in. No, that's unfair or, as they say in libel cases, 'not fair comment.' It is just that Court 13 and all its contents are worn out with Ramsden & ors v MGN Ltd Pt Hd. When will it be Al Hd?

When it is, there will be a big bag of videotapes, four televisions and six sets of blue and black jury bundles going cheap. The light bulbs have done well. There they are, still shining. Osram should use them in an advert.

At 10.20am, Mr Justice Morland turns to face the jury and, for the best part of four hours, virtually ignores everyone else. Voyeurs are allowed to watch if they want to. Jack Ramsden has rejoined Lynda Ramsden on the front bench, and Kieren Fallon has rejoined both of them. Further along sit Tom Clarke [editor of *The Sporting Life*] and Alastair Down, separated by a solicitor.

'The law is for me, but the facts are for you,' Mr Justice Morland advises the jury. He can't say fairer than that. Later, the court will be introduced to the tricky question of, "What is a fact?" I'm sure we got asked that in a history lesson once, but I can't remember what the answer was. Messrs Morland, Milmo and Hartley find it a bit of a teaser, too.

'I am sure you will not be prejudiced against Mr Ramsden because he is a successful gambler,' Mr Justice Morland remarks to the jury. Point taken, my Lord. How many times have you been standing in a betting shop, screwing up your latest pink slip, when some smart arse insists on telling you that he's just had £100 on the winner? Of course you hate him; it's only natural.

The jury is given advice on what qualifies as 'evidence' and what does not. It is told that 'libel is defamation in written form,' and that the article complained of 'is clearly highly defamatory.' The defendants maintain that it is true in substance and fact, or is fair comment on a matter of public interest. The public interest bit is easy, but the fair comment part later provokes fierce and impenetrable debate. I am told that I cannot report the debate, which is lucky, because I don't understand it.

It turns out that Mr Patrick Milmo QC is joint-editor of *Gatley on Libel and Slander*, which is similar to the Form Book, but makes even less sense. As Mr Milmo wages polite war with Mr Justice Morland over Gatley, Groucho Marx comes to mind – 'The party of the first part and the party of the second part ... and there ain't no sanity clause.'

'The all-important race is the Swaffham,' states Mr Justice Morland, baldly, confirming what I've always thought. 'I suggest to you that you concentrate on the Swaffham.'

Unfortunately, it doesn't stop him going, in his slow, engaging way, over the mysterious affair of Captain Carat and the six air-shots, Rafferty's Rules' trip to Nottingham, and the strange case of Top Cees and the Edinburgh hurdle.

'The first main question,' says the judge, 'is, has the defence established that Top Cees was deliberately dishonestly ridden by Mr Fallon with the intention that it should not obtain the best possible placing, on the Ramsdens' deliberate and dishonest instructions?' It's a jolly long question and, by 4.30pm, the jury still hasn't answered it.

Before that, the judge has said what he's got to say about the vital matter of

Derek Thompson's evidence; the evidence that Fallon had been told by Jack Ramsden to stop Top Cees. 'The defendants strongly rely on the evidence of Derek Thompson,' Mr Justice Morland suggests, and he has two important points of law to make. 'First, if you accept it, it is evidence against Mr Fallon alone, not against the Ramsdens. Second, you must treat the evidence with caution.'

The conversation took place nearly three years ago, Thompson made no note of it, and his testimony in the witness box differed from the details given in a written statement. 'That inconsistency throws serious doubt on the reliability of what Mr Thompson said.'

Ears prick up, hopes are raised and lowered yet the court clerk soon gives every appearance of having nodded off. We are a bored but well-behaved class.

My eyes drift to the day's cause list. In Court 69, a particularly racy venue, Lord Justice Judge, a man born to the bench, does not preside over Galaxy Energy International Ltd v Novorossiyk Shipping Co., which is next door in Court 70. Nearby, Lady Justice Butler-Sloss considers the case of White v Russell Farm Racing Ltd. I wonder if Lord Justice Pill specialises in medical malpractice?

Mr Justice Morland deals with Messrs Maxwell, McGrath and Amies, the expert witnesses. As lunch approaches, the summing-up hangs heavy over the public benches. Chins are placed in hands, eyes are rubbed, foreheads stroked. I think I may have lasagne for lunch.

The morning's proceedings, or possibly the turkey baguette, have taken their toll. At two o'clock, attendance is down, although it recovers later. Regarding fair comment, the judge advises that 'the comment has to be fair having regard to the facts that are true.' I hope the jury is following. If it is, and finds for the plaintiffs, it is advised that damages of £50,000 each would be 'niggardly,' while £125,000 would be deemed 'extravagant.'

The judge places the jury in the position of ordinary readers of *The Sporting Life* and, at 3.13pm, despatches them to a monastery to consider their verdict. One last buttered scone.

The jury found for the plaintiffs, awarding damages of £75,000 to Lynda Ramsden, £50,000 to Jack Ramsden and £70,000 to Kieren Fallon, plus costs estimated at £300,000.

2
FIRST BUY A HORSE

A madman armed with a hammer: David Pim.

Michael Jackson had Neverland; horseracing has the sales ring, an arena awash with human fantasies and foibles. Occasionally, I have been told that it's a very serious business and I should treat it more seriously. I almost managed to, when reaching Ocala in Florida, but, on the whole, I can't.

If you do put your hand up and buy a racehorse, you need to name it, choose your racing colours, choose a trainer, and choose a religion; one that involves a lot of praying is ideal. Good luck (you never know).

NEWMARKET: GRAPPLING WITH SALES TALK *Racing Post*, 7 October 1998

John O'Kelly can speak seven languages. Unfortunately, he speaks them all at once, pointing with one hand and waving a wooden hammer with the other. O'Kelly is obviously mad, but this is the Houghton Sales at Newmarket, so no one notices.

'At 110,000 I get. 120, 130 now. A tremendous walker. Yes, sir, I'll come back to you. 140, 180 now. Yes, sir, 200 bid, 210 if you like. 250 I have, against you. Every inch a two-year-old. 290, only 290, round it off now. Yes, well done, sir, 300. What a purchase. I'm selling this fine colt. I sell behind.' Bang goes the hammer and Bruno Schutz has bought the first lot of the second day for just 300,000gns.

O'Kelly's spectacles balance on his nose, and mine would be balancing on my nose, too, if I hadn't just walked past a sign warning, 'No glasses in the sales ring.' Sheikh Hamdan has a pair of Bertie Wooster glasses, hanging on a chain, beneath his flat cap. Flat caps are popular, as are sales catalogues, which are free. Everything else starts at 5,000gns, but doesn't stop there.

It's a curiously casual atmosphere, with visitors chatting over their catalogues while bloodstock empires are gained and lost. Outside the round ring, the next lots are walked around a paddock. Lot 97 has a sticker on her rump, like an apple. I thought it would say 'Granny Smith' but it didn't.

'Take him over if you like. 200. A tremendous colt. 280, 300. The dam a hell of a racemare.'

Richard Hannon is leaning over the railings around the pre-sales ring, so I ask what he's looking for. 'Not her,' he says, 'with the front wheels she's got.' They look okay to me. One on each side. Not like Mick Channon's. He'd be lucky to pass the abattoir, let alone the vet.

Back in the ring, it's impossible to tell who's bidding. Is anyone bidding, or is O'Kelly making it up? Why doesn't he tell people to stand up and shout, 'Cooee, over here?' But he doesn't and, soon, he falls back exhausted and David Pim takes over.

Pim is good, so good they've named a drink after him. He holds the head of the hammer, raises his other hand artistically, and puts up two fingers. 'You're going to be on the wrong leg if you don't look at me. I sell him right-handed this time at 90,000. I sell him now.' He seems to be mad, too.

O'Kelly has probably popped out for dinner. 'Is that eight guineas I have for the steak and kidney, and you couldn't ask for a better one, it's with you now. No sir, the pie's outside, on my right, at nine guineas. It's a tremendous pie, and it's with you now, sir. You won't regret it, and a great vegetable on the side plate.'

John Magnier sits on a step, next to Demi O'Byrne. What happened to the other half of him? Where's Michael Tabor, and where's Sheikh Mohammed? He came in for lot 73, but let the Germans have it for 750,000gns, which was a bit feeble.

I ask Anthony Stroud if there's a lot he particularly likes and he says 114, which is a funny thing because I'd just asked Angus Gold, Sheikh Hamdan's man, the same question, and he came up with the same answer. Maybe it's their favourite number. It's a Rainbow Quest. That's how they talk about them. If the Princess Royal came up, they'd say she was a Prince Philip.

Philip Freedman has a Machiavellian coming up seven lots before the Rainbow Quest, and he's looking a bit twitchy, in Freedman's gentle, *Wind In The Willows* way. If he's forced to guess, which he is, he thinks his Machiavellian, a prince of a horse, will fetch 75,000gns. When it fetches 30,000, I wish I hadn't asked.

If you didn't know, you probably wouldn't guess that Freedman was, well, filthy rich. They should have a game where you line up six of the Houghton crowd and have to say which one's the richest. Here's a tip. Go for the ones in jeans.

'Will anybody open with a terrace? A small terrace. A semi. A large semi. A small detached, with you, sir. Thank you, sir, four bedrooms. Do I hear five? Five and three bathrooms. With a paddock, to my right. A tremendous colt, don't stop now, sir. A small country estate. I sell now, for a small country estate. Thank you, sir. Next lot.'

Joss Collins, red cardigan and yellow trousers, a bit like Noddy, stands in the entrance-way. On the terraces, Tim Bulwer-Long, alias Wafic Said, looks out from beneath his Norman Wisdom cap. Wally Sturt studies his catalogue, with more yellow stickers in it than there are lots. What do they all say? 'Pay milkman.' 'Buy more stickers.'

'I sell him on the end of the cage, and rightly so. The first progeny of one of the great racemares of all time. 300,000.' Bang goes the gavel, and John Oxx has just bought Ridgewood Pearl's first foal.

3.55pm and I spot Sheikh Mohammed. He's wearing a white T-shirt, faded jeans (what did I tell you?), and chewing chewing gum. I wonder if it's Wrigley's. If it is, they'd be able to advertise, 'As chewed by Sheikh Mohammed.'

4.06pm. John Magnier speaks into a mobile phone. Timmy Hyde, another of the Coolmore collection, leans nonchalantly against the railings.

4.08pm. Sheikh Mohammed bides his time in the Chifney Restaurant.

4.09pm. I say hello to a bloodstock agent I know and she says, 'I didn't recognise you.' 'No, I've aged a lot.' 'No, you've put on weight a lot.' Ow.

Objection. Lot 113 is described as 'bay or brown.' I submit that she's grey, but no one takes any notice. John Gosden stands talking to Sheikh Mohammed, his hand in the half-open catalogue. 'Everything from here to the end, sir?'

Michael Tabor is squatting where John Magnier once squatted. Edmond Mahony (pronounced Mahny, but he'll soon be able to afford the 'o') has succeeded Pim, and gives a good impression of a ventriloquist as he introduces lot 114. I haven't quite got the guts to make the opening bid.

'100,000 I have. 180. 200 now. 225 I have. 250 gone.' And so it goes on, 'Now 800, 925, 950, one million, and another two.' Lot 114 expresses his opinion, which the man responsible for collecting opinions sweeps up and puts in a bucket, for which I consider making an offer. The droppings look disappointing to me, but Messrs Magnier and Fusao Sekiguchi are undeterred. 'One million four, one million six, one million eight.'

The law of diminishing returns is packed off to bed. 'Two million on the stairs. Two million one is the bid now. One more if you want, sir. Two million two, a stunning colt. Sold to John Magnier.'

I feel like wandering over and saying, 'Well done, John. You couldn't lend me 40 grand, could you?'

Outside, Lady Lloyd Webber, the vendor, looks as if nothing much has happened, and so does the Rainbow Quest. A man taps my catalogue, points to Red God in the pedigree and says, 'I wouldn't touch it with a bargepole.' I feel a terrible urge to shout out, 'Snaafi Dancer!' [bought for $10.2 million in 1983 but never raced and a flop at stud] but don't and, as I leave, behind me in the distance I hear David Pim, four brass buttons on his cuffs, '260 on the rail, you all done with him?'

They are all barmy.

The 2.2 million guineas yearling, named Good Heavens, won three races for trainer Aidan O'Brien, the best a-listed race at Cork, before being sold to race in Hong Kong, where he won once.

KEENELAND: BEAUTIFUL CALM BELIES STORM THAT WAITS AHEAD *Racing Post*, 18 July 2000

We haven't bought a horse yet but, last night, we bought two rather nice pork chops. We were going to buy a lobster, but couldn't meet the reserve.

Keeneland is class. Maple trees line the driveway to the best-looking parking lot in the US, watched over by an executive committee made up of James E Bassett III, John A Bell III, William T Bishop III and Louis L Haggin III, probably under chairman Napoleon III.

The July Selected To Cost You An Arm And Four Legs Yearling Sale proudly boasts that 59 per cent of the yearlings sold between 1990 and 1998 have won a race. The bad news is that 41 per cent haven't. The trick is to find out which is going to be which. It's about $600,000 a go.

The first thing to do is to get a catalogue and stroll along through the trees, under the sun, to the long, neat, grey-green barns housing the finest yearlings in Kentucky. The horses are walked up and down between the barns, while agents, owners and trainers stare at them and make notes.

James Delahooke, famous for buying Dancing Brave and Rainbow Quest, is staring at lot, or, as they say here, hip, number 152. Hip 152 is the property of Wayne G Lyster III, for the time being. When I ask Delahooke what he's looking for, he goes quiet for a long time and then suddenly says, 'Symmetry, balance, poise, quality. The relationship of the different parts of the horse. A lot of people do it with a tape measure. Also attitude, willingness. That's important. I watch them later in the day to see which ones are still coming out willingly. And motion, movement, I am very influenced by that.'

Hip 152 motions that she would like to go back into her box. 'She's a lovely filly,' says Delahooke. 'She's one of 20 on my list. I've got to get it down to one.'

Delahooke won't say which is the one. No one will. 'Not while we're still at the poker table,' explains Craig Bandoroff. Craig, short as a jockey, curly grey hair, has his name underneath eight of Denali Stud's offerings, a couple of Storm Cats, an AP Indy, that kind of thing.

'I sold Royal Academy for $3.5 million when I was still young,' says Bandoroff. 'I had to look for a wall to lean against. You can tell the class ones. They show it to you young. The way they handle themselves. Every time they show, they show with class. They know they're special.'

Hip 128 walks up and down, but the white blaze down her nose isn't quite straight. I make a note in my catalogue, 'Wrong in nose.'

Nelson Bunker Hunt, once famous for buying soya beans, looks as if he's eaten most of them. Hunt is looking old but still won't tell me which is the hip for him. Nor will Kay Shigeta, looking at hips for Silky Green Inc. Shigeta, slim, pink-shirted, white crocheted hat, asks the man who's holding hip 179 to jog him up and down. The man says he's not allowed to. Walking only.

'We like him,' Shigeta explains, 'but look at the top of his tail. It's a very funny shape.' She's right, it is. There's a sort of dent there. That would put me right off, especially as the Gone West colt is described as 'dark bay or brown.' All that money, and they don't even know what colour he is.

'It's very difficult,' Shigeta says, when I ask which is her favourite lot. 'We are buyers, you see. Hip number 20, we like that. Pleasant Colonys are usually huge. He is not too big and a very nice mover. A good mover is the most important thing. If a horse looks beautiful but doesn't walk well, I don't buy.' Me neither. That's an absolute rule with me. If it can't walk, I won't buy it.

It's beautiful at Keeneland. Sugar maple, hornbeam, white pine and crab apple, pin oak and Chinese elms shimmy in the breeze, grey squirrels scamper, tan-breasted birds scoot from tree to tree.

'She's got a pretty good scar on that back leg,' says Cecil Borel, a local trainer, 'but she looks the part. A bit light on pedigree, but that's all right.' And hip 132 does a spot more walking. Satish Sanan, short and wearing shorts, jokes with his family while D Wayne Lukas, in long trousers, examines a few pasterns.

'Which one do you have a soft spot for?', I ask the Eaton Sales representative. Eaton Sales are the biggest consignors at the sale. 'I don't have soft spots,' he replies, and you realise, the quiet of the yearlings walking in this lovely spot will soon be gone. Serious money is gathering.

KEENELAND: LADIES AND GENTLEMEN, PREPARE TO YUP AND HUP *Racing Post*, 19 July 2000

Kick off for the big show is at 7.30pm. Cars pull up and valets park them. Theatregoers mill in the foyer, circle the corridor, peer through the glass screens into the sales ring, play spot the billionaire. Ladies and gentlemen, welcome to another world.

'Ladies and gentlemen, good evening, welcome to the Keeneland Sales.' Scott Caldwell, hair as short as a GI on a Sergeant Bilko show, sits on the top of a tall, wooden-slatted rostrum, nervous in his tuxedo. Right outfield in the waiting semi-circle, D Wayne Lukas, slick as an aftershave advertisement, leans on an elbow and talks the fight with Satish Sanan. Left outfield, John Magnier, oiled grey hair curled up at the nape of his neck, rests his jaw in his hand.

At 7.42pm no bell goes, but hip number 1 walks on to the small, roped stage in front of the rostrum. Caldwell opens his mouth and a ticker-tape of foreign words and numbers spews out like a video on fast-forward. No one says, 'Hold it right there, this man needs a doctor.'

'At 30, 40, Roxanne 50, close pub, help yourself, at 70, wheel set on fire, blood sir, at 75 leave at 80, no one else, all done, thankyou.'

They're called ringmen, standing like dinner-jacketed bouncers, white cuffs showing, backs to the rostrum, faces to their own section of the theatre, urging their boys on, spotting the bids.

Roger, tall, angle-jawed, playing piano keys in the air with his fingers, lets out a 'yes' which comes out 'yep,' like a fox's bark. Pete, a little bit Frank Sinatra, a little bit Bob Hoskins, black jacket bulging at the chest, thinning black hair flat to his skull, waves one finger in the air, hustles a few steps up the aisle, dances a set of stubby, wiggling fingers, eases back down the aisle. All in good time, we're in this together. The first three hips don't make their reserves but the hip replacement is a Mr Prospector, and Caldwell pulls out all the commas. '200 now who'll give me 50 at 75 who'll bid 400 525 Arkansas gentlemen 575 oh she's good 700 help me I want 50 725 help yourself 790 thank you.' But six figures is for boys, seven's for men.

The crush of watchers sitting on benches behind the glass at the back of the ring, standing in the corridor, staring into the fishbowl, know what they're waiting for, and they don't have to wait long. Hip 8, out of Winning Colors, the champion three-year-old filly in 1988. '775 800 one million,' and the audience claps and cheers and Pete waves one arm and dances with the fingers of his other, 'hup, yep, hup,' and Roger 'yeps' back and in a cacophony of yelps and barks the red figures on the screen reach $2 million. At $2.4 million Anne Sanan shakes her head as if to say, 'That's enough, Satish, remember we've got to go shopping later.'

And so, at $2.5 million, a Mr Jones allows himself a small smile, as photographers take pictures of his 78-year-old grey head and check shirt and journalists cluster round. 'Aaron U Jones' he says, and tells them about his timber business back home in Oregon.

Two hips later, Mr Jones hands out another $850,000 of pine trees but, like a gambler needing the stakes to rise for his adrenalin to pump, the ring needs a million to feel a thing. Suddenly, $500,000 is boring. That's what Silky Green Inc pay for hip 20, that nice moving Pleasant Colony colt that Kay Shigeta, acting for Silky Green Inc, had told me she liked on Monday.

Soon, John Ferguson, buying for Sheikh Mohammed's Kentucky Derby dream, raises an eyebrow at $1.2 million, scratches his nose at $1.3 million, winks at $1.5 million, as does Demi O'Byrne, fighting out of Coolmore. They leave hip 37, a Mr Prospector, to the Japanese, inscrutable and unspellable.

By then, Caldwell's brother Cris's sing-song bass has taken over the rostrum. 'I'm bid 325, 350. I have 375 and 400. I've got 425. Dem bones dem bones dem, dry bones. Dem bones dem bones dem, dry bones. I have 450 and 500 bid.'

Pete and Roger yup and hup, hip 45 kicks the rostrum, Nelson Bunker Hunt takes off his jacket and prepares to corner the market in hip 54, which he does, for $240,000. It's not much, I know, but it's more than the $35,000 which Joss Collins lashed out on hip 27, the sale bottomer. The restaurants close early in Lexington. I expect Joss will get together with a few friends for a barbecue later.

With the catalogue closing, Mrs Sanan finally loses control of her husband and, before she knows it, Satish has paid $2.15 million for a Seeking The Gold. Everyone claps, then troops out, as if they're leaving church, which, in a way, they are. 'See you tomorrow, 1.30pm start,' says Scott Caldwell.

Straight out of the doors, turn left for the real world.

The $2.5 million yearling, named Dr Litin, raced three times, never finishing better than fourth. He won $5,520 in prize money and was retired to stud in Oregon, at a fee of $750. The Pleasant Colony colt, bought for $500,000, was named Preston Swan and exported to Japan, where, in a long career, he won 21 races, although no major ones. Joss Collins' $35,000 purchase, named Spanish John, won six races, including two listed events.

OCALA, FLORIDA *Racing Post*, 27 August 2009

Sheikh Mohammed isn't here; nor John Magnier. It's a pity; they could have given each other a lift.

The horses for sale at Ocala, just like Sea The Stars, all trace back to one of the same three stallions, the Godolphin Arabian, the Byerley Turk or the Darley Arabian but, judging from the bids, most of them don't seem to trace back in quite the right way, or maybe there's something awry with their pasterns, or fetlocks, or gaskins. Then there's the depression, but we've all got that.

Royal Ascot winner Jealous Again was bought here, for $30,000, and so was the Dubai Golden Shaheen winner Big City Man, for $45,000. They now grace the covers of book 1, the Selected Sale of Yearlings (hips 1-200), and of book 2, the Open Sale of Yearlings (hips 201-1151). You wouldn't want to be hip 1151.

In the long barns, under a hot blue sky and green corrugated roofs held up by cream coloured girders, hopes and fears wait for the bidding to begin. It seems quiet. 'The traffic's much lighter,' says consignor Janie Roper, in a turquoise shirt and blonde hair. 'There's a big difference from previous years. If you have a nice individual with a good pedigree, you can still sell well but below that ...' Quite.

Boards hang from chains at the end of each barn, bearing the names of the consignors. 'Woodside Ranch. Bryan and Holly Rice,' 'All Dreams Equine,' 'Peggy S. Dellheim. Agent.' Juan Centeno is All Dreams Equine, with three horses in the select sale and seven in the also-rans. 'I think the sale is a little hard, like any other business,' says Centeno, dark hair, dark moustache, dark sunglasses, light smile. 'We think positive. We work extra hard to prepare our horses and to give them good manners. You have to work harder than before and try to be a little better than the rest. I feel glad when we sell a horse and it do good. It make me feel good, it's my pride.'

Centeno moved from Mexico 20 years ago. Now, he has a small farm in nearby Morristown where he prepares horses, his own and other people's, for the sales. Centeno buys weanlings and sells them as yearlings. If they don't sell as yearlings, he sells them as two-year-olds. 'I am not looking for a lot of money,' he says. 'I try to make a bit from each group each year. We are hoping to survive. I am happy. You are happy if you make the best of things, and make the best of your neighbours and friends.' Confucius said the same thing, I think.

Hip 14, a colt by Macho Uno, is not owned by Centeno, but he has prepared it. 'Whoever gets him will have a nice horse,' he says. 'He's very athletic, well balanced, and good temperament. People get a decent horse.' For how much, Juan? How much will you be happy with? It is not a question sellers want to answer. Finally, he says, '$50,000. If he brings $50,000 I will be happy. He is one of the nicest.'

From a stall in barn 6, hip 278 is led out. 'Tony, look at this horse,' says a woman in an extra large T-shirt, the smaller sizes being unable to contain her. Tony watches as the bay Indian Ocean filly is trotted one way, then trotted the other. Here and there, yearlings are walked and trotted this way and that, while potential buyers, wise or foolish, look on.

A long walk away, in the outback, a sign hangs from barn 14. 'University of Florida Equine Science Program.' Richard Hays, rebellious hair sprouting from beneath his U of F baseball cap, sits, undisturbed, in a beach chair. Hays, the university's farm manager, explains that they keep a band of mares and, every year, students prepare their yearlings for the sales. This week, the university is selling 16 yearlings. What is the highest price you have ever got? 'Over $20,000,' says Hays. 'The money might not be here this year but the people will be here, not like last year, when a hurricane kept them away.' That was Hurricane Fay. It was jolly windy, evidently.

In the walking ring, Centeno waits. On the podium, Ryan Mahan, the senior auctioneer, warbles in the alien, machine-gun language taught at the School of Auctioneers. '32, 32, 32, 35, dem bones dem bones dem dry bones, 35, 35, 37, dem bones dem bones dem dry bones.Virgil's in at 37.' Virgil must have got fed up with writing poems, and decided to buy a yearling by Exchange Rate, instead. I don't blame him. It must have been murder, writing in Latin.

In the sales pavilion only about 100 seats, out of hundreds more, are occupied but in the walking ring, there is a much busier buzz. Hip 14 is led forward to meet his market. Mahan warbles and rat-tat-tats his way to $35,000 while bid spotters snap their 'yaps' and 'hos' and 'ay-ups.' 40, 45, 50. Centeno's Macho Uno colt goes for $55,000. Juan will be happy.

Time passes. Mahan has either been replaced by another auctioneer, or he's put a toupee on. The prattle's much the same. Either all the auctioneers are mad, or my ears need to see an otologist.

Centeno is happier than most vendors, because only 113 of the 200 hips are sold, for an average of less than $33,000, 34 per cent down on last year. Only three hips break the $100,000 barrier, with hip 108, a Medaglia d'Oro filly, like Rachel Alexandra, topping the sale, bought by Live Oak Plantation for $275,000. Charlotte Weber, whose grandfather founded Campbell's Soup, owns Live Oak. I expect she's got one of those Andy Warhol pictures of a Campbell's soup tin on her living room wall; tomato, perhaps.

With 28 hips going for less than $15,000 (£9,150), what will it be like by Thursday? I might go to a cash machine, and take out $100.

As a two-year-old, the $55,000 Macho Uno colt, named Classic Legacy and trained by Bob Baffert, won two races at Woodbine before finishing third in a Grade 3 race at the same track, then fifth in the Grade 3 Delta Downs Jackpot. In November 2011, at Keeneland, the $275,000 Medaglia d'Oro filly, named Fru Fru, was sold, unraced, for $11,000.

Now that it's yours, there's the pleasure of naming it. Nothing would surprise me.

WHAT'S IN A NAME? *Racing Post*, 7 December 2002

Understandably, Rostropovich has ducked out of a contest with Beethoven at Chepstow today, but Prokofiev is taking on Oliver Cromwell at Sandown. If it comes to a war, my money's on Cromwell. After all, he won the civil one, chopped Charles I's head off, more or less, and, although his own head was chopped off eventually, at least he was already dead when they did it.

God Forbid that a racehorse should ever be mistaken for a Squirrel. Oh, it already has been, and for a Bee, Seagull, Persian Cat, Bullfinch, Arctic Penguin and March Hare. Robin Dickin even trains a White Dove, although it isn't white, and isn't a dove.

How could you mistake a horse for a Macaw, or a Snow Leopard? But people do. Somebody, not long ago, looked at a horse and mistook it for a Parachute. Somebody else thought it was a Tin Cup, or a Bayonet, a Metal Detector, a Chandelier, or a Negligee. If it wasn't one of those, then it was a Bus.

Someone looked at other horses, and were reminded of Stanmore, Istanbul, Arizona and Africa. It's a funny thing to do, call a horse a place, like Marble Arch or Hyde Park, Caterham Common or Strathclyde, but people do.

Knowing what happened to Archduke Ferdinand (shot), Lawrence Of Arabia (motorbike accident), Ned Kelly (hanged), Rommel (forced suicide) and Robespierre (guillotined) might have been expected to put some owners off, but it didn't.

Strange to think that Oscar Wilde can't talk and can't write but can jump open ditches. It's hard to imagine. No wonder he was tailed off at Folkestone last time out, but if Grandma Lily can win, there's still hope. At four, Grandma Lily must be the youngest Grandma in the world.

You think they're only horses, but it turns out they're not. They might be a Barman, a Flying Instructor, a Curate, Cabin Boy, Archbishop, Attorney, or even a Harlot. That might be better than being an Ice Cube, or A Piece Of Cake.

Whole banquets have been built around horses, without ever eating horsemeat. The Country Chef starts off with Potted Shrimp, then offers Beef Or Salmon, perhaps with a bit of Asparagus, Black Pepper and Mango Chutney, before moving on to Peach Sorbet, washed down with Riesling. Then it's Blue Cheese and Coffee Time, with Highland Toffee. Pass The Best Port, please, or a spot of Sloe Gin.

I don't know what the wittiest current name is but I remember some favourites from the past. One of Busted's offspring, out of Amazer, gloried in the name of Amazing Bust, while Toby Balding once trained a horse called Cleavage, out of a Busted mare called Divided.

Denys Smith, recently retired, used to train a lot of horses for Joe Lisle, who managed to slip both Sixty Nine and Soixante Neuf through Weatherbys' vetting system. They weren't the only ones. Two of the more subtle ones were Rhett Butler, by Bold Lad out of Pussy Galore, and Entire, a gelding out of Tactless. Clever, that.

The cleverest of all, though, is still one of those thought up by Louis Freedman, the late owner of the Cliveden Stud. In 1973, Freedman had a yearling filly by Reform out of Seventh Bride, a full-sister to the cleverly named Polygamy. Freedman called her One Over Parr. Catherine Parr was Henry VIII's sixth wife.

Then there are your colours. You might consider lime green.

LIME SILKS *Racing Post*, 16 October 2004

Eight years ago, the British Horseracing Board had a wheeze. It decided to invent some jockeys' colours and auction them. Not any jockeys' colours but very distinctive ones; the sort of colours for which rich owners would pay a lot of money.

So, in November 1996, at Sotheby's, three 'cherished colours' went under the hammer; cerise, terracotta and lime green. The winning bid for the lime green colours was £18,000. It was made by Blair Down, of Bridgetown, Barbados.

A few months earlier, Incitatus had won the Barbados Derby sporting Down's white colours, for Down was a wealthy man, a Canadian with a $17 million mansion at St James Beach, Barbados. (And therefore no relation of our own Alastair Down.)

What Down had bought was the right to register the lime green colours in his name. Weatherbys waited for the colours to be registered, and waited, but nothing happened. Under the terms of the sale, the right that Down had bought would expire after one year. One year expired.

Weatherbys contacted Sotheby's, who informed them that Down had given his address as Direct Management Systems, Bridgetown. He was no longer at the end of the telephone numbers he had given, and the Barbados Turf Club told Weatherbys that Down no longer lived in Barbados.

Weatherbys didn't know what to do. They were reluctant to enforce the terms of the sale and deprive Down of his colours, so they carried on waiting, wondering what had become of him. If only they had known.

For Down also had a wheeze, a profitable, utterly unscrupulous one. Starting in 1989, in Canada, he sent mail-shots to elderly US residents, informing them that they had won a prize. All they had to do was send a few dollars to cover administrative costs. You may have received similar mail-shots. Those who sent the $5 or $10 were asked to send more, and more, and more. For Down had other schemes to offer, including the chance to pool resources to buy foreign lottery tickets.

By 1992, Down's enterprises were being investigated, but it wasn't easy, because he used 57 different company and trade names. The US Postal Service imposed a string of 'cease and desist' orders. US Customs seized materials. Down switched between Canada and Barbados, employing 500 telemarketers to befriend his elderly victims and get their money. There were a lot of victims, 42,000 in the US, 400,000 worldwide, and a lot of money, at least $120m, perhaps $300m, with one victim alone losing $329,000.

In 1997, Down had more pressing matters to attend to than registering his lime green colours. He was indicted in Seattle and, in 1998, pleaded guilty to criminal conspiracy. By operating across state and national borders and concealing his assets offshore, Down frustrated justice. He was sentenced to just six months in an Oregon prison and ordered to pay $12m, prompting a judge to remark that he would leave prison 'a very wealthy man.'

He did, pursued by Interclaim, an Irish asset-recovery company acting on behalf of some of Down's victims. They tracked down $100m of assets in a dozen countries and, in 2000, hired the law firm of Ness Motley to pursue a class action on behalf of the victims.

In 2002, Ness Motley, to the fury of Interclaim and the victims, reached an extraordinary settlement with Down. Under it, Ness Motley received $2m, another $2m was allocated to administrative costs, and just $6m was made available to Down's victims, but only if they met near impossible conditions. Professor of Law Lester Brickman, also outraged, wrote, 'If there were an award for the most abusive class action settlement of the decade, if not the century, this settlement would be an odds-on favourite to gain the prize.'

So Blair Down, now 60, is still free, and still very rich. He could easily afford another set of lime green colours and, on 3 November, at Sotheby's Olympia sale room, he has the chance to buy them again. A dozen sets of distinctive racing colours are up for sale, plus an additional lot, lot 575A – lime green (estimate £30,000 – £50,000).

The lime green colours were bought by racehorse owner John Fretwell for £60,000.

YOUR FIRST RACEHORSE, AND YOUR FIRST TRAINER

The Sporting Life, 27 December 1988

The great advantage with having bought a yearling is that you don't know quite how bad it is. It's your trainer's job to make sure that it stays that way.

It won't be long before he advises you that yours is 'not an early type.' This is good news. You don't expect next year's Derby winner to be running at the opening meeting at Doncaster. What is more, 'he has done nothing wrong.' Note that there is no reference to your champion having done anything right. It is the equine equivalent of being told that your best friend has not murdered his mother but that, for the time being, he is not allowed out of the police station.

This early disappointment is tempered by the comforting news that 'he needs more time,' mainly for eating and running up bills. The beauty of this is that it delays the evil debut while conveying the promise of better things to come. Given the more time that he needs, who knows what dizzy heights might be scaled? As a general rule, you should give them until their 11th birthday and, if they still need more time, get out the Yellow Pages and look under 'A' for 'Abattoir.'

The great day arrives. Granted, to those who don't know any better, 14th of 15 in what has the appearance of being a desperate Wolverhampton maiden race may seem somewhat unpromising but this is where inside knowledge is invaluable, that is, the opposite of valuable.

What the hard-nosed student of form is apt to overlook is that the horse is still 'a big baby,' ran 'as green as grass,' and will 'come on a ton.' He also 'needs more time.'

The important thing is that the ability is there. Expressions such as 'useless,' 'of no account,' 'ungenuine' and 'temperamental' are all very well in racing annuals but have no place in the delicate relationship between owner and trainer. The horse has ability; that goes without saying. The problem is finding it. Even with a good trainer, it can be a desperate race against time. If you haven't found the key after about five seasons you should consider replacing the door.

Good trainers are humble people. They will readily admit that they have not yet found the right trip/going/tactics/feed/bit/shavings or training routine for your pride and joy but they are willing to devote a lifetime to finding the right trip/going/tactics etc. Never forget that your horse may be only the right bag of horse nuts away from the Prix de l'Arc de Triomphe.

True, the horse is pure sprint-bred. However, its utter inability to sprint proves that it is a genetic freak. Clearly, it needs a trip. Well, maybe not a real trip but somewhere in that tricky area between six furlongs and a mile and a quarter. By the end of the season you may have to face up to the fact that the horse 'doesn't have a trip.' What this means is that there is no distance recognised by the Jockey Club over which your horse can go faster than its rivals. It is an open question whether, as your trainer suggests, he would be a world beater over six furlongs 101 yards.

What we do know is that he is not suited to Newmarket's relentless galloping straight any more than he is to Chester's tight turns. He doesn't act left-handed, nor right-handed. In addition, he's not very good at galloping straight or, indeed, at galloping. It may be worth fitting him with blinkers and then with a visor. Visors were introduced so that, when blinkers failed, there was something else to try.

Racing folk hold widely differing views about horses' intelligence. Personally, I don't think the signs are very encouraging. Nevertheless, if your horse refuses to show anything remotely resembling 'form,' it may be worth trying to reason with him. If that doesn't work, try reasoning with him while holding a pair of gelding irons.

After your horse has spent two or three seasons troubling everybody except the judge, you should consider switching codes. This is an exciting time. Those obstacles could well be the making of him. Why, only last week, didn't your trainer say that he had always thought of the gelding as a National type?

3
NO ORDINARY OWNER ...

The wonderful Wilfrid Hyde-White (right) with John Dunlop and Lester Piggott.

For years, it was my dream to have a horse in training with Sir Mark Prescott and, until spread betting arrived, I lived the dream, along with other dreamers, including fellow racing journalists Alastair Down and Chris McGrath. Prescott did us proud. Our first horse, Quinsigimond, won four times in 1993 and our second, Petomi, won three times in 1994 and once the year after, before being sold to race in Italy, where she won another four races. It was all terrific fun and, if Sporting Index would give me my money back, I'd do it again.

Here is a small flavour of my experience of ownership, and bigger flavours of some of the extraordinary racehorse owners who have added colour, and eccentricity, to the sport.

PETOMI *The Sporting Life*, 7 May 1994

After the mighty Quinsigimond, who was wonderful, we clubbed together and bought a yearling, called Petomi. She's ill; she's had the virus. Sir Mark Prescott's very good about it. He rings up every Sunday, except when he's bullfighting, and we talk about how ill she is. To begin with, she was quite ill, but now she's hardly ill at all. Soon she may be well.

He talks about scoping and the bacteria count and whether it's a good idea to canter her this week or wait until she's got really good at walking. I tell him that I haven't been feeling too good, either, and wonder if it's the same thing, and we decide it may be best to stick to the walking.

Last week, I went to see Petomi. She didn't recognise me but she walked out of her box and back in again really well and I said those things you say to make it seem as if you know what you're talking about. 'She's grown, hasn't she?' (This is a fairly safe one, since she's been eating solidly for two months), and 'She's still a chestnut, then?' Then you pat her on the neck and say, 'Feeling better?', and she doesn't say anything. Probably feeling too ill.

I don't mind. You don't really feel you've been an owner until you can say, 'Oh, she's had the virus,' and everybody nods and talks about all the viruses they've known and then you get on to rape seed and, after that, vaccinations. Then you think of all those races she might have lost if she hadn't been ill and start thinking about all the ones she's going to win when she's better and how it was probably for the best in the long run, anyway.

By the way, when does the season end?

THE AWFUL TRUTH *The Sporting Life*, 13 May 1995

As we stand in the parade ring at Doncaster, it doesn't seem possible that so many people can own such a small horse. There aren't enough legs to go round. 'I've seen more,' says George Duffield. Owners, not legs.

Petomi has been sweating. She's worried. What's she worried about? Bosnia? All she's got to do is run as fast as she can for a minute, then she can go home and have dinner. I think it's oats again.

'It's quite warm,' says fellow part-owner Jo Willis-Bund, making excuses for Petomi and telling me off for calling her 'it.' No, it's not, it's quite cold. It's quite cold but it's not raining, because God, in his infinite indifference, doesn't seem to care that Petomi likes it soft and it's good to firm, firm in places.

Sir Mark Prescott gives George his instructions. I want to hear him say, 'Right, George, we've got a race in mind for this one in November and we've got to get her dropped 27lb in the handicap. See what you can do, will you?' But he doesn't say that.

We're geared up for defeat. The ground's probably too fast, Petomi's got the worst of the draw, the opposition looks quite strong, and this is the yard's first runner after being hit by the virus. We're geared up for defeat but the inside of my head keeps running a picture of Petomi sticking her neck out to clinch victory. Silly, I know, but she's game, and can quicken, and won all three of her races last year. Some clever placing. She's not as good as the handicapper thinks she is. Maybe she's improved.

We thought she'd run well but get beaten. We were right about the last bit. Her form figures now read 111-11, but the last ones stand for eleven.

Prescott tells us that Jack Waugh used to say, 'The longer people talk about the race afterwards, the worse the horse has run.' We talked for ages. Duffield and Prescott told us the truth. I like that. There's the awful possibility that she hasn't trained on.

The next time I looked, Petomi had been entered for a couple of claimers. Goodbye dreams, hello reality. But, somehow, I like that, too.

WHERE IS SIENA? *The Sporting Life*, 28 October 1995

Tuesday was the day for selling Petomi, so we set off for Newmarket Sales, trying to work out what one eighth of 8,000 was, and one eighth of 12,000, and one eighth of 16,000, and one eighth of 160,000, in guineas.

The auctioneers are incredible. After a few years, I wonder if they get stuck in the mode, come down to breakfast, and say, 'Shredded Wheat, Shredded Wheat, will someone start me off with the Shredded Wheat, who's going to start me off, do I see some milk, is that some milk there, is that your milk, whose going to help me with some milk, lovely Shredded Wheat, where's the sugar, do I have the sugar, where is the sugar, have you got the sugar, that's your sugar, it's with you, do I hear a spoon, where's the bloody spoon?' Only more quickly.

Anyway, just before Petomi walked in, the group of Arabs we'd been pinning our hopes on walked out and no one but us seemed very interested in lot 570 apart from Paola Forzanti, who bought her for an insulting 6,200gns.

I think Paola only bought her because of her name. It sounds Italian, doesn't it, Petomi? Actually, she was named after Peter and Tommy Mines, who owned more of her than the rest of us. I knew we should have called her whatever Flower Of Dubai is in Arabic.

Paola couldn't speak English but a friend of his told us that Petomi would be raced in Siena. I don't know how like Wolverhampton that is but Jo Willis-Bund, who owned part of Petomi until the auctioneer brought his hammer down, prematurely, was racked with worry that Petomi might not be happy. The rest of us were racked with worry that an assortment of banks and bookmakers might not be happy.

Anyway, Sir Mark Prescott bought us all dinner, which was nice of him under the circumstances. The circumstances being that, having trained Quinsigimond and Petomi, combined price 15,000gns, to win eight races, and then fetch 34,000gns, some of us were pleading poverty and baling out. You just can't please some owners.

A dreadful woman, but a good subject.

DOROTHY PAGET *Racing Post*, 18 January 2010

More than 20 years ago, I drove along Nightingales Lane, between Chalfont St Giles and Little Chalfont, in Buckinghamshire, until I reached a lodge at the entrance to a sweeping drive. It was almost 30 years since Dorothy Wyndham Paget had lived at Hermit's Wood but the owner kindly agreed to show me the rooms that the extraordinary Miss Paget, the owner of Golden Miller, once occupied.

We examined the shed fitted with a heated floor for the comfort of Paget's great danes, then stood on the balcony at the rear of the house, overlooking the neat garden. 'It was in a dreadful state when we arrived,' the lady told me. That was because Mr Hall, the gardener and odd-job man, was rarely allowed to cut the lawn during the day, when Paget was asleep, and it was difficult to cut the grass at night, when it was dark.

In Little Chalfont, Hall was known as 'the eunuch,' because locals could not believe that Paget, a dedicated spinster, would tolerate an 'entire' on the premises. There were no other men on her staff, both racing manager and chauffeur being women and, when Hall received his instructions, they arrived from one of a team of secretaries, each allotted a colour, blue, yellow or pink, but not green, which Paget regarded as unlucky. 'Tell Hall to grow gladioli,' and a message, in duplicate, would be issued, to join countless others. Messages announcing Paget's impending visit to the toilet, messages instructing a trainer to load a horse into a horsebox, followed by a message instructing the same trainer to unload the same horse.

Paget did as she pleased, to the frequent displeasure of others. It was a reward for having been born, in 1905, the second daughter of Almeric Paget, the first and last Lord Queenborough, and Pauline Payne Whitney, a wealthy American heiress. Whitney died in 1916, leaving Dorothy a fortune large enough to make any skill beyond that of signing a cheque superfluous. Later, Paget employed a secretary to sign the cheques for her, while she prepared for adult life by getting expelled from six schools in England by the age of 15, at which point she turned her inattention to the French education system. In Paris, she was tutored by the Russian Princess Vera Meshchersky, emerging sufficiently accomplished as a singer to perform, at Christmas 1924, before 400 inmates of Wormwood Scrubs prison.

Whitney's family belonged to the elite of American racing society while, in

1922, Lord Queenborough won the Two Thousand Guineas with St Louis. Dorothy became an accomplished horsewoman, riding side-saddle to hunts and in point-to-points, an achievement hard to imagine in later life, when Paget appeared to have eaten a horse rather than ridden one. Hunting foxes was certainly more to her taste than chasing men, for whom she had a strong aversion, confiding in a cousin that the worst experience of her life was being kissed by a drunken Frenchman.

Sober Englishmen were barely more welcome and, when forced to travel by train during the Second World War, Paget appealed to the Minister of Transport for special dispensation to reserve a carriage to herself, on the ground that sitting next to a strange man was liable to make her vomit. The danger of unwelcome contact was reduced by booking more than one seat for herself at Wimbledon and the theatre, the spare seat being occupied by Paget's handbag, a thermos flask and sandwiches, while her visits to the local cinema, in Amersham, were notable for Paget's habit of booking the entire auditorium.

In her twenties, Paget developed an enthusiasm for motor racing so strong that, on occasion, she shared a car with the charming Sir Henry 'Tim' Birkin, bankrolling his failed attempt to win the 1930 Le Mans 24-hour race with a supercharged Bentley. The engine blew, Paget withdrew her support, and Birkin went on to burn his arm on an exhaust pipe, contract blood poisoning and die, aged 36, in 1933.

Paget switched her passion, and cheque book, to racehorses, slower than Bentleys but easier to bet on. In 1931, after a series of expensive failures, she paid a reputed £12,000 for two geldings, Insurance and Golden Miller. At the time, the Cheltenham Gold Cup was worth less than £700.

Insurance had recently completed an impressive hat-trick over hurdles and went on to win the 1932 and 1933 Champion Hurdles but Golden Miller's future success was less predictable. When trainer Basil Briscoe's £500 acquisition first arrived from Ireland, Briscoe complained, 'I wanted a likely chaser, not a three-year-old cart horse.' Sent hunting, his rider reported, 'We went through the roots of every fence we jumped.' Things gradually got better and, when Paget bought Golden Miller, as a four-year-old, he had won two hurdle races and finished second in his only chase.

Paget and Golden Miller had little in common, although Golden Miller also ate like a horse. Both out of the ordinary, their names became inextricably linked. Paget's cousin, Jock Whitney, owned Easter Hero, winner of the 1929 and 1930 Cheltenham Gold Cups, but Golden Miller soon outshone him, rapidly establishing himself as the greatest steeplechaser of his era. A relentless galloper with a devouring stride, who jumped quickly and economically, Golden Miller won his first Cheltenham Gold Cup as a five-year-old, in 1932, on only his sixth race over fences. He won the Gold Cup again in 1933 and 1934, when, uniquely, Golden

Miller also won the Grand National, carrying 12st 2lb and knocking eight seconds off the course record. He is still the only horse to have won the Gold Cup and Grand National in the same year. Golden Miller won the Gold Cup again in 1935, narrowly beating Whitney's Thomond II.

Three different jockeys had partnered Golden Miller in his first three Gold Cups and, following an argument after the 1935 Grand National, Paget's horses were moved from Briscoe to Owen Anthony's yard at Letcombe Bassett, where Tim Forster later trained. 'Training horses is child's play,' Briscoe remarked, 'but it's a hell of a bloody job trying to train Miss Paget.' Under Anthony's care, Golden Miller won the Gold Cup for the fifth successive time in 1936 and finished second on unsuitably firm ground in 1938, the 1937 race having been abandoned because of flooding.

Following the 1934 National, Miss Paget declared herself 'terribly pleased' with her champion's performance and presented Briscoe and jockey Gerry Wilson with large chocolate effigies of Golden Miller, who received an appreciative kiss. It was, one wag remarked, the first time she had ever kissed a member of the opposite sex. To be fair, no others had won a Gold Cup and Grand National.

Briscoe and Wilson thoroughly deserved their chocolate, for dealing with Paget was a trying and exhausting ordeal. Her daily routine followed an unconventional pattern, with dinner at seven in the morning, followed by bedtime. Meals were substantial – 'there were an awful lot of larders here when we first arrived,' I was told during my 1989 visit – with breakfast at 8.30pm. As well as fish and chips, Paget had an insatiable appetite for discussing her horses with her trainers, with a tendency to open the discussion at midnight, while taking a break from all-night card sessions with her staff. When Briscoe attempted to escape her tyranny by taking his telephone off the hook, Paget despatched a messenger at 2.30 in the morning, with instructions to replace it.

Paget's unusual timetable resulted in a correspondingly curious arrangement with her bookmaker, William Hill. Since Paget was usually asleep during racing hours, it was agreed that she would be allowed to bet, as it were, posthumously, after the racing was over. It was testimony to Paget's honesty, if not to her betting prowess, that the arrangement did more for Hill's bank balance than for Paget's. She bet on a gargantuan scale. At a time when the average price of a house was less than £1,000, Paget regularly bet several houses at a time. Sometimes choosing to strike a bet to win £20,000, she once put £160,000 on an 8-1 on shot. Fortunately, it won. Many did not and, in 1948 alone, Paget lost over £100,000, equivalent to about £3 million today.

The choice of Hermit's Wood was particularly appropriate because, before Paget moved in, in 1939, the estate was occupied by Sir Reginald Blair, a Conservative MP and founder director and later chairman of the Racecourse Betting Control Board, which ran the Tote.

For Paget, outings from Hermit's Wood to the racecourse were not straightforward. Her choice of clothes was easy enough, since she invariably confined herself to a shapeless tweed coat and dark beret. According to Alice Wilson, who lived nearby, Hermit's Wood was one of the few places boasting stockings during the Second World War, but when asked if Paget wore them, Wilson exclaimed, 'No, she'd never have got into them, she had the most enormous legs.' This may have been malicious local gossip, for Paget discouraged visits from strangers and did not encourage them from relatives. When I approached Paget's nephew, Sir Gawaine George Hope Baillie, busy in Leeds Castle amassing one of the world's largest stamp collections, he told me that he had met his aunt only twice, and gave the impression that twice was sufficient.

A trip to the races was preceded by a flurry of notes and instructions, including one to Hall, the gardener, to stand in the middle of Nightingales Lane to ensure that Paget's chauffeur-driven Rolls-Royce made an unobstructed exit. Watches were synchronised, a precaution that failed to guarantee Paget's arrival at the races on time. Once, when her car broke down, she promptly bought the local butcher's delivery van to get her to the races and, subsequently, insisted that a 'spare' Rolls-Royce form part of the convoy.

In June 1939, Miss Paget, still only 34, set off for Royal Ascot, buoyed by trainer Fred Darling's glowing reports of Colonel Payne's prospects in the Cork and Orrery Stakes. Colonel Payne had cost Paget 15,000gns as a yearling, and was about to cost her a great deal more. After having one of the biggest bets of her life, Paget watched Colonel Payne finish well beaten, then rushed into the unsaddling enclosure to confront her trainer. 'Where's Mr Darling?' she demanded of jockey Gordon Richards. 'I wouldn't be quite sure, Miss Paget,' Richards replied, 'but I've a pretty shrewd idea he's on the top of the stand, cutting his throat.'

In that year, Golden Miller joined Insurance in retirement at Paget's Elsenham Stud, in Essex, where her 1943 Derby winner, Straight Deal, was bred. Three years earlier, Solford and Roman Hackle had given Paget a Champion Hurdle-Gold Cup double at Cheltenham and she would win both races again, the Champion Hurdle with Distel in 1946 and the Gold Cup with Mont Tremblant in 1952. The following year, carrying 12st 5lb, Mont Tremblant finished runner-up in the Grand National.

Fulke Walwyn, Mont Tremblant's trainer, was responsible for 365 of Paget's grand total of 1,532 winners but, despite imposing a 'no phone calls after 9.00pm' rule, Walwyn found it an exasperating experience. 'She was,' he told me, kindly, 'so trying.' One day, when Walwyn won five races at Folkestone, Paget complained that he should have won six, an episode that may have contributed to a lengthy spell when trainer and owner were not on speaking terms. Instead, Paget used Peggy Whitehead, a huntswoman and international showjumping rider, as an intermediary. On one occasion, with Walwyn in a nearby room, Paget gave Whitehead her instructions, then added, 'Kick him in the balls if you've got the guts.'

After eight years, Walwyn resigned and Paget's body, subjected to up to 100 cigarettes a day, soon followed his example. Paget died at Hermit's Wood, of heart failure, in 1960, aged 54. She did not leave a will, only 'The Heaps,' rooms full of messages and old copies of *The Sporting Life*. The lodge at the entrance is still there but, in 2006, Hermit's Wood was demolished, to be replaced by a block of luxury apartments, called Ellwood Hall. Paget Hall would have been more fitting, and more fun.

The father of my newsagent, a lovely man.

UJAGAR SINGH DHARIWAL *Racing Post*, 17 February 2004

Every morning at 6.00am, Harbhajan Singh Dhariwal opens his newsagent's shop in Taplow, near Maidenhead. He is a dignified, kindly, gently spoken man, working on, together with his friendly wife Bhupinder, well past the age when most people have retired.

It is a family business; nothing is too much trouble. Every morning, for over ten years, I have bought my *Racing Post* at Mr Dhariwal's shop. Upstairs, in a bookcase, among the scrapbooks and photograph albums, is a small, battered, maroon coloured notebook. On the cover, it reads, 'Jarabub. Racing career of Jarabub in Kenya. A scrapbook kept by Harbhajan Singh Dhariwal.'

Hidden beneath the everyday comings and goings of his newsagent's and general store, Mr Dhariwal has an extraordinary story to tell.

Born in the Punjab in 1928, Dhariwal moved to Kenya with his parents when he was six. His father, Ujagar Singh Dhariwal, became a bookmaker, and Harbhajan his helper. 'Because of racial discrimination, my father was not allowed to bet at the racecourse,' says Harbhajan. 'Only white bookmakers could bet there but, in Nairobi, on Government Road, he had a betting shop.'

It was a thriving shop and, in 1944, Ujagar became the first Asian in Kenya to own a racehorse when he bought a two-year-old called Jarabub for £425. Jarabub's grandsire was Hurry On, winner of the 1916 St Leger; his granddam was Fifinella, winner of the 1916 Derby and Oaks.

Jarabub was trained by Captain Spencer Tryon who, in 1928, during the Prince of Wales's visit to Kenya, had supplied the future King Edward VIII with a winning ride on Merlin in the King's African Rifles Cup. Jarabub won four races in a row before being ambitiously switched from six furlongs to two miles for the Kenya Gold Cup. Barely a three-year-old in Southern Hemisphere terms, Jarabub finished second.

Harbhajan went with his father to the racetrack, sometimes to Nairobi, sometimes to Nakuru, 100 miles away, but the reception for turbaned Sikhs was not always friendly. 'One day at Nakuru, my father sent me to get a drink,' he remembers. 'I joined the queue in the restaurant and, when I got to the front, I asked for a cup of tea. 'We are not serving tea,' said Mr Green, the restaurant manager. But I noticed that he was serving tea to other people, so I rejoined the queue. When I got to the front again, I again asked for a cup of tea. 'I have told you already,' snapped Mr Green, 'We are not serving tea.'

When Harbhajan told his father, he was furious and set off for the restaurant but, on the way, was met by Lord Delamere. Lord Delamere strode to the restaurant and ordered Green to serve Harbhajan, but it was not a happy experience.

In 1945, Jarabub ran in the Civil Service Gold Cup. 'He was ridden by Arthur Orchardson,' Harbhajan remembers. 'Captain Tryon told him to kick on when he got to the straight but the jockey waited until half a furlong out, and got beaten a short-head. In the unsaddling enclosure, Tryon told Orchardson, 'You can look for another mount in the Derby.'

'My father asked Tryon, "Who is going to ride Jarabub, then?" "I am," replied Tryon, who was then 65 years old. "I will give you a cheque. If I don't win, you can fill in the amount".'

In his scrapbook, Harbhajan copied reports of Jarabub's exploits from the *East African Standard* and *Kenya Weekly News*, which had described Jarabub as 'clearly the best of last season's two-year-olds.'

True to his word, Captain Tryon rode Jarabub in the East African Derby, and won, sitting bolt upright, by four lengths. Harbhajan has a faded photograph of him doing it. Later that year, when trained by Major Kirkham, Jarabub won the Kenya St Leger and Governor's Conference Cup. Early in 1946, he won the Kenya Gold Cup and was then loaded onto the *SS Shirala* at Mombasa and shipped to Bombay, where he won the Brabourne and Aga Khan Cups.

Although Jarabub was Ujagar's star, he had other successful horses in training, both in Kenya and India, including Panoi, a half-brother to Ballymoss, the winner of the 1957 Irish Derby and St Leger and of the following year's King George VI and Queen Elizabeth Stakes and Arc de Triomphe.

Panoi was flown from Bombay to Nairobi to run in the City of Nairobi Cup. His trainer, Captain Bruce McLaren, worked Panoi and told Ujagar that he was not good enough to win. On the day of the entries, Harbhajan was at home on his own when Mr Day, the secretary of the Kenya Jockey Club, phoned to say that they had received no entries from Captain McLaren.

'My father was out,' says Harbhajan, 'so I asked Mr Day to enter Panoi. At midnight, there was a knock on the door. I answered it, and it was Captain McLaren, to see my father. "I'm sorry," he said. "I have made a blunder. I forgot to enter your horse".' It was lucky that Mr Day had phoned, and that Harbhajan had answered, because Panoi won, at 33-1.

In 1952, Harbhajan's grandfather died and his father went back to the Punjab to manage the family farm. Harbhajan stayed in Nairobi but his mother did not want him to work as a bookmaker, so he got a job with an oil company, in the accounts department.

One day, he was told that the trade unions wanted Asian workers to be replaced by Africans and, in 1965, he and his family moved to Britain. For the past 30 years, Dhariwal has run his grocery and newsagent's business and been a prominent figure in the Lions charity organisation.

'I am still interested in horseracing,' says Dhariwal, one of life's gentlemen, 'and still hope that one day, if God gives me the chance to stay alive long enough, I may own a racehorse again. I have still got my father's colours.'

Endearing, charming, life-enhancing souls. The day I interviewed Robert Morley was a day I cherish.

ROBERT MORLEY AND WILFRID HYDE-WHITE
Racing Post, 20 January 2010

Robert Morley and Wilfrid Hyde-White, instantly recognisable figures in their day, both appeared in an enormous number of plays and films, partly the result of trying to satisfy the demands of both Ladbrokes and the Inland Revenue. It was a difficult task, with Morley managing to avoid the need to emigrate or appear in the bankruptcy court, and Hyde-White not managing to.

I have fond memories of visiting Morley at Fairmans, the actor's family home at Crazies Hill, near Henley-on-Thames. It was 1991, Morley was a comfortable 83, sitting in a deckchair at the end of the garden, smoking a cigar and intermittently pondering the scrapbook that rested on his lap. 'No, I don't go to the theatre any more,' he said, when I asked him if he did, 'but I go to the occasional memorial service.' I can still remember the distinctive cadence of his voice, the perfection of the pause.

Warm-hearted, witty and whimsical, an instantly endearing man, Morley was bred to bet. His father, Major Robert Morley, was an accomplished loser, and took Robert junior to the casinos in Deauville and Monte Carlo, as well as to their local racecourse at Folkestone, to demonstrate how it was done. Major Morley could either gamble or own racehorses but not both so, when he took his son to Tattersalls' Sales and presented himself as a prospective buyer, the action was confined to inspecting the horses in their boxes. There wasn't any money to actually buy one.

Intent on a career in acting, Morley presented himself at the Royal Academy of Dramatic Art, where Helen Haye, an established actress, found the efforts of his group unbearable to watch. 'Not a winner in this lot,' she'd say, turning her attention to *The Sporting Life*, 'perhaps I can spot one at Sandown Park.' It was a habit Morley soon adopted, eventually consolidating his links to the sport by marrying the daughter of Herbert Buckmaster, a director of Ladbrokes.

Hyde-White, five years older, had no racing connections, his father being canon of Gloucester Cathedral. When Wilfrid expressed an unwelcome interest in acting, Canon White despatched him to uncle Joe Fisher White, himself an actor, to dissuade him. Fisher White, 54, took Wilfrid in his chauffeur-driven limousine to visit his 24-year-old mistress. 'I was very impressed,' Hyde-White recalled. 'I thought, the sooner I am an actor, the better. I wanted Rolls-Royces, mistresses, and racehorses.' Later, he would have all three. Like Morley, Hyde-White set off for the Royal Academy of Dramatic Art, where he learned two things – 'First, that I couldn't act; second, that it didn't matter.'

Both Hyde-White and Morley regularly played themselves, urbane English gentlemen with a flair for light comedy and a champagne lifestyle, to which acting was a generally agreeable, if uncertain, passport. Early in his career, Morley joined the Cambridge Festival Theatre Company, whose director, Norman Marshall, remarked that he was 'as unpromising an actor as I have ever seen.' Marshall changed his mind after Morley registered a string of successes in the later 1930s and 1940s. When *Edward, My Son*, a play Morley co-authored, was a long-running success, he bought his first racehorse and called it The Gloomy Sentry, after a line in the play.

In 1951, Morley appeared in the classic film, *The African Queen*, as the Reverend Samuel Sayer, brother of Katharine Hepburn's prim missionary. The Reverend suffered an early death, which left Morley free to take Lauren Bacall, Humphrey Bogart's wife, to the races. Celebrities were different in those days. Bacall, who really was one, was approached by only one racegoer, a policeman.

Morley became friends with John Huston, the film's director. Inevitably, Huston was also taken racing, to Newmarket's July meeting – 'except for the flies, it was delightful.' Morley persuaded Huston to buy the winner of a selling race. 'I said, 'bid for it, John,' and the horse immediately fell down dead.' Huston, as he tended to in hopeless situations, offered the reassuring opinion, 'He'll be just fine.'

On another memorable day, the same year, at Worcester, Evan Williams, the trainer of The Gloomy Sentry, told Morley, 'We're going in.' The Gloomy Sentry won by a short-head. 'Going in was a wonderful experience,' Morley recalled. 'It involved standing in the winner's enclosure after having done absolutely nothing.' Two years later, Williams retired. 'His wife couldn't bear to meet the owners,' Morley explained.

Hyde-White, meanwhile, spent his early acting days working for Tom Walls' theatre company, at the Aldwych. It was a good match because Walls divided his time between working as an actor-manager and training racehorses. In 1932, he won the Derby with his own April The Fifth. Six years later, Hyde-White appeared in the film I've Got a Horse and, somewhere along the way, attracted the attention of Dorothy Paget, the eccentric owner of Golden Miller.

Paget would book a box at the theatre, arrive when the play was over and the cast were taking their bow, then escort Hyde-White to the Cafe de Paris to discuss racing. Morley was once invited to join them. He watched, in amazement, as the pair became so immersed in discussing breeding that Paget uncharacteristically postponed her attack on the lobster thermidor, then asked Noël Coward to delay his cabaret performance to enable them to finish their conversation. When Coward pointed out that he wasn't actually due to perform that evening, Paget offered to pay him, anyway. Morley asked Hyde-White if he didn't think Paget's behaviour a bit strange, to which Hyde-White replied, 'Wouldn't you be strange, if you owned Golden Miller?'

Racing was a subject so close to Hyde-White's heart that, according to Morley, 'his enthusiasm for performing in Shakespeare never recovered from the shock of being asked to rehearse while the Derby was being run.' Both men were prone to improvise but only Hyde-White, having acquired a yearling, departed from the script in order to discuss the choice of a name with the audience. Finally, he settled on Coal Scuttle. 'Wilfrid thought that it might amuse them,' said Morley, pausing before adding, 'I'm not sure that it did, though.'

In 1954, now regular racing companions, Morley and Hyde-White appeared together in a play called Hippo Dancing and a film called The Rainbow Jacket, filmed largely on racecourses, with both men playing owner-stewards. It provided ample opportunity for experiencing the real thing and, when *Hippo Dancing* proved to be a success, it was agreed that Wednesdays' matinee performances at the Lyric Theatre would be moved to Thursdays, an adjustment that enabled Morley and Hyde-White to watch Never Say Die win the Derby.

Combining afternoon racing with evening acting was difficult, but Morley and Hyde-White were determined. 'It was wonderful fun watching the 4.30pm and then trying to get back to the West End in time for the evening performance, especially if the 4.30pm was at Wolverhampton,' Morley remembered. 'They used to hold the curtain for us, which was an added thrill.'

The following years were full of work and play, with Hyde-White's career peaking in 1964, when he played Colonel Pickering in *My Fair Lady*. In constant demand, the money rolled in and, during the 1960s and early 1970s Hyde-White had horses in training with Ian Walker, enjoying success with Soft Collar, Lend An Ear and Three Sevens.

While Morley described himself as 'a nervous punter,' Hyde-White was a reckless one. When they went racing together, which was often, Morley would occasionally venture £100, a sizeable sum at the time. Hyde-White's approach had more zeros. 'He put £1,000 on every time one of his horses ran,' Morley recalled, 'but it became difficult for the bookmakers to compete with the Inland Revenue.'

By the time Hyde-White appeared in *The Jockey Club Stakes*, which enjoyed a successful run on Broadway in 1973, he had moved to the USA. When Morley asked his friend why he was moving, Hyde-White replied, 'I really cannot stand another winter in England with the income tax and Violetta [his girlfriend].' Then Hyde-White paused and apologised. 'Sorry, that was a very caddish thing to say about the income tax.'

In 1979, Hyde-White returned to face the wrath of the Inland Revenue, which entailed several bankruptcy hearings. At one, the official receiver asked why Hyde-White was staying at the Savoy Hotel? 'Two reasons, dear chap,' Hyde-White replied. 'One, it is the finest hotel in London and, two, it is the nearest to Carey Street.' 'But how are you going to pay for it?' asked the incredulous receiver. 'Well,' said Hyde-White, 'you're the financial expert. You tell me.'

At another hearing, held during Royal Ascot, the official receiver attempted to establish how Hyde-White had managed to get through so much money. Having failed in his attempt, the receiver asked, 'If you cannot tell us how you spent such a large sum in so short a time, perhaps you could tell us what will win the Gold Cup at Ascot this afternoon, since I understand you would already like to be on your way?'

'Of course, dear fellow,' said Hyde-White, welcoming the change of subject, and recommending Le Moss. 'But only have a small bet. We don't want to have to change places, do we?'

Le Moss won and, in 1980, Hyde-White cleared his tax debts but by then, well into his seventies, prosperity was beyond recall. He returned to California, where Morley periodically visited him, combining the visits with trips to Las Vegas, a favourite venue. In 1985, Hyde-White moved into the Motion Picture and Television Hospital but his debonair wit and love of racing survived. When a visitor asked if he ever watched any of his old films, Hyde-White exclaimed, 'Good God, no. I'm not as ill as that,' but when Royal Ascot came around, he put on a top hat, tails and a carnation.

Morley was better off, partly because, for ten years from the early 1970s, British Airways paid him handsomely for a series of commercials screened in America. He remembered, fondly, being told during filming, 'I'm sorry, Mr Morley, we can't get you into the Ritz for lunch today. Will the Dorchester be all right?' During the 1980s, Morley also presented a successful television programme in the US, called *Celebrity Chefs*. 'The celebrities cooked something, and I added the salt.'

Never out of work, Morley entertained himself, and others, with several more racehorses, latterly trained by Freddie Maxwell and Ray Laing: Anything and Just Ennis, Greek Skittle and Trample, Bobby Dazzler and, finally, Class Struggle. 'Nearly all my horses won, once,' Morley remarked. 'They weren't monotonous winners. To be an owner, you have to have hope. After that it needs faith and a certain amount of charity. It's very good for your character.'

When Laing offered little encouragement for Bobby Dazzler's prospects at Epsom in 1984, Morley backed him anyway, at 12-1, and thoroughly enjoyed the success, along with his final one, when Class Struggle won a seller at Windsor, at 14-1, in 1988.

Hyde-White died in 1991, aged 87, and Morley the following year, on Derby day, aged 84. He left instructions that his credit cards be buried with him. Margaret Morley, his daughter-in-law, arranged for a bench at Windsor racecourse, 'his spiritual home,' to bear Morley's name. After our meeting, Morley wrote me a charming letter, which I cherished. When my car was broken into, and my briefcase stolen, the letter went with it. I didn't mind about the other things that were taken, but I minded about the letter.

The most dangerous woman in the world!

JOSEPHINE ABERCROMBIE *The Sporting Life*, 17 June 1993

And in the blue corner, fighting out of Houston, Texas, weighing in at 5ft 4in and one hell of a woman, let me introduce, formerly Mrs Hudson, Mrs Segura, Mrs

Robinson, Mrs Ryan, Mrs Bryan – but that's all over now – Josephine Abercrombie.

Mrs Abercrombie, in her sixties and looking good, former cattle breeder, horsewoman, boxing promoter, Vogue model, skier, multi-millionairess, owner of the Pin Oak Farm and Stables, and a woman with so much energy she makes you feel tired, is over here for Royal Ascot. On Tuesday, Winged Victory came close to putting her royal blue and grey stripes into the winner's enclosure.

She loves life, and she's lived it to the bottom of the barrel. 'Life is fun,' says Mrs Abercrombie, neat and poised in a blue dress that looks a million dollars, and probably was. 'It's certainly better than the alternative.'

Josephine is the only child of James Smith Abercrombie, who was a good man to be the only child of. 'Life as a child was wonderful,' Josephine remembers. 'My parents were delightful and I didn't have to share anything.' That was quite a bonus because Jim Abercrombie invented a device for capping 'blowing' oil wells. The industry showed its appreciation by making him one of the richest men in Texas, where they know how to be rich, and a leader of Houston society.

'My mother would have liked me to put on a nice hat and a white dress but I used to go out on the ranch with my father and ride, ride, ride. When I was seven, I started showing horses; American saddle horses, five-gaited and three-gaited. I did it for years, and held the record for prizes at Madison Square Garden.'

That was appropriate because Madison Square Garden is where boxers go to beat the hell out of each other, and Josephine likes boxing. 'In 1938, my parents went to New York to watch Joe Louis fight Max Schmelling. It took three days on the train from Houston. My mother had just finished arranging her skirt, looked up, and Schmelling was lying on the floor.' Schmelling was hooked, and so was Miss Abercrombie, although her mother wasn't too struck.

'I used to listen to all the fights on the radio and, in 1951, my father and I went to Paris and saw Sugar Ray Robinson fight. He was like a black panther and drove around in a big purple Cadillac.'

For a while, Josephine was diverted from boxing by men. 'I think men are wonderful,' she says, and she did her level best to find the right one. She was Mrs Hudson for a year, Mrs Segura for 18 months, Mrs Robinson for six months, Mrs Ryan for a year and Mrs Bryan for ten years.

No one can say she didn't try, but now she's through with husbands. She has decided she wants to be Mrs Abercrombie, instead. 'I've done that,' she says. 'I don't have to do it again. There will be no husband number six,' a decision which left Mrs Abercrombie free to concentrate on racehorses and boxers.

She set up the Houston Boxing Association, sat through 435 bouts at the 1984 Olympics, and launched herself as a promoter. Promoting boxing is something you normally do only if you are one of the most unpleasant men in the world. Stalin would have been good at it, but he isn't around so Bob Arum and Don King are standing in for him.

Arum once described Mrs Abercrombie as 'the most dangerous woman in the world,' which was some kind of compliment. 'It was difficult,' she says, with masterly understatement. 'Bob Arum is the toughest, and very smart. You have to watch everything with him.'

And cuddly Don King? 'Well,' says Mrs Abercrombie, raising the odd eyebrow, 'we used to wave to each other and say, "Hi."'

World featherweight champion Steve Cruz, who took the title from Barry McGuigan, world welterweight champion Joe Manley, and 1984 Olympic gold medallist Frank Tate were in her boxing stable, as well as Tony Tucker and Carl 'The Truth' Williams. Mrs Abercrombie had an unconventional approach to boxing. She sent her boxers to university and gave them lessons in etiquette. Even if they got caught with a right, they knew which one was the fish knife.

When she lost her main venue in Houston, Mrs Abercrombie decided it was time to quit. 'It was tough,' she says, 'and exceedingly expensive. The big boys didn't really want me around.' No, I suppose not.

So Mrs Abercrombie switched her attention to her other great love, horses. 'In 1949, my father, myself and some friends had set up a syndicate to buy yearlings at Saratoga. Slim Pearce advised us and trained them and we did quite well. We thought, "This is easy; it's not tough at all." Then we decided to breed. We bought Pin Oak Farm and discovered just how tough it can be.'

In time, things got better. Pin Oak bred Touching Wood, the 1982 St Leger winner, and, in the same year, Mrs Abercrombie's Grease finished second in the Coronation Stakes before winning three Group races in France.

Eight years ago, she took on Joe Osborne, son of Kildangan Stud manager Michael Osborne, as Pin Oak's manager. 'He is a wonderful man, a complete horseman. I hadn't been concentrating on the horses but now I spend more time in Kentucky than Texas and, together, we've got it on the right tracks.' Sky Classic, the Canadian champion who won the Belmont Turf Classic and finished second in the Breeders' Cup Turf in 1992, stands at Pin Oak.

Mrs Abercrombie suddenly says, 'Feet are one of our big things. Dr Rick Reddon is our blacksmith and he believes in elevating horses' heels. I'm crazy about him. I think he's a genius. We're also into nutrition and weigh our horses every week, which is unusual in the States.'

Danny Vonhemmel and Bill Mott train the horses in America while, in England, Mrs Abercrombie uses John Gosden and Sir Mark Prescott. 'Racing in the States is very commercial,' she says, 'and that's fine, I like that, but it hasn't got the elegance of racing here. I love the big grass courses and the fact that not all tracks are oval. The scene here is so attractive but the thrill is just the same. I'm a competitor and nothing gives me a bigger thrill than seeing my horse coming down the stretch two lengths in front.'

When it does, you'll see Josephine Abercrombie leaping up and down. She's a real lady but she's not a lady who just stands quietly by, on life's sideline, saying, 'Oh, that's nice, how exciting.'

Josephine Abercrombie and Pin Oak Stud are still going strong. One of Pin Oak's stallions, the 1995 two-year-old champion Maria's Mon, bred two Kentucky Derby winners – Monarchos (2001) and Super Saver (2010).

4
... NOR TRAINER

John Manners and Cavalero in conversation.

Trainers come in many forms, from many backgrounds, rich and famous, poor and obscure, honest and crooked, capable and incapable, the racehorse a bond between them. Imagine the following trio together around a table.

JOHN MANNERS *Racing Post*, 15 April 2000

Down the twisty grey track, across the cattle grid, into a strange land. Higgledy-piggledy buildings, higgledy-piggledy people, where you expect the ducks and dogs and horses to speak. They probably speak when visitors have gone.

'Thought Hitler was going to invade, just over there,' John Manners points. 'Nothing to stop him. Father used to go over to the clock tower and stand guard with a shotgun.'

Manners, with his Wiltshire burr, tousled grey hair, mad-cap hat, all his own teeth, doesn't take his coat off and sits in the museum kitchen, with the caged bird singing, wall-clock ticking, cat sleeping and walls looking like the Thames rose up them and forgot to clean them on the way back down.

The walls are covered in pictures of Killeshin and Cavalero, who missed out on his chance of glory at Aintree, but runs in the Ladbroke Casinos Scottish Grand National at Ayr today.

'Suppose you're a bloody socialist,' says Manners, with far too much life for anyone to believe he's 73. 'Let's face it, we're a wonderful country. Tony Blair's only a f***ing Tory really, isn't he?'

If Manners ever writes a ******* dictionary, the biggest entry will be 'asterisk.'

Manners has discovered how to breathe without stopping talking. It's a wonderful discovery and he makes the most of it. 'Wonderful parents. Bought this bloody place after the war for f***-all. Father loved a gamble. A friend used to tell him, "Lester will not be beaten," so he'd have £200 on. If it won – well, they did sometimes, didn't they? – whisky all round.'

Then Manners leans forward on his kitchen chair, and says, 'Duodenals. It was the excitement. Died at 69. If only he'd have gone and been a bit sensible, but silly old dad. Put me clean off backing horses.' Edward VIII, Dunkirk, Stalin. Opinions fly around the kitchen like shot from a blunderbuss. Manners probably has a cleaner in the morning to sweep them all up. There would be plenty of time for it because he doesn't get up until 10 o'clock. Feeds the horses at lunchtime, again at midnight.

There's wife Audrey in leather trousers, hoping the rest of the family will appear normal provided she does. Daughter Heidi looking lovely, cooking lunch.

'I rode a few winners, point-to-point,' Manners machine-guns on. 'Used to ride until the horse was tired out, then went arse over head. Permit 1950, first winner under Rules Market Day. I'd train a winner, then have a row with a steward and we'd trot off to Portman Square. "Manners, your permit to train will be taken away until further notice."'

In 1989, the stewards took it away for three years. 'Absolutely stupid thing I did,' he recalls, 'fiddling about with the weights at a point-to-point. The one good thing about it was that we went to Florida on holiday. Took my own eggs. Poured with rain, but it was hot water. I've got a full licence now. I'm amazed they gave it to me. The Licensing Committee said, "Oh, you don't look as old as we thought you were."' It's true, he doesn't. And he doesn't stop. 'The way we train is a joke. We hack them round our 400 acres and I gallop them on the neighbours' farms when they aren't looking, and occasionally I take them to Lambourn. It does the horses good to go for a ride in a lorry.

'Our staff get run away with regularly.' One just has. No harm done. 'No one else but me rides Cavalero at home. Sunday before the National, I took him down to the river and he whipped round and I fell on my back. He galloped off and I lay on the ground and thought, "This is it. I'm f***ed. That's the end of the National, and a bloody good show." My boots were full of water and I had to walk back.' So did Cavalero.

'I love breeding things. Bred Cavalero ourselves, and his mother, Jolly Lass. An absolute cow, unrideable, couldn't get her on the racecourse. And Cavalero was an a******e to start with. I'm a hunting man, winning the Foxhunter was my dream. Have you seen the Cup? It's the most disgusting thing.'

Manners shows me into the dining room. You need a dining room with a big door and a high ceiling if you're thinking of putting the Cheltenham Foxhunter Cup in it. The Cup's huge. Huge and silver. Manners taps it with his knuckles. 'Of course, it's 100 years old. Country was at its peak. They could afford it.' Disgusting, but he loves it. Proud as punch, really.

They almost withdrew Cavalero from the Cheltenham Festival when the ground dried up. Manners didn't go. Audrey went, but closed her eyes and stood by a noisy dustcart with her fingers in her ears so she couldn't see and couldn't hear. The only person who knew they had won was Alex Charles-Jones, the winning jockey.

'I tell him he's too bloody old,' says Manners. 'He should pack up. We've had top jockeys ringing to ride Cavalero, but I'm going to stick with Alex. He does ride well for a 40-year-old, and he paints nice pictures.'

Remarkably, as well as the Cheltenham Foxhunter, Manners has won the Aintree version twice, with Killeshin and Cavalero, who had to be pulled up in last year's National when the saddle slipped and narrowly missed the cut for this year's version. Now he's seeking compensation in the Scottish equivalent.

'I might go to Ayr myself,' says Manners, 'because I'm feeling a bit cock-a-hoop after Cheltenham and Cavalero must stand a great chance. There are a hell of a lot of buggers in it, but it doesn't look a very strong race.'

Then we go out in to the yard and Manners introduces me to Cavalero and Audrey introduces me to Killeshin. No one could visit them without feeling that life was suddenly a bit richer, and hoping that Cavalero wins the Scottish Grand National.

Cavalero unseated his rider at an early fence in the Scottish Grand National but, five days later, won a hunter chase at Cheltenham. John Manners died, much lamented, aged 83, in 2009.

Next, a very different trainer: bullfighting and cock-fighting, hare coursing and opera are just some of the Baronet's interests.

SIR MARK PRESCOTT *The Sporting Life*, 4 May 1989

Sir Mark Prescott has fought bulls in the streets of Pamplona. At least, he's been chased up Pamplonese drainpipes by them. But that is nothing compared to the extraordinary feats he has performed with horses.

In 1980, the stable's Spindrifter won ten races in a row and 13 in all to equal Nagwa's record for the most victories by a two-year-old. Prescott then sent out Misty Halo to win 21 of her 42 races; Marching On and Mandalus won 13 races apiece and Dawn Review, Heave To and Herradura nine each. Yet none of these horses possessed exceptional ability. Spindrifter was allotted just 7st 11lb in the Free Handicap, while most of Misty Halo's successes were achieved with a Timeform rating of less than 90.

What his horses have lacked in ability, Prescott has made up for with careful planning and brilliant placing. He studies the racing programme with the same intensity that W. C. Fields once studied the Bible – 'Just looking for a loophole.' Who else could have piloted Misty Halo to 21 victories without one of them being in a handicap?

'I used to love it when there were different handicappers for different meetings,' he says. 'The excitement of finding you'd been given a chance by one of them. I miss that. Then, in a few races each year, geldings got an allowance. I loved beating a colt by a neck with a gelding which was getting that 3lb allowance. It appealed to my rather unpleasant nature.'

Prescott's ability to recognise and exploit opportunities for moderate horses reaped a rich harvest in amateur riders' races. 'Trainers were reluctant to run good horses in amateur races,' Prescott recalls, 'and most of the races were conditions races restricted to horses that had not won a certain amount of prize money. Each season I'd select a two-year-old with some ability and make sure that it didn't win too much money. By the following June, I'd have the best mile or mile and a half horse in England that hadn't won £1,500.' With Elain Mellor on board to outride most of her rivals, it proved an irresistibly successful recipe.

Sadly, Prescott acknowledges that those loopholes are a thing of the past. That doesn't mean that his placing skills are redundant. 'If it's true that I am a good placer of horses,' he says, 'if I have any skill, then it's in being right in judging their ability before they run. To be right about how good they are, that is the key factor.'

Having made his judgment, Sir Mark meticulously studies and plots their programme. 'Every horse goes where it's got its best chance,' he says, and that is why he spends so much time in Scotland.

'My owners' geography improves out of all recognition,' he says. 'I don't mind in the slightest going to Hamilton and back in a day if I think we can win but to go to nearby Yarmouth to watch a horse that cannot win unless the stalls fail to open for all the other runners, that would be a most gloomy prospect.'

With the scope for exploiting loopholes in the programme much reduced,

Prescott has switched his attention to the veterinary side of the business. It is an area where he can still steal a march on his rivals and he applies the same meticulous eye to the data on scoping and blood testing that he once devoted to the Racing Calendar.

'It's up to me,' Prescott says, 'to eke out from each horse whatever it can do,' and no one does it better. Nevertheless, his ambition is to train better horses. 'I'd like to have a top horse, a proper horse, at any distance; one that, when you galloped it, it went like hell in the night. I've never had one like that. It's a gap. I worry about the fact that I haven't come up with a top horse when I've had so many winners.'

That one good horse may be a long time coming but, one day, it will surely arrive at this multi-talented trainer's yard. In the meantime, Sir Mark is not grumbling. He hasn't done, he says, since he recovered from a broken back. 'I enjoy every day of it, which is a marvellous thing. It's endlessly interesting. When I hear some trainer say, "Oh, hell, tomorrow I've got to go to Pontefract," I think, "how lucky." Can you imagine saying to someone screwing in bolts in a factory in Dagenham, "I've got to go to Pontefract races tomorrow"? How lucky can you be?'

Evening Stables

'This one had three runs last year. Ran badly, poorly and dreadfully.' Perhaps only half in jest, Prescott adds, 'I'll have to find the worst race of the season for it and then tell George that if he gets beaten less than half a length and doesn't get done for excessive use, he's fired.' Into the next box. 'This one looks as if it's going to be Catterick, G. Duffield, low draw, big stick, pray for a miracle.'

Then there is the inmate that Prescott ran without G. Duffield on board. 'It's the only video I've ever bought,' says Prescott, 'so that I could see the full horror of it. I told the jockey not to hit the front until inside the final furlong. He cruised into the lead two out, then gave him two enormous cracks. He veered across to the far rail, switched his whip, and gave him another crack which sent him back across everything he hadn't crossed already, and got beaten a short-head. As I was standing waiting for him, the rider of the winner turned to my jockey and said, "I don't like the look of your man." "I think we may just have held on, sir," said mine.'

Prescott is marvellously entertaining but it's the confident humour of an enthusiast who loves his job and knows that he does it well. It's the best hour in Newmarket.

'The Heath House equation this year is that, with the exception of Serious Trouble, who is too high in the handicap, the three-year-olds are no good. They'll each have their Derby but it will probably be in a claimer at Carlisle. Last year's three-year-olds were a grand crop' – they included the Cambridgeshire winner

Quinlan Terry, Teeming Shore, Plain Fact, Milligan and St Elmo's Fire – 'but they are now thoroughly exposed.'

Prescott on George Duffield

When Sir Mark Prescott was assistant to Jack Waugh, George Duffield was the stable's apprentice. On Waugh's retirement, in 1970, Prescott took over at Heath House, becoming Newmarket's youngest trainer. With the exception of a single season, Duffield has been the stable's jockey ever since. In the last ten years, he has averaged over 80 winners a season, yet Duffield has never been regarded as a fashionable jockey.

'As a man, I don't know better,' says Prescott. 'He and Colin Nutter, the best head lad in England, are honest to the nth degree. If the whole world told me that Duffield had stopped one, and he said that he hadn't , that would be it. That's a very rare thing to be able to say.

'In all these years, George has never been jocked off one of my horses, ever, nor will he ever be. When a new owner arrives, the number one condition is that Duffield rides, full stop. It's a source of amazement to me that he hasn't been snapped up by one of the top trainers and has only had one Derby ride. How can people be so blind?'

And his qualities as a rider? 'He's fearless and has always been able to impart a sense of urgency to his mounts. Even when he was a moderate horseman, horses went up the gallops faster for him than for anyone else. He never loses fitness in the winter, never lets himself go. I can't say that I've never looked at another woman but I've never looked at another jockey. I'd just love Duffield to ride the big winner he deserves.'

George Duffield on Prescott

'You couldn't ride for a better man, ever. You get no pressure whatsoever. If I ride a bad race, I know I'm not going to get a real earful or be embarrassed in front of other people. Later, all he would say would be, "I thought you rode a bad race. Never mind, there's another day."

'He instils a tremendous amount of confidence and, consequently, you make very few mistakes. We've survived so long because we've got respect for each other. We can communicate and admit our mistakes. I think of him as a good friend as well as an employer.'

And his qualities as a trainer? 'Eye for detail. He's so meticulous in whatever he does. He's always thinking well ahead and he's second to none in placing and planning. If a horse is capable of winning, he'll win with it, and he tells his owners the truth.'

Prescott on Hare Coursing

Over the last 15 years, Sir Mark Prescott has played a leading role in reviving the popularity of what was once a major spectator sport. He resurrected the Newmarket Club and is a key figure on the committee that runs the Waterloo Cup.

Whatever your own views may be, no one can doubt that coursing has been fortunate to have Sir Mark as its advocate. I asked him to sum up the case for the defence.

'The hare is better off with coursing than without it. The Newmarket Club, for instance, has conserved hare stocks enormously and this is now the premier area in the country for hares. We have educated farmers not to shoot them and not to spray their fields with Gramoxone [a herbicide containing paraquat, highly toxic to mammals]. At Chippenham Park, during the ten years before coursing started there, 2,860 hares were killed in the annual shoot. In the ten years since, 63 hares have been killed, there is no more shooting and no Gramoxone.'

Prescott is critical of animal welfare groups for ignoring hare shoots, in which over 300,000 hares a year are killed and an equal number wounded, while raising an outcry about coursing, in which less than 300 hares a year are killed.

'There's never been a wounded hare in coursing,' he says. 'It's either dead or it's alive. And it's not 'ripped to bits' – they're not marked. The hare screams if it's not killed outright and, to urban man, that is very shocking, but if you or I knew that when we died we would suffer for no more than 40 seconds, we would settle now and be very grateful. In nature, to suffer for 40 seconds is very short.

'If you want to ban it as morally wrong then, fair enough, but don't think that you'd be doing the hares a favour. The total welfare of the hare is better on a coursing estate than it is anywhere else.'

Prescott continued, with great consistency and success, to get the most out of the horses he trained, regularly achieving an outstanding strike rate. There were good horses, including three in 2006, when Pivotal was champion sprinter, and Last Second and Confidential Lady leading three-year-old fillies. Alborada won the Champion Stakes in successive years, in 1998 and 1999 and, in 2010, Hooray was champion two-year-old filly.

Duffield remained as stable jockey until his retirement, in 2005, aged 58, when he was succeeded by Seb Sanders. Hare coursing was banned from 2005.

CAPTAIN TIM FORSTER *Racing Post*, 19 January 2010

Captain Tim Forster was sitting in his battered Range Rover at the top of the gallops, on the Downs near Letcombe Bassett, waiting for his slow-coach chasers to lumber into view. When the first of them finally did, ears flopping, it was a horse about to run at Sandown's annual military meeting, where Forster regularly had runners. Sitting next to him, I asked why he liked the military races so much. 'It's because I used to be able to ride in them,' he said. 'I was excited about it for weeks beforehand. It was a tremendous thrill, falling off at the first fence.'

That was Forster. I met him only a few times but, when I did, he made me laugh, as he made many others laugh. What he said, the way he said it, the way he looked, the lugubrious, bloodhound expression, the droll tone, the impeccable timing, the fatalistic pessimism. Forster had that rare, wonderful quality, of making you feel better as soon as you saw him, and ready to laugh, before he said anything. He was also a kind man. On the other hand, he was said to have delivered some fearsome bollockings. A legacy of his army days, perhaps.

Forster seems to have been born at Cold Ashby Hall, in Northamptonshire, in 1934, the son of Lieutenant-Colonel Douglas Forster. He went to Eton, went into the 11th Hussars, possibly because they had taken part in the Charge of the Light Brigade, served in Malaya, Cumbria and Northern Ireland and, in 1957, rode a winner at the Vale of the White Horse Hunt's point-to-point meeting at Siddington, in Gloucestershire. Over 30 years later, when I asked what his ambition was, Forster replied, 'To win the Gold Cup and own the winner of the maiden at the Torrington Farmers' point-to-point.' Asked to name his best day's racing, he found it difficult to choose between winning the Grand National, three times, and the Stag Hunts Cup at the Devon and Somerset point-to-point, with When In Rome. 'I love it down there and got a hell of a kick out of it,' he explained.

It was fitting that, having taken out a licence in 1962, and moved into the Old Manor House in Letcombe Bassett, near Lambourn, his first winner as a trainer was in the United Hunts' Chase at the 1963 Cheltenham Festival, with the redoubtable hunter chaser Baulking Green. Forster, a man of principle, had firm views about what constituted a proper horse, and a proper racecourse. Proper racecourses had fences and unsuccessful drainage systems. Towcester was a particular favourite, resulting in the sort of going (soft) that proper horses required to be rewarded for their fine qualities, which included a substantial physique, sound jumping, ample stamina and a resolute attitude. Speed was not highly prized, despite the fact that his father had owned Light Harvest, winner of the 1956 Wokingham Stakes at Royal Ascot. When Jeremy Tree, a Classic-winning trainer of well-bred Flat horses, described Forster as 'a brilliant judge of a very slow horse,' Forster regarded it as a compliment, and glowed with rare pride.

'I don't know anything about Flat-race breeding,' he once told me, pointing, not altogether approvingly, at Cheerful Aspect, who had recently won a juvenile hurdle.

'Evidently he's by Cadeaux Genereux, who I'm told was a sprinter.' Singularly unimpressed by the bluest of bloodlines, Forster preferred to dwell on the memory of two trainers standing together, watching a selling hurdle. As the leader galloped by, one remarked, 'He's by Nijinsky, you know, beautifully bred.' 'I'm beautifully bred, too,' replied the other trainer, 'but I'm f***ing useless, as well.'

Forster might have enjoyed training Nijinsky, but only if he could jump an open ditch. Sprinter was a word that rarely passed his lips, and hurdlers were tolerated only on condition that they did the decent thing, and matured into proper horses, called chasers. Forster thoroughly approved of Tom Dreaper, Arkle's trainer, not least because of Dreaper's contention that 'there'd only be one thing worse than a Flat race, and that would be a hurdle race.' Forster famously declared, 'One day I'm going to stand for Parliament and, if I get in, my first Bill will be to abolish Flat racing and my second to do away with hurdlers.' He dismissed the Triumph Hurdle, saying, 'it doesn't count. It's a Flat race.'

Whenever one of his horses won a hurdle race, he seemed slightly embarrassed and, when Sun Surfer won the valuable Tolworth Hurdle at Sandown in 1993, Forster confessed, 'It's a terrible thing to say but, although I was thrilled to bits, I'd rather have seen one jump the last really well in the novice chase.'

The slow maturing chasers that got Forster's blood flowing required owners with healthy lifespans and plenty of patience. Looking forward to overseeing the education of the stoutly bred Ring For Rosie, Forster remarked, 'When she was two, I told her owner that she'd be no good until she was seven or eight.' To his surprise, Ring For Rosie won a novices' hurdle when she was six, a victory he regarded with mixed feelings, as he did when, a few weeks later, Holloa Away unexpectedly won a bumper on his debut. 'I can only suppose that it was one of the worst bumpers run in the British Isles in the last 25 years,' said Forster. If he was the beneficiary of a stroke of good fortune, Forster seemed to feel that the natural order had been disturbed, and was more comfortable relating that he had placed one horse 'appallingly' and 'totally ballsed up' another. For Forster, disaster was the normal state of affairs.

Pinned to the shelves of the bookcase behind his well worn armchair were cards declaring, 'The situation is hopeless and getting worse,' and 'Yesterday was a dead loss, today is even worse, tomorrow is cancelled.' Ambrose Bierce, author of *The Devil's Dictionary*, would have approved of Forster, and Forster of Bierce, who defined an optimist as, 'A proponent of the doctrine that black is white.' A dedicated pessimist, Forster was fatalistic about his pessimism, explaining, in a resigned, accepting tone, 'You're either an optimist or a pessimist. I'm a pessimist. You can't do anything about it. It's the way you're born. It's much better to be an optimist, except that, if you're always expecting the worst and something good happens, you're extra chuffed.'

Forster was not, therefore, prone to sending jockeys on their way buoyed up by encouraging predictions of the experience that awaited them. Memorably, before Ben Nevis won the 1980 Grand National, he instructed jockey Charlie Fenwick, 'keep remounting' and, before Last Suspect won the 1985 National, Forster told owner Anne, Duchess of Westminster, 'I'll meet you at the back of the stands, after they've caught him.'

In 1972, there hadn't been much time to give winning jockey Graham Thorner his instructions on Well To Do, because Forster only decided it was worth running him 15 minutes before the race. Forster owned as well as trained Well To Do, who had been left to him by Heather Sumner when she died the previous year. The Sumner family were stalwart supporters, for whom Forster trained literally hundreds of winners, including those by John Sumner's Royal Marshall II and the hugely popular Dublin Flyer.

With hindsight, Forster regarded his fine early record at the Cheltenham Festival as a puzzling aberration, and the barren period that followed as a fascinating display of fate's inevitable mockery. With Baulking Green winning the United Hunts' Chase four times, Forster had Festival doubles in 1964 (Baulking Green and Take Plenty), 1973 (Denys Adventure and Hinterland) and 1979 (Casbah and Redundant Punter). Although it was 18 years before his next Festival winner, he had few runners, and several that were placed. Forster believed that Drumadowney, who finished fourth in the 1985 Gold Cup, might have won had he not hit the third last fence hard, while Cherrykino, owned by Anne, Duchess of Westminster, fell and was killed in the 1993 edition of the race. The following year, in the Arkle, Coonawara, unbeaten in his previous nine races, fell at the third last, when leading.

That year, Forster moved to Downton Hall stables in Shropshire, owned by Michael Wiggin, a lifelong friend and chairman of Ludlow racecourse. When asked if it had taken him long to get used to the new gallops, Forster replied, 'There weren't any.' Having installed an uphill all-weather gallop and adopted Martin Pipe's interval training methods, he reported, dolefully, 'you know the worst thing about it? It works.'

There had always been a steady flow of fine chasers and big race successes – Royal Marshall II in the 1974 Hennessy and 1976 King George, Pegwell Bay in the 1988 Mackeson Gold Cup and AF Budge Gold Cup, Dublin Flyer in the 1994 Tripleprint Gold Cup and 1995 Mackeson and, then, towards the end, Martha's Son.

In 1991, after Martha's Son won a novices' hurdle at Stratford, Forster told owner-breeder Michael Ward-Thomas, 'I will never, as long as I train, win a steeplechase with this horse. He will never jump fences.' Later, Forster took characteristic pleasure in relating, 'Martha's Son then won nine chases in a row.' In 1994/1995 they included the Peterborough Chase at Huntingdon and the Victor Chandler and Comet Chases at Ascot but, in December 1995, a leg injury scuppered plans to run Martha's Son in the King George VI Chase. 'So that solves the jockey problem,' Forster observed.

When Martha's Son returned, at Kempton in February 1997, he fell at the second fence. Less than three weeks later, he ran in the Queen Mother Champion Chase at Cheltenham. Martha's Son had never run at Cheltenham before and, with his tendency to jump flat and low, was far from certain to shine. My final memory of Forster is of bumping into him immediately after Martha's Son's victory. 'I never thought he'd get round,' I said. Forster's face lit up, as if everything was suddenly back where it belonged. 'Neither did I,' he said, animatedly. 'I was sure he'd clip the top of one and turn over.'

Martha's Son went on to win the Melling Chase at Aintree while, the following year, Forster received the George Ennor Trophy for outstanding achievement, marking the occasion by registering a plea for jump racing to be protected, 'before I burst into tears.' In the 1999 New Year Honours list, he was awarded the OBE for services to horseracing.

By then, Forster was seriously ill. With stoic courage and undimmed humour, he defied multiple sclerosis and cancer for as long as they could be denied and, when he died, aged 65, in 1999, the tributes that poured forth were a telling measure of the huge respect and affection felt for him, as great as the affection he felt for steeplechasing.

5
BRIGHTON AND OTHER LOVES

Rocking Billy. A Brighton special.

I have a soft spot for Brighton. It's the town, as well as the racecourse, and the fact that it's a place, and a trip, I associate with having a good time, often in the company of my old friend and fellow writer, Ian Carnaby. In 1997, to celebrate happy days there, we launched the Ashforth-Carnaby Selling Handicap, although it appeared in the Programme Book as the Ashford-Carnaby Selling Handicap. Whatever it was, it was repeated annually until my credit cards all reached their limits, after which it continued, equally gloriously, as the Ian Carnaby Selling Handicap.

There were plenty of other racecourses I was fond of and, between 2005 and 2007, I undertook a tour embracing every racecourse in Britain and Ireland, 86 in all, writing articles about them along the way. The rich variety of our racecourses is often cited as one of the sport's great attractions, and it's true. From the self-conscious elegance of Goodwood to the humble charms of grandstand-less Bangor; the bread-and-butter fare of Wolverhampton and

Ludlow to the high peaks of Royal Ascot and the Cheltenham Festival. A huge range of venues and experiences, bound together by the horses and the people fascinated by racing.

In Ireland, where jump racing reigns in the affection of race fans, there is an engaging, egalitarian atmosphere at virtually every racecourse, from Punchestown and Leopardstown to Listowel and Killarney. There is a lot of fun to be found at racecourses.

I love the great festivals but I also love days at smaller, less well publicised, gems.

BRIGHTON: THE ASHFORTH-CARNABY SELLING HANDICAP *Racing Post*, 15 August 1998

Stan Clarke [chairman of Northern Racing, which manages the racecourse] and his amazing smile were on display at Brighton on Wednesday, along with lots of badges saying 'Welcome to Brighton.' It didn't stop all six favourites getting stuffed, which was a shame for my mate Mart, who started the afternoon by announcing that there was bound to be at least one winning favourite, and bet accordingly. I thought of comforting him by saying, 'There's always the next time, Mart,' but he'd just told me he was 51, so I kept quiet.

Sir Michael Stoute was the only posh trainer with a runner and he didn't have one in the Ashforth-Carnaby Selling Handicap, although William Hattersley, presumably Roy's brother, owned one of them and Mike A D'Arcy Quinn added a touch of class by owning another.

We were banned from giving an award to the stable lass we fancied most (the one who walked Muja's Magic round in the race before ours), and were told we were supposed to be deciding which horse had been washed and dressed best. 'Stand and try and look knowledgeable,' said Pete Thomas, helpfully. 'No, it's not working.' Alan Potts decided that Thomas O'Malley was the best turned out, so we gave his lass 50 quid and agreed that she'd probably have won the other award as well.

Everyone said Martin Pipe would win the big race with Highbury Legend but everyone was wrong because, to general astonishment, Mrs S Lamyman won it with Modest Hope. I bet Modest Hope was surprised, too, although he didn't say anything. When it came to the auction, neither did anyone else.

Mrs S Lamyman wasn't there, which was a pity, because she could have settled the argument about what the 'S' stands for. Mr McManamon, the owner, wasn't there either, which meant that Basil Richmond, who trained Modest Hope before Mrs S Lamyman did, got all the prizes, including the stick of Brighton rock.

Basil was delighted, Antonio Polli, the winning rider, was delighted, we were delighted, and most of the bookies except Fred Honour were delighted. Fred said he'd lost £490 on the race. I'm worried about Fred. Early on, he had a big cigar in his mouth and, later on, he didn't. I think he may have paid it out.

Everyone was very good to us and, later, inevitably, we ended up at the Chequers in Preston Street to see Rocking Billy (Wednesdays, Saturdays and Sundays) playing Gene Vincent records in his long red jacket and brothel creepers. Rocking Billy wears glasses nowadays, and I think his days of brothel creeping may be over, except possibly on Mondays, Tuesdays, Thursdays and Fridays.

In the meantime, Dion and The Belmonts were given another spin before Ian Carnaby said he was worried about the casino and felt he ought to check that it was all right. It was good fun, and we're going to sponsor the race properly next year, unless we're dead, in which case it can be called the Ashforth-Carnaby (Posthumous) Selling Handicap.

S for Sue Lamyman.

ROCKING BILLY, CUTE KATE, AND STICKS OF BRIGHTON ROCK *Racing Post*, 11 August 2001

Like debt and betting shops, once you get into Brighton, it's very difficult to get out, which means that I'm poorly placed to tell you about the Shergar Cup [staged at Ascot that day], but ideally placed should you want a stick of rock from that shop near Brighton pier called, revealingly, 'The Rock Shop.'

Before I forget, if you were wondering what had become of the William Hill shop that was always next to the Chequers on Preston Street but isn't anymore, they've moved it round the corner. The shop's moved, but I expect the results in it are just the same.

On Thursday, when a hurricane reached West Sussex, it rained so much that the biggest pool of water you've ever seen collected on the far side of the pier. It was so big, there were boats on it. The woman in The Rock Shop, who looked as if she'd just been dealt another 14 when the dealer had a picture, nodded at the monsoon and said, 'It always rains on racedays. That'll be £7.90.'

You know someone's a regular at Brighton when they stand in the pouring rain and say, 'I expect they'll come up the stands' side,' which is what Ian Carnaby said, as we tried to work out what was going to win the Ashforth-Carnaby Selling Handicap.

There's something perversely satisfying about having 18 runners for a 0-60 handicap and the top-rated on 47. The *Racing Post* Spotlight verdict said, 'They don't come much weaker than this. Having said that, something has to win.'

Having studied it, I wasn't so sure.

George Duffield was what journalists call 'an eye-catching booking' for Milton Bradley's Lokomotiv. Lokomotiv hadn't won for a long time, but then most of them hadn't won at all, including Scenic Lady, who likes Brighton, and finished first. Royal Satin, who doesn't like it, finished last. All the others finished in-between. For some reason, I've got a betting ticket in my pocket that reads, 'Sam Harris. £100 win, Stiletto.' Either it isn't mine, or I shouldn't have gone back to the cash machine.

I think that G Sparkes (7), who won later on Dodona, rides well, and I expect that L. P. Keniry, also (7), who won on Tapau, does too, although I didn't actually see that race.

After giving out the sticks of rock, we did what we usually do and trundled along to the Regency Tavern, where Mart produced this fantastic quiz. Which biscuit won the 1975 Dante for Geoff Wragg and Willie Carson? On which course are there no six-furlong races? Which King George winner had previously won two Brighton Challenge Cups? That sort of thing. Question nine was rather rude about me and the answer was Six Mile Bottom. He won the Ormonde Stakes in 1982.

In the Chequers, they've got a new manageress, called Kate, who comes from Birmingham but still looks gorgeous. I think I may have fallen in lust with her just after Rocking Billy played Twist And Shout and just before Hit The Road Jack. Rocking Billy, who got dressed as a teddy boy in the 1950s and forgot to change, has the most amazing record collection. He told me, in his kindly way, that I don't know my Billy Furys from my Eden Kanes, and proved it by playing Halfway To Paradise, which was Billy Fury, and Forget Me Not, which wasn't.

But then it's difficult remembering that far back, as anyone trying Mart's question number 87 will know. Which E. L. Doctorow novel and early 20th century music craze won the 1964 Richmond Stakes?

Eventually we ended up in the casino at the bottom of Preston Street, where a lady at the door smiled one of those welcoming smiles which, roughly translated, says, 'Here's another one,' and, when you smile back, becomes, 'silly sod.'

Anyway, after a while Ian had a big pile of chips next to him at the roulette table, even if they were only yellow ones; Howard was pushing his on to a rich variety of numbers, according to some deeply scientific system, and Pat was doing rather well at poker. I admire a woman for that. Both the blackjack tables were occupied by a colony of permanent residents who sat on, grimly determined, even after the dealer dealt himself a six, then a picture, and then spoilt everything with a five. After that he promptly followed up by dealing himself another six, followed by a picture and a four.

Mercifully, I never did get a seat but, when I got back to my hotel, I did have a long conversation with a woman standing on the favoured side of the front door, while I stood on the unfavoured side, trying to remember what the secret code number was to get in. It was 1-9-7-6, which I should have known from Mart's question 15, in which year did a book of verse by Ted Hughes win the St Leger?

That's easier than on which racecourse did Brigadier Gerard win two races as a two-year-old? I've no idea what the answer is, but I do know I've got a thumping headache. If you don't mind, I think I'll give Ascot a miss, and see if that nice little coffee shop on the front, along with the sea breeze, make any difference. They didn't last time.

PS. According to Mart, the answers are Hobnob, Sandown, Park Top, Ragtime and Newbury, in that order. Oh, and Ted Hughes's book of verse was called Crow.

PPS. Will the woman who was in the Chequers with a raincoat with a label in it that says 'Harrods' please get in touch. God knows how but, as well as my own raincoat, I seem to have got yours. It's a lot nicer than mine, but it doesn't fit.

The Chequers had long been a regular part of visits to Brighton but the course of true love had not always run smoothly. Once, after describing the pub's unusual ambience, I received a humourless letter threatening legal action.

THE CHEQUERS: A LEGAL CHALLENGE *The Sporting Life*,
24 August 1996
In a recent column (3 August), while looking forward to a trip to Brighton, I mentioned a pub called the Chequers, a favourite haunt of Ian Carnaby and myself over the years. I affectionately described the regular clientele as consisting of 'six lesbians, four gays, a retired greyhound and a man in loafers playing Billy Fury records.'

I have since received a letter from Devonshire Business Management Services, acting on behalf of the current proprietors of the Chequers. The letter acknowledges that, 'Prior to September 1995 the premises could have been described in the manner indicated,' but points out that, since the present owners took charge, the description is no longer accurate. 'My clients have invested a considerable sum of money in changing the premises both in decor, clientele and public relations to overcome its previous reputation.' As a result of my remarks, the author's clients are allegedly now experiencing 'social stigma.'

Funnily enough, during our trip to Brighton, and to the Chequers, Ian and I remarked on the changes that have, indeed, been made to the pub. I apologise for having depicted it as a place where a collection of colourful characters could be found and can confirm that, on our visit, the first since before September 1995, there was no sign of customers of unconventional sexual orientation, greyhounds, or players of Billy Fury records, although the sample was small.

If anyone knows which pub they have gone to, please let me know.

Some favourite venues from my racecourse tour.

KELSO *Racing Post,* **9 April 2007**

Kelso is a racecourse in *Alice in Wonderland*. Everyone there seems to regard it as perfectly normal but eventually you can't resist asking, 'Isn't it all a bit, well, odd?'

Richard Landale, the cheery managing director, spends most of the afternoon with one leg (the broken one) up on a bench, which means that someone else has to hand out the bags of carrots presented to every winner. The tweed-jacketed staff all walk round smiling; drugs, I suppose.

Landale is one of five shareholders in the company that owns Kelso racecourse – well, not the racecourse, exactly, but the car park. Another shareholder, the 10th Duke of Roxburghe, properly referred to as 'His Grace,' owns the track. His Grace also owns Floors Castle, the Roxburghe Hotel and the Roxburghe golf course, all rather more luxurious than the Roxburghe racecourse. Now that the former three have been invested into good shape, perhaps His Grace would care to focus his funds on the latter one.

In 1822, a former Duke built the stone grandstand now variously known as 'the main stand' or the 'Duke and Duchess's Stand.' It's a cross between a small stately home and Dotheboys Hall. Whatever crimes Wackford Squeers inflicted on his pupils at Dotheboys, someone has inflicted worse ones in and around the Roxburghe Stand (there, that's a better name).

On arrival, I suggest you close your eyes and ask to be escorted to the Duke's Bar, which is up a rather splendid stone staircase. The Duke isn't there (having seen a picture of the Duchess, he may be otherwise engaged) but a fine open fireplace is and, despite the fact that it's warm and sunny outside, the fire is blazing away.

Above the fireplace is a photograph of an elderly gentleman (anonymous) presenting a large trophy to an even more elderly lady (also anonymous). They both look pleased. Duke's Bar is one of several locations supplying tea for £1 in a real cup or mug, plus somewhere to sit down to drink it. Excellent, a bonus mark. See, it can be done.

Unfortunately, it has to be said that the innards, and several of the outards, of the Roxburghe Stand (you can call it what you like, but that's what I'm going to call it) are defective. The wonderfully named Doody Room, adjacent to Duke's Bar, is something of a microcosm of the whole racecourse – a complete hotch-potch, in this case of furniture and fittings of the kind that appear at auctions where, just as you are saying to your neighbour, *surely* no one will buy that, someone does.

Criminally, Heath Robinson-type structures and stairways have been attached to the sides of the Roxburghe Stand in a way that makes you want to weep (admittedly, I didn't see anyone weeping).

The whole racecourse, in fact, is awash with temporary-looking buildings. What Kelso needs, but has clearly never had, is an architect and designer; plus a large sum of money. Instead, it looks as if, every time there has been any money (never very much, nor very often), something else has been erected in the Portakabin tradition.

Today, in the Charity Tea Room (a Portakabin on skis), soup, sandwiches and scones are being sold in aid of Macmillan Cancer Support. On the walls are rather nice old photographs, several featuring the famous owner and rider Reg Tweedie, who lives on in the form of the Tweedie Stand, opened in 2000. Next to the Charity Tea Room is the Hamilton Room (Kelso is full of rooms). I don't know who's in it, Lord Nelson, perhaps.

The Tweedie Stand, an upmarket pink breeze block structure, is more like it, with the first floor boxes providing a terrific view of the track, and the ground floor food bar providing rather nice hot Scotch pies and hot mince pies, for £1.50. The Scotch are beef and the mince are lamb. I had the mince. It was good, and there were plenty of televisions to enable me to watch my bet on Dalucci go down by a neck. Thank you, God.

Luckily, Kelso has the country's finest clerk of the course, Anthea Morshead, as evidenced by her ability to tip the winner of the second hunter chase of the day, Natiain. She said he would gallop them into the ground, and he did. Thank you. Clerking's not all about stabbing the ground with a stick, then lying about it.

Above all, Kelso rises totally, idiosyncratically, even gloriously, above its defects. Like a character in *Alice in Wonderland*, the crowd seem joyously oblivious of any faults, ignoring the awful grey plastic seats and everything else that contributes to the desecration of the Roxburghe Stand, staring resolutely forward with eyes only for the wonderful view.

In case someone asks you, the pointed obelisk (you wouldn't want to sit on it) on the horizon is something to do with James Thomson, who wrote the poem on which Rule Britannia is based.

It comes as no surprise that there are no plans to do what some people would like them to, and change the curious configuration of the long, Aintree-type, run in; nor to make the deliberately stiff fences less stiff; nor to dispense with the Chicken

Hutch Bar, a semi-open, wood and corrugated iron structure that stands (just) as proof that racegoers can rise above their surroundings. They seem to love it.

There are, however, plans to build something containing restaurants and bars between the strange building currently housing Landale's broken leg, and the equally strange Doody Room, hopefully in two years' time, money permitting.

The best, and perhaps only way to judge Kelso is to look at the crowd – remarkably large for a Monday afternoon (Landale proudly explains that Kelso barely has a population in its catchment area), and remarkably happy. An amazing place. On the way back, I think I saw a golden eagle. I certainly saw a crow.

A certainty for any list extolling the virtues of the glorious variety of British racecourses. Close, or even cursory, inspection of the architecture is not advised. Instead, have a drink and a hot meat pie, and enjoy yourself. Maybe the Duke of Roxburghe will come good with some money.

KILLARNEY *Racing Post*, 23 July 2007

If you are thinking of dying, it's worth putting it off until you have visited Killarney. The view feels as if it is part of the racecourse, and the view is beautiful. The mountains are called Tomies, Purple, Shehy, Mangerton, with glimpses of Lough Leane and Ross Castle.

It's no more than a walk from Killarney town where, in the McSweeney Arms Hotel, Tony McSweeney, a twinkle never far from his eye, muses on the generations of jockeys who have stayed there. 'Twenty years ago,' he says, 'jump jockeys wouldn't be seen dead in a gym. Yesterday, even ****** went.'

You don't need directions to the racecourse, simply follow everyone else, quickly by foot, slower by car. If your hobby is studying ferns, lichen, moss and ivy, walk on past the entrance and enjoy the collection growing out of the racecourse wall.

Manager Con O'Mahoney, impersonating an ill-sitting hen, flits here and there. 'We reconstructed the track 12 years ago,' he says. 'It had notoriously bad bends leading to numerous stewards' enquiries. Now it's 30 metres wide, with a cambered bend.' It still looks sharp enough.

A new entrance has recently been built, as part of a five year plan. Nearby is a reasonably new grandstand. 'There used to be a timber one,' O'Mahoney explains. 'The roof blew off and, after we held a meeting without a roof, the stand burnt down.' Outside its replacement, an ambulance stands with 'Feidhmeannacht Na Seirbhise Slainte' on its side, perhaps as a reading test for jockeys with suspected concussion.

At one end of the stand is Ladbrokes' betting shop, with lots of live screens, and one dead one – the results screen. They probably want to avoid upsetting their customers.

The five year plan envisages bridging the gap between what the racecard calls the 'Stand' and what it calls the 'Stand Complex.' At the moment there is a single-storey tote building between them. The Stand Complex includes the Jim Culloty Bar, opened last year. 'He was born in Killarney, a Killarney man,' says O'Mahoney, adding, 'he had a bad fall here.' Culloty will be able to go to the bar, and reminisce about his fall, knowing that he will never be short of a drink, nor of a job behind the bar, above which are large pictures of Culloty and Best Mate.

A partition separates the bar from the self-service canteen, with its choice of sit down or stand up tables. The food isn't cheap – €3.50 for a plate of chips, €4 for a sandwich, €13.90 for a not very appetising (I know, I ate it) battered cod, with vegetables and mashed potatoes. The mashed potatoes defeated me.

In May, a new building was opened, housing the Killarney Racegoers Club – an excellent spot – weigh room, jockeys' room, stewards' room and, above them, a corporate suite with a magnificent view of the magnificent view. If you want to eat, that is the place to do it, although you had better book now for next year. All the seats are taken.

The setting produces a sense of space but the enclosure occupies a fairly narrow strip of land, and O'Mahoney says there is no room for expansion, except in the fixture list. This year, there is a three-day meeting in May, a four day festival in July, and a single day in September which, next year, will be two days.

The course is owned and run by the Killarney Race Co. Ltd, with unpaid directors and all profits reinvested. In 1995, a golf course was opened in the centre of the track, 'a small club but a very good spirit' says O'Mahoney, and a driving test centre is based at the course. A sign on the stand reads, 'Driving Test as Normal. Applicants Proceed to Applicant Parking Area Ahead.' There don't seem to be any applicants this evening.

In the pleasant parade ring, there are two palm trees, and roses with rose hips nearby. Look between the palm trees towards the mountains, and you could be on a Caribbean island (you're not).

In a persuasive bid for the title of 'least useful signpost on a racecourse,' the one in the middle of the betting ring boasts ten signs. There is some doubt as to whether all the featured destinations exist (where is the Horseshoe Bar?), and few exist in the directions indicated. The sign for the weigh room points towards the sponsors' lounge – a nice place for a sit down and a drink but lacking in scales. The sign marked 'Jockeys' points towards the toilets. Luckily, the enclosure isn't big enough to get lost, and no one is in a hurry.

Swallows fly in and out of the stables, children skip up and down with painted faces (it's Kids' Day), hot beef rolls are available, as ever, for €7.50, and the winning posts are topped by fluorescent red circles. And, always, there are the mountains.

According to the racecourse's website, Michael Kinane once described Killarney as his favourite racecourse in the world. Kinane's not here to ask if it still is and, while I'm waiting to talk to another jockey, I realise that the next race is the one in which I was told to back Newton Bridge, the first reserve, if he got a run. He did. I stood and waited until I could wait no longer. It was the jockey or the bet. I tried to be a proper journalist, and waited, and Newton Bridge tried to make enough mistakes to lose, but failed. At least he was only 5-1.

The course is awash with tips. Someone tells me that Ruby Walsh has given up food to do the weight on Davenport Democrat. I'm not convinced. I think it might just be that he looked at himself in the mirror and realised that he was horribly fat.

PS. Why weren't the Toblerone ladies here?

When it came to awarding marks. Setting 6/5. Magnificent. If you know someone who never stops moaning, send them to Killarney. If that fails, justifiable homicide would seem a reasonable next step.

MARKET RASEN *Racing Post*, 21 November 2005

Don't stop at the cemetery, unless you have to, but carry on down the lane. At first sight, it looks a bit like a 1960s school, or secret government research station, but turns out to be Market Rasen racecourse. It's rather nice, in a higgledy-piggledy sort of way.

The entrance was opened by Lord Oaksey in 1977 and people still pass through it today, often on a Sunday. Next year, eight of Market Rasen's 20 fixtures are on Sundays and five on Saturdays, which is handy if you hate shopping and church. The clock on the top of the entrance is working, which is always a good sign.

It's one of those courses which looks as if it's never had enough money to build everything at once, in harmony, but every few years, when they've got some money, either build another bit or refurbish what's already there. None of the major buildings look particularly new but a lot of the insides do.

Pip Kirkby, the managing director, says that Racecourse Holdings Trust, which owns Market Rasen, is developing a 15 year plan, a bit like the old Soviet Union but with fewer deaths. They don't seem to have quite decided what's going in the Plan but I suggest that they act boldly, and probably expensively, and end up with a stand with a big glass front to exploit the smashing view of the track and countryside.

Before that, they're thinking of fiddling around with the enclosures, currently separated by rather unattractive metal railings, including down the middle of the stands, and are about to introduce a new logo. There's also going to be two music nights next summer, instead of one.

It's a compact course, with the racecourse stables next to the pre-parade ring, which is near the winner's circle, which is in front of the weighing room, which is in a bungalow like the one elderly relatives sometimes live in. The course is said to be full of flowers in the summer and a bed of purple pansies is still battling on bravely near the team from Racing UK, who are also battling on bravely. It's a bit cold. I hope the jockeys have brought their gloves.

If you are a member, for £7.45 you can have warm goat's cheese and red onion tart served with fig chutney in the pleasant, non-smoking restaurant on the first floor of the Brocklesby Suite. If you're not, for £4.95 you can have Grimsby seafood pie with crispy potato topping and vegetables in the not non-smoking Red Rum bar and buffet on the ground floor, which is what I did.

The pie was nice but £1.05 for some hot water in a plastic container with a tea bag in it is a scandal. First Iraq, now this. For some strange reason, you can get a cup of tea in a proper cup for 75p in the members bar and buffet opposite the winning post. Go figure, as some people say. (I expect it's from a television programme).

There are some nice photographs on the stairway between the Grimsby pie and the goat's cheese and, in the 'archive corridor' to the members' viewing area , there are more old photographs, and race cards, and press cuttings, although the people in some of the photographs are anonymous.

This is the territory of trainer Michael Chapman (181 runners at Market Rasen in the last five seasons) but, today, is also the land of JP McManus, Michael Tabor, Sir Robert Ogden, and David Johnson, all represented but, unfortunately for the 24 bookmakers in the ring, and two on the rails, not in person.

According to bookmaker Paul Johnson, who will not be sending Betfair a Christmas card, 'Most of the big punters have gone, a £500 bet is a rarity, but there's usually a lot of small bets, like a good Silver Ring. In terms of the racing, I think it's about the best small course in the country. The quality has improved and the management is progressive.' Even so, the winning posts are very small, especially given their importance and influence on the suicide rate. Any chance of bigger ones?

Caroline Hurley didn't need to be able to see them since, wherever the winning posts had been, she and Parisienne Gale would have passed them first. For men looking for wives, the first race wasn't a bad place to start, since all the riders were 'Miss,' and most still seemed to have their own teeth.

I'm not sure why racecourses persevere with those boards that someone has to fill in, saying what the SP of the winner was in each race, information readily available elsewhere (the racecourse betting shop).

The seller was pretty awful, as sellers should be, but it didn't stop the auctioneer from singing the praises of the winner, Lazy Lena, which is what auctioneers are supposed to do. If Stalin had won, I expect we'd have been told that he was a good sort, too. 'Only a six-year-old and a mare, too. She'll do well, do another turn, a useful sort.' 3,600 guineas, bought in.

No one protested, possibly because they'd read the notice that read, 'Annual and daily members are asked to behave in an orderly and reasonable way and to be smartly dressed.' I didn't notice a similar notice in Tattersalls or the Silver Ring, so maybe disorderly behaviour and torn jeans are okay there. Personally, I always keep a tie in the car, in case I'm forced to wear one.

In the middle of the track, as well as a nine hole golf course, there were some white birds (seagulls) and some black birds (crows). They seem to like jump racing – they were at Taunton last week. I don't suppose they've got much else to do.

When you leave, there are signs saying, 'Thank you for visiting Market Rasen. Next meeting Thursday 1 December.' That's all right, I enjoyed it.

When the final scores were tallied, and awards made, Market Rasen was judged to have the best toilets, which led to another enjoyable visit, and the following news item. I felt proud.

TOILETS TO BE PROUD OF *Racing Post*, 13 November 2007

At a short ceremony at Market Rasen on Sunday, a plaque identifying the toilets in the Brocklesby Suite as the 'David Ashforth toilets' was unveiled by the *Racing Post*'s columnist himself.

The ceremony, which took place between the entrances to the gentlemen's and ladies' toilets, was attended by Charles Booth and Pip Kirkby, the racecourse chairman and managing director respectively, and by a steady stream of bemused toilet users.

SALISBURY *Racing Post*, 15 August 2005

Salisbury is one of the quiet treasures of British racing and, as a bonus, it always seems to be sunny.

Set off early, to give yourself time to appreciate the local roadworks, then pop into the Victoria & Albert pub near the course, at Netherhampton. They've got something there called Moles Molennium. It helps build up misplaced confidence, a bit like London Pride before a fall.

If you think praying might help, Salisbury Cathedral is magnificent and contains one of the finest collections of dead bodies in England, as well as the Magna Carta, and the tallest spire (404 feet).

As you turn up the narrow lane to the racecourse, trees on one side, cornfields on the other, you sense that Salisbury's setting will be lovely, and it is. When you arrive, it's well worth an early visit to the top of Tattersalls' grandstand. Swallows (or it might be swifts, or house martins) nest there, swooping and gliding. You look out across the Wiltshire countryside, with the cathedral in the distance. It's enough to stop you throwing yourself off.

Parking is free and, if you are completely skint, you can park and watch the racing from a distance for nothing. It costs £6 to get into the 'course,' £11 for Tattersalls and £18 for the 'club,' although you have to be wearing the right clothes for that. Smart jeans are okay but faded jeans aren't. I don't know what happens if you turn up wearing smart faded jeans.

The names of the enclosures need to be reviewed. What are new racegoers to make of the 'course,' or of 'Tattersalls'? And a 'club' with a 'members stand' suggests something exclusively for members but, as Salisbury's website points out, 'Members is our premier enclosure which can be used by the general public.' Maybe it would be better to call it the Premier Enclosure.

It's worth walking across the track just to look down it. The grass is lush and the view wonderful, unless you want to follow what the horses and jockeys are doing during a race, in which case the big screen operating at 15 of Salisbury's 16 meetings is essential. The odd meeting out is the second meeting of the year – take binoculars and hope that Richard Hoiles is commentating again; he's very good at it.

There is something intimate about the track's relationship with the stands and parade ring, so intimate that, in races over one and three quarter miles, they start, stalls-free, from near the winning post, then go up the track the wrong way. It's politically incorrect but rather nice, unless yours gets left.

The parade ring is pretty, well sited, will be rubberised for next year and is always well attended (there's a bar a few feet away). Just outside it, there's a carpet with a sign reading, 'Warning Trip Hazard.' Too late, I'd already tripped over a manhole cover marked, curiously, 'Clark-Drain.Com. Inspection Chamber.' Maybe they should organise underground tours, a bit like the tours of the sewers in Paris; which reminds me, the gents toilet in the infield, featuring Twyfords Adamant urinals, was rather smelly.

At the furthest end of the enclosures is an ancient, derelict stand, home only to climbing ivy, 'No Admittance' signs, and Erica Ferrari, who was sitting reading John Francome's *Rough Ride*. According to Erica, his best book is *Outsider*. If the stand had been made out of wood, instead of iron and concrete, it could have been sold as coal by now.

The next stand along is Tattersalls, pistachio green with emerald green trimmings, followed by the members stand and then Salisbury's new pride and joy, the Wiltshire Stand, opened by Lester Piggott in June. I wonder if Lester said anything, apart from, 'Could I have the cheque, please?'

It's a cream building with a nautical flavour. The terraces that provide fine views down the track, and over the parade ring, look like the railed decks of ships, with a splendid new owners and trainers bar on the ground floor.

It's a fun course, boasting a decent-sized crowd and a relaxed atmosphere. If you like ice cream, I can recommend the ones sold by the effusive man in Lovington's ice cream van ('A taste of the West Country'), parked, unpromisingly, outside the old brick toilets. If you like burgers, there are burger vans and, if you like the aristocracy, there's Viscount Head, acting as one of the stewards. The Viscount used to train Border Incident and Uncle Bing but I don't think he does much nowadays, apart from suspend the occasional Flat jockey.

While Richard Quinn was in front of the Head, Kerrin McEvoy was busy demonstrating his considerable race-riding skills, and Robert Havlin was timing things perfectly to prove that Aoninch isn't totally opposed to the idea of winning, after all.

If you like to bet in euros, George Cooper, betting in the 'course,' is the bookmaker for you. Cooper has a sign reading, 'euros taken,' presumably in case someone from Belgium turns up. In the main ring, Derek Barnes, betting under an umbrella reading Norman Barnes (they're never who you think they are), says, 'Business is very hit and miss here, with good days and bad. There's decent business at the evening meetings, which are very popular.'

Later, Barnes reports that business has been quite good but that Aoninch wasn't. A few pitches along, Gary Wiltshire says that business at his Tote pitch hasn't been great but Tote were sponsoring the big race and at least he'd flown the flag. Nowadays, it's a lime green and red one.

If they'd had a sweetie kiosk I'd have had a packet of chocolate buttons (not the white ones) or maybe a Mars bar but they didn't have one, so I didn't. I had a half of Castlemaine XXXX instead, for research purposes. It tasted like Castlemaine XXXX. Still, never mind.

A gem of a racecourse for both enthusiasts and casual visitors. There is plenty of scope for further improvement in facilities in Tattersalls and the 'course' (and for changing the names of enclosures) but a progressive management offers hope of better to come. A good track to introduce someone to racing.

TOWCESTER *Racing Post*, 8 February 2006

It was bad luck being assassinated by an anarchist in 1898 but at least the Empress Elizabeth of Austria has had a grandstand at Towcester racecourse named after her, the Empress Stand. Elizabeth helped to found the racecourse and I expect she'd have approved of the architectural style, a sort of Chinese art deco.

Towcester, rather like its maverick owner, Lord Hesketh, does things differently. It doesn't charge people to go in, and it doesn't belong to the Racecourse Association. A real jump enthusiasts' course, it has always been one of my favourites, and not only because I once backed a 100-1 winner there.

With or without a grandstand, Towcester's a wonderful track to look at, with the horses disappearing steeply downhill on one side and plodding steeply uphill on the other, if they've got the strength. That telling hill into the finishing straight is Towcester's signature.

It's a pity the course is built on clay, which tends to offer a choice of going, either hard or suet, usually suet. Chris Palmer, Towcester's chief executive, reports that it is now much improved, as a result of all sorts of things having been done to it, and I expect he's right. Last year the average field size was over ten, so trainers must be reasonably content.

In recent years, they've pretty much knocked everything down and started again, at a cost of almost £8 million. It's probably just as well that Hesketh has recently sold about £45 million worth of surplus country estates.

For a small jumps course, it's pretty amazing. You arrive to discover that, although Hesketh is a former Tory minister, there's no preferential parking. The next shock is that admission is free, and the next that you don't even get your shoes covered in mud anymore, they've replaced it with tarmac.

They had planned to introduce a £5 admission charge this season but a lot of racegoers said they preferred to pay nothing, so they've let them. Palmer insists that it's a business model that works. What the racecourse loses on admission charges it gains on bigger crowds, fewer staff and higher sales of food, drink and betting tickets. During the last financial year they made £250,000 profit and they expect to make £500,000 during the current one.

As well as the big new Empress Stand, there's the quite big and quite new Grace Stand, in similar architectural style, and a new and impressive stable block, with a nice clock on top. It's got over 100 boxes, a veterinary treatment unit, sampling unit, dedicated wash down facilities and, according to the Jockey Club official at the entrance, is on a par with Cheltenham.

The same, unfortunately, can't be said of the horses but there's the usual welcome collection of big slow things, as well as Jamaican Flight, that small, bonny enthusiast who won at Towcester in 1997, and was having his 173rd start. Before they set off, they all walk round a rather dull parade ring (how about getting a gardener in, or a sculptor, or Diane Keaton, she's rather nice?).

The marquees behind the parade ring, which currently house the owners and trainers and various other bars are due to be replaced by a permanent building, which will include a new weighing room. The old one is going to be turned into a 'themed bar' (I hope it has lots of nice old black and white photographs). They've also got a 100-bedroom hotel in mind, to boost the conference centre side of the business, and are toying with the idea of applying for a licence to open the betting shop seven days a week, along with the themed bar.

The betting shop (open plan, Ladbrokes) is at one end of the Empress Stand's large but still not large enough ground floor, which has underfloor heating. You probably have to take your shoes and socks off to appreciate it properly. Unfortunately, the ground floor also contains a design flaw. To reach the gents, gents have to elbow their way through other gents staring at a bank of television screens, to their mutual irritation. As Edward VIII said during the 1930s depression – it was about the only sensible thing he ever did say – 'something must be done.'

Upstairs, the Empress Suite restaurant offers nice views across the course, in pleasant surroundings, as well as a menu (£55) boasting a 'melee of dressed Atlantic prawns.' Further upstairs there are roomy hospitality boxes, and a box reserved for owners and trainers with runners that day.

In the Grace Stand, you can either stay at the bottom, and have a cup of tea for £1.20 or a bottle of champagne for £20 or, also for £20, promote yourself to the Pomfret Suite and have a private chair, bar, balcony and betting counter, with the option of ordering a Cumberland sausage or something called Cajun chicken ciabatta, possibly from New Orleans, or Northampton.

Something interesting always happens at Towcester. On this occasion, it was Kim Bailey having a winner. Bailey looked delightedly amazed, as did everyone else apart from Glen Thyne, who looked as if he couldn't care less, which was how he'd looked during most of the race.

The same was not true of John Willoughby, standing under a bookmaker's sign reading 'John Lovell,' who openly welcomed the outcome, at 28-1. Willoughby was one of five bookmakers with pitches situated between the weighing room and parade ring. 'It's been good for the last few meetings, since we moved here,' he said. 'The expenses here are low and, overall, I'm content. There are a lot of £2 punters but our average ticket today has been £10 and there are one or two big punters.'

It's not really a betting crowd, more a country sports crowd, without the fishing and shooting. I expect Lord Hesketh will be introducing those next year.

Towcester is a unique treasure, and curiosity. All racing enthusiasts should take the trouble to experience it at least once. The new facilities, with more on the way, aren't perfect but they are impressive for a small course and the continued free admission is a wonder of the modern world.

6
COURT 11

The Royal Courts of Justice – horseracing's second home.

Graham Bradley was a top jump jockey, stylish and successful, who won some of the sport's biggest races, including the Cheltenham Gold Cup on Bregawn in 1983, the King George VI Chase on Wayward Lad in 1985, and the Champion Hurdle on Collier Bay in 1996.

Colourful and popular, but also controversial, Bradley retired in 1999 and became a bloodstock agent but, in 2002, the Jockey Club disqualified him for eight years for several offences committed while he was a jockey, including passing information for reward to Brian Brendan Wright who, in 2007, was sentenced to 30 years in prison as the leader of a cocaine smuggling gang.

In 2003, on appeal to the Jockey Club Appeal Board, Bradley's disqualification was reduced to five years. He then appealed to the High Court, alleging that the ban was 'unreasonable, unlawful, disproportionate and massively excessive.'

DAY ONE *Racing Post*, 29 June 2004

Court 11 of the High Court has many law books, much wood panelling, but few spectators. If there was a jury, the jurors would outnumber everyone else, but there isn't a jury, there is only Mr Justice Richards, who wears spectacles and a bright red sash and listens attentively to what Timothy Higginson, for Graham Bradley, and Mark Warby QC, for the Jockey Club, have to say, intervening regularly to keep them on their legal toes.

Bradley is wearing grey hair and a rather darker suit. However well or badly Bradley may have behaved in the past, his behaviour today is impeccable. His side goes first. Mr Higginson proceeds slowly, the ungenerous may say somewhat ponderously. His client does not shout, 'spit it out.' Perhaps he is paying by the word, rather than the hour.

Mr Higginson invites the judge to consult bundle seven. Mr Justice Richards has an accident with bundle seven, which slips out of his judicial hands and into the more fickle hands of fate, which send it in the direction of the court usher below. Refreshingly, the blame culture has not yet infected Court 11, where the usher does not turn to the judge and say, 'I'll see you in court.'

Water, if not the drink of choice, is the drink of supply. Mr Higginson takes a sip and encourages the judge to adopt the 'current, correct and modern approach' to domestic tribunals, as exemplified by the case of Colgan v Kennel Club, which he recommends for the judge's consideration and approval. Sixteen Newfoundland dogs were placed in an unsuitably hot van from which only six emerged alive.

Curious to think that Bradley's fate may depend on ten dead Newfoundland dogs, about which the court is united in acknowledging its collective ignorance. Perhaps they will have died in van, but not in vain.

By 11.30am, eyelids are already heavy under the weight of Mr Higginson's submissions on the existence and nature of the contractual relationship between Bradley and the Jockey Club, if there was one. The gentleman behind me is engaged in a crossword puzzle. The gentleman in front of me, Mr Warby, is busy wielding his armoury of pens. He makes notes with a black pen, then with a red pen, then highlights vital points with a yellow marker pen. There is strong circumstantial evidence that Mr Higginson favours a pink marker pen. At the moment, he is wielding his spectacles.

It would be a mistake to use the expression 'courtroom drama.' Despite his wig and cloak, Mr Higginson is very much in favour of the modern approach, which he suggests can best be pursued by Mr Justice Richards stepping boldly into the shoes of the Jockey Club Appeal Board, and giving his client an appropriate sentence. By 'appropriate,' Mr Higginson has something rather different in mind from the 'draconian penalty' of five years imposed by the Appeal Board. Perhaps something closer to the 35 days imposed on John Francome in 1978 for having passed information to John Banks, the bookmaker.

The judge asks why another appeal hearing is needed when a right of appeal is already available, including on the grounds that the penalty was not proportionate? Mr Higginson explains that it is needed in case the first appeal went wrong. He does not say whether he thinks there should be as many appeals procedures as it takes to get it right.

Hopefully, it won't go wrong, because Mr Justice Richards confesses that racing is 'a world I don't follow,' unlike Mr Edward Cazalet, chairman of the Appeal Board, who is said to have a long and close association with the Jockey Club, although not a member, unlike two fellow members of the Appeal Board. All of which leads Mr Higginson to conclude that the Appeal Board 'cannot properly be characterised as an independent tribunal.'

The judge glances at the clock. It is 12.30pm. I confess I had beaten him to it. He does not say, 'Good Lord, is that the time? Court adjourned.' Instead, he says, 'The sooner we get to grips with the main authorities, the better.'

After lunch, in the unfortunate absence of his witnesses, Mr Higginson advances into the world of 'comparables,' a world populated, in Mr Higginson's opinion, by people doing things just as bad as Mr Bradley did but hardly being punished at all. The Jockey Club, he submits, has failed to take proper account of comparables. Mr Warby, I suspect, may not agree.

DAY TWO *Racing Post*, 30 June 2004

This is more like it. A real trial, with witnesses and cross-examinations, and one barrister shouting, 'I put it to you, Mr Foster, that your testimony is nothing but a tissue of lies. You have lied and lied and lied again, to save the Jockey Club you love.' Then the other barrister leaping up, 'Objection!' And the judge banging his hammer on his bench, 'Order, order.' Just pretending. They didn't actually say that, but there were witnesses, starting with Charles Patrick Evelyn Brooks, better known as Charlie, who was soon on sparring terms with Mark Warby QC, for the Jockey Club.

They settled into a routine. Mr Warby would invite Mr Brooks to agree to a proposition, and Mr Brooks, confident and combative, would decline the invitation. Having failed to agree the date on which Brooks ceased to be a trainer, they went on to fail to agree on everything else.

While Brooks insisted that he had never met Brian Wright, Declan Murphy admitted to knowing him, without being close to him. 'You were visited by Brian Wright in hospital?' 'I don't know,' replied Murphy, 'I was unconscious at that time.'

The clock in Court 11 tick-tocks. Clocks in courtrooms always work, to avoid the frequent danger of time standing still. I've just remembered who Mr Justice

Richards reminds me of. It's Alan Bennett. 'A fascinating document,' he says, of the Jockey Club's Rule Book. Warby's Rule Book is full of stickers, some yellow, some blue, one red, perhaps for a particularly bad rule.

Christopher Norman Foster takes the stand, takes the Bible, and takes his seat. The Jockey Club's executive director is not a betting man. He has no betting accounts. He does not read tipsters' advertisements. All of which makes it difficult for him to answer Timothy Higginson's questions, which feature an advertisement by 'Britain's top tipster,' boasting the kind of privileged inside information liable to breach the Rules of Racing if put into the wrong hands, for reward.

Foster is ignorant of tipping lines, of the fact that large numbers of people are prepared to pay £500 for access to them, and of whether or not any tipsters have ever been written to by the Jockey Club, although he has a dim recollection that they might have been. He does not know where either Derek Thompson or Jim McGrath get their information from, or whether they pay for it, but he suspects that it may be from gossip ('conversation is perhaps a kinder word') or the Form Book.

These are matters on which Nigel Macfarlane, secretary to the Disciplinary Committee, may be able to help. He may also be able to help with the fate of a list presented to the Disciplinary Committee by Graham Bradley, a list of jockeys and trainers and others who were allegedly friends of Brian Wright. It is a long list, containing names such as Lester Piggott, Steve Cauthen, Walter Swinburn, Kieren Fallon, Frankie Dettori, David Elsworth, Richard Hannon, Michael Tabor – most people in racing, in fact, except Nigel Macfarlane.

Macfarlane, 31 years with the Jockey Club, tall and thin, thought Bradley's list may have been passed to the security department, possibly by Nigel Macfarlane, although he wasn't sure. Mr Warby QC taps the fingers of one hand against the knuckles of his other hand, leans backwards against the bench behind him, then forward on to the bench in front of him. 'I confess I remain unsure where all this evidence is to take Mr Bradley's case,' he says, before spelling out why the Appeal Board's procedures were 'impeccable' and, one way and another, its findings independent and unimpeachable.

Warby glances at the clock, which shows 12.50pm. Time has moved more quickly today. Even so, I wonder if, were my stomach to rumble loudly enough, Mr Justice Richards would be minded to adjourn for lunch. It doesn't, and he isn't. Warby smiles at the judge. Not, I am sure, as a reward for favours hoped for. The smile and the sniff are Warby's stock in trade. 'Francome, tab 12, bundle three, page 511, M for mother,' he says, for the judge's benefit.

Messrs Warby and Higginson are as unable to agree about John Francome as they are about everything else. While Francome's case, circa 1978, reminds Higginson strongly of the case of Graham Bradley, circa 2002-4, and suggests to him that a similar sentence, viz, a 35-day ban and £750 fine, would be equally fitting, Warby sees few, if any, points of similarity. At last, they agree, to disagree again at 10.30am tomorrow morning.

DAY THREE *Racing Post*, 1 July 2004

A mere tube strike cannot obstruct the wheels of justice, possibly because they do not start turning until 10.30am.

Mr Justice Richards arrives bright and breezy into Court 11, where counsel for the Jockey Club (Mark Warby QC) and counsel against the Jockey Club (Timothy Higginson, not QC) are waiting to persuade his lordship of the soundness of their own submissions and the laughably flawed nature of their opponent's.

Warby opens by addressing 'the sore thumb case,' the thumb being the lengthy ban imposed on Graham Bradley that, Higginson contends, sticks out like one. After directing a few pointed thrusts at Higginson's balloon, Warby sits down and Higginson stands up to deal with several points of 'housekeeping.'

When someone says 'and seventhly' you know you are in the company of lawyers. Higginson advances seven reasons why the evidence of Messrs Brooks, Murphy and Foster is admissible. His audience is small. The case has not, we must be frank, captured the imagination of the public, only four of whom are present, three of them awake.

Curiously, given his choice of dress, Higginson insists, 'We live in the real world.' It is a world in which jockeys are forever issuing tips and spreading information and the Jockey Club is forever turning blind eyes to the fact, except when an eye alights on Bradley. Higginson's contention amounts to this, does it not? Sorry, it becomes infectious. That the evidence on which Bradley was handed a five-year ban did not justify a five-year ban, although (see case of John Francome, 1978), it might have justified a ban of 35 days. Mr Justice Richards has the power to quash the outrageous penalty and substitute a fair and reasonable one, and he should.

That covers, as it were, London and New York, but omits the Atlantic Ocean, diligently rowed by Higginson, whose ports of call include the unfortunate cases of Associated Provincial Picture Houses and the urine produced by Diane Modahl in Lisbon. The judge looks engaged, almost fascinated. When he frowns, it is not a condemning frown, but a pondering one. He is a rather likeable judge.

Higginson returns – 'relatively briefly' – to comparables. He promises not to mention Francome again, which will please Francome, and, instead, submits that the 16 comparable cases submitted by Warby are of absolutely no use or relevance, in striking contrast to those presented by himself, which are exceedingly germane and helpful.

At noon, precisely, there is an exciting development. A new spectator, a rather bemused-looking gentleman, joins us. He sits down and pushes a finger into his left ear. At 12.01pm he leaves, along with his ear. At 12.20pm, two of the four remaining spectators leave. They are a young couple, who look as though they may have eloped but had been thwarted by the Central Line. Declan Murphy arrives. He joins Higginson's party, which heavily outnumbers Warby's, which doesn't exist.

Higginson passes through the doctrine of restraint of trade en route to five concluding submissions, calling in on the nature of contractual relationships along the way. At 12.50pm (sorry to keep looking at my watch), the Court is told Bradley's livelihood would be ruined were the ban to stand, that no good could come of it, and that the best thing to do would be to cross out 'five years' and substitute 'five weeks.'

Just as a prawn salad and an apple seem within reach, Warby announces he has 15 points to make. The two remaining spectators throw in the towel.

Luckily, Warby's points are short and, suddenly, Mr Justice Richards is thanking counsel, remarking, 'You've left me with quite a lot of reading to do,' and promising to announce the winner as soon as possible. Pity, I was enjoying it.

Graham Bradley lost his appeal.

7
GRAB-A-GRAND 2002 TO 2009

An old bald bloke cheering home Cetti's Warbler, at 100-1.

In 1999, someone at the *Racing Post* had the bright idea of sending someone else, who boasted (not quite the right word) over 30 losing years in a row, off racing for a week to win a grand for Christmas. It was like asking Dr Shipman to visit a few more patients in the hope that he'd come back and say, 'I did much better than usual, only three dead.'

It was very enjoyable but a bit vague financially. My final report explained,

'I'd like to be able to tell you how it's all ended up but I've lost track. You know how it is. When you're winning, you keep count. When you're not, you miss a few things out. This is one of the many reasons why Jim McGrath [of Timeform and Channel 4] makes his betting pay and I don't. We're a bit up, but not £1,000 up. On the other hand, the editor has said that, despite my incompetence, and thanks to Towcester's generous offer of £500, one way or another, racing's charities will be getting a grand.'

That seems to have been enough for the editor for a while. Either that, or I can't find the articles. Anyway, from 2002, Grab-a-Grand became an annual event and, though I write it myself (no one else is going to), a popular one. People still come up to me and ask whether I'm going to be doing another Grab-a-Grand. I suppose it's the attraction of watching another punter make a fool of themselves, for a change.

Each year, I'd approach it with mixed feelings. On the one hand, it was good fun. How many jobs require you to go off for a spell of racing and betting? It was nice meeting people at the racecourse and provided good writing material. On the other hand, there was always the possibility (well, probability) that, after two days I'd be £700 down and after five days I'd be feeling badly in need of a coronary.

That was why I chose to punt with my own money rather than the paper's. I knew that, if I was well down after a couple of days, the fact that I was losing the *Racing Post*'s money would prey on my mind and affect the way I bet.

Usually, the plan was to stand any losses myself and give half of any winnings to charity. As this note from 2009 indicates, it depended a bit on how flush or skint I was at the time. 'David Ashforth will stand any losses himself and give half of any winnings to charity. He may give all of any winnings to charity, depending on what mood he's in and how much is in his bank account.'

Amazingly, five of the next eight Grab-a-Grand weeks were winning ones, and four times I reached the magic grand. By the end of 2009, I was showing a grand total profit of almost £5,000. Given what happened, without fail, during the other 51 weeks of every year, the question arises – how?

I'm not really sure but I've got a few theories. The main one is that even the most hopeless punter has a good week now and again, and I just happened to hit the right weeks. Another theory, which I prefer to believe, is that I try harder than usual, although I try quite hard normally. I watch a lot of racing and study the form a lot, although that's nothing new, either. Maybe I am more disciplined, or more concerned about my indiscipline being exposed to view. When people are scared, it's amazing what they can do. That could be it.

2003: MY FINEST HOUR *Racing Post*, 16 December 2003

Here on the finest day of the year, the finest jump racecourse in Britain (Towcester) features the appearance of Jimmy McCarthy, the finest jockey ever to put boots in stirrups.

What a wonderful thing it is to be alive, and what a wonderful place to be alive at. How likeable everyone is, and how sadly misunderstood Saddam Hussein is, and President Bush. I'm sorry I said all those rude things about you. Funny to think that, at 12.39pm, I was convinced that this lunatic attempt to win another grand for Christmas, after last year's unexpected success, was doomed to humiliating disaster.

Admittedly, there's still time. Since I last visited Towcester, they've taken the stand away, and bookmaker Gary Wiltshire. I preferred it when they were both here, but evidently they're about to build a new stand and maybe another Gary Wiltshire as well, if they've got enough bricks left.

The first at Towcester was between Bourbon Manhattan and one of those French things trained by Nicky Henderson, Mon Villez, until Mon Villez was withdrawn, when it was between Bourbon Manhattan and however many hurdles there were. He was 1-10 not to fall over.

It was one of those races where you look for something to back each-way, can't find anything, but keep looking until you do. The rest were, well, not very good (although all very lovable in their way), except for number 13 (what a wonderful number that is). Cetti's Warbler, stoutly bred out of that nice mare Sedge Warbler, ran with more promise than most of her rivals in a novice hurdle over further at Towcester a month ago, and wouldn't have to improve much, if at all, to stand a decent chance of finishing second or third to the winner, Bourbon Manhattan.

So I went to see her in the parade ring, which confirmed that she was grey, and looked rather nice, although she didn't say much. Better ask Mrs P Robeson, who is probably married to Paul Robeson, so good at singing *Ol' Man River*. I may sing it myself later. Mrs P Robeson also bred, owns and probably feeds and generally entertains Cetti's Warbler.

Wearing a rather splendid animal on her head, Mrs P Robeson turns out not to be P Robeson at all, but Rene Robeson. When I tell her that I am thinking of backing Cetti's Warbler each-way, Rene (wonderful woman, fine trainer, excellent wife, splendid daughter, etc.) says, 'I'm hoping she'll make a three-mile chaser. I'm running her here because I thought it might be heavy, but it's dried out.'

That wasn't quite what I was hoping to hear, which was, 'well spotted. I'll eat my fur hat if she's out of the first three. If you can get 2-1 a place you really must put your flat on it.' Fortunately, the whole point of asking trainers what they think isn't to take any notice of what they say but to confirm your own prejudices. So I ignored Rene's advice and, assuming that none of the racecourse bookmakers would be betting each-way, took myself off to Ladbrokes' betting shop. What a splendid company Ladbrokes is, and what an outstanding betting shop the one at Towcester is. How attractive the staff, and how attractive the betting slips. Cetti's Warbler was 66-1. I had £20 each-way, SP. If you don't speculate, you can't accumulate.

Passing the stand, Cetti's Warbler was in the lead and, passing it again, Cetti's Warbler was still in the lead. She wasn't going very fast but, then, neither was Bourbon Manhattan. You've probably guessed the end of this story (one which I intend to recount at regular intervals, complete with embellishments, for the foreseeable future). The result was announced, followed by the SP, 100-1.

I've never backed a 100-1 winner before, although I did once back Ben Nevis to win the Grand National at 40-1. (A grand race but hardly on a par with the Alphameric Red Onion Novices' Hurdle. Class E. Div. I. What wonderful vegetables red onions are. I intend to eat some tonight.) Ladbrokes was struggling to find enough £20 notes so Eileen, the manageress, made out a cheque for £2,440 and handed it to me, which none of Ladbrokes' manageresses, or managers, has ever done before.

The rest of the tale is quickly told. I'd sold distances for £10 a length at 47 but closed at 42 after four races, having tried to walk across the track and got stuck, which made me lose my bottle. Then, after speaking to Derek Shaw (lovely man), and not getting huge encouragement for Rayware Boy in the seller, I had £20 each-way on anyway, followed by the same again on Follow The Flow in the 3.10pm. He was one of the horses disqualified after running out. After that I felt slightly smug but, mainly, relieved. Roll on tomorrow. Southwell. Marvellous racecourse.

What do you do when you are over £2,000 up with four days still to go? As I put it, 'I scratched around like a nervous grandad,' and ended the week up £2,323.87. Cetti's Warbler went on to win three chases, including a valuable chase at Uttoxeter in 2005 at 25-1.

Another glory.

2004: THE FINAL DAY *Racing Post*, 18 December 2004

Yippee! (see later). Uttoxeter, the finest racecourse in the world; 17 December 2004, the date of its finest meeting; Polar Gunner, the finest horse in training, unless Steve The Fish wins the race with the very long name, in which case he will be joint-finest.

This morning, I placed blobs of varying sizes next to selected names in the *Racing Post*'s racecards. This is it, my last chance. I've got to win another £525. A blob in the wrong place, of the wrong size, could be fatal.

Uttoxeter's card looks easier than Catterick's yesterday (thank God); Windsor's fails to tempt, as a grand-winning medium; Wolverhampton attracts one large blob, Madge in the 1.40pm. That might just be the day's big punt, if it comes to the crunch. Luckily, it doesn't come to the crunch or, rather, the crunch unexpectedly comes much earlier, in the first. I quite like the first, a conditional jockeys' hurdle. Scarface looks like a well-placed Martin Pipe hotpot and, since it's Pipe, the 461 day layoff is barely a deterrent. Tom Malone says that Scarface will love the ground (heavy, and being rained on), but there are others with squeaks and I'm not going to put several hundred on Scarface at 11-8 or shorter.

I give a chance to Vallica, Polar Gunner and Little Villain. I have a chat with Alison Thorpe, Vallica's trainer. Alison doesn't take up my invitation to agree that Vallica has a decent chance. Expressions such as 'However much you've got on you, put the lot on' are conspicuous by their absence. Anyway, it's too late, I've already backed it, with Betfair. £33 at 20-1, the same on Polar Gunner, at almost 14-1, £7 on Little Villain at prices up to 69-1, and £22 Little Villain for a place, at 9-1.

As the rain falls, the distance market comes to mind. Usually, you shouldn't buy distances, not least because most of us have a psychological inclination to do so, but when it's heavy at Uttoxeter, horses often finish legless. I can't remember whether they've done something to the drainage or not recently. Anyway, when the rain starts bouncing off my bald head, I decide the moment has come, and buy them, £10 at 57.

Then I ask Jim Old about the horse I expect to be the make-or-break of the day, Steve The Fish. I want to ask if Steve The Fish has learned how to jump properly yet because, if he has, I think he's got a great chance of winning the novices' handicap chase. He made a promising return over hurdles last month, and is rated 31lb lower over fences. 'He's a major mystery,' says Old, 'because he jumps beautifully at home yet, on each occasion on the track, he's made a catastrophic balls-up.' Jim thinks that, today, he has a very good chance. £150 at almost 9-2.

It's funny how things work out, because if it hadn't been for that opening race, the day might have panned out very differently. If you were watching, you'll know that Polar Gunner led them a merry dance, and was still dancing, 29 lengths clear of Little Villain, when they passed the post, the one whose red and white top later blew off.

Perfect, an after-commission profit of about £578. The grand achieved! Eureka! Then there were the distances. Normally, I might have let the bet run but I wanted to make sure I didn't drop below a grand, so I sold them at 76, for a profit of £190. That's £768 up on the day, with Steve The Fish to go.

It's an odd feeling, because I'd expected to be battling all afternoon, feeling the pressure, to the wire. By about 12.30pm, I'd done it. In a way, it's an anti-climax, welcome, but unexpected. All that's left is to resist the temptation to back the things I would have backed if I'd needed to. Just as well, because Madge is beaten, that could have been £300 down the tubes.

The seller looks awful, as sellers should, but the auctioneer gets very excited, as auctioneers should. 'Just the sort you want,' he tells his audience, after Fleetfoot Mac had run less slowly than the others. 'If you can get a horse who goes in heavy going, that's the sort you want.' Someone agreed, and forked out 7,400gns. I'm spared another empty pocket because I'd probably have backed Steppes Of Gold, beaten thanks to a fine training feat by Nicky Henderson, who sends out Dungarvans Choice after 594 days off to make Steppes Of Gold look like a horse to watch rather than back, for the time being.

As Steve The Fish lines up, the sky turns black, the wind blows and the sleet sleets, for the Lord was angry, and did cause Steve The Fish to run as if, all things considered, he'd rather not jump fences for a living but might be prepared to consider dinner invitations instead. It's disappointing for Old, who thinks Back Among Friends, one of three blessed or cursed with a small blob in the bumper, has a good chance if he settles. Firm of resolve, if rather dull, I don't have another bet, but it's great to see Back Among Friends win for Old, who has endured his fair share of disappointments.

And that's it. It's been great fun, I've really enjoyed it, and everyone has been very helpful. Next year again, maybe.

Polar Gunner, with a handicap rating of 68 that day, was eventually rated 120. He won 11 more races, over hurdles and fences, mainly on soft ground, winning for the final time, aged 14, in 2011.

Normal service resumes.

2006: TRY, TRY, TRY AGAIN ... BUT IT DOESN'T HELP
Racing Post, 13 December 2006

You wouldn't believe how hopeless some racehorses are, unless you've been to a banded race meeting at Southwell. The 13 horses running in the first have raced 139 times between them, and won twice. Soon, they'll have raced 152 times, and won three times, so maybe they're getting better.

I couldn't sleep last night, either through excitement, or because the shower was dripping. As well as the dripping shower, Southwell's Saracen's Head Hotel, opened in 1460, boasts the creakiest floorboards in Britain. It would be hopeless trying to murder someone in their bed.

At 6.30am, I was already studying the first, so at least I've tried. I'm using the blob system, a big blob for a big fancy, a small blob for a small fancy. There aren't any big blobs, and there aren't any small ones, either. It's tempting to leave a blank space, with 'Nothing today' in the middle. Eventually, small blobs sit beside Stoneacre Fred and Franky'n'jonny. Stoneacre Fred's price (11-4) puts me off (there's something about backing a favourite in a banded stakes race), so I back Franky'n'jonny, at 9-1, instead.

In the weighing room, trainer Michael Attwater is giving Dale Gibson his instructions. I've heard some Reith Lectures shorter than Attwater's address to Gibson. It's lucky the race is only over seven furlongs. I was going to ask about Franky'n'jonny's disturbing habit of starting slowly, but first Attwater fills me in on the filly's other problem, the pulled muscles in her quarters. While I wonder whether I've got time to lay her for twice as much as I've just backed her for, Attwater says, 'Hopefully she's all right now and, if she is, I think we've just got Stoneacre Fred to beat.'

I feel a brief frisson of excitement when Franky'n'jonny doesn't start as slowly as she sometimes does, and then watch her run a respectable sixth, while Stoneacre Fred runs a more respectable first.

In the bar, Milton Bradley is having a cup of soup, possibly minestrone. This could be an omen, because I've awarded Bradley's Ulshaw a blob in the 1.30pm, and his Vlasta Weiner a blob in the 2.00pm, and have already backed them both, at 19-1 and 32-1.

The sort of comment I'm hoping for is, 'I've brought the big horsebox, so there's enough room for the money.' Instead, when I ask him if it's a tip that the trainer's here, he replies, 'No, I had nothing else to do today.' Evidently the 'old lad' (Ulshaw, not Bradley), is being retired after today's race. 'Do you think he'll go out with a bang?' 'I'm not full of confidence,' says Bradley. The conversation isn't going quite as I'd hoped, but Bradley does say that Vlasta Weiner would stand a good chance if he found his old form. 'Is he finding it?' 'Not really.'

What's the point of asking trainers what they think if they're not going to confirm what you thought? When Ulshaw finishes a narrowly beaten third, it's worth £230 to me, and £302 to the owner. Hang on a minute while I see whether or not Vlasta Weiner finds his form. No, he doesn't. Somehow, I've managed to accumulate a deficit of, well, quite a lot, so I gird my loins for the second time in two days, and have £333 Misbehaviour for a place, at 1.7. It's a pretty stupid bet, and I'm lucky that Misbehaviour staggers into a distant third.

I've done my best, now it's up to Tacid and Boucheen in the last, trained by Dr J D Scargill and Ms Deborah J Evans. That's the only nice thing about banded racing, you get to see trainers you don't normally see, although somehow I managed to miss both of them. I do bump into a man who says, 'You'll never win a grand here,' and another who adds, 'If you do, you can buy two of these horses.'

Tacid finishes second but Boucheen runs disappointingly, which is a pity, because I bought him for £10 at 15 on Sporting Index's 50-30-20-10 index. Stupid. After a ridiculous amount of adding and (mainly) subtracting, I can reveal that I've lost £289 today. I suppose suicide's out of the question.

By the end of the week, I had lost £400.

Abnormal service resumes.

2009: GOING SWIMMINGLY *Racing Post*, 11 December 2009

Now that I'm a grand up, what should I do? Phone in sick? Just do a £1 Placepot? They sound attractive options to me but, of course, that's not what I've done. No, I've done a bit of this and a bit of that and, if all the bits go wrong, I'll be back to where I was before glorious Leicester on Wednesday. What a horrible thought.

Huntingdon's improved a lot since I last came but it won't count for anything if Racing Demon finishes first or second in the Peterborough Chase, because I've laid him; nor if, at Ludlow, Sambulando fails to finish in the first three in the novice chase. Oh, he just has failed to, creeping nicely into contention turning for home, then weakening horribly. One way (Betfair) and another (Sporting Index) that seems to have cost me £217.30.

While I'm waiting for nervous apprehension to creep up, closely followed by depression, I ask Wayne Hutchinson what chance he thinks Balzaccio and Raduis Bleu have later on. I rate Hutchinson highly and, luckily, I back Balzaccio before he tells me that he's got a chance but 'is what he is, a typical four-year-old moving into handicaps. I think he'll improve a bit from Leicester and should handle the ground. It depends on whether he's good enough.' It's not quite the same as, 'It's very shrewd of you to have picked him. I know the boss is planning to have the biggest bet of his life on him, and I don't fancy going to work tomorrow if he doesn't win,' but it'll have to do.

Hutchinson rides a characteristically capable race, bringing Balzaccio with a timely challenge. I wasn't sure he'd beaten First Avenue but he had, by a nose.

Strange things, photofinishes. Sometimes you lose eight in a row and tell God that he might as well stop messing about and fire off a bolt of lightning now, while at other times, well, you win them. 'I thought I'd won,' said Hutchinson. 'We got into a dog fight down the back, and he loved it.' So did I; a £370 profit.

When things go well, it seems easy; when things don't, it seems impossible. Better savour the going well bit before the other bit surfaces. People ask how I'm getting on and I'm able to tell them that it's going swimmingly. I was right about Racing Demon but he kept drifting in the betting and, through incompetence, I suppose, most of my lay bet was still sitting there on Betfair, unmatched, when they set off. I made a pathetic £41.27, less commission.

Hutchinson was slightly more hopeful of Raduis Bleu than of Balzaccio, and I've bought him for £10 at 15 on an index. 'Choc Thornton told me he was too gassy at Market Rasen,' says Hutchinson. 'He should stay and hopefully he's got improvement in him. If it turns out to be just an ordinary novice hurdle, he should run well.' Fair enough.

No one else seems to eat sweeties much nowadays, just bottles of special water. So far I've eaten a Lion (the reverse of Stanley Holloway's monologue, Albert and the Lion, in which the lion eats Albert) and a Dairy Milk (contains Fairtrade sugar, Fairtrade cocoa butter, Fairtrade cocoa mass, not forgetting E442, possibly Fairtrade). According to the wrappers, I've just eaten a grand total of 537 calories, less the two bits of the Dairy Milk I gave away. It takes me another step closer to The Biggest Loser show (It's American. Danny Cahill just won the latest series. He started off weighing 430lb and ended up weighing 191lb. I don't suppose he ate many Lions.) Admittedly, this doesn't have much to do with the racing but I'm trying to distract myself, to prevent getting drawn into a punting disaster. I've reached that frame of mind where I'd like to win more but, even more, I'd like not to lose.

Another good ride from Hutchinson, who is rarely where you don't want him to be in a race but, after looking likely to go close, Raduis Bleu tires and finishes a well-beaten third. Pocketwise, that's okay. I've won £50. That just leaves Dawn At Sea in the amateur riders' hurdle at Ludlow. He finishes fourth. I'm shutting up shop now. Thunderstorm has just won the bumper, it's getting dark and I've already started thinking about the two days coming up at Beulah Park in Ohio. I hope someone there knows what they're doing. It certainly won't be me.

It's been good fun this week. Thank you to everyone who helped, while everyone whose advice was hopeless is forgiven.

I made £165 profit that day, and ended the week up £1,233. If only it was always like that.

8
NO ORDINARY JOCKEY

You know who.

Lester Piggott and the Duke of Alburquerque had little in common, except that both sat on racehorses; often, in the Duke's case, not for very long. He had trouble with fractures, Lester with the Inland Revenue, Guy Packer with his name, and Kieren Fallon with the Old Bailey. For some jockeys, the saddle is the safest place to be.

With Lester, there was his riding (very good), his approach to income tax (very bad), and the stories about him (very likely).

LESTER PIGGOTT
THE STORIES
The Sporting Life, 7 May 1994

Lester had been booked to ride a horse at Nottingham for trainer Johnny Haine, formerly a top class jump jockey who held a Flat licence for a few years in the 1970s. When Lester arrived in the parade ring, Johnnie said, 'Lester, this horse has to be held up until the very last moment. The only way it can win is if you put its head in front on the line.' Lester nodded.

The stalls opened and Lester promptly kicked his mount into the lead. By the time they reached the straight, he was five lengths clear. The horse faded in the last 50 yards, and was caught on the line. Haine was furious. He marched into the unsaddling enclosure, ready to tell Piggott what he thought of him. Lester got off, turned to Haine and said, 'You were right, you know.'

The Sporting Life, 14 May 1994

Lester was writing a column for a newspaper or, rather, a journalist was writing it for him. The hack was getting pretty hacked off because it was difficult to get Lester to tell him anything.

The journalist lived on the South coast and, on a day off, he drifted across to Brighton races. Walking back to his car after the last race, he heard a familiar voice behind him. 'Hello,' said Lester, 'are you driving back to London? Can I have a lift?'

'I'm sorry, Lester, I only live a few miles away. I was going back home.'

'That's a pity,' said Lester, 'I've got some good stuff for your column.'

The journalist took a deep breath. 'All right, then.'

They got into his car, drove down the hill and turned on to the London road. 'No, not that way,' said Lester, 'go this way.'

They turned this way and that, through the back streets of Brighton, with the journalist getting more and more irritated. 'Stop here,' said Lester, finally.

Lester got out, crossed the road and went into a small shop. He came back, sat down and started to lick the ice-cream he had just bought. 'They sell the best ice-cream in the country there,' he said.

It was too much for the journalist. 'I don't suppose you thought to buy me one,' he said, a touch sharply.

'Oh,' replied Lester, looking surprised. 'I didn't know you liked ice-cream.'

The Sporting Life, 21 May 1994

Robert Ellis, a racehorse owner, has sent me a lovely Lester Piggott story.

'Back in the 1970s, the master rang up Ron Vibert, my trainer, and asked to ride a horse of mine called Pirate Way. Lester had seen it ridden badly in its previous race. I was in Brazil at the time and don't normally let my horses run when I am not able to see them. However, it was a dream to have a horse of mine ridden by Piggott so I gave permission. Pirate Way won, at 100-8. As a present, I brought back a most attractive Brazilian stone set of ashtrays and, a few days later, presented them to Lester at Windsor.

'He looked at them rather unenthusiastically and, after a pause, I asked if he liked them. "I'd rather have a cheque," said Lester. I wrote the cheque out on the weighing room table and went home. I still have the ashtrays.'

UPON RETIREMENT *The Sporting Life*, 11 September 1995

'What's Lester riding?' For years, for thousands who knew little about the strange world of horseracing, Lester Piggott was the one name that sparked curiosity and gave the sport meaning. A near mythical figure, Piggott bridged the gulf between racing enthusiasts and the outside world. When the Derby came round, once-a-year punters wanted to know only one thing: what was Lester riding? That was what racing professionals wanted to know, too.

A genius in the saddle, an enigma out of one, people longed to know what Lester was really like, and the longing lasted from the beginning to the end of his 47-year career, because Old Stoneface has never provided an answer.

Distant, detached, wearing his emotions in the inside pocket of his inside pocket, people forever wondered what lay behind Piggott's taciturn expression. Was he uncommunicative because of his partial deafness and speech impediment, or was he monosyllabic by choice? Was there more to him than met the eye, or less than people imagined?

For every point, there was a counter-point. Piggott was a misery; no, he was full of dry humour. He was mean; no, he was regularly engaged in acts of quiet charity. He was selfish; no, he was generous with advice.

On and off the racecourse, Lester Piggott has always made his own rules, but the rule he never broke was that second wasn't good enough. As a personality, Piggott may remain a mystery but as a jockey he left his mark everywhere he rode; an individualistic talent that amounted to genius, wedded to an unbending will to win.

Piggott could be unattractively materialistic and shameless in his pursuit of a coveted mount but he was also enormously brave and disciplined, forcing his weight way beneath its natural level, and shrugging off a string of life-threatening falls. His precocity – he rode his first winner at the age of 12 and won his first Derby, on Never Say Die, in 1954, aged 18 – captured the public's imagination. He has never left it since.

Tall for a Flat jockey, Piggott developed his own inimitable style; short-stirruped, high-bottomed, supremely effective. As trophies and records, Classics and championships piled up, racefans came to believe that their hero was capable of anything, and he often was.

Piggott did his homework before racing, and was a master of pace and timing. He could control a race from the front, but punters loved to see him swoop late, with arrogant accuracy. They had enormous confidence in his ability and, at his peak, during the 1960s and 1970s, and when it really mattered, Lester rarely let his fans down.

On occasion, he brought a skewed fierceness and machine-gun whip action into play, never more tellingly than when compelling Roberto to master Rheingold in the 1972 Derby. Piggott made Epsom his own, first in company with Noel Murless and then with Vincent O'Brien, partnerships which attracted their own superlatives.

His insularity and single-minded dedication to the life of a professional jockey made Piggott an unlikely candidate either for a training career or retirement, although he tried both. Only Piggott could have retired at 50, staged a comeback at the age of 54 and, within a fortnight, won the Breeders' Cup Mile on Royal Academy. Although he landed his 30th English Classic success when Rodrigo De Triano won the 1992 Two Thousand Guineas, Piggott's powers were inevitably waning, and he is right to retire, but there really never will be another.

Lester Piggott was one of a group of jockeys at Newmarket for a special presentation to mark the 125th anniversary of the Champion Stakes. Yves Saint-Martin and Geoff Lewis were also there.

A REUNION *Racing Post*, 19 October 2002

Twenty-five years ago, Lester may not have been at his very best. He had just paid a visit to Stevenage Magistrates' Court on a speeding charge, for which he held two previous convictions. His solicitor, Jeremy Richardson, presumably without bursting into an uncontrollable fit of the giggles, appealed to the magistrates not to ban Lester because of the hardship it would cause the racing public and 'the whole bloodstock industry.'

It wasn't just owners, trainers, racegoers and punters who would suffer, Richardson warned. Lester's hectic timetable meant that, if he had to employ a chauffeur, the chauffeur would have to work 'extremely unsocial hours.' Out of compassion for the racing industry and for the as-yet-not-employed chauffeur, the magistrates restricted Lester's punishment to a £60 fine. Unfortunately, two days later, Piggott appeared at Linton Magistrates' Court on another speeding charge. This time, it wasn't just the future of the bloodstock industry that lay in the balance but the future of Lester himself. Asked what effect a ban would have on him, Piggott replied, 'I'll retire.'

The magistrates banned him for six months and, true to his word, Lester did retire, but not until 1985, and then again in 1995.

Lester, Yves Saint-Martin and Geoff Lewis will be able to have a good laugh reminiscing over the 1973 Benson and Hedges Gold Cup. Lester was due to ride Roberto, the previous year's winner, for Vincent O'Brien. However, O'Brien considered that overnight rain had made the ground too soft for Roberto and withdrew him. Lewis had been engaged to ride Moulton for Harry Wragg, with the proviso that, should Roberto not run, Piggott would have the mount. Lester rang Wragg and told him that he would ride Moulton.

When Lester arrived at York, he was approached by the connections of Rheingold, who was due to be ridden by his regular partner, Saint-Martin. Piggott agreed to switch to Rheingold, the odds-on favourite, leaving Lewis to ride Moulton and Saint-Martin without a ride, and very cross. Saint-Martin lodged an official complaint and the stewards issued a statement deploring the late change in riding arrangements. *The Sporting Life*'s columnist Jack Logan, alias Sir David Llewellyn, argued that 'The remedy is to make the overnight declaration of jockeys compulsory and only to allow substitutes on medical grounds.'

The race dispensed its own justice. Moulton won, at 14-1, with Rheingold third.

It was another 15 years before the overnight declaration of jockeys was introduced, in 1992.

THE DUKE OF ALBURQUERQUE *Racing Post*, 21 January 2010

Before the 1928 Grand National, jockey Bill Dutton heard a friend yell out, 'Billy boy, you'll only win if all the others fall down.' And they all did, leaving Dutton and Tipperary Tim, at 100-1, to beat the only other finisher, the remounted Billy Barton. The Pathe News newsreel showed the field streaming over Bechers Brook, with its then formidable drop, and a melee at the Canal Turn, where many runners were baulked and refused, and the crowd pressing in on the winning horse and rider as they returned, elated.

A little later, in Madrid, an eight-year-old boy watched the newsreel in awe. 'It was the most exciting thing that I had ever seen,' he recalled, 64 years later. 'From that moment on, I was determined to ride in the race. It was my obsession.' It was an obsession that carved a unique footnote in the history of the Grand National, and in that of Liverpool's Walton Hospital, an obsession that bore the exotic name of Beltran de Osorio y Diez de Rivera, the 19th Duke of Alburquerque.

When Beltran told his parents of his ambition, his mother told her already lanky son that jockeys needed to be short, not tall. So Beltran slept curled up in a tight ball, to make himself as small as possible. It didn't work but, by the time he was 11, the future Duke of Alburquerque was already hunting on horseback, and soon a regular wearer of neck braces, the result of an early aptitude for injury. Nothing stopped him.

The family were monarchists, loyal to Alfonso XIII, King of Spain. When the monarchy was overthrown, in 1931, the house of Alburquerque supported the exiled king and, during the Spanish civil war, the Duke of Alburquerque, in company with other monarchists, fought on the side of the Nationalists, led by General Franco. Alfonso XIII died in exile in 1941 and, during Franco's long rule, the Duke of Alburquerque acted as head of the household of Juan, Count of Barcelona, Alfonso XIII's son and claimant to the throne.

The Duke rode regularly in Europe, as an amateur jockey, and in equestrian events. By the late 1940s, in preparation for his dream, he had horses in training in England, with John Goldsmith and Peter Cazalet. Finally, in 1952, aged 32, the Duke of Alburquerque rode Brown Jack III, trained by Cazalet, in the Grand National. He fell on the first circuit, at Becher's Brook, cracked two bones in his spine and made his debut at Walton Hospital, just down the A59 from Aintree. That August, he represented Spain at the Helsinki Olympics, for the Duke, although regularly down, was rarely out.

It was important to have the right horse for Aintree and it was 1963 before Alburquerque, then aged 43, found another one, in the shape of Jonjo. Two years earlier, the fences had been altered, prompting *The Times*'s racing correspondent to declare that Ayala's victory signalled 'a new order of Grand Nationals. The change in the shaping of the fences has reduced by more than half the number of falls in all races over them.' Perhaps that was why Jonjo didn't fall until the 21st fence, and the Duke of Alburquerque, unusually, did not require a visit to Walton Hospital.

Two years later, when Groomsman fell at Valentine's Brook, the Duke broke a leg, bringing his career tally of fractures to 22. Utterly undaunted, in 1966 he was back, this time on L'Empereur, trained by Toby Balding. As tall as a basketball player, as thin as a rake, Alburquerque somehow managed to ride at 10st 2lb, partly by resorting to a fibre glass saddle. 'He was a total kamikaze pilot,' Balding recalled, 'and brave as a lion.' L'Empereur reached the fourth fence from home before being pulled up.

Issuing riding instructions was not easy. 'If he didn't want to listen to you,' Balding said, 'he suddenly wouldn't remember any English.' This also made it difficult for journalists although, in those days, extended interviews with jockeys were uncommon. Luckily, *The Sporting Life*'s John Clark spoke Spanish and, in 1992, the obsessive Duke spoke to him from his castle near Madrid.

'I didn't have the horses for the race,' the Duke told Clark. 'Then I bred Nereo.' He sent Nereo to Fred Winter, who had already won the Grand National four times, twice as a jockey and twice as a trainer. 'A giant among jockeys and among English sporting men,' Alburquerque observed. 'A great person and a very great friend of mine.'

With the long-bodied, long-faced Duke on board, Nereo won on his hurdle debut at Hereford in 1970 and, two years later, won the Dick McCreery Chase at Sandown. Alburquerque had finally found the right horse. In 1973, when Nereo was seven and the Duke 53, he tried again to win the National. While stablemate Crisp, carrying 12st, jumped magnificently in the lead, only to be cruelly caught by Red Rum, carrying 10st 5lb, the Duke of Alburquerque fought his own battle with a broken stirrup leather. At the eighth fence, the Canal Turn, he lost. At least he was not required at the hospital.

On the long drive back to Lambourn, the Duke remembered, 'Fred never said a word but, when we arrived home, we had the most wonderful meal I have ever had in my life. There was champagne and caviar. It was party time. That was what made Fred so great; he was such a brilliant loser.'

The following year, Red Rum was back at Aintree, and so was Nereo. More remarkably, so was the Duke of Alburquerque, who had recently had 16 screws removed from his leg and, a week before the National, broke his collar bone in a fall at Newbury. On the day of the race, *The Times* reported, 'The Duke of Alburquerque may have to pass the course doctor's medical check this morning but Aintree finds him still undaunted and none can say that he does not approach the Grand National in the try, try again spirit of Robert the Bruce.'

'Fred was furious that I was riding in the race,' said the Duke, 'and his instructions were monosyllabic. Ironically, it was my best performance in the National, when I was in the worst condition. The poor animal had to do everything on his own. He didn't have a jockey on board, but a sack of potatoes.' The 55-year-old potatoes arrived at the finish in eighth place after, perhaps anecdotally, having given Ron Barry and his mount Straight Vulgan a hefty bump at the Canal Turn. 'What the **** are you doing?', Barry shouted, to which the Duke replied, 'My dear chap, I haven't a clue. I've never got this far before.' Forty-six years after being inspired by a newsreel of the Grand National, the Duke of Alburquerque had finally succeeded in completing the course. 'It gave me enormous satisfaction,' he told Clark, 'and, if I had been in decent shape, we wouldn't have been far away.'

A multiple compound fracture of his right leg forced the Duke to miss the 1975 National, although he had something to celebrate that year, when Franco's death was followed by the restoration of the monarchy. Juan Carlos, the grandson of Alfonso XIII, became king of Spain, while the Duke continued to serve as head of the king's father's household.

In 1976, with another seven screws securing a metal plate in his leg, the Duke of Alburquerque partnered Nereo for a third time in the National, falling at the 13th fence. Nereo was unscathed but the Duke was taken to Walton Hospital. The next day, the hospital issued a bulletin, 'The Duke's fracture of the right thigh bone and concussion have been dealt with and he is comfortable. It is hoped he will be fit to travel within a few days.' 'I spent most of my time there unconscious,' the Duke recalled, 'but when I did wake up, the staff were charming.'

Diana Winter, the trainer's wife, believed that the Duke's shape was against him. 'People who are that tall don't fall very well,' she suggested. 'They tend to splatter.' The Duke preferred to put his multiple fractures down to bad luck, and over-excitement.

Early in 1977 he travelled to London to hear the Jockey Club stewards decline to renew his riding permit. The Duke of Alburquerque, aged 57, was outraged. 'I was in brilliant physical condition,' he insisted. 'I had trained hard and was ready to ride. I couldn't understand the decision. It was my body, my horse and my responsibility.' Fred Winter was less outraged. 'I am both very sad and very relieved,' he said.

If the truly iron Duke had been allowed to ride on, the hospital might have run out of screws, and the Duke out of legs.

That year, the Duke went to Aintree as a spectator, an experience he described as 'one of the saddest days of my life.' Denied the pleasures of Becher's Brook, he rode on, in Spain, and was still riding competitively in 1985, aged 65. In 1991, aged 71, the Duke walked 721 kilometres to complete the pilgrims' path to Santiago da Compostela. Two years later, the rarely awarded Order of the Golden Fleece was conferred on this extraordinary man by King Juan Carlos. The Duke of Alburquerque died a few months later, in 1994.

GUY PACKER *Racing Post*, 3 October 2007

Hitler had shot himself, and thousands of soldiers returning from the war were determined to enjoy themselves, some of them on Cambridgeshire day at Newmarket's Rowley Mile course. The soldiers had more money to spend than Guy Packer, a 15-year-old apprentice who had never ridden a winner in his life and was earning two shillings and fourpence a week working for Bob Colling.

He had reached Colling's yard by bicycle which, as a schoolboy, he mounted early every Saturday and Sunday morning in Cambridge in order to ride out on Newmarket Heath. The son of a bookmaker, Packer was soon working full-time for Colling, but was apprenticed to his son, Jack, because Colling snr was a bankrupt. So, very nearly, was Packer.

Today, in his Berkshire bungalow, Packer, now 77 and renamed Guy Hart, produces a small apprenticeship certificate, dated 18 August 1944, marking the start of a riding career remembered largely by himself.

'I had two rides in 1944, both for Major Holliday, and a few early in 1945,' Hart recalls. 'Then I got beaten a short head on one of Holliday's horses, after giving the horse a couple of slaps with the whip. Major Holliday told me that he wouldn't have his horses hit and that I wouldn't be riding for him again. I was in good company, because he sacked Gordon Richards and Michael Beary for the same thing, and sacked most of his trainers, too.'

It wasn't a promising start to the 1945 season, which threatened to end with both Packer and Esquire, his mount in the Cambridgeshire, still maidens. 'Bob Colling trained Esquire and I rode the horse at home,' says Hart, a lively, compact figure, who still swims every day, partly to ease a back injury sustained in a fall. 'Esquire had been bought for export to Brazil, but couldn't be exported until he had won a race.' By the time the Cambridgeshire arrived, on 31 October, Esquire had tried and failed a dozen times, although in his previous race he was the 3-1 favourite, and several professional punters had already backed him for the Cambridgeshire.

'It was very different in those days,' says Hart. 'Now there is a good betting handicap every Saturday, but there wasn't then. The Cambridgeshire was one of a handful of big betting races and, after the war, there was a lot of money about.'

On his son's advice, Packer snr had backed Esquire and when he was beaten on 16 October, finishing tenth, Guy told him not to worry. Esquire still had a good chance in the big race. 'The jockey gave him a terrible ride that day,' says Hart, 'but as a result, Esquire drifted in the betting for the Cambridgeshire and eventually went off at 40-1.'

Built into the price was the jockey, a winnerless 7lb claimer, weighing less than six stone, and riding at 6st 3lb. 'If the horse had won his previous race, he'd have carried a penalty, and a heavier jockey would probably have got the ride,' says Hart. 'I told my father that Esquire would win, and got him to put £40 each-way on for me, which was a huge bet then, especially for a 15-year-old. Of course, we weren't supposed to bet, but all the jockeys did, and I'd been brought up in a betting family.'

Packer's confidence was increased by the soft ground. 'That was what Esquire wanted,' he says. 'I was drawn next to Gordon Richards. He said to me, "I know your stable fancies your horse. Don't chase me, because mine won't get home. When I get to the Bushes, I'll look round and, if you're there, kick on".' Packer did, and won by half a length. 'Richards was the first to congratulate me,' he says. 'He was a lovely man.' Packer's view of the trainer was less flattering. 'Colling told me that I'd taken a long time to pull up and get back, but the owners sent me £300 as a present, and Esquire went off to Brazil.'

It wasn't the start of something bigger, except Packer's waistline. He put on weight and, when his five-year apprenticeship was over, he approached Jack Colling for his indentures, and his share of riding fees. 'Bob was sitting there,' he says, 'and Jack said, "I've taught you a trade in life, you can get a job anywhere in the world. There's your indentures", but no money. I didn't get anything. I walked to the cafe across the road and cried.'

Three years later, in 1952, still broke, Packer went to Lingfield on the day of the Derby Trial. 'I went into the weighing room and saw Charlie Smirke, who used to ride for Colling sometimes, and who I got on well with. He told me to back his mount, Tulyar, that afternoon, and to beg, borrow and steal to back him for the Derby. That's what I did. I put credit bets on with a Cambridge bookmaker who thought I was putting them on for university undergraduates, and backed Tulyar to win £4,000. It was spunky, because there was no way I could have paid if he'd lost. I was skint.'

Fortunately, Tulyar didn't lose, and Packer subsequently joined forces with Sheila Hart, and enjoyed a lively life in London. They bought several properties, drove a green and beige Jaguar, and became lucratively involved with greyhounds, playing on the edge. Packer changed his name by deed poll to Hart, turned to the antique business and, in 1960, married Sheila. The marriage eventually ended, but the gambling carried on, one way and another.

Lucian Freud, one of Britain's most highly regarded artists, was also a gambler and, through gambling, met Hart. 'He loved gambling,' says Guy. 'He'd have £200 doubles and trebles, and loved to back Jeremy Tree's horses, which was a good way to go skint. I used to put the bets on for him with Michael Tabor, when Tabor was a bookmaker.

'When I first got to know Freud, he told me that he'd paint me one day, but not until I was older. About ten years later, he suddenly said, "I'm ready to paint you now." It took him five weeks to paint one hand, and 18 months to finish it. He was unbelievably slow.'

Freud painted Hart several times. Unfortunately, the sitter wasn't also the owner of the paintings, which came to be worth a lot more than Esquire's win in the 1945 Cambridgeshire.

The most prized of Lucian Freud's portraits of Guy Hart is 'Guy and Speck' (1981), showing Hart holding a Jack Russell terrier. In 2010, the painting was sold at Sotheby's for £1.3 million.

KIEREN FALLON *Racing Post*, 31 August 2009

Napoleon Bonaparte only had two major ups and downs, but Kieren Fallon has regularly met his Waterloo. Diligent and wayward, charming and intimidating, generous and careless, endearing and exasperating, with a body of iron and feet of clay, Fallon's capacity for casually destroying what he has worked hard to create makes you want to shake him and say, 'Kieren, for heaven's sake.' It's been tried, often. On the other hand, between bouts of hara-kiri, Fallon has won six jockeys' championships and 15 English Classics.

Having graduated from Kevin Prendergast's and Jimmy Fitzgerald's yards to that of Lynda and Jack Ramsden, for whom he won the 1993 Lincoln on High Premium and the 1994 Gimcrack on Chilly Billy, Fallon first put a serious blot on his copy book in September 1994, at Beverley. Offended by Stuart Webster's behaviour during a race, Fallon pulled Webster out of the saddle immediately after it. The altercation continued in the weighing room while, in the stewards' room, Fallon was suspended for six months.

Riding for the Ramsdens provided plenty of practice in the art of weaving through a field of rivals and, in 1997, Fallon took up the cherished post of stable jockey to Henry Cecil. Despite winning his first Classic in that year's One Thousand Guineas, on Sleepytime, it was not a smooth transition to the big time. When Bosra Sham was beaten in the Coral-Eclipse, neither Cecil nor owner Wafic Said were impressed, and Fallon lost the ride to Pat Eddery. Fallon was not a stylist, nor yet the acknowledged master of race-riding that he later became but he was, for the first time, champion jockey.

He spent the first part of 1998 in court, successfully pursuing a libel action, with the Ramsdens, against *The Sporting Life*. The paper had accused Fallon of not riding to win on Top Cees in a race at Newmarket in 1995, prior to the horse's success shortly afterwards in the Chester Cup. Fallon was awarded £70,000 in damages.

There was another considerable 'up' in 1999, when Fallon won both the Oaks and Derby for Cecil on Ramruma and Oath. A month later, Ramruma and Fallon won the Irish Oaks but, in August, when the filly won the Yorkshire Oaks, Eddery took the honours. Cecil had sacked Fallon for personal reasons never publicly disclosed. Having been pushed out of the window, Fallon was still flying through the air when Sir Michael Stoute stuck out a hand and grabbed him, stable jockey Gary Stevens having decided to return to the US. Fallon started 2000 as Stevens' successor.

Having launched the partnership by winning the Two Thousand Guineas on King's Best, the pair were moving along nicely when Alhawa's fall at Royal Ascot left Fallon with a career-threatening shoulder injury. Fallon's determination ensured that his injury only temporarily interrupted his sequence of jockeys' championships, while Stoute's loyalty helped him through an alcohol problem that led to a month's stay in a rehabilitation clinic.

Fallon and a quiet life seemed incompatible, every up needing to be contradicted by a down. Sandwiched between two successive Derby wins, on Kris Kin and North Light, was a disastrous short-head defeat on Ballinger Ridge at Lingfield in March

2004, a ride which prompted a public debate about whether Fallon was guilty of an intentionally or unintentionally inept finish. To make matters worse, Fallon had been set up by the *News of the World*, in a sting in which reporters posing as Middle Eastern high rollers subsequently claimed that Fallon had told them that Ballinger Ridge would not win. What it actually revealed was Fallon's vulnerability, his openness and willingness to share the company of people who would be avoided by wiser and more self-respecting champions.

While the Ballinger Ridge debate rumbled on, September opened with Fallon's arrest, along with 15 others, as part of a police investigation into alleged conspiracy to defraud. The champion jockey was promptly released on bail and, the following month, was back at the top of the ladder, at Lone Star Park in Texas, winning the Breeders' Cup Filly and Mare Turf on Ouija Board. As another 'up,' the Jockey Club decided that the evidence presented by the *News of the World* did not justify disciplinary action.

Stoute had been prepared to take a chance, calculating that the risks that accompanied Fallon were outweighed by the benefits, and so was Coolmore. John Magnier and his associates offered Fallon financial rewards too great to resist, plus the lure of Ballydoyle and Ireland, and he spent 2005 as Jamie Spencer's successor at Aidan O'Brien's.

The safest spot for Fallon and the best antidote for turmoil was always in the saddle, whether on the gallops or on the racecourse. Freed, for a while, from his demons, Fallon had a striking capacity for exhibiting his talents even while the Sword of Damocles was poised above him. The 2005 season drew to a close at Longchamp, with a Group 1 treble on Hurricane Run, in the Arc, and Horatio Nelson and Rumplestiltskin. Two days later, he was at Bishopsgate police station in London, answering bail.

The largely self-inflicted roller-coaster accelerated in 2006, lurching wildly from triumph to disaster. Having won the Two Thousand Guineas on George Washington and the Oaks on Alexandrova, Fallon had barely added the Queen Anne Stakes and Gold Cup at Royal Ascot before being charged with conspiracy to defraud and suspended from riding in the UK, although not elsewhere. Two weeks later, he won the Irish Oaks and, in September, the Irish Champion Stakes, on Dylan Thomas. Three weeks later, he was at Southwark Crown Court.

The pressures were immense and, whatever Fallon's outward demeanour, they took their toll. At the end of November, the French authorities banned him for six months for substance abuse. The ban was worldwide. A new dimension had been added to the crazy mix. The script was already barely believable but it had yet to reach its climax. Fallon returned to win the 2007 Irish St Leger on Yeats and, on 7 October, won the Arc with a daring ride on Dylan Thomas. The following day, he appeared in the dock of the Old Bailey, where he would spend the next two months, until Mr Justice Forbes ruled that there was no case to answer, and directed the jury to return not guilty verdicts. Within 24 hours, Fallon faced the prospect of another worldwide ban, this time for 18 months, having failed a drugs test in France for a second time.

Fallon had slipped down the well-worn snake again. Now, his 44-year-old feet are climbing back up the ladder. You really couldn't make it up.

In 2010, Fallon finished third in the jockeys' championship, with 140 winners. In 2011, he finished third again, with 145 winners.

9
... *NOR JOURNALIST*

Jeffrey Bernard with friends.

Some racing journalists have been very out of the ordinary. Few can have been more extraordinary than the trio of Jeffrey Bernard, Donald Adams and John McCririck.

JEFFREY BERNARD *Racing Post*, 22 January 2010

On 3 October 1970, reading *The Sporting Life* suddenly became a different experience. That was the day Jeffrey Bernard's first column appeared and, for exactly a year, until he was sacked, Bernard was a revelation. He wrote about racing in a way that no one else did, irreverently, as a losing punter. He wrote about the things he liked – women, drinking, gambling – and about the things he disliked, including trainers who took themselves too seriously. Not all his pieces were good but Bernard could be, and often was, very funny.

His first venture into racing came in 1948, when he was 16. 'Another boy and myself laid Dramatic for the Stewards' Cup,' Bernard recalled. 'We lost 237 weeks' pocket money and, if you've never tried welshing on 150 boys at a boarding school miles from anywhere, then don't.'

As well as illegal betting, Bernard had already discovered the joys of Soho and sex, both of which he indulged in enthusiastically for the rest of his life, body permitting. Handsome and amusing, his many drinking companions included Francis Bacon and Lucian Freud, Dylan Thomas and John Hurt, Peter Cook, Tony Hancock and even, on one occasion, Marlene Dietrich. His list of bedmates was a long one. As Graham Lord, his biographer, observed, Bernard 'had a lot of wives, four of them his own.'

What Bernard lacked was money, which he begged and borrowed but rarely repaid. During the 1950s, he worked, but usually not for long, as a dishwasher, model, fairground worker, boxer, labourer and stagehand. After the Old Vic sacked him, for drunkenness, he got a job sticking stars on the dancers' nipples in the Folies Bergere show. There were 40 of them.

Encouraged by his second wife, Jackie Ellis, he pursued photography, fitfully, and in 1962 obtained an advance of £100 for a collection of his work, *Soho Night and Day*. Bernard lost the £100 in ten spins of a roulette wheel, was thrown out by his wife and tried to commit suicide, a pattern periodically repeated. Friends invariably bailed him out and took him in, which was often a mistake, as Cook discovered when Bernard promptly seduced his wife. Bernard was a charming and entertaining man but, particularly when drunk, could also be an unpleasant one.

He got his first job in journalism in 1964, with *Queen* magazine. The following year, he was sent to interview Prince Monolulu, the famous racecourse tipster. The Prince was in hospital and, when Bernard put a strawberry cream chocolate in the 80-year-old patient's mouth, Prince Monolulu choked to death. Fortunately, Bernard also had a part-time job at a Soho pub. One evening the publican took Bernard to the nearby Pickwick Club where, after a few drinks, Bernard recalled, 'he emptied an entire sauceboat of sauce tartare into my jacket pocket.' Bernard walked to a table occupied by the actor Peter Finch and asked if he would like some sauce tartare with his fish. When Finch said 'yes,' Bernard picked up a spoon, dipped it into his pocket, and put a dollop of sauce on Finch's plate. The next day, wrote Bernard, 'I took the jacket to a cleaner and a terrible old bag with a deadpan face behind the counter just wrote out the ticket saying, "Gentleman's jacket. Sauce tartare in right-hand pocket."'

In 1966, when he married his third wife, Jill Stanley, Bernard borrowed £100 and went to the Derby intending to back Charlottown. Unfortunately, he changed his mind and backed Sodium, instead. Things briefly looked up when *Town* magazine sent him to the Dorchester Hotel to interview Raquel Welch, the semi-naked star of *One Million Years BC*. Distracted by the actress's thighs, Bernard poured a pot of tea over her sandwiches. It could have been worse, and often was. At Royal Ascot, in 1971, he was said to have been sick over the Queen Mother's shoes.

By then, he was in full flow for *The Sporting Life*, a job offering all that Bernard desired. At the racecourse, admirers of his column provided an endless supply of free drinks, which Bernard rarely declined. As a result, the morning after a race meeting at Huntingdon, he woke up in bed with jockey Barry Brogan and a woman he didn't recognise. Bernard wasn't sure what had happened but he was asked never to return to Huntingdon, to make sure it didn't happen again.

Drink and memory don't mix well and, after another racecourse outing, Bernard wrote, 'Would the married lady who wasn't with her husband, but with the other chap, please contact me? I enjoyed drinking with her at Lingfield, have forgotten her name and wish to repeat the performance.' He found Chester particularly appealing. It 'really was wonderful,' he enthused. 'I'd like my ashes to be scattered on the run-in, if there's room.' On the other hand, after two days at Newmarket, Bernard lamented, 'It's always very depressing to discover that the best racing crumpet is usually accompanied by racehorse trainers and/or millionaires.' Reflecting on the fact that Fred Archer was in Newmarket when he shot himself, Bernard observed, 'Knowing the place pretty well, I suspect he was trying to attract the attention of the staff in the Rutland Hotel.'

He bet often, and generally badly, although during his year with the *Life*, he did strike a bet with a Brighton bookmaker that the winner of the Miss World contest would have a bosom measuring 36 inches. She did, at 5-2. During a bad run, he declared, 'I want to bet on how many more bets I've got to strike before I make a winning one.'

Bernard counted Fred Winter and Lester Piggott among his heroes, musing, 'what's Lester really like? As one of the 50 million people in this country he doesn't want to meet, I can only guess.' When Piggott gave him a lift in his plane, from Newmarket to Newbury, Bernard was delighted. A week later, he received a bill for £35. Winter was more accommodating. When he showed Bernard around his Lambourn yard, Bernard, wanting to say the right thing, ventured, 'Your horses look healthy.' 'Yes,' replied Winter. 'They don't stay up all night playing cards and drinking vodka.'

Drinking was Bernard's core activity and a reliable source of disaster, for himself and others. Periodically, *The Sporting Life* reported, 'Jeffrey Bernard is ill. It is hoped that his column will be resumed shortly.' The end came when Bernard was invited to present a trophy at a point-to-point dinner, armed himself with too much Dutch courage and, depending on one's choice of witness, either fell asleep on a sofa in the hotel lobby or stood up to speak and fell, head first, into his soup. A dozen years later, in 1983, Bernard would return to the fold, with a column in the *Weekender*.

Meanwhile, in 1972, having graduated to two bottles of whisky a day, Bernard entered an addiction clinic, where a fellow patient advised him that, if he ever resorted to surgical spirit, 'for God's sake drink Boots' and not Timothy White's. It's got a better looking label and doesn't look as sordid on the sideboard.' His wife (the third one), left him in 1973 and, after punching a woman in the Coach and Horses pub in Soho, Bernard shocked himself into two and a half years of abstinence. During this untypical period, he wrote to the *New Statesman*, to which he was a contributor, 'I have been commissioned to write my autobiography, and I would be grateful to any of your readers who could tell me what I was doing between 1960 and 1974.' The autobiography was never written.

He wrote for various publications, including *Men Only*, where, in a column entitled Bedtime with Bernard, he claimed to have visited a church in Suffolk and seduced the vicar's daughter while she was playing Bach on the organ. Another claim, made under the byline of Colonel Mad in *Private Eye*, was that 'England's largest open-air lunatic asylum, Lambourn, is shortly to be wired off in an attempt to stop the spread of drunkenness and wife-swapping that is becoming a national disgrace.'

1978 was an important year, in which he was sacked by the *Daily Express*, married his fourth wife, Sue Ashley, moved to East Garston, near Lambourn, and launched his Low Life column in the *Spectator*, which made his name. Memorably described by Jonathan Meades, in *The Tatler*, as 'a suicide note in weekly instalments,' Low Life achieved the remarkable feat of making a weekly account of a life based largely around a refilled glass of vodka engaging. After giving up driving, 'for fear of killing somebody between Lambourn and Great Shefford,' Bernard obtained a daily lift to the Queen's Arms, whose buckled railings bore the imprint of his car, by posting an envelope addressed to himself, then getting into the postman's van when he delivered the letter to Bernard's home at Crane's Farm. Tony Lovell, the pub's landlord, obligingly opened the back door at 9.00am.

Decades of heavy drinking translated themselves into a range of ailments, including diabetes and pancreatitis, so that, by 1982, Bernard reported, 'When the doorbell rang this morning, I was sure it was the grim reaper but, luckily, it was the milkman.' Admitted into the John Radcliffe Hospital, Bernard managed to get expelled for secretly eating jam sandwiches, which didn't form part of his treatment for diabetes. Later, when a doctor asked him, 'Why do you drink?' he replied, 'To stop myself jogging.'

By the end of 1980, his wife (the fourth one) having finally left him, Bernard was back in London, mainly in the Coach and Horses, although in 1983 he accepted an invitation to Barbados, where his companions were amazed when they visited a run down-bar in a wooden shack and the barman turned to Bernard and said, 'The usual, sir?'

When he left Lambourn, Bernard was still a good looking man and, into his 50s, had no difficulty charming a succession of much younger women to his new home, which he called 'the Great Portland Street Academy for Young Ladies.' He posed for *Naked London*, clutching a carefully placed Timeform volume, yet, by the end of the 1980s, Bernard looked like an old man, with two large, disfiguring lipomas on his neck. Drink and diabetes had taken their toll. 'Last week, I had an erection,' Bernard reported. 'I was so amazed, I almost took a photograph of it.' Rising to the challenge of the weekly deadline for his column became even more difficult. In 1987, the *Spectator* informed readers, 'Jeffrey Bernard's column does not appear this week, as it is remarkably similar to that which he wrote last week.' When Keith Waterhouse completed his script for a play based on the Low Life columns, Bernard was seriously concerned that he might not live to see the play performed, a concern widely considered to be justified.

Jeffrey Bernard is Unwell, its title based on the note which appeared in the *Spectator* when the Low Life column was absent through alcohol, opened in Brighton in September 1989, moved to Bath and made its triumphant debut at the Apollo Theatre in Shaftesbury Avenue in October. Bernard, magnificently played by Peter O'Toole, gets locked in the Coach and Horses for the night, with his reminiscensces, a bottle of vodka, and a collection of ghosts for company. Very funny, yet scratching, with increasing sadness, at the line between comedy and tragedy, the play ran for a year, with a successful revival in 1991.

It gave Bernard great pleasure and financial security, although the Inland Revenue, already pursuing him vigorously, took most of the money. In 1986, Bow Street Magistrates Court had taken more, after Bernard pleaded guilty to illegally taking bets in the Coach and Horses. Two months later, the police officers who had arrested him invited Bernard to their Christmas party. Bernard, inevitably, accepted.

I met him twice, equally inevitably in the Coach and Horses, where he took four large vodkas to establish contact with the day, dismissively discarded written offers from attractive women who had sent photographs of themselves for his consideration, and mulled over an offer of £2,000 to write 350 words about a pub. You would have laid 10-1 against him living another five years but, minus one leg, he did, dying, aged 65, in 1997.

DONALD ADAMS *Racing Post*, 31 March 2010

On 16 January 1939, an article titled 'Introduction and Growth of Juvenile Racing' appeared in *The Sporting Life*. The author was identified by his initials, D.O.R.A. Less than six months later, Donald Owen Reginald Adams was charged with spying for Germany.

Adams, 56, had started writing about horseracing before the First World War, under the nom de plumes of Flying Fox and Arbitrator, as well as D.O.R.A. The police reported, 'For many years past, he has been a freelance racing journalist and has contributed to well known racing publications.'

Adams was an unsavoury character. His first wife, Emma, described him as unfaithful, violent and abusive. Within two years of their wedding, in 1905, he had allegedly punched her in the face, threatened to shoot her, terrified her into jumping into the River Thames at Richmond and, finally, forced her into prostitution.

In 1915, Adams joined the Army and, in 1917, obtained a commission in Egypt. When the war ended, Adams stayed on. In 1924, the exotically named Hyacinth Louis Rabino, British Consul in Cairo, reported that arrangements were being made to return Adams to Britain at the expense of the British Charitable Fund. 'He is an exceedingly undesirable character,' Rabino wrote, 'not only on account of his habitual drunkenness but because he has victimised more than one woman in Cairo, having lived on their earnings and then abandoned them and their illegitimate children.'

Eight years later, when Adams applied for a passport to enable him to revisit Egypt, an official who interviewed Adams described the 'sporting journalist' as 'a most unsatisfactory individual.' Reluctantly, they issued him with a passport.

In 1936, Adams approached the War Office and, optimistically, offered his services as a secret service agent in Palestine. The War Office turned him down. Adams' motivation was not patriotism but a want of funds. Well known in ex-servicemen's clubs in the Richmond area, 'Captain Adams' smoked expensive cigars and, according to the *News of the World*, was 'always ready with an appropriate racing anecdote.' He claimed to make money betting but when the police and MI5 came calling, at 8.00am on 30 June 1939, Adams was living in an attic bedroom. He was a racing journalist, but not a successful one.

The previous November, writing from his attic at 11 Friars Stile Road, Richmond, Adams acknowledged the receipt of £10 from E. Fricke, whose address was a hotel in the Netherlands. Four days later, on 9 November, the Post Office was instructed to open all Adams' mail, the justification being that 'this individual is strongly suspected of being a German espionage agent.' Adams had offered to spy for Britain. When his offer was rejected, he offered to spy for Nazi Germany, instead.

Later that month, Adams travelled to Germany, visiting Hamburg, Hanover and Dresden. MI5, Britain's security service, believed that he made contact with representatives of Germany's espionage organisation. A letter from 'Fricke,' dated 29 December 1938, read, 'Thanks for *Sporting Life* issue 38, which I think is the last in the course of this year. I have asked our mutual London friend Captain P. and Mr Struck each to forward £10 for the next races.' Three days later, in a letter addressed to D.O.R.A., Captain P. duly enclosed £10, 'this being part of the bet I won in the mentioned sire line of Stockwell. I hope you won't consider me being rude if I let you take part in this bet.'

On 18 January 1939, in a letter addressed to Karl Radeler & Co., in Hanover, Adams suggested a secret code, together with an example based on the phrase, 'Irish horses are most suitable for the work.' It was a simple code, with numbers representing letters. Its simplicity reflected the amateurishness of Adams' work as a spy.

He received irregular payments of £5 and £10 from his German employers, equivalent to roughly £230 and £460 today, but Adams sometimes expressed dissatisfaction with the payments while his paymasters expressed disappointment with the information received. 'Not a single useful order has come through from you yet,' the Germans, masquerading as export merchants, complained. Adams apologised, claiming, 'I have worked very hard in your interests,' and reminded them, probably untruthfully, that 'I resigned my journalistic employment to accept your agency last November and I recently refused two different contracts to resume newspaper work when the racing season opened up on 20 March.'

The spy and his spymasters used racing and betting as a thin, unconvincing mask for the real reason for their communications. On 18 May 1939 Fricke wrote, 'Thanks for your Derby tips. I'll back of course the two Woodward horses and would ask you to put the enclosed USA$60 on Foxbrough II and Hypnotist.'

Adams was a hopeless spy and the information he passed on, mainly about military training and equipment, was all available in published documents, some of which Adams ordered from WH Smith. In an attempt to get more for their money, Adams' contacts suggested more direct involvement. In a letter from Fricke, enclosing £10, a meeting in Cologne on 12 April was suggested and, in a coded message, Adams was instructed, 'Join territorials or any army job. There is big money for you.' Adams did visit Germany that month but, apart from some superficial information about London's barrage balloon defences, he supplied nothing of consequence. It was a fruitless exercise for the Germans and a costly one for their spy.

On 30 June 1939, Detective Inspector William Gagen of the Metropolitan Police, accompanied by two other police officers, together with Lieutenant Colonel Hinchley Cooke of MI5, arrested Donald Adams in his attic bedroom. According to the police report, written that day, Adams, when cautioned, said, 'I see, right ho.'

A large quantity of material and correspondence relating to defence matters was seized, along with a £5 note. A code was found on the inside back cover of a copy of *Cassell's Concise Cyclopaedia*. Adams was taken to Richmond Police Station and subsequently appeared at a special sitting of the petty sessions, charged that he did, 'between November 1938 and 30 June 1939, feloniously record information relating to His Majesty's forces which is calculated to be or might be, directly or indirectly, useful to an enemy,' contrary to the 1911 Official Secrets Act. Adams' response, at the police station and in court, was, 'I am not guilty of giving information away. Certainly not guilty. I am not guilty of giving away anything that is not in the public press. I am a journalist.'

He was remanded in custody and when his case reached the Old Bailey, on 25 September, Adams, reported to be in poor financial circumstances, pleaded guilty. He told the judge, Mr Justice Oliver, 'I did not know I was doing anything wrong, really. I had not seen an Official Secrets Act. I only sent news to Germany which was public.'

From Adams' point of view, the trial could not have been more badly timed. Earlier that month, Germany had invaded Poland, triggering the start of the Second World War, and the judge took a serious view of the offence. Adams had acted for money at a time 'when it was apparent that this frightful war was coming.' He had pleaded guilty to 'one of the most shocking charges' and was worse than a murderer. Fortunately for Adams, the punishment was less severe. He was sent to prison for seven years.

Adams served most of his sentence at Camp Hill prison, on the Isle of Wight. In November 1943 he petitioned for early release, pointing out that, while in prison, his (second) wife had died 'under tragic circumstances,' his only daughter had been killed during an air raid and his adopted son killed in action. He had lost all his worldly possessions, although they could not have amounted to very much. The petition was rejected and, a few months later, an official remarked, 'Adams is a thoroughly bad individual who will do anything for money.'

By that time, Adams, a convert to Roman Catholicism, was in Wakefield prison, confident of being released on 12 May. His thoughts immediately turned to racing. He wrote to his sister, Lena Adams, asking her to buy a copy of *Horses in Training*, and added, 'From personal opinion, a horse named His Excellency will be well worth following whenever he appears in public. Another of quite inferior class, named Scratch, may run away with a spring handicap at Pontefract, if given any burden up to 8st. I will tell you about a Derby outsider when I have actually seen a few colts at work.'

Adams' appearance on the gallops would have to wait because government officials were concerned about public reaction if they released a convicted spy while plans were being made to open a new front in Western Europe, plans leading to the D-Day landings in Normandy on 6 June. That month, having already asked his sister to obtain catalogues for Tattersalls' July Sales at Newmarket, Adams petitioned for a definite date for his release. He was freed on 3 August 1944 and, after a short spell living with his sister in Fulham, moved to a furnished room in a nearby property. Now aged 61, Adams's prospects were bleak. He applied, unsuccessfully, for a job with the British Bloodstock Agency in Charing Cross Road and early in 1945 was working at the Royal Automobile Club in Pall Mall, 'and also does a little work for *The Sporting Life*.'

Adams died, aged 70, in 1953.

JOHN MCCRIRICK *Racing Post*, 26 January 2000

It's going to be quiet when he's gone. There'll never be another. Pointing finger and jutting face, ranting at the camera. Big Mac. And he is big. How many shoppers would recognise a photograph of Tony McCoy or Kieren Fallon, Martin Pipe or Henry Cecil? But they'll smile and give a name to John McCririck, then say what they think of him, in black or white, like Big Mac's own opinions.

He trumpets opinions, he provokes responses. That is why television loves him. When the ripples of a racing story reach beyond racing's pond, the first opinion outsiders seek is McCririck's. The ungrey voice of racing, big enough to be put on dreadful TV shows, like 'Noel's House Party'.

Big Mac stands in his clown's outfit, a shield as well as an attraction, a man whose bombast and aggression is one side of a coin, the other side of which is vulnerable and fragile. Part of him seeks attention, part of him fears it. An eternal child.

His mews house, The Trap, a shrine to himself, shared with a mothering wife happy for McCririck to be the centre around which both their lives revolve; no children – McCririck doesn't like them. He refuses to reveal his age, which would be to acknowledge ageing. He will soon be 60. Under the always unremoved hat, perhaps his hair is thinning. Like a schoolboy, nicknames are everywhere. 'Greatest jockey' [John Francome] and 'my noble lord' [Lord Oaksey] are part of a long sequence. And, of course, the 'Booby' – Jenny McCririck, married almost 30 years.

She is his faithful, unfailing, essential rock. Drives him, waits on him, organises him, cherishes him, protects him, accepts him. The only person he lets in. He has friends, including Robin Cook, the Foreign Secretary, and Peter Jones, the Tote chairman. McCririck, socially nervous, is respected by serious people, but the Booby is his true friend.

His wife doesn't seem to mind McCririck's sexism, and the women who work with him like him. Self-centred, yet a team player, and a kind man. But the sexism is real. 'I would sometimes like to put his head through a mangle,' says one female colleague, for McCririck says things to women that are offensive to many. In some workplaces, it would not be laughed off. He either doesn't realise it, or doesn't care, or views it, cynically, as useful self-publicity.

Who knows? For who knows where McCririck's curious, damaged personality ends and the performance begins? One is an extension of the other.

An unconventional childhood was rounded off at Harrow, where McCririck taught himself bookmaking and emerged with three 'O' levels. After a brief spell as a trainee at the Dorchester Hotel, he spent six years, from 1965 to 1970, as private handicapper for Formindex and Racing Data. He had worked part-time in betting shops and, when Mill Reef won the 1971 Derby, he was working at a pitch on the Hill at Epsom during an avowedly unsuccessful spell as a cheap-ring bookmaker.

Joining *The Sporting Life* in the early 1970s was the making of McCririck and, in a way, the making of *The Sporting Life*. His brashness and arrogance made him unpopular with the staff, but Ossie Fletcher, the *Life*'s editor, recognised his worth. McCririck brought investigative reporting to the *Life*, and racing has never had a better exponent of it.

In 1978, McCririck was voted the Specialist Writer of the Year in the British Press Awards; in 1979, the Campaigning Journalist of the Year. In 1978, McCririck had exposed a sting based on the fact that Extel, who used to broadcast commentaries into betting shops, gave the off-times for greyhound races in minutes, without the refinement of seconds. By briefly delaying the commentaries, criminals were able to back dogs after a race had started. The same year, McCririck took the lead in covering the Rochester greyhound coup, which would have won £350,000 for its clever architects, and should have done, but bookmakers refused to pay out.

In 1979, McCririck hit the jackpot with 'Totegate.' On 4 July, at Carlisle, Shine On, at 11-1, and Tinas Gold, at 20-1, finished first and second in an 18-runner handicap. The dual forecast paid 45p to a 10p stake. Persistence enabled McCririck to establish that the Tote had developed a practice of putting winning off-course bets into the racecourse pool after the race result was known. Further persistence persuaded a reluctant Home Secretary, Willie Whitelaw, to set up an independent inquiry from which Woodrow Wyatt, the Tote chairman, was lucky to escape with his job.

At the *Life*, McCririck revealed what he still displays, a tremendous feel for what matters to punters, and what stands at the core of racing and betting issues. It was McCririck who issued an early, 1983, warning against computerised SPs.

The following year, he hit the buffers. Rumours that McCririck, by now a regular on television, was in trouble with bookmakers created tension between Fletcher and his star journalist. On 5 March 1984, the *Daily Star*'s front page proclaimed, 'TV Star's Gambling Debts.' Describing McCririck as an 'obsessive gambler,' the *Star* claimed that he owed money to the John Power chain and to Colin Webster. The paper went further, and alleged that, in the case of one bookmaker, debts were being repaid by giving the bookmaker media publicity.

McCririck sued for libel and, in May 1986, Express Newspapers accepted that the allegations were untrue and agreed to pay 'a very substantial sum.' The settlement gave a decisive boost to McCririck's finances which, despite overwhelming evidence to the contrary, he still insists are in a parlous state. Too poor to own a racehorse; that is for fat cats. McCririck's gambling did not end completely. Asked recently what his best investment had been, he replied, 'When Zafonic won the Two Thousand Guineas.'

McCririck lost his job at *The Sporting Life*, but soon gained a new one at Channel 4. He has been centre stage ever since. Love him or loathe him, and people do, McCririck's populism is underpinned by a deep understanding of racing as a betting sport. Fearless and outspoken, unfailingly well-prepared, the most penetrating interviewer (in a weak field), he has more often been right than wrong.

When he dies, Big Mac wants his ashes to be scattered at the furlong pole at Ally Pally. Some would like to scatter them now but a lot more wouldn't.

McCririck's subsequent appearances on 'Celebrity Big Brother' and 'Wife Swap' provided ample fuel for his critics. Channel 4 Racing cut down his appearances, much to McCririck's annoyance but, for good or bad, he remains an instantly recognisable face of racing.

10
THE CHELTENHAM FESTIVAL

A panel of experts, possibly.

There is nothing like it in the world, and few events as keenly anticipated. The tangible passion of the Cheltenham Festival exercises a powerful grip, for there is a depth about people's love of jump racing, its heroes, its memories, its cliff-hanging excitements, that Flat racing can rarely match. Those depths inform every visit to Cheltenham, enriched by the presence of the Irish.

It begins with the course itself. You stand and stare, in awe and delight, at the familiar, evocative signature of the track, the fences and features that have raised spirits to the heights, and broken hearts, and pockets, against the background of Cleeve Hill. You can see it all, without even needing to climb a stair, simply by standing in front of the stands.

TEN THINGS I LIKE ABOUT THE FESTIVAL *Racing Post*, 2 March 2010

1. It means that another year's gone by, and I'm still alive. Yippee! From Arkle to Kauto Star, without a coronary. It must be awful to survive a winter of Southwell, only to die just before they set off for the Supreme Novices' Hurdle. It was sad when actress Dame Thora Hird died, aged 91, but her timing was as impeccable as it had been in those wonderful Alan Bennett monologues, *Talking Heads*. She died on 15 March 2003, two days after Best Mate won his second Gold Cup; 15 March, not 10 March. It makes all the difference. Worth bearing in mind, if you're not feeling well.

2. The anticipation. There is nothing to compare with the build-up to
    Cheltenham, which starts immediately after the Supreme Novices' Hurdle
    has finished, when Ladbrokes offer 10-1 against the winner for next
    year's Champion Hurdle. In life (it doesn't matter so much afterwards),
    it's important to have something to look forward to, and the Festival is a
    great annual treat to look forward to. As the races take shape, and potential
    champions and championship battles emerge, the expectation builds,
    reaching fruition in ....

3. Four days of racing in which every race poses intriguing questions, finally
    about to be answered; championship races where true champions clash.
    Admittedly, I've never cared much what wins the bumper, possibly because
    I've never had a bet in it, and the same goes for the juvenile handicap hurdle
    and some of the handicap chases, and the Cross Country Chase, the one that
    Enda Bolger always wins, and the ... but even these races have their value,
    offering time to see if the queue for the toilets has got any shorter, or the one
    at the Arkle Bar any longer (probably not possible).

4. The setting. When I arrive, I like to stand on the lawn in front of the stands,
    and stare at the marvellous natural amphitheatre, with Cleeve Hill as its
    backdrop. Magnificent, unique. It's quiet now but the knowledge that, soon,
    it will be seething with nervous hopes, to be fulfilled or dashed, and the noisy
    welcome of champions, starts the week off perfectly. Standing and thinking
    about ...

5. The past. At Cheltenham, the present adds to the past, and the past to the
    present, in a rare way, each winner taking its place in a pantheon of gods,
    small and large. The Festival's enormously rich, emotion-filled history adds
    to the meaning of each new victory, for the connections of every Gold Cup
    winner know that memories of Arkle, and Desert Orchid, have been conjured
    up again, and they have become part of a continuing story. For each of us
    who have been to the Festival before, returning jogs memories of victories
    cherished and defeats rued, of bets won and lost. For some reason, I always
    end up thinking about Dawn Run's 1986 Gold Cup triumph. I backed
    Wayward Lad, even though I didn't think he'd quite get up the hill. He didn't,
    quite, and I tried my best, not altogether successfully, to feel as elated (very
    elated) as everyone else seemed to feel. Now I stand and think how lucky it
    was that Betfair didn't exist, because I'd probably have laid Dawn Run, at

15-8, for more than the limit on my credit cards. I still don't think she can win – even if she stays, her jumping's not up to it, you see. Oh, well, it pleased ...

6. The Irish. The Festival wouldn't be the same without them even though, in the old days, they were a bit of a nuisance because they brought horses over that were far more of a mystery to us than Irish horses are today. Not that knowledge is necessarily bliss. Two years ago, on the opening day of the Festival, I bumped into trainer Tom Hogan in the car park. Hogan told me that he fancied Silver Jaro in the County Hurdle but, by the time the County Hurdle arrived, the final race of the meeting, I'd forgotten, which was a pity, because Silver Jaro won, at 50-1. I'd met Hogan, briefly, during a tour of Irish racecourses, when I met a lot of other likeable horsemen, too, which gave me fond memories and brings me to ...

7. Bumping into people. That's a very enjoyable part of Cheltenham, where you bump into people you haven't seen for a while, most of whom are in a good mood, because most people are during Cheltenham week. Everyone's been looking forward to it, is excited to be there, and generally feels well disposed towards mankind, at least for a few hours. As part of the ritual, they tell you what they fancy (you don't take much notice) and you tell them what you fancy (they don't take any notice). It's even nice to see ...

8. The bookmakers. I'll look at the front row in Tattersalls, and wish Freddie Williams was still there, but his daughter Julie will be, as well as John Hughes and Adrian Pariser, and the rest. The results at Cheltenham matter a lot to their businesses, and I like chatting to them. Some complain about Betfair, and some complain about other things. I'm the same, although I always promised myself I'd save complaining up for old age, something not yet afflicting ...

9. Jump jockeys. A generally admirable bunch whose admirableness (possibly not a word, until now) seems to be even more conspicuous at Cheltenham, where there is no mistaking how much a Festival winner means to every one of them. Jump jockeys know how to celebrate victory and, a more difficult feat, how to celebrate the victory of others. And what a generation of jockeys, led by Ruby Walsh and Tony McCoy. Something to savour before making a beeline for ...

10. The sweetie kiosks. A life saver. Getting something to eat or drink can be a problem, but there's always a bar of Dairy Milk waiting for you, full of natural goodness, possibly, at one of the sweet kiosks. Such a comfort, in victory and defeat.

Speaking of Dawn Run …

DAWN RUN AND THE 1986 CHELTENHAM GOLD CUP
Racing Post, **7 February 2005**

Great races are full of emotion. They bring nervous, impatient waiting, eager wanting, hope, fear, anticipation, anguish, debate. The 1986 Cheltenham Gold Cup was riddled with emotion, awash with adrenalin. Spectators and participants were drained, for Dawn Run's victory was one of racing's great, suspenseful moments.

There are the actors and actresses, and there is the stage. In 1986, both were extraordinary and, on a fine March day, they came together for a unique performance. One of those days that all who were there will always remember.

Twenty years ago, there was an even greater sense of an Irish gauntlet thrown down each March, a challenge where victories and defeats mattered in the edgy friction between the British and Irish nations. Dawn Run, more than any champion since Arkle, was Ireland's horse, and every Irish man and woman had a small right to claim her, proudly, passionately, as their own. Dawn Run was for Ireland.

So, fiercely, was her owner, Charmian Hill. An Irish patriot with a feisty, awkward, opinionated spirit, in a diminutive body, Hill was never going to be merely a signer of cheques. Sixty-one when she bought the three-year-old Deep Run filly at the 1981 Ballsbridge Sales for 5,800gns, Hill was clutching a letter refusing a renewal of her rider's licence when she won a bumper on Dawn Run at Tralee the following June.

Part of what rouses a crowd is the history that comes to a race. Dawn Run brought a lot of history, woven around Hill and the Mullins family. Unlike Dawn Run's trainer, Paddy Mullins, Hill was not a quiet, tolerant soul but a horsewoman with views, especially views about jockeys. She had views about Tony Mullins, Paddy's son, the jockey who rode Dawn Run more times than anyone else, and won on her more times. When Dawn Run appeared in the 1983 Sun Alliance Novices' Hurdle at Cheltenham, Hill believed that Mullins, then 21, was too young and inexperienced for the task. Ron Barry, an Irishman in Britain, replaced him. 'I would never employ an English jockey,' said Hill. Dawn Run finished runner-up to Sabin du Loir.

Mullins was restored to the saddle until a trip to Ascot in November. This time his replacement was a different Irishman, the talismanic Jonjo O'Neill. 'It's no disgrace to lose the ride to someone as good as Jonjo,' said Mullins, with dignity and generosity. Universally known as Jonjo, O'Neill, twice champion jumps jockey, could drive hard as well as skilfully in the saddle, and charm with a twinkling smile and wry lilt out of it. People loved Jonjo. In 1984, the new combination won the Irish and English Champion Hurdles.

Then, with Jonjo injured, Mullins won the Sandeman Aintree Hurdle and Grande Course de Haies d'Auteuil, the French Champion Hurdle. It was a unique and remarkable achievement, not least because the Grande Course de Haies was over different obstacles, over three miles one and a half furlongs. Dawn Run was a versatile as well as gutsy champion, the only horse ever to land the treble of Champion Hurdles.

Jumping fences presented a different test. Fast and flat over hurdles, with a distaste for being organised, Dawn Run was not a natural jumper of fences. When Hill told Paddy Mullins she wanted the target to be the Cheltenham Gold Cup, Mullins was uneasy.

In November 1984, at Navan, Dawn Run made a winning debut over fences, ridden by Tony Mullins, but a leg injury then kept her off the track for over a year. In December 1985, Dawn Run returned to win at Punchestown and Leopardstown but in January, sent to experience Cheltenham, she reached the open ditch at the top of the hill, and unseated Mullins. Hill was not impressed.

Jonjo was booked for the Gold Cup but fierce weather scuppered plans for another prep race. When O'Neill schooled Dawn Run, he emerged believing that the mare did not like jumping fences. That was one of the teasing ingredients of the 1986 Gold Cup. The horse who was supported with the fiercest passion, the 15-8 favourite, was having only her fifth race over fences, and she looked like a hurdler.

Wayward Lad, in contrast, was a wonderfully athletic, smooth, accurate jumper, three-time winner of the King George VI Chase, with a different fear for his admirers. He didn't really stay three and a quarter miles. There was no such doubt about John Spearing's Run And Skip, who had improved into an exciting front-running stayer, leading all the way to win both the Welsh National and Anthony Mildmay, Peter Cazalet Memorial Chase. Forgive'n Forget had won the previous year's Gold Cup for Jimmy FitzGerald, while David Elsworth's Combs Ditch had only just been beaten by Wayward Lad in the King George.

Dawn Run, who had never raced over as long a trip before, duelled for the lead with Run And Skip, both mixing good jumps with bad. After a bad mistake at the water, and a worse one at the top of the hill, five from home, Dawn Run fell back and came under strong pressure. Attention switched elsewhere, to the strong-travelling Wayward Lad and Forgive'n Forget.

O'Neill, at his most powerful, forced Dawn Run back into the battle and, with a great leap two out, back into a narrow lead. It was quickly wrested from her, as Wayward Lad and Forgive'n Forget quickened ahead. At the last, there was little between the trio, with Dawn Run landing third, and Run And Skip still at their heels but, as they set off up the telling hill, Wayward Lad and Graham Bradley forged on, two lengths clear. Then, suddenly, as Wayward Lad faltered, O'Neill conjured a spine-tingling thrusting rally from Dawn Run. With the crowd delirious, she nosed ahead. The only horse ever to win both the Champion Hurdle and Gold Cup, the latter in a course-record time.

In a hat-trampling stampede, Charmian Hill was carried aloft and so, after he had weighed in, was Jonjo O'Neill, who hoisted Tony Mullins on to his own shoulders. It was a unique occasion, a race for memories, but one with a sad aftermath. Three months later, at Auteuil, ridden by Michel Chirol, Dawn Run fell and was killed.

Festival previews have become an established part of the build-up to Cheltenham, with panels of experts (hopefully) giving audiences, sometimes small, sometimes huge, the benefit of their opinions. They are a good way of getting into the mood, and into the races, and fun to write about.

Here are samples from the 2007 collection.

DUBLIN *Racing Post*, 6 March 2007

What you need are strong and conflicting opinions, forcefully expressed, with panellists sparking off each other. Welcome to the Stillorgan Park Hotel, Dublin, for a rollicking, good-humoured exchange of profound disagreements in front of a very big and partly boozy but well-behaved audience.

The MC is MC – Matt Chapman – bullet headed, hair oiled to encourage punches to slide off (it can only be a matter of time) while racing's new showman balances precariously, but entertainingly, on the line that separates boldness from offence, teasing from insult. Forever on the brink of going too far, Chapman is certain to do so, sooner or later, but there is still enough vulnerability to make you want him to swim rather than sink, and he has done his homework.

The 8.00pm start becomes an 8.30pm start – they must be waiting for a second ambulance. When it arrives, a boxing contest is announced. 'The great Tony Mullins – let's hear it for Tony!' We hear it. 'Let's hear it for Davy Russell!' We hear it. We'd hear it for Andy, too, but Thornton is still on his way from Bangor.

Meanwhile, journalist Jonathan Powell says that he would like Amaretto Rose to win the Supreme Novices' Hurdle for 'Nicky and Fitzy,' while Matty is about to describe Fair Along, favourite for the Arkle, as 'a tiny little rat.' It's an excellent panel, full of opinions and humour, with trainer Mullins and jockey Russell, both prone to strong views and giggling, an edgy double act, and not a dud among them. Mullins and Russell do agree about Fair Along – 'I don't think he's going to see another horse,' says Russell. 'He'll jump out, make all, win on the bridle,' says Mullins.

Grey has been barred for the evening, in favour of black and white. Damien McElroy, the *Irish Independent*'s racing correspondent, a treasure chest of engaging phrases, explains, 'Lennon doesn't do hills. He's like Beef Or Salmon, we just don't do them.'

Thornton arrives just in time to put the stuffing into Straw Bear, who Russell says he'd hate to ride – 'bags of pace but he's going to flatten out something wicked.' Detroit City is widely admired, while McElroy admires Hardy Eustace – 'you don't see him take off till he's landed.' Makes you think.

At the Stillorgan Park Hotel, horses are either heroes or hopeless, with enormous winning distances. 'Well Chief will win by a fence,' says Mullins, 'an absolute certainty. He won't come off the bridle.' Mullins thinks it's a waste of time debating the Champion Chase any further. Russell, on the other hand, insists, 'Newmill is a superstar. He's streets ahead of Nickname. If he had a big-name trainer, he'd be joint-favourite.'

Rob Hartnett, now with sponsor Sporting Index, having formerly been with everyone else, believes that Denman will also win by a street. It's a view shared by everyone, although Thornton, who holds the strange belief that Denman is a machine, thinks Dom D'Orgeval is a good each-way bet for the Royal & SunAlliance Chase at 12-1. When Chapman remarks on Dom D'Orgeval's rather plodding success at Hexham, Thornton says, 'McCoy's great at making horses look hard work. He just can't sit still.'

Mullins, who trains Aranleigh, reports that his Champion Bumper contender 'certainly hasn't disimproved' since he beat brother Willie's Mad Fish, who reportedly gurgled. With favourite Cork All Star having had a wind operation, Mullins says, 'They'll have to have an oxygen tent for both of them.'

11.00pm. It's past my bedtime and we've only just reached day three. Paraphrasing the panel's views, Black Jack Ketchum may not turn up for the World Hurdle, and won't win even if he does. In the Gold Cup, L'Ami is great value at 25-1 (Thornton), Beef Or Salmon is great value at 33-1 (Russell), Kauto Star will definitely not win (Hartnett), Kauto Star should be odds-on and will waltz in (Powell), Kauto Star is the lay of the meeting (Mullins).

As midnight comes and goes, Russell announces that the bet of the festival is actually Star Performance, 14-1 for the Sporting Index Cross-Country Chase. 'He will win.' More sitting on the fence, then.

To salvage something from the wreckage of the panel's predictions, Denman won easily, Aranleigh finished third in the Bumper, at 8-1, and Straw Bear ran badly and was pulled up. Kauto Star won the Gold Cup, vindicating Jonathan Powell but doing the reverse for Rob Hartnett and Tony Mullins.

CARLISLE *Racing Post*, 8 March 2007

Tables full of punters and pints, but the panelists' table is equipped only with water and orange juice. Amazing to think they said those things when sober.

The unobtrusive chairman, Paul Clarkson, seems normal, and so does jockey Tony Dobbin, hotfoot from yesterday's preview in Belfast, but after that . . . There's journalist John Budden, who would make a wonderful uncle, comfortable in his pullover, full of goodwill and good cheer, an old world Mr Pickwick, not a malevolent bone in his body, mellifluous, enthusiastic, warm. 'My advice for the Supreme Novices' Hurdle would be to have a long lunch,' he says.

Then there's trainer Len Lungo, affable, unique, bespectacled, revealed as the man who once babysat for the Pipes, when the baby was David Pipe. It's difficult to see beyond Lungo's hair, or hear beyond his Scottish dialect. What does loquacious mean? I think he might be loquacious.

Then there's Paul Jones, the author of *Weatherbys Cheltenham Festival Betting Guide*, an extraordinary man, his striped black and white shirt making him look like a sweet. Jones's brain is overflowing with knowledge, bursting to get out (I do hope he does sometimes). He waits patiently for his turn, then the dam bursts and the contents of his head pour out in a torrent of facts and statistics, analysis and assertion.

'Only one front-runner has won the Arkle in the last 25 years,' he says. 'That was Azertyuiop, and he wasn't really a front-runner.'

'I can't add to what's been said,' says Lungo, then does. 'At Cheltenham, of course, it's that reddish clay that holds them down.' Dobbin maintains that Faasel 'has more brains than I have,' brains generally being considered a bad thing when occupying a racehorse. Even with brains, he thinks Faasel has a great each-way chance.

We move on. 'I'm not sure she was off a yard last time,' says Jones. (The identity of the horse in question has been concealed, on the grounds of legal costs. Ditto several similarly voiced suspicions.)

'By a process of elimination,' says Budden, 'the winner of the Champion Hurdle, ladies and gentlemen, will be Straw Bear.' It's a ridiculous suggestion but it makes me suddenly remember who Budden reminds me of, it's Nigel Bruce as Dr Watson, when Basil Rathbone played Sherlock Holmes. He'd be perfect.

Much more sensible is his advocacy of New Alco for the William Hill Trophy. 'He keeps being beaten by a whisker.' That's okay. A Whisker isn't running this time. 'Cheltenham can be red-clay sticky,' Lungo reminds us, while advocating Heltornic.

Jones believes that the cross-country chase is one of the best betting races of the Festival and that Never Compromise, at 12-1, cannot be knocked out of the frame, unlike Granit Jack in the Supreme Novices' Hurdle, who he thinks is 'useless, a talking horse.'

On the mute television screens, it's Liverpool 0 Barcelona 0. 'Any views, Len?' It's like asking Jade Goody if she'd like to pose for a photograph.

'Swings and roundabouts,' says Budden, possibly stepping down memory lane again, having already reminded us of Ron Barry and Man Alive. 'Denman's an appalling price,' says Jones. 'He's had his own way up front against nothing. The bet of the race is Cailin Alainn. If she jumps, she cannot be out of the first three.' When you put it like that.

No six year-old has won the Champion Chase since 1973, and 11 of the 14 runnings of the bumper have been won by an Irish runner, Jones tells us, so it's goodbye Voy Por Ustedes and hello Cork All Star, although Dobbin and others are fans of Tot O'Whiskey.

Jones (sorry, but it's difficult to ignore him) has a habit of suddenly announcing striking news or, at least, striking rumours. 'Black Jack Ketchum is rumoured to have a physical problem . . . I've heard Mountain might not run . . . Ouninpohja's likely not to run, so Desert Quest won't run.' With or without Mountain, Jones likes Degas Art for the Triumph Hurdle. 'I'm quite confident he will be first or second,' he says, but Dobbin questions Degas Art's attitude and sings the praises of Katchit. 'He looks very, very willing,' says Dobbin.

So am I, but I've run out of space. It's Liverpool 0 Barcelona 1.

Least said, soonest forgotten. To focus on the positive, Katchit won the Triumph Hurdle, at 11-2. So well done, Tony Dobbin.

BIRMINGHAM *Racing Post*, 9 March 2007

This is a proper club, the Midlands Racing Club, meeting at the Barn, near Aston Villa, under the engagingly enthusiastic leadership of Chris Pitt, who wrote that splendid book, *A Long Time Gone*.

The Barn sells mild at the bar, has dancing lights strung across the ceiling, and a picture of Buddy Holly on the wall. It would be nice to hear him again. That'll be the day. Waitresses wander to and fro among the good-sized, good-humoured audience, issuing banana splits.

It's a no nonsense, let's get on with it approach, with a panel devoid of trainers or jockeys but featuring that rare creature, a woman. Lydia Hislop, of *The Times* and the telly, has easily the best teeth and the most hair, a commodity sadly lacking in the case of Betfair's bruiser, Tony Calvin, and Cheltenham's new communications director, Andy Clifton. Stuart Machin (telly), in a pyjama shirt, looks clean and well-mannered, while Steve Mellish (telly, again) in a green shirt and sports shoes, looks less well ironed than Machin.

It's soon apparent that the audience are going to get tremendous value for money. If I hadn't heard Ronan Graham in Belfast, I wouldn't have believed anyone could talk as quickly as Hislop, until Mellish starts. Either he's going to have to slow down, or I'm going to have to learn to write with both hands. They must have terrific lungs.

We're soon on to the Arkle, in which Hislop expresses her admiration for Fair Along but fears that all those big leaps using little legs will take their toll. 'I don't have a strong view,' Clifton admits, about the Champion Hurdle. Can't you pretend? He thinks that Detroit City is the most likely winner, partly because he is 10 kilos lighter than when he won at Sandown. I wish I could say the same. Hislop scratches her head. I hope she hasn't got nits.

Mellish, full of well-informed advice, warns against backing Aran Concerto at 2-1 for the Ballymore Properties Novices' Hurdle. 'You go skint backing horses at 2-1 in races like that.' Instead, he draws listeners' attention to the merits of Scotsirish, at a more palatable 16-1. Hislop concurs, adding that, while there isn't generally much to be gained from listening to trainers, Willie Mullins, Scotsirish's trainer, is an exception, being less prone to 'fluff and hype.'

When the panel move on to the Royal & SunAlliance Chase, a near-consensus emerges. No one loves Denman, apart from Clifton, who was impressed by the fact that, when he visited Paul Nicholls' yard, Denman dribbled on his shoulder. It's a persuasive argument but fails to sway the unromantic hearts of his fellow panellists, who want to oppose the hot favourite but can't think of anything to oppose him with.

Hislop thinks that Monet's Garden's connections are 'daft' for running him in the Ryanair Chase when they should be running him in the Champion Chase. Pitt asks if the Ryanair will be going off an hour late.

At 9.15pm, the audience and panel are let out on parole, with the interval occupied by a raffle. The holder of winning ticket 696 is in for a doubly good time. Mellish looks as if he's about to bounce off for a game of tennis but has another pint instead.

Admirably, Pitt pursues a policy of audience interactivity, with questions submitted on slips, and surveys conducted by a show of hands. All that is lacking is a division of opinion. There isn't one about the World Hurdle, in which Inglis Drever emerges victorious, nor the Triumph, for which Mellish declares Lounaos to have 'the best form by a country mile,' with Hislop adding that Eoin Griffin's filly gets a 7lb allowance, 'gold dust'. Only Clifton prefers Katchit. Maybe he was sick on him.

And then the panel disagree about Kauto Star. Calvin believes that Kauto Star will win the Gold Cup, and win it well. So does Clifton, but Machin has his doubts, while Mellish and Hislop are non-believers. So it's over to the audience. For every hand that believes that Kauto Star will win, two hands believe that he will not.

I enjoyed that. It was good fun.

Steve Mellish was right to warn against backing Aran Concerto, 5th in the Ballymore when 5-2 favourite, but Scotsirish managed only 8th, at 12-1. Inglis Drever did the panel proud, winning the World Hurdle at 5-1. Andy Clifton was right to prefer Katchit to Lounaos in the Triumph. The former won, the latter finished 10th, at 7-2 favourite.

EAST GARSTON *Racing Post*, 11 March 2007

Either the outside wall of East Garston village hall isn't straight, or I'm sitting at an angle. The hall's wooden floor is back in fashion, but it may take a while for the bum-numbing old school chairs to catch on.

The audience is different from that at previous previews, younger, more women, less baldness. Good.

On the stage, Ed James provides brisk, capable chairmanship. Colin Brown is wearing a striped shirt and mad-professor hair. It's time to forgive him for going too fast on Desert Orchid in the 1987 King George. However old Carl Llewellyn is, he looks younger, and however much Pat Murphy's left ear sticks out, his right ear sticks out further. Leighton Aspell is wearing a light-blue pullover and Phil Smith, the BHB's head of handicapping, is wearing a darker one.

While the panel discusses the Supreme Novices' Hurdle, a man with a camera on a stick photographs the back of Aspell's head. Maybe they're doing a documentary on it. Aspell plumps for Amaretto Rose. Phil Smith says that Amaretto Rose is rated 146 but that Hide The Evidence is rated 150, though he doesn't trust the handicapper's rating. Actually, he didn't say that, I made it up, but he has doubts about the rating, and likes Osana, who is progressive.

Speaking of Fair Along, in the Arkle, Llewellyn opines that 'he's done nothing wrong,' thereby instantly incurring penalty points for an irritating cliche. 'I couldn't have it on my mind' soon makes its dreaded appearance.

When Smith talks, a respectful hush descends. I think it's to do with figures. They bring a seductive sense of certainty to the impenetrable uncertainty of racing. 'It boils down to whether you believe in the weight-for-age scale,' says Smith. Now is the time, surely, for James to announce, 'Hands up everyone who believes in the weight-for-age scale.' He doesn't, so Smith explains that Fair Along, a five-year-old, is rated 163, 'incredibly high for a novice.' Smith thinks that Fair Along will win. Aspell, a big Fair Along fan but an even bigger My Way De Solzen fan, thinks 'it will be a crazy race for the first mile. There could be carnage.'

Carnage, not a word popular with Cheltenham's management, pops up again when the Royal & SunAlliance Chase is being discussed. 'This has got carnage written all over it,' warns Smith. 'They'll go a hell of a pace.' Miriam Francome is scribbling away on a big notepad. She's either working out her bets or writing her autobiography.

Brown's habit of putting in good words for several runners is abandoned in favour of sticking his neck out in the Champion Hurdle. 'Detroit City, he will win, no bother. An absolute steering job,' he says. Aspell also opts for Detroit City, but Llewellyn and Murphy prefer Hardy Eustace. Smith has ratings for all of them. They tell him that Brave Inca, 'an incredibly consistent 167 but I wonder if all those tough races are catching up with him,' will find it hard to beat Hardy Eustace, 'a solid 170. I can't see past him.'

Llewellyn thinks that Aran Concerto, hot Irish favourite for the Ballymore Properties Novices' Hurdle, is one to lay. 'He's a bridle horse,' he says. 'He's won slowly run races and Noel Meade talks horses up and then they get stuffed.'

In the Royal & SunAlliance Chase, Brown likes Cailin Alainn, on the grounds that 'she's done nothing much wrong, apart from fall.' Mmm. A strong body of opinion believes that My Way De Solzen could win either the Arkle or the Ryanair Chase.

What else do you need to know? According to Brown, 'Kauto Star has been the same weight all season, more than you can say about his trainer.' According to Smith, Kauto Star's rating (176) suggests that he'd have won the last five runnings of the Gold Cup and will win this one, if he can replicate his best form.

At 10.05pm, panellist Stan Moore arrives. The preview ends.

Those who opted for My Way De Solzen to win the Arkle were right, those who preferred Fair Along were wrong. Sublimity's unexpected victory in the Champion Hurdle was ... unexpected, unlike Kauto Star's in the Gold Cup.

The search for a Cheltenham winner also took me to racing stables, among

them that of Jonjo O'Neill, trainer to legendary punter JP McManus.

JACKDAWS CASTLE *Racing Post*, 5 March 2011

Jackdaws Castle. There don't seem to be any jackdaws, nor any castles, but that's a small mystery compared to the identity of the resident horse we should back at Cheltenham. Go on, Jonjo, just between you, me, JP McManus and anyone reading this, which one is it?

The speed limit on the long drive to the five-star horse hotel near Stow-on-the Wold is 10mph. I think it's to make the horses look fast. There are plenty of them, all ridden by riders wearing the sponsor's name 'Jewson' on their blue jackets. The riders' coats are all blue while most of the horses' coats are bay. Sitting in Jonjo O'Neill's jeep, Jonjo studies the messages coming from the way in which the horses put one hoof before another, before another, before another, while I pray that he doesn't suddenly ask, you recognise that one, don't you? Is it Albertas Run? No, it's Adare Manor. He's rated 98 and hasn't won since 2008. Luckily, he doesn't ask.

Jonjo is a very likeable man, a lover of life, easy to be with, a giggle never far away. But that's no good, that won't bring home the bacon, nor the Coral Cup. What will? O'Neill has trained 17 Festival winners. He should know.

Jonjo is holding a clipboard with a list on it, possibly full of secrets, but I haven't got my spectacles on, and can't read it. He points to a horse in a field and says, 'that's Don't Push It, parading as if he thinks he's won another National. He's in grand form, on target.' That's all very well but Don't Push It's not going to win the Pertemps Final, is he? What about Albertas Run for the Ryanair, which he won last year? Granted, he's been running like a soft-boiled egg this season. 'He's had a few problems,' says O'Neill, an expression trainers use to describe a horse that has gone in his wind, legs, liver and skeleton. 'He was very sore after the King George at Kempton but I think he's in good form now.' He'll need to be, because O'Neill says that he may run in the Gold Cup rather than the Ryanair. Naah, that's not it.

What about Sunnyhillboy in the Stewart Family etc. etc. Chase? He's a grand horse, second in the Byrne Group Plate last year and a good third at Cheltenham before Christmas, although this would be his first run over three miles. 'He's had joint problems,' says O'Neill. That's the trouble with horses, they've got so many joints. 'Hopefully he's right now and he likes Cheltenham. I think he probably wants the step up to three miles because he hasn't quite got the speed he had.' Not a ringing endorsement, but a definite maybe.

Hughie is very close to Jonjo, with him all the time, has big ears, and must have heard something. Maybe he can let me in on a secret. Unfortunately, like most Jack Russells, Hughie is saying nothing. Jonjo does reveal that JP McManus drinks camomile tea. Peter Rabbit was just the same, but it doesn't really help us. What about Get Me Out Of Here, who looked so good last year, and was just beaten by Menorah in the Supreme Novices' Hurdle, but has run badly this season? 'Fierce disappointing. He's run shocking, as the fella says,' says O'Neill, who explains that Get Me Out of Here has had his soft palate cauterised and will probably have another operation in the summer. 'I don't know if he'll make Cheltenham. If he does, it will probably be in the County Hurdle.' To make matters worse, the handicapper hasn't relented much. No, that's no good.

Backspin was to be the stable's next superstar novice but, sadly, he died suddenly and unexpectedly earlier this week, and O'Neill is hoping that, among the almost 100 horses in the yard, another potential star may yet emerge. That's the future, Cheltenham is the present (well, the very near future). So I try a long shot. 'If I was JP, and I asked you which one I should back, which would it be?' Jonjo smiles that endearing smile but, instead of a neat side-step, says, 'I'd like Mister Hyde if he gets in the Pertemps. He was a bit disappointing at Sandown last time but it wasn't because he didn't stay the trip. Our horses weren't flying then but he's in grand form now and has had a clean prep, which is what you need for Cheltenham. He's improved all season and, with a bit of cut in the ground, I think he'll run a blinder.'

That's more like it although, if Mister Hyde doesn't make the cut in the Pertemps, or the ground turns soft, he may end up in the Martin Pipe Conditional Jockeys' race. Nothing's straightforward, is it?

Oh, and a little bird (well, Jonjo, actually) tells me that Rock Noir might run in the Arkle. That's if he doesn't run in the Byrne, the Jewson or the Grand Annual.

JP usually turns up at Jackdaws Castle on the Monday of Festival week, which might be a good time to hide in the back of the jeep. 'He just loves Cheltenham,' says Jonjo, 'we all do, and you're desperate to get a winner for him, and for other owners. The Festival is the pinnacle, and you never get sick of it. The only time you get sick is when you think everything is right and then you get stuffed. Then you come home and want to be sick in your tea, but if you have a winner ... If I have one winner, I'm happy.'

So that's Mister Hyde then, is it?

There was a winner, and almost another, although I failed to spot them. Albertas Run won the Ryanair again, at 6-1, and Get Me Out Of Here was beaten a nose in the County Hurdle, at 7-1. Mister Hyde ran in the Martin Pipe Conditional Jockeys' race, and was brought down, while Sunnyhillboy fell in the Stewart Family Chase.

Finally, the Festival arrives, in this case, in 2009:

TUESDAY *Racing Post*, **11 March 2009**

The crowds are streaming in to escape from the recession outside, oblivious to the danger of depression inside. I like the earlier, 1.30pm start. There's less waiting. While we are, a kiosk in the Centaur is offering 'Foot long hot dogs,' for anyone with a foot long mouth.

Some racegoers are already queuing up to launch a rescue package for the bookmakers while others are in the shopping village, to see what Katherine Hooker's got to offer. It turns out to be clothes. Nearby, Norton & Townsend are offering a free shirt worth £120 if you buy a suit to go with it. Suits start at £495. Jenny McCririck's just bought a pair of boots from Dubarry of Ireland; a left one and a right one. Beatrice von Tresckow's here again, with her oriental-hippy collection, and so is the Master Butchers Band ('A cut above the rest'), as jolly as ever, but playing in a garden shed this year. They don't seem to mind.

There are a lot of clothes stalls, although most people already have their own, apart from a girl in the Guinness Village, who seems to have lost the bottom half of her skirt. Just outside the village, the Goodwood Organic Food van is sizzling with organic burgers while, just inside, the Flaming Cactus Mexican Food van is serving nachos grande. A sweet van is serving bars of Dairy Milk chocolate. I know, because I've just bought one.

The first horse on to the course at the 2009 Festival is Medermit, in case it crops up in a quiz. Shortly after 1.30pm, the traditional Festival roar goes up, to mark the end of hope and the start of experience. The lawn in front of the grandstand seems fairly full, although I don't think racegoers are as fat this year. I've backed Medermit and Copper Bleu each-way, and they finish second and fourth, which isn't bad, although the man who's backed Go Native seems even more pleased, as does Paul Carberry, who rode him. His injured leg's feeling better, then.

In the Arkle, I've backed Forpadydeplasterer, Planet Of Sound and Golden Silver, all each-way, and the first two finish first and third, which makes me feel better than Julie Williams, standing where her late father Freddie stood so memorably for so many years. Julie wanted Medermit to win the photofinish in the first race and Kalahari King to win the photofinish in the second, but neither of them did. 'I'm breaking even,' she says, cheerily, under the circumstances.

I'm glad I asked her before Tony McCoy McCoyed the third, the William Hill Trophy, forcing Wichita Lineman forward with an unmatchable intensity of strength and will to spoil things for Maljimar's connections. The crowd on the tiered steps around the winner's enclosure applaud the returning, placed horses, which is nice, then give an enthusiastic reception to McCoy, although the ride he gave Wichita Lineman deserved an even more rousing one. There's trainer Jonjo O'Neill and there's owner JP McManus, but McCoy doesn't kiss either of them. Instead, he kisses a lady in a lemon-yellow coat, Mrs McManus. Now would be a good time for her to ask JP for another coat, with green and orange hoops, perhaps.

The Champion Hurdle is a cracker. I don't remember Punjabi getting much of a mention at all those Cheltenham previews but I do remember backing Celestial Halo each-way, so it would have been nice if Barry Geraghty could have found it in his heart to have, well, lost. I expect Ruby Walsh feels the same. He's walking back to the weighing room, saddle over his arm. There's a lot of difference between the attention paid to the winning jockey, and to the one a neck behind him. A couple of journalists approach Walsh. It's not a long conversation.

All isn't lost, though, unless you put everything to win on Binocular. I hope JP McManus didn't, but saved a few million to back his horses in a tricast in the Cross Country race.

THURSDAY *Racing Post*, 13 March 2009

Dark clouds are gathering. It's either the end of the world, or we're in for a spot of rain.

That red airship with Ladbrokes.com on it is still floating overhead. If only someone had got a really long arm, we could pop it. At Estribos Argentina, in the shopping village, Lizzie has sold 70 hats so far. It's not bad but she says she sells 140 at Punchestown. Maybe they've got more heads there. At Jackson's Shoes, Mr Jackson, a Yorkshireman, has sold 100 pairs of shoes. 'It's down,' he says, rather dourly. The trouble with shoes is that they are nothing without feet and, this year, there just aren't the feet. Perhaps, in view of the recession, Mr Jackson could offer to sell his shoes in instalments, one at a time.

There's Terry Biddlecombe, and there's Henrietta Knight, in case you were looking for them. And here, in the Guinness Village, is Laurence Robertson, the affable local MP. A band called Black Velvet (guitar, banjo, flute) is playing that circular music that goes round and round until one of the players decides it's gone on quite long enough and it's time to stop.

Chapoturgeon won the first race easily. Paddy Power had given Paul Nicholls a £500 charity bet and Nicholls had £250 each-way on Chapoturgeon, at 12-1. But that's enough about Chapoturgeon. Let's concentrate on the one I backed, Naiad Du Misselot, who was desperately unlucky. If he hadn't jumped poorly and run too slowly he would surely have gone close. Responsibility now passes to Ballydub and Rhys Flint. They don't win, either. In front of the big screen near the parade ring, a man no longer in the first flush of middle age shouts Kayf Aramis home, apoplectically. 'Come on, go on, come on, go on! Keep it going!' Luckily Aidan Coleman heard him, and did. I'm glad the triumphant punter didn't have a coronary. I don't think I could have brought myself to give him the kiss of life.

Just as I was beginning to think I was a hopeless punter, the Ryanair Chase came along, and it turns out that I'm a genius. I've backed Imperial Commander each-way, laid Our Vic and bought Imperial Commander in a match bet with Our Vic. A treble. The important thing now is to tell as many people as possible, even though none of them are remotely interested, and wish you wouldn't. I do tell as many people as possible and they aren't remotely interested. Sir Robert Ogden's in the parade ring, and I think of telling him, then realise that he may be more interested in Voy Por Ustedes. On board, Robert Thornton grimaces, probably in physical as well as mental pain. Paddy Brennan, on Imperial Commander, looks delighted. Did you realise that, so far, Sam Waley-Cohen is the only British-born rider to have won a race at the Festival this year?

Right, what's next? When you've had a winner, somehow the next race suddenly seems more appealing. Oh, good, the World Hurdle. Will Christophe Pieux put his critics in their place? Will Fair Along at least finish placed, which I want him to? 'Come on, go on, come on, go on! Keep it going!' Right, better watch the race. I don't suppose the jockeys could have got their colours muddled up, could they? Pity, but another tremendous finish. We are lucky to have a generation of great jump jockeys to watch, Ruby Walsh peerless among them.

Now it's time for the race named in honour of the legendary bookmaker Freddie Williams, a wonderful man, whose daughter Julie, delightful herself, is running the pitch. I wish Freddie was here to try to sort out his own race, a race, appropriately, likely to fill bookmakers' satchels. I've backed Three Mirrors and Turkish Surprise. Other people have backed other horses. The ones who backed Something Wells are thrilled. I'm relieved; Three Mirrors ran on into fourth.

Say not the struggle naught availeth. Save that for tomorrow.

11
THE GRAND NATIONAL

Happy Day! Charlie Fenwick jr on Ben Nevis. 1980.

Everyone knows about the Grand National. Well, maybe not quite everyone.

AINTREE IN LOUISVILLE *Racing Post*, 2 April 2009

The world's most famous horserace. That's how Lord Daresbury, Aintree's chairman, describes it in the information pack.

So I walk up to Day's coffee shop, my favourite, on Bardstown Road, Louisville, and ask Stella Wade, serving the coffee and bagels, if she's heard of the Grand National. Stella, in that tricky age group that horseracing would like to enthuse, gives the question serious thought, then says, 'Is it a band?' It may be, although not a world-famous one.

Day's coffee shop is only four miles from Churchill Downs, the home of the Kentucky Derby, in a city that has an attachment to horseracing, but Day's may not be typical of Louisville. After all, on a table is a book by Elyn R Saks and on the front cover is a quote from a review, 'Saks's descriptions of her descents into psychosis are riveting' – *Entertainment Weekly*.

So I give it another shot, at the Cherokee Animal Clinic, the home of veterinarian Dr James Grace. While Grace examines Martha's ears to see if they are fit to be given a dog licence, two of his assistants respond willingly, but ultimately blankly, to the words 'Grand National.' It is left to Dr Grace to gamely have a stab at it. 'Is it a dog show?' Lord Daresbury would be turning in his grave, if he wasn't still alive.

Correct me if I'm wrong (on second thoughts, don't), but didn't Battleship memorably win the Grand National for the US in 1938, and the American Tommy Smith win it on triple Maryland Hunt Cup winner Jay Trump in 1965, and Charlie Fenwick repeat the feat on double Maryland Hunt Cup winner Ben Nevis, in 1980? Wasn't Raymond Guest, the owner of L'Escargot, the 1975 winner, an American, along with Lois Duffey, who owned Mr Frisk, the 1990 winner, and Betty Moran, who owned Papillon, the 2000 winner? Wasn't this the race beloved of Gregory Peck and Tim Durant, Paul Mellon and George Sloan?

Admittedly, none of them were from Louisville, unlike Cheryl, a jolly and helpful lady who works in the main branch of the Louisville Free Public Library. 'Cheryl, do you know what the Grand National is?' 'Yes,' says Cheryl, in an encouragingly confident tone. 'It's a golf tournament, isn't it?' It might be.

The library is a splendid one and offers an impressive array of local and national newspapers, all of them filled to the gunwales with basketball but seemingly oblivious to the world's most famous horse race, due to be run on Saturday. Maybe it's the recession; maybe they've dropped their Grand National page, to save money.

The race is a mystery in the halls of the library, and in the aisles of Old Town Liquors, where Kenny does his best to help, but can't. He's fine on Beaujolais but, to be honest, hopeless at Becher's. 'The Grand National? I don't know,' he says, frankly, before moving on to the Derby, the Kentucky one.

Maybe Indiana, across the mighty Ohio river, is more into the world's most famous horse race than Kentucky. At the Indiana University Southeast, near New Albany, a seat of learning and treasure trove of information, I finally hit gold. Librarians Nancy Totten and Phyllis Nachand, although helpful, are not au fait with the term 'Grand National' and raise the possibility of a car race, but Martin Rosen, director of library services, knows exactly what the Grand National is.

Rosen is a race fan. Eureka! It's a small sample, and maybe I'd have had better luck in Maryland, home of the Maryland Hunt Cup, but there does seem to be some way to go before the Grand National achieves recognition in the US, which makes me wonder about watching it. At Churchill Downs on Saturday, there is simulcasting from 17 tracks, starting with Tampa Bay Downs and finishing with Charles Town, but, ominously, the gates don't open until 11.30am, which translates into 4.30pm British time, which is 15 minutes after the Grand National starts. Parsons Legacy will have won it by then, granted fast ground.

I phone Churchill Downs and ask if they're showing the Grand National there, or if there's anywhere in Louisville I can watch it. Is the Grand National on TV? 'Sorry,' says the lady at the other end of the phone, 'the what?' Then she explains that the first simulcast is from Tampa Bay Downs at 12.25pm.

No, here in Louisville, the Grand National is definitely not the world's most famous race.

Still, it was a reminder of Ben Nevis's victory in 1980, a year when the race excelled itself. I backed Ben Nevis, at 40-1. Happy day!

BEN NEVIS: 30 YEARS ON *Racing Post*, 9 April 2010

In Cockeysville, north of Baltimore, a man in his early 60s, trim, fit, still riding and playing squash competitively, spends the day managing his car sales business then returns home and watches a film of the 1980 Grand National. This weekend, friends are holding a party to celebrate the 30th anniversary of Charlie Fenwick jr's victory on Ben Nevis. 'It was a life-defining moment,' says Fenwick, 'a great thrill.' He is still a fitness enthusiast, still steeped in Maryland's steeplechasing traditions, still thinks back to the day when he won the greatest steeplechase in the world.

Fenwick grew up in Baltimore County, hunted foxes, rode over Maryland's daunting timber fences, as generations of his family had done, worked as an investment banker, and harboured an ambition to ride at Aintree. 'I was very familiar with Jay Trump,' he says. 'Tommy Smith and Jay Trump paved the way.' That partnership won the Maryland Hunt Cup three times before winning the 1965 Grand National. It could be done, across the Atlantic.

Fenwick's father-in-law, Redmond Stewart jr, bought Ben Nevis in England after a day's grouse shooting and an evening's conviviality, and gave daughter Ann and Charlie the dubious pleasure of turning the white-blazed chestnut into a chaser. 'He was a difficult, tough horse,' Fenwick recalls. 'He pulled like a ton of bricks, was always going at top speed, and there was nothing pleasurable about riding him. It was a while before he matured and became manageable.'

Yet even when approaching fences too fast, Ben Nevis was a safe jumper. 'It was nerve-wracking,' says Fenwick, 'but he never made much of a mistake.' To win the Maryland Hunt Cup twice, as Ben Nevis did in 1977 and 1978, when he lowered the course record by over eight seconds, a horse has to jump well, because the 22 fences on the course are not only big but unyielding, made of solid timber poles. After Ben Nevis's second Maryland Hunt Cup success, Stewart agreed to send his ten-year-old to Captain Tim Forster's yard at Letcombe Bassett, near Lambourn, to be prepared for the following year's Grand National. 'The whole of foxhunting America,' said Stewart, 'would rather win your Grand National than any other race.'

'Our horse had done everything in the US,' Fenwick remembers, ruefully, 'and I naively assumed that the great run would continue. I got a rude awakening. Everything was different. I was overwhelmed. The racing was far more competitive than I was used to. I am not sure I ever got comfortable with it.'

Graham Thorner, Forster's stable jockey, who had won the National on Well To Do in 1972, became Fenwick's mentor and friend. 'Charlie was a very, very good horseman,' Thorner remembers. 'There wasn't a better horseman but his jockeyship was wanting, because of a lack of experience. He was used to riding in races in which the fields were fairly small and the pace steady for most of the way. It was a shock for him when he lined up with a lot of runners who went fast from the start. In the beginning, he found it difficult.'

Ben Nevis made his English debut in December 1978, in an amateur riders' chase at Devon and Exeter. Carrying automatic top weight of 12st 7lb, Ben Nevis was challenging for the lead when unseating Fenwick at the final fence. He then ran in the King George VI Chase. 'Graham told me that I would be caught out by how fast they went and, sure enough,' says Fenwick, 'they started fast and got faster. After that, I told myself that I had better listen to what Graham said. He lived and breathed the National and we talked about it incessantly.'

Fenwick says that it was before his next race, the John Bull Chase at Wincanton, rather than before the 1980 National, that Forster issued his memorable instruction, 'keep remounting.' Ben Nevis needed to complete a third chase in order to be given a handicap mark and avoid carrying automatic top weight at Aintree. 'In the paddock,' Fenwick relates, 'Forster told me, "I don't care what happens but keep remounting, even if you have to chase the horse up a hill to get back on him, and finish the race".' He finished fourth.

Narrowly beaten by Royal Frolic, the 1976 Cheltenham Gold Cup winner, in his final race before the 1979 National, Ben Nevis started at a respectful 14-1. All went well until the 15th fence, the biggest on the course, the intimidating Chair. 'There was a horse in the ditch,' Fenwick remembers vividly. 'It was moving along the ditch. I had to jump the horse, the ditch and the fence, and I couldn't do all three, but Ben Nevis didn't fall, I came off in the mêlée.'

A year later, now a 12-year-old, Ben Nevis's chance seemed to have gone. He was still a capable performer, as he showed when just beaten at Warwick by Peter Scot, that year's Welsh National winner, and had an attractive weight of 10st 12lb, but the going turned against him. Ben Nevis was considered a top of the ground horse and the going for the 1980 Grand National was heavy. 'With the ground as it was, I thought it would be a disaster,' says Fenwick, 'but it turned out that he went as well on that ground as he did on fast. Maybe he wasn't as fast himself by then but he had wonderful stamina. He was a dour galloper.'

'I told Charlie that, because of the ground, there would only be a few finishers and that he should hunt round for the first circuit and ride a race on the second circuit,' says Thorner. 'He was last jumping Becher's the first time around, then crept forward. I was always happy with the way he was riding the race.'

'Graham felt that a lot of jockeys would go too quick, and that's exactly what happened,' says Fenwick. 'When we went round a second time, everyone who had been in front of us was suddenly behind us. It was amazing, absolutely amazing.' Ben Nevis seized the lead approaching Becher's for the second time, and galloped further and further ahead. 'Towards the end, I remembered what Graham had told me,' says Fenwick. 'That, no matter how far in front I was, no matter what, to keep riding, never let up.' He won by 20 lengths, with only three other finishers.

Michael Seely, *The Times*' racing correspondent, reported, 'Fenwick is a Corinthian in the true sense of the word. This remarkable character looked jet-propelled rather than jet-lagged as he sailed over the Aintree fences on Ben Nevis,' a horse 'possessed of tremendous courage, unlimited stamina and cat-like jumping ability. He possessed infinitely superior credentials to any other horse in the field.'

'With the presentation and questions from the press, there was no let up afterwards,' says Fenwick, 'and it took a while for me to realise what had happened. It wasn't until I got in the car and was driving back, and heard it on the radio, that I thought, "Gee, we really did win this damn thing!" It was so exciting. About 40 of us, joined by John Francome and Andy Turnell, had dinner in Burford. It was an awful lot of fun.'

Fenwick, 32 when he won the Grand National, carried on riding in the US for another 14 years, winning the Maryland Hunt Cup five times in all. Two years ago, his son, Charlie Fenwick III, maintained the family tradition when winning the race on Askim. Ben Nevis died in 1995, aged 27, and, last year was elected to the National Museum of Racing's Hall of Fame. 'I looked at the film of the National again last night,' says Fenwick. There are some things one never tires of watching.

That was the last National seen by the racecourse's former owner Mirabel Topham, who sold Aintree in 1973 but continued to live in Paddock Lodge until her death on 30 May 1980.

A ROOM WITH A VIEW *Racing Post*, 8 April 2007

On Saturday afternoon, Nicholas Ryan will enjoy one of the most extraordinary views on an English racecourse. As he looks out of his first-floor window, Ryan will see the runners for the Grand National circling the parade ring a few yards in front of him. For a sum in excess of £1.25 million, the view, from inside Aintree racecourse, could be yours, permanently.

Paddock Lodge, unprepossessing but rich in history and unique in location, is being sold, 70 years after Arthur Ronald Topham and his wife Mirabel made the converted and extended bailiff's cottage their home.

'Ronnie' was the titular head of the Topham family and manager of Aintree racecourse, but Mirabel, an altogether more formidable character and presence, stamped her authority on both her husband and Aintree. Among the documents Ryan has unearthed in the Lodge are the minutes of Tophams Limited's 1937 annual general meeting chaired, not by Ronnie, but by Mirabel. The minutes record that Mrs Topham stated that 'she would not permit petty obstructional methods to hinder the proper conduct of the company's business.' Mirabel, a former actress, was a woman used to getting her way.

Ryan knew Mirabel as Mirrie, for she was Ryan's great aunt and, later, he was sometimes invited to attend board meetings. 'Only two people ever said anything,' he remembers, 'Mirrie and the finance director.'

Tophams Limited bought Aintree racecourse in 1949 and added the Mildmay course and a motor racing circuit. Framed black and white photographs in a room full of relics of Aintree's past show Stirling Moss and Juan-Manuel Fangio duelling for the lead in the 1955 British Grand Prix.

Ryan spent his childhood in Rhodesia but, after returning to Britain in the 1950s, he often visited his great aunt and watched car and motorbike races, as well as the Grand National. 'My first National was in 1959,' he recalls, 'when Michael Scudamore won on Oxo. I came every year and Mirrie had magical lunch parties in Paddock Lodge that went on for ever. It made it very difficult to get out and put a bet on.

'I used to think what a wonderful display of daffodils there was in the garden. Guests would comment on them. Later, I discovered that Mirrie's assistant used to go out and buy a lot of jam jars and a lot of daffodils, bury the jam jars in the flower beds, and stick the daffodils in them.'

Ronnie died in 1958 and Mirabel later shared Paddock Lodge with her nephew and niece, Jim Bidwell-Topham, who was clerk of the course, and Pat Bidwell-Topham, who organised the catering at Paddock Lodge.

In 1960, the Grand National was televised by the BBC for the first time and Peter Dimmock, the programme's presenter, was a regular guest at Mirabel's parties. 'He was very debonair,' says Ryan, 'and provided Mirrie with an enormous television set and, later, with a colour one.' Among the papers is a draft agreement from 1967, granting the BBC exclusive world broadcasting rights for four years.

By then, the future of the Grand National hung on what seemed a permanently fragile thread, with Mirabel first announcing the course's sale in 1964, by which time Aintree's matriarch was in her seventies. 'She was a very dominant figure,' Ryan recalls, 'but deep down had a heart of gold. When Aintree got into financial difficulties she was too old and tired to manage it on her own, but she didn't want to let go.' One sign of Mirabel's advancing age was the appearance of a strange, battery-operated lift, still there today, which carried her from the hallway to a room above. 'I was never allowed upstairs,' says Ryan. Nor was anyone else.

In 1973, Topham sold the racecourse to Bill Davies, a local property developer, heralding another decade of uncertainty until Aintree was finally taken over by the Jockey Club and its future secured. Paddock Lodge was not included in the sale, and Mirabel continued to live there until her death in 1980, after which the house passed to Jim and Pat Bidwell-Topham. Pat died in 1982 and, although her brother lived on until 2005, in his later years he rarely received visitors.

'Due to ill health, he lost his zeal for life,' says Ryan. 'In the past, he had been very keen on cars and, when he died, and I inherited Paddock Lodge, there seemed to be a vintage car in every garage.'

Paddock Lodge unarguably needs some attention. Its spacious rooms contain the remnants of a past both distant and recent, with photographs and documents, paintings and prints, books and badges, accounts and cuttings, some dating back to the mid-19th century, each telling small parts of the story of Aintree, the Grand National, and the Tophams. A framed photograph of Henry Seymour 'Atty' Persse, who rode Aunt May into third place in the 1906 Grand National and was later a celebrated Flat trainer, bears Persse's inscription, 'Good luck to Aintree. I hope it will remain as it has always been in the past.'

Paddock Lodge now looks out across the new parade ring towards the new Lord Sefton and Earl of Derby Stands. 'I think it is absolutely wonderful,' says Ryan, 'and I know that my great aunt and my great-great-grandfather, Edward "The Wizard" Topham, the Grand National's first handicapper, would be so happy.'

Mirabel might have been less happy about the state of affairs in the Aintree Pavilion.

GRAND NATIONAL DAY *Racing Post*, 8 April 2002

It's all change in the Aintree Pavilion where, rather optimistically, they have opened a Tetley Tea Bar, complete with a teapot on the top. 'Tea as you make it at home.' I hope not. I haven't washed that mug for weeks.

Nigel Twiston-Davies passes by, possibly on his way to watch the entertainment, 'Sister Act.' There are three of them, one with a big ginger mop of hair, one with a big black mop of hair (not Twiston-Davies) and one with a big blonde mop of hair, although they all have completely bald armpits.

'We're going to heat things up a bit for you,' shouts the ginger one. 'Here we go,' shouts the black one. 'Burn, baby, burn. Just can't stop when the spark is hot,' shouts the blonde one. A few girls swing their hips in the marquee, rather more effectively than the one brave (but not really at his best, even though it's only 2.00pm) man, whose leer is better developed than his jive.

The Sisters are pretty good, although, personally, I preferred The Big Town Playboys, who were giving Shake, Rattle 'n' Roll a good shaking and rattling (and quite a bit of rolling) while, on the big screen behind them, Ovation was winning the Martell Cup in Hong Kong. It was surreal, and paid $382.50 for the win.

Outside, a man dressed in jockeys' silks sits on the top of a pole juggling balls, waving and smiling, and generally giving a persuasive demonstration of what psychiatrists call 'being bonkers.' I expect they'll take the pole away later.

It's a good place for observing people, and there are so many of them. 'Sue Barker's looking older, isn't she?' 'I bet that jacket of hers cost a lot.' 'And that face. Look, there's a woman putting stuff on her lips for her.'

Tony, sitting not doing much, well, nothing at all really, in the cab of the Bootle and Netherton fire engine, has had £20 each-way on Frantic Tan, although I'm not sure why, and I'm not sure he does either. 'I'll be looking for 1,200 quid,' he says. I think he may have trouble finding it.

A girl doing a survey comes up and says, 'What's your name?' 'Ashforth.' 'Ashfroth?' 'Yes, that's pretty much it.' At least no one has said, 'You're Salman Rushdie, aren't you, mate?' There's still time.

There are long queues at the cash machines, and we've only just had the first race. The queues for the ladies (a bit of a misnomer after about four o'clock) are even longer, confirming my suspicion that the only two good things about being a woman are that you don't get prostate cancer and you don't get sent to the Western Front. One of the ladies, whose high heels seem to be in a state of rebellion, is wearing a backless top, but I expect she'll turn it round later.

Up on the screen, TJ Murphy and AP McCoy are having a chat about the finer points of the finish of the novice chase, possibly with particular reference to the methods employed by Mr Murphy in denying victory to Mr McCoy. While the stewards have a little chat with both of them, Norrie Drummond shortens Armaturk from 1-8 to 1-14 to keep the race.

Charles-Edouard Walsh de Serrant, probably related to Ted Walsh, must have been thrilled at Ilnamar's success, having bred him, and a woman in a once white dress must have backed it, because she's just kissed a policeman. The policeman seems totally bemused. I don't suppose it was covered during training.

Bookmaker Bill Farrell, from Cleator Moor, says that he doesn't want Beau, Blowing Wind or Smarty to win the National, so he must be happy, because they don't. Paris Pike is the first home, with Richard Guest on board, arriving back before the rest have even completed a circuit. Unfortunately, he missed the last 29 fences. For a while it looked as if Beau might win, then as if Kingsmark might win, then as if What's Up Boys might win but finally, in case you don't already know, it was Bindaree who won.

I could have kicked myself because Twiston-Davies was the first trainer I saw in the Pavilion, and you're supposed to back the first trainer you see.

One man who picked Bindaree was none other than Sherlock Holmes. He approached 2003 full of confidence.

SHERLOCK HOLMES SEEKS A WINNER *Racing Post*, 5 April 2003

Looking pleased with himself, Dr Watson stroked his tidy moustache, coughed, and ventured, 'They say that it is a case of, the bigger the field, the bigger the certainty.' The fire in the living room at 221b Baker Street flickered gently. Sherlock Holmes, still wearing his dressing gown at ten in the morning, frowned and sucked a little harder on his pipe. 'My dear Watson, I fear that you are mixing with the wrong people. How often have I said to you that when you have eliminated the impossible, whatever remains, however improbable, must be the truth?'

Dr Watson's well-polished brown shoes shuffled on the worn carpet. 'Yes, Holmes, but I do not see ... '

Holmes, knocking his pipe on the fireplace fender, interrupted. 'And that, dear fellow, is your problem. The bigger the field of possibilities, the greater the need for elimination.'

Watson had not noticed the newspaper resting on Holmes' knees, which the famous detective now opened at the racing page. 'It is exactly a year today, Watson, if you remember, that you asked my advice on the case of the Grand National, which I believe you described to me as more of a puzzle than that of Silver Blaze, which I resolved some years ago.'

A broad, rather childlike smile beamed across Dr Watson's affable face. 'How could I forget it? When I told my friends you were adamant that Bindaree would be the winner, they could not believe it.'

'That does not surprise me, Watson, although the choice of Bindaree was entirely elementary. I believe you set up your practice as a result of it.'

'Yes, Holmes, I did. I cannot tell you how grateful I am.'

Holmes languidly flicked his long, thin fingers at the smoke billowing from his pipe. 'I have been looking at the sporting press,' he said, 'to see if I cannot repeat the trick. First, Watson, we must eliminate the impossible.' Watson nodded.

Holmes picked up a quill from the walnut table, dipped it in an ivory inkpot and struck a bold line through Empereur River. 'C'est impossible,' he declared. He then scored quickly through the names of Bramblehill Duke, Robbo, Red Ark, Burlu, Djeddah, Wonder Weasel, Tremallt, Supreme Glory, Royal Predica, Gunner Welburn, Mantles Prince, Good Shuil, Cregg House, Polar Champ, Montifault, Amberleigh House, Majed, Monty's Pass, Southern Star, Red Striker and Katarino.

Holmes dipped his pen into the inkpot again and, with a flourish, expunged all the hopes carried on the withers of You're Agoodun and Blowing Wind. 'It is a remarkable fact, Watson,' he said, 'that this annual extremity numbs the faculties of the sanest and most successful of England's trainers.'

Returning to his task, Holmes struck through The Bunny Boiler, Carbury Cross, Ballinclay King and Fadalko. 'Watson, I know you follow the Turf, although I have advised against it. Please give me your opinion on the remaining dozen.'

Watson pulled on the lapels of his tweed jacket, leant over the newspaper, tweaked the ends of his moustache and, standing upright again, said, 'Well, Bindaree did very well for us last year, Holmes. I would be sorry to abandon him.'

'You would be sorry if you did not, Watson. Emotion is the enemy of detection. Think of Bindaree as a flash of lightning. The claim that lightning does not strike in the same place twice is one of the less stupid of our English sayings, and I fancy this year's lightning is rather weaker than it was last year. No, Watson, we must look elsewhere.'

'Behrajan?' Watson suggested.

'A very fine horse, Watson, with a fine performance in the Gold Cup to his curious name, but there is another Turf expression you will be familiar with, that weight will stop the *Flying Scotsman*.'

'Ah, yes,' nodded the Doctor. 'No, Watson. We must not prostrate ourself before every dubious epigram, but it is a point. We must lay him aside, reluctantly.'

'Killusty?' 'It would be a remarkable training performance.' 'Yes, indeed.' 'And that is why we must eliminate it. We are not seeking the remarkable but the commonplace. The remarkable, by definition, is unlikely; the commonplace, predictable.'

While Watson grappled with the puzzle, Holmes pressed a wad of tobacco into the bowl of his pipe. 'It would also be remarkable,' he said, 'if Iris Bleu were to win.' 'But Mr McCoy is the finest of jockeys,' Watson protested.

'Only,' replied Holmes, dismissively, 'if you consider two completions from seven attempts to be fine. We are dealing with probabilities, Watson. You will be familiar with fractures of the clavicle.'

'The collar bone,' declared Watson, happy to be on home territory.

'Mr McCoy appears to be fully recovered but we, Watson, cannot afford to risk his clavicle, even if Mr McCoy can.'

Holmes scratched his pen across the page at the expense of Maximize. 'Worthy, but dull,' he mused, moving on to Youlneverwalkalone. 'Dreadful song,' said Dr Watson. 'We are not considering names, Watson,' retorted Holmes. 'It is the ground, among other things, that may find out your disliked song.'

Holmes laid his pipe on the table, and stared towards the heavy, purple brocade curtains. Watson knew better than to interrupt his reverie. Finally, Holmes said, 'Value, Watson. We must also consider value.' And, to the silent sound of Dr Watson's dropping jaw, Holmes's quill carved its way across Ad Hoc and Shotgun Willy.

'Now,' said Holmes. 'We are on the run for home. Our little exercise has reduced the question to Chives, Gingembre, Goguenard and Torduff Express.' Leaning over the detective's shoulder, Dr Watson suddenly said, triumphantly, 'Good Lord, Holmes. Three are trained by women.'

'These are changing times, Watson,' replied Holmes, looking unusually uncomfortable. 'As you know, I am not a man for romance. Mrs Hudson is a landlady worth her weight in gold but . . .'

Sherlock Holmes suddenly, and rather violently, made three scratches with his quill. 'There, you have your answer, Watson. Torduff Express.'

A rare defeat for the great detective. Torduff Express, at 33-1, led at the 17th fence but his saddle slipped and Timmy Murphy was later unseated. Monty's Pass, among the first to fall in Holmes's analysis, triumphed. Holmes was better with dogs (see *The Hound of the Baskervilles*).

12
COURT 14

John Kelsey-Fry clutching his bag of barrister's tools.

In July 2006, champion jockey Kieren Fallon and others were charged with conspiracy to defraud. The Horseracing Regulatory Authority suspended Fallon from riding in Britain until the case had been heard, a decision confirmed following an appeal to the Appeal Board of the HRA. Fallon challenged the decision in the High Court.

KIEREN FALLON AND DR HAROLD SHIPMAN *Racing Post,*
28 July 2006.
Court 14. That just leaves court 68, and racing will have been heard in every court in this splendidly Gothic building. [The Royal Courts of Justice in the Strand.]

There's Mark Warby QC, tall, slim, a race-case regular, and there's another, John

Kelsey-Fry QC, who doesn't say anything, even though at one point Mr Justice Davis asks him if he'd like to. Kelsey-Fry leaves it to David Pannick QC, 'batting' for Kieren Fallon, as the judge puts it.

Disappointingly, no one is wearing a wig, except perhaps the lady at the back. It makes the barristers look rather like preachers, an impression reinforced by the length of their sermons. Legal precedents are like Africa, vast and repeatedly explored. When barristers enter the hinterland, you wonder if they are ever going to emerge.

Pannick cites the case of Dr Harold Shipman in Fallon's support, without suggesting that they have mass murder in common, before moving on to Tesco. 'Is this one of the numerous South Wales cases?' asks the judge. 'No, Oxfordshire,' replies Pannick, adding, 'not far.'

If Warby had been Perry Mason, he'd have leapt up and shouted, 'Objection, my lord. It's nowhere near South Wales.' But he doesn't.

Plums are briefly discussed, as is the case of Ridge and Baldwin, but the pace is slower than a non-trier in a banded race. One journalist finishes his crossword and disappears. Maybe it's a prize one and he wants to get his entry in. Another journalist sits down and immediately starts another crossword. Kelsey-Fry scribbles a note in red ink and passes it to Pannick. Perhaps it says, '3 across is judiciary.'

The court clock was made by Gillett & Co of Croydon. When it shows 12.05pm, a letter is passed to the judge. It's from the Crown Prosecution Service. The judge passes it to Pannick, Warby and Kelsey-Fry. I want to say, 'Can I look at it?' but don't. Two minutes later, another letter arrives. The judge keeps it to himself. At 2.58pm, a package marked 'urgent' arrives. Ian Burton, Fallon's solicitor, opens it. It's a copy of the *Racing Post*.

Pannick contends that the Horseracing Regulatory Authority have acted illegally. They should have looked at 18 videos, studied 297 pages of transcripts, and heard as many witnesses as Fallon wanted them to, before deciding to suspend him, which they shouldn't have done anyway, because he'd have to be mad to break the law with a trial hanging over him, which meant there was no risk at all in allowing him to carry on riding.

Pannick doesn't contend that Fallon isn't mad, but nor does Warby suggest that he is mad. There is what lawyers call 'common ground' on Fallon's lack of madness. When Pannick finally sits down, Warby stands up, and warns us that he is going to take as long as Pannick did, although what barristers actually say is that they hope to be brief. In life, hopes are so often dashed. Warby takes Pannick's points, dissects them, and finds them sadly wanting.

When barristers are about to insult someone, they start by declaring their respect for them. As Pannick puts it, 'the police point, with great respect to them, is a rank bad point,' and 'respectful as one is of the CPS, there is nothing whatsoever in the points they seek to make.' In the legal lexicon, 'great respect' is a term used to indicate 'nincompoop, or the argument deriving therefrom.'

At 4.20pm, Mr Justice Davis declares that this is a case that calls for a swift judgement, then says it's too late for one. 10.15am tomorrow.

Mr Justice Davis dismissed the appeal.

13
OBITUARIES

Walter Matthau ringing his bookmaker, again.

One of the strongest arguments against immortality is that it would spell the death of obituaries, often the best read in a newspaper. I know I like them.

GETTING TO KNOW SOMEONE WHEN IT'S TOO LATE

Racing Post, 16 September 2000

As regular readers (if there are any) will know, I'm a regular reader of obituaries, a habit I picked up from my late next door neighbour, Gladys Petty. Gladys's particular interest was the deaths column in the *Bradford Telegraph & Argus*. She wasn't alone in appreciating the attractions of the obituaries page. Dorothy Parker, also late, had a predictably acerbic line in posthumous put-downs. When told that the colourless President Coolidge had died, she replied, 'How could they tell?'

So I'd have read the obituaries of Sir John Astor, who died earlier this week, even if he hadn't been a prominent owner-breeder, boasting two St Leger winners, Provoke and Cut Above. I didn't know him, but that's part of the beauty of obituaries. They enable you to get to know someone when it's too late.

In Astor's case, that's a pity because it turns out that he was not only a brave man, both during the Second World War and through the trials of Parkinson's disease, but an amusing one. When his formidably idiosyncratic mother, Nancy Astor, threatened to write an autobiography, Jakie, as he was known, suggested that she call it 'Guilty but Insane.'

In 1937, Astor was knocked out in a car crash. 'I've lost my memory,' he muttered. 'Has anyone got it?' Even when he was dying, Astor retained his humour. 'The good thing about dying is that you don't have to pack.'

It's been a sad week on the obituaries front, because Sir Julian Critchley also made an appearance. If Critchley didn't have anything to do with racing, and he probably didn't, it's a pity, because he would have been a welcome source of amusement.

A Tory MP deeply unsympathetic to many things Tory, especially Mrs Thatcher, Critchley once memorably described Kenneth Baker as 'a man who can strut sitting down.' I can't remember there being much about racing in Critchley's autobiography, *A Bag of Boiled Sweets*, but I remember laughing a lot, before moving on to the latest Groucho Marx biography.

It includes *A Day At The Races* and the day when Marx's mother shouted out, 'There's a bookmaker at the door.' 'Tell him we don't want any,' said Groucho. 'If we want books, we'll go to the library.'

I can't tell you much about *A Day At The Races*, because that's not until page 206, but Groucho's already had his first date (page 23). She was called Lucy and, when they arrived at the streetcar to go home, in a snowstorm, Groucho only had enough money left for one fare. Marking the start of a lifetime of misunderstandings with women, Groucho told Lucy that he would toss his last coin to decide who had to walk. Lucy lost, he got on the streetcar, and she never spoke to him again.

Sir John Astor would never have done that.

THE DELIGHTS OF DEATH *Racing Post*, 27 December 1999

The reason they stop racing over Christmas is to give us time to work out which horses haven't been 'off' for six months but are going to be 'off' today, possibly at Hereford.

Unfortunately, I haven't got my form books with me. On the other hand, I have got *The Daily Telegraph Fourth Book of Obituaries – Rogues*. It's a cracker. I can't wait for more people to die, so I can read the Fifth Book.

Obituaries are people's lives with the boring chunks taken out, and I can strongly recommend them. Racing is under-represented by Charles St George and Jeffrey Bernard but there are nice walk-on parts for Raymond Blackburn MP and Jessica Mitford, not MP.

The gist of the piece on Charles Anthony Barbaro St George is that he was jolly good at owning racehorses and also chairman of the first underwriting firm in the history of Lloyds to be forced into receivership. Some people thought he was a bad boy. To be fair, when Jeffrey Bernard was in hospital, showing off what remained of his liver, St George slipped £200 under Bernard's pillow, 'for toothpaste.'

Bernard is the only obituaree to comment on his own obituary, which ends, 'Jeffrey Bernard writes: May I add a few words to your excellent obituary of Jeffrey Bernard ... ' If you don't know who Bernard was, then you're four days too late to find out by watching *Jeffrey Bernard Is Unwell* on the telly.

Raymond Blackburn was a Labour MP and solicitor who also liked bets and bottles, a combination that led him towards the Bankruptcy Court but made it difficult for him to locate the entrance. Rehabilitated, Blackburn joined Lord Longford's campaign against pornography. He took the film *The Language of Love* to court, but failed to persuade Judge Neil McKinnon, whose daughter was a topless model, of its indecency.

Jessica Mitford's link with horseracing came through her sister Pamela, who wanted to be a horse. Another sister, Unity, fell in love with Hitler and, when the Second World War broke out, shot herself. Deborah, the youngest Mitford, became the Duchess of Devonshire and, presumably, Lord Hartington's mother, although I haven't been able to check this with either of them. I suppose they'd know. I hope so, because Pamela would have been pleased that, as the first chairman of the British Horseracing Board, her nephew was more or less in charge of horses, even if he didn't become one.

Other sports are represented, notably by the test cricketer, Bob Crisp. When Crisp went to Buckingham Palace to collect his Military Cross, having been invalided out of the army, King George VI asked, 'Has your bowling been affected?' 'No, sir,' Crisp replied. 'I was hit in the head.'

I wish that RD Laing, the psychiatrist who believed that madness was an expression of sanity, had been a racing man. Then I could have told you about his habit of howling at the moon and how, in a bar in California, another drinker responded by hitting the psychiatrist over the head with a shovel. 'I don't blame the man,' said Laing. 'I only hope I can still play the piano.'

One obituary I would rather not have been writing.

ARTHUR JONES *Racing Post*, 8 July 2000

Sadly, Arthur Jones died this week. In racing's record books, he will be remembered as the trainer of Merry Deal, the winner of the 1957 Champion Hurdle, but his friends will remember him as a lovely, gentle, unassuming man, with a twinkle in his eye and a cheeky smile, and a wry sense of humour. Eyebrows raised and head tilted to one side, Arthur made you smile.

His yard, at Pentre David, near Oswestry, was the first racing stable I ever visited. It was a tucked-away, tumbly Shropshire farmhouse, with barns and boxes, and sheep in the fields and dogs in the kitchen, and owners and friends drifting in and out.

Arthur had lived there since he was a child, and trained there since 1952, when a friend offered him a broken-down racehorse called Lumiere, on the condition that, if it ever won a race, Jones would give him £100. Lumiere won nine races, which encouraged Arthur to buy an unbroken three-year-old called Merry Deal for 145gns. Merry Deal won twice at the Cheltenham Festival. The second time was as a 12-year-old, in the 1962 Spa Hurdle, and Arthur's champion raced on until he was 16, winning 19 races.

There were other good horses at Pentre David, like Donnadeala, Man Of The East and Take Cover, but for most of Jones's years at the stable, it was a life of working to get little races out of modest horses. In the days when I used to spend the mornings studying *The Sporting Life*, I followed the fortunes of names I came to know, from a distance, names like William The First and Prince Reviewer, Gun-Carriage and High Port. Sometimes 'Miss D Jones' appeared on the right. Diana was one of the very best female riders but, in those days, the late 1970s and early 1980s, she rarely got the rides to match her ability. Eventually, I wrote to her, and Diana invited my wife and I to visit Pentre David. They were wonderfully welcoming.

Life for Arthur and his wife, Isobel, and his three daughters, Diana, Victoria and Alex, revolved around the challenges standing in their stables. There was Frankie, fifth to Wollow in the 1976 Two Thousand Guineas but bought by Jones for just 900gns, out of love with racing and vicious with people, and Prince Reviewer, a cast-off from John Dunlop's yard, who would only gallop when chased by their whippet. Prince Reviewer won the 1983 Ladies' Derby, as a five-year-old maiden, and Frankie won two hurdles at Bangor. 'He never won anything very brilliant for us,' Diana told me, 'but he gave his owner a lot of fun and came to like it here, and to trust people. It's lovely to see a horse that is happy.'

I saw Russian Winter, the stable star, who had won a seller for Pat Haslam on his 16th start on the Flat, been pulled up three times out of four over hurdles, given Don Plant his first winner for three seasons when landing a small sprint at Hamilton, then gone in his wind. Sent to the 1979 sales, a reserve of 2,000gns proved too much and Russian Winter became another challenge for Arthur.

When Russian Winter was retired, in 1988, he had won 16 races for Pentre David, including eight at Ayr, where a race was named after him.

For Arthur and his family, as for many small trainers, there were pleasures beyond winning, other achievements, shared with friends. Making horses happy, getting the best out of them, even if they didn't win, friendships with their owners. And, when there was a winner, it meant so much more than it possibly could for one of the big Newmarket yards.

My good fortune to have known Arthur is one of the reasons why a Derby winner could never make me feel as excited as when Diana won a handicap hurdle at Bangor on the seven-year-old maiden Billion Melody, or when Shy Mistress, starting as slowly as she always did, with her dodgy knee, won an amateur riders' race at Redcar in 1989.

Diana finally got the recognition she deserved, winning the Lady Amateur Riders' Championship in 1993. Arthur retired a year later but, 25 years after her first ride, Diana, now assistant to Les Eyre, is still riding, and Victoria and Alex are still involved with horses. When I visited them recently, Thundering (Hamilton seller 1990, 33-1, no bid; Wolverhampton Amateur Riders' 1992; Nottingham Amateur Ladies' 1993), the subject of so much talk, was enjoying a spoilt retirement.

Even in illness, Arthur was still Arthur, with his smile and dry, wry lines. 'Training's not been any good to me financially,' he had told me, years ago, 'but it's what I've spent my life at, and I would do it again, because you meet so many nice people.' He was one of them.

WALTER MATTHAU *Racing Post*, 15 July 2000

Walter Matthau couldn't half act, and he couldn't half gamble, too, but now it's too late to ask America's best comedy actor about it. When you are born with a name like Matuschanskayasky, a face like a rubber puppet, and feet at ten to two, you'd better be born with a sense of humour, especially if your father disappears when you are three, and your mother works in a New York sweatshop and is so poor she has to steal toilet paper from cafés.

When someone tried to teach Matthau method acting, he retorted, 'I don't want any method to tarnish the way I used to make my mother laugh, by imitating the landlady asking for the rent.'

During the war, part of which he spent in England, Matthau once won $20,000 at poker. He took the whole barracks to the Palace Hotel in Norwich for a night with silver knives and forks.

That was nothing. Fifteen years later, in Florida, Matthau achieved the remarkable feat of losing $183,000 in two weeks, betting on exhibition baseball games. He had to borrow the money from a loan shark and it took him six years to pay it off. He didn't fare any better with real games. He once put $20,000 on the New York Yankees and, when they lost, put $80,000 on their next game, which they also lost; after 18 scotches, Matthau could still remember.

'I thought the only reason you made money was to give it to bookmakers,' he said. 'I always had one ear offstage, listening for the call from the bookie.' Or making one. According to Jack Lemmon, his regular co-star, 'If you couldn't find Walter on the set, you could look in the phone booth and he'd be placing a bet.'

Matthau was a loser (he once reckoned $5 million), and he knew it, but he couldn't stop. 'The first time I went to a greyhound track in England, I put £75 on, and my dog stopped and raised its leg halfway around. It was then I knew I was a loser but, when I don't gamble, I get mean and irritable and, when I win, somehow I feel I've cheated.'

While filming *The Fortune Cookie*, in 1966, Matthau had a heart attack. 'My doctor gave me six months to live and then, when I couldn't pay the bill, he gave me six months more.' Advised to stop smoking and gambling, Matthau stopped smoking.

Ten years later, by which time *The Odd Couple* had made him a star, he had heart surgery. 'One doctor told me to take it easy and get plenty of rest, the other said I needed to exercise more, so I did press-ups in bed.' But he still gambled. The cover of the first edition of *Gambling Times*, in 1977, featured Matthau with Telly Savalas and Howard Koch, also big gamblers. They invited him to share a horse with them. Matthau declined and Telly's Pop, who cost $6,000, went on to win more than $300,000.

A racetrack regular, Matthau once described his approach. 'I bet $20 a race until about the seventh, when there's something I like. I put $1,000 on it, and it's nipped at the wire. I bet $2,000 on the last and it's caught by an absent-minded 7-1 shot.'

Several of his film roles involved playing bookmakers or punters and, in 1977, in *Casey's Shadow*, Matthau played a trainer modelled on Lloyd Romero, a part which gave him the line, 'When we win this race, and we're rich, we're goin' ta Tahiti, where the women don't wear no top.'

His wife, Carol, was remarkably tolerant, until Walter's eyes strayed to a Swedish actress, beautiful from the waist up, but heavy-legged. When Matthau asked how old she was, his wife burst out, 'For God's sake, Walter, why don't you chop off her legs and count the rings.'

In 1993, Matthau announced that he had given up gambling (again). Dallas Cowboys had just won the SuperBowl. 'I had Buffalo,' he explained.

The only good thing about Matthau's death is that they might show *The Odd Couple* again on the telly. If they do, don't miss it. It's a great performance.

THE HONOURABLE MERVYN GREENWAY
Racing Post, 29 September 2001

There are three things I know for sure about The Honourable Mervyn Stephen Kelvynge Greenway, four if you count the waitress at Walthamstow. He was born on 19 August 1942, there were an awful lot of people at his memorial service, and a race is being run in his memory at Lingfield on Friday. It's a bugger that he'll miss the tax-free betting. [Betting duty was abolished from 6 October 2001.]

Mervyn owned racehorses and greyhounds but I'm not sure they were his prime interest, although the other one seemed to fit in pretty nicely that evening at Walthamstow, which was the second and, as it turned out, final time I met him. On the one hand, there was the constant dashing off to place the next bet, done with enormous enthusiasm; on the other, there was the young, slim waitress, ditto.

I think she may have been aware of the fact that Mervyn had been born in 1942, whereas she hadn't, but Mervyn didn't allow such minor details to stand between his twinkling eyes, cheery, plummy chat-up, and the knowledge that, sometimes, long-shots come in.

Searching for Mervyn on the internet, I found just one reference. It recorded the result of a cricket match in 1998 between a team from the Lords and Commons, and Roedean School. Mervyn, captaining the Parliamentarians, scored 50. So it was probably another year when, overtaken by one of the dizzy spells that came with his heart surgery, Mervyn collapsed at the crease, came round, looked up, saw a circle of girls in white leaning over him, and decided he'd gone to heaven.

Once, invited to a concert at Wigmore Hall, he developed a passion for the music or, at least, for the young lady who was turning the pages for the pianist. The next day, Mervyn rang the concert hall and asked for her name. When they refused, he introduced himself as the Honourable Mervyn Greenway, secretary of the Stockbrokers' Operatic Society, keen to offer her some work. I don't know what happened after that.

I think it was 20 March, exactly a month after Walthamstow, when Mervyn went to Fontwell, saw his horse, A Chef Too Far, finish second, and then set off to watch his dog run at Wimbledon. Between the two, he died. Not such a bad day to go. On Friday, his friends are invited to use Pavilion 4. If I were you, I'd ask the Tote to pay for your drinks; Mervyn often paid for theirs. Anyway, have a good time, because he certainly would have done.

HUNTER S. THOMPSON *Racing Post*, 26 February 2005

Having spent most of his life putting everything else that was life-threatening into his body, this week Hunter S Thompson finally tried a bullet. The bullet succeeded where years of whisky and cocaine had narrowly failed. Thompson liked firearms, and his last request was to have his ashes fired from a cannon.

Memorably, Thompson once said, 'I hate to advocate drugs, alcohol, violence or insanity to anyone, but they've always worked for me.' He also described the loathsome president Richard Nixon as a man who 'could shake your hand and stab you in the back at the same time. His body should have been burned in a trash bin.'

That was Hunter S Thompson, a model American citizen, and the founder of what was called 'gonzo' journalism. When Thompson wrote about an event, he was always in it. You didn't always learn much about the event but you had an enjoyable time reading about Thompson's latest self-inflicted disaster, real or imagined.

It would be an exaggeration to say that Thompson (started 18 July 1937, ended 20 February 2005) was a racefan but, from time to time, he was a racegoer and, more often, a gambler. Like Muhammad Ali, Thompson, whose best known work was *Fear and Loathing in Las Vegas*, was born in Louisville. Like Ali, he punched his way out of it, but occasionally returned for the Kentucky Derby. Thompson came back, not to praise the Derby but to heap abuse upon it, and all those who attended it. For Thompson, returning to Louisville was a punishment for having been born there.

'The Derby is not my favourite sporting event of the year, despite my deep Kentucky roots and my natural lust for gambling,' he once wrote. 'I have had more truly heinous experiences linked to Churchill Downs than any other venue. Derby week in Louisville is a white-knuckle orgy of booze and sex and violence. Going to the Derby in person is worse than volunteering to join General Pickett's famous charge at Gettysburg, and just about as much fun. Horse people have very short attention spans for anything involving humans. The best thing about the Kentucky Derby is that it is only two minutes long.'

It was an article about the 1970 Derby, entitled, promisingly, 'The Kentucky Derby is Decadent and Depraved', that helped popularise Thompson, who regularly lived up to his own title.

In his account, Thompson arrives at Louisville airport, pretending to be a photographer from *Playboy*. When the big day arrives, Thompson, *Scanlan's Monthly*'s reporter, is in no fit state to report, so relies on the whisky-stained notes in his mangled notebook. When Ralph Steadman, a sometimes vicious caricaturist and Thompson's illustrator, said he wanted to see some Kentucky colonels (such as Louisville's Colonel Sanders, of Kentucky Fried Chicken infamy), Thompson 'told him to go to the clubhouse men's rooms and look for men in white linen suits vomiting in the urinals. Watch the shoes, that's the tip-off. Most of them manage to avoid vomiting on their own clothes, but they never miss their shoes.'

The race itself figures only briefly, just long enough for Steadman to back Holy

Land, Thompson to back Silent Screen, and Dust Commander to win. The duo then resume drinking. Later, 'such horrible things occurred that I can't bring myself even to think about them. I was lucky to get out at all.' Unsurprisingly, the final sentence reads, 'We can do without your kind in Kentucky.'

DOUG MARKS *Racing Post*, 14 June 2007

Doug Marks, who died last week, was one of racing's great characters. I know that, even though I'm not sure whether I ever met him. I certainly interviewed him at his Lethornes yard in Lambourn, in 1989, although Marks wasn't there at the time.

His daughter Kelly, a character in her own right, explained that Doug had gone to Haywards Heath to play in a charity golf tournament. Kelly, who had done some fairly amazing things herself, did her best to pretend to be Doug, while I did my best to pretend that she was. It seemed to work all right.

Kelly ran through the highspots and lowspots of her father's life, including training the winner of the 1962 Cesarewitch, Golden Fire, at 25-1. Doug told the encircling journalists, 'You can quote me as saying, "I don't have to work again".'

Golden Fire was awarded the race on the disqualification of Orchardist, and Marks remembered how happy Orchardist's lad had looked when leading him in. Afterwards, he went to trainer John Benstead's yard, gave the lad the then huge sum of £100 and took all the stable staff to the Talk Of The Town. That spirit of generosity was an important part of Marks's make-up. More than 20 years later, when Kelly was working for Geoff Lewis, a man walked up to her and said, 'If you need anything, just tell me. I was the kid who did Orchardist.'

Marks knew how to train good horses, as his handling of the top-class sprinters Fireside Chat, Shiny Tenth and Singing Bede showed, but his was also a gambling yard. He took that seriously.

Jockey Peter Madden, who served his apprenticeship with Marks, told me, 'If Doug Marks said, "He'll win today," he was never far out. The night before, he'd have me in and draw a plan of the course on a blackboard and tell me exactly what was going to happen. He schooled me well.'

One day, Madden asked Marks for a day off to go fishing. Marks insisted that he ride at Sandown, then wait for him after the last race. Madden waited a short while then dashed off to meet jockey Richard Dicey for a trip to Brighton.

The next day, Marks confronted Madden, who told him that they had gone fishing. 'I know where you went,' said Marks. 'You had a couple of women, didn't you? Just remember, I'm entitled to half of everything you get.'

Another apprentice, Nicky Howe, once rode a winner for Marks and later received one of the presents Marks was famous for. Howe wrote to express his gratitude.

'Dear Mr Marks. Thank you very much for the golf balls. I don't play golf but I am sure that they will come in very useful.'

When jockey Tony Clark suggested that a drink might be in order after he had given Marks his first winner for a while, Marks promised to send him a present. Sure enough, Clark subsequently received a letter. It was from the Ethiopian Appeal Fund and read, 'Thank you very much for your kind donation of £100.'

On another occasion, Marks told two riders to canter to a particular tree, then turn back. When they got there, one rider said, 'I wonder where the old bastard is?' 'He's up here,' replied Marks's voice, 'keeping his bloody eyes on you.'

There were other stories, including one of Kelly's about Stan Mellor when he was a jockey. It's nothing to do with Doug, but I like it, and I'm sure Doug did. Evidently Mellor hated being photographed without his false teeth but, on safety grounds, jockeys weren't allowed to wear them when riding. Mellor kept his teeth tucked up his sleeve ready to slip them in his mouth for the post-race cameras. One day he had a fall and lay on the ground, in agony, clutching his arm. Elain, his wife, dashed up. 'Have you broken your arm?' she asked. 'No,' groaned Stan, 'they bit me.'

No wonder Marks managed to persuade several show business personalities to have horses with him. According to Frankie Vaughan, once a very popular crooner, one day he received a letter from 'D Marks, Trainer Extraordinary, Lambourn.' Marks told Vaughan that he was a big fan of his, while he himself was a brilliant trainer.

Vaughan invited Marks to his show at the London Palladium and, before long, Vaughan, Jimmy Tarbuck, Edmundo Ros and Danny La Rue were the puzzled owners of a two-year-old called Jazz Singer, later followed by Razzamataz and Water Rat. 'We had some wonderful times,' Vaughan told me.

As I left Lethornes, I asked a stable girl what Marks was like. There was a long pause. 'Well,' she replied, 'he's not boring.' Doug Marks must have given a lot of people a lot of pleasure.

FREDDIE WILLIAMS *Racing Post*, 23 June 2008

Freddie Williams will be missed as a unique presence in the racecourse and greyhound-track betting rings, but he will be missed even more as a lovely man, rich in qualities that made him both respected and liked. He was honourable, reliable, warm and good-humoured, with the rare ability to be the same in victory and defeat. He was a generous, lovable man.

In 2000, a year after he first appeared at pitch number two at the Cheltenham Festival, Freddie agreed to relate his daily betting experiences to the *Racing Post*. When I first spoke to him, on the telephone, two things struck me. The first was that I couldn't understand most of the words he was saying. The second, that the ones I did understand revealed an open, straightforward man. It was Freddie's nature to trust you to keep private what he didn't want revealed.

Each day, we would have a chat before racing and, eventually, I got to semi-grips with his strong Ayrshire accent. After racing, he would step wearily, and sometimes lamely, off his box, and tell the day's tale.

Standing all day in the ring at the Cheltenham Festival is draining. The first thing you want to do afterwards is not spend time talking about it to a journalist, especially if the afternoon has gone badly. Freddie was a very big and brave layer. When an afternoon went badly, it sometimes went six-figure badly. However badly it had gone, Freddie was always the same.

He wanted to be helpful, and he was. He never ducked out and he told the truth. I always felt I could believe him. All he kept to himself was the name of the clients who had struck the bets. Their privacy was to be respected.

Freddie was enormously philosophical about misfortune, however much it cost. On the first day of the 2002 festival, Adamant Approach looked the likely winner of the opening Supreme Novices' Hurdle until falling at the last, leaving victory to JP McManus's Like-A-Butterfly. Freddie had laid a bet of £225,000 to £100,000 on the winner. He didn't utter a word of complaint.

In sharp contrast to most present day bookmakers, Freddie told me he bet 80 per cent to his opinions, and that he invested a lot of time and effort to ensure that they were soundly based. Before racing, he would tell me what his opinions were. They weren't always proved right and Freddie lost at every Festival from 2003 to 2005, although he scored some notable victories in other years.

Three weeks before the 2006 Festival, he had a hip replaced. It didn't stop him, just as major heart surgery had not stopped him, because Freddie loved Cheltenham with a fierce passion.

I liked walking up to Freddie's pitch and chatting to him and Julie, his delightful daughter, who Freddie was rightly proud to have working with him. For her, and the rest of Freddie's family and friends, his death will leave a terrible gap, and there will be a sad absence at the Cheltenham Festival.

14
BURROWING IN THE ARCHIVES

Stanley Wootton (right) thinks about £10 million while Charlie Smirke talks to him.

In a former life, I was an academic historian. Studying neglected documents in archive collections is still my idea of an enjoyable way to spend a day, or a year. Some of the fruits of my labour appeared in *Ringers and Rascals* (2003) and in a history of the Tote, *For the good of racing: the first 75 years of the Tote* (2004). Here are the results of some later detective work and, first, of an earlier investigation.

In 1999, a small item in a newspaper reported that a Cardiff solicitor was seeking to overturn the conviction for murder of a bookmaker called Danny Driscoll. It intrigued me, so I contacted the solicitor, who kindly gave me access to the case papers he had collected.

THE CASE OF DANNY DRISCOLL *Racing Post*, 2 September 1999

Danny Driscoll, a licensed bookmaker, looked up at the sky and said, 'Well, they've given us a nice day for it. Which noose is mine?'

There was one waiting for Danny and another for Edward Rowlands. There would have been a third, for Edward's brother John, but he had been declared insane, and sent to Broadmoor. All three had been found guilty of murdering David Lewis, 30 years old, once a professional boxer and captain of a Cardiff rugby club. 'As cruel and as beastly a murder as could possibly be imagined,' said counsel for the prosecution.

Yet more than 250,000 people, including MPs and archbishops, signed a petition calling for Driscoll, 35, and Rowlands, 38, to be reprieved. Eight of the jurors who had returned a verdict of 'guilty' made their own eve of execution plea, but to no avail. Sir Austen Chamberlain, the acting Home Secretary, rejected all appeals for clemency, and Driscoll and Rowlands were executed at Cardiff prison on 27 January 1928. 'A terrible blunder, a gross miscarriage of justice,' declared Thomas Power O'Connor, MP for Liverpool and Father of the House of Commons.

Now, over 70 years later, Chris Driscoll, the son of Danny's youngest brother, Dennis, is trying to get his uncle's conviction overturned. He has employed a Cardiff solicitor, Bernard de Maid, to urge the Criminal Cases Review Commission to refer Driscoll's case back to the Court of Appeal. 'I am very confident,' says de Maid. 'A more staggering miscarriage of justice you'd be hard pushed to find.'

The Murder

It was a two-day meeting at Monmouth racecourse, 28 and 29 September 1927. At the end of the second day, George Dyer, John Hughes, David Lewis and Edward Rowlands piled into Dyer's car and drove back to Cardiff.

They were all racecourse regulars. Dyer was a bookmaker, 'Jockey' Hughes his clerk, Dai Lewis hired out bookmakers' stools while 'Tich' Rowlands, although not a bookmaker himself, had an interest in Ernest Long's book. Several of the party had been drinking at the races, and they stopped off and topped up on their way back to the Blue Anchor Hotel in St Mary Street, Cardiff, arriving at about 8.00pm.

At about 9.45pm, they were joined by Danny Driscoll. On Bank Holidays, Driscoll worked as a bookmaker at Cardiff and Newport races but, that afternoon, he had been playing cards in Cardiff's Colonial Club. Closing time was 10.00pm. Dyer bid his farewells but the landlady allowed Driscoll, Rowlands, Lewis and Hughes to stay on. They left the Blue Anchor at about 11.10pm.

As they emerged on to St Mary Street, John 'Jacky Tich' Rowlands and William Joseph 'Hong Kong' Price appeared from the Express Cafe, opposite. They, too, had been to the races and Price was very drunk.

St Mary Street was a busy, well-lit spot, and the men, close to a taxi rank, were watched by an assortment of cab drivers and passers-by, and by two policemen. At about 11.30pm, a violent fight erupted. Lewis was attacked with a knife, probably a razor. One blow left a horribly deep cut, 7in long, from his jaw to above his left ear. It was all over in 30 seconds. Lewis collapsed, his attackers fled, and, while police constables David Evans and David Roberts hurried to the spot, Eileen Latchford, a local prostitute, tore off a piece of her petticoat and tried to staunch the flow of blood. Lewis was driven to Cardiff Royal Infirmary, arriving at about 11.40pm.

Within three hours of the assault, the Rowlands brothers, Price, Driscoll and Hughes had all been arrested. There was blood on John Rowlands' hands and in his trouser pocket. At 5.30am the following morning, the arrested men were taken to the hospital, to be identified by Lewis in the presence of a local magistrate. Lewis refused to incriminate any of his attackers. He insisted that he didn't know how he had been injured.

'Who on earth has done this to you?,' asked his wife. 'Hush,' replied Lewis.

At 11.20am, he collapsed and died.

The Trial

John Hughes was soon released, leaving the Rowlands brothers, Price and Driscoll to appear together at Glamorgan Assizes on 29 November 1927, charged with the murder of David Lewis. All pleaded not guilty.

There had been plenty of witnesses to the attack, but witnesses willing to testify were in short supply, as was consistent identification evidence. The prosecution relied heavily on PCs Evans and Roberts, the only witnesses to name Driscoll as an active participant, and their testimony was in conflict. Evans maintained that Driscoll had held Lewis's arms from behind, while Edward Rowlands struck the fatal blow. Roberts testified that Driscoll was facing Lewis. The blow had been struck by a short man.

The Rowlands brothers were both conspicuously short. Edward was 5ft 2in and John a diminutive 5ft. Driscoll, in contrast, was 5ft 10in and powerfully built. John Rowlands confessed to having wielded the knife but, in his summing up, Mr Justice Wright told the jury, 'If one man strikes a blow and it is part of a concerted action, then the others are guilty.'

The jury took just 48 minutes to reach their verdict. Price, deemed too drunk to have taken any part, was found not guilty. The Rowlands brothers and Driscoll were convicted of murder and sentenced to death.

The Appeal

On 11 January 1928, Driscoll and Edward Rowlands were taken by train to London to attend the appeal hearing, presided over by Lord Chief Justice Lord Hewart.

Artemus Jones KC, representing Driscoll, alleged that Lord Halsbury KC, the prosecution counsel, had prejudiced the jury against Driscoll by describing him as a member of a racing gang, present at Monmouth races on 28 and 29 September, and on bad terms with Lewis. But Driscoll had not been at the races and, according to Jones, 'It was utterly untrue to say that Driscoll was at any time a member of a racing gang.' Nor was he engaged in a feud with Lewis. The prosecution produced no evidence to support its claims, yet the judge did not warn the jury to dismiss them.

Mr Justice Wright had also failed to highlight either the discrepancies in the policemen's evidence, or the fact that no other witnesses identified Driscoll as a participant. Instead, he had emphasised points favourable to the prosecution.

The Appeal Court judges gave short shrift to Jones's arguments. The Lord Chief Justice declared, 'It is quite impossible to say that the evidence was not sufficient to support the verdict which the jury returned.' Mr Justice Wright's summing up had been 'careful and entirely adequate,' and, although the prosecution counsel's opening speech did 'overstate the case,' it was 'idle' to suggest that this had influenced the verdict given by the jury three days later.

The appeals were dismissed and Driscoll and Rowlands returned to Cardiff prison, to await execution.

The Police Files

Not everyone joined the wave of support for Danny Driscoll. Arthur Evans, MP for Cardiff South, controversially refused to sign a petition calling for a reprieve. The *Daily Mail* insisted that this was not a suitable case for sentiment. 'The three were guilty beyond a doubt. The verdict of guilty was the proper one, and the sentence was just.'

South Wales was a notably depressed area in the 1920s and the men who met in the Blue Anchor Hotel on 29 September lived a harsh, hand-to-mouth existence. Edward Rowlands had a string of convictions, including for assaulting the police, who regarded him as a 'clever, daring, violent and unscrupulous thief, an associate of the lowest type of the racing fraternity and of all classes of criminals.'

According to a report by detective sergeant Gerald Broben, Rowlands was the leader of a gang of racecourse roughs, the 'Forty Thieves.' Helped by his brother John, 29, who 'frequents racecourses and preys upon bookmakers,' and by David Lewis himself, Rowlands had driven two bookmakers out of the area. In 1923, the gang had tried to push one of them out of a third-floor window, but no one was prepared to press charges, or give evidence.

The following year, Edward Rowlands and Lewis were convicted in connection with an assault on a tram conductor. They and three other men had called at James Jones's house in Newport, to demand money. Jones, another bookmaker, was out and, when the men confronted his wife, a tram conductor went to her aid. He was then attacked. Rowlands was sentenced to three years for grievous bodily harm and Lewis, who also had a string of convictions, to six months.

When Lewis was released, he returned to the racecourse, making money hiring out bookmakers' stools and calling out the horses' numbers. Rowlands claimed that Lewis had agreed to hand part of his income to Rowlands' wife, until Rowlands was released. Lewis retorted that his own wife had received no help while he was in prison, and he could not afford to sacrifice the money.

This dispute was thought to have led to an assault on Lewis by William Price, a criminal associate of the Rowlands, at Cowbridge races in April 1927. During Cardiff's race meeting in May, Lewis was replaced as number caller. Rowlands and his associates also wanted to replace Lewis as the supplier of bookmakers' stools. On the first day of the Monmouth meeting, 28 September, Edward Rowlands threatened Lewis with one of the iron spikes bookmakers used to make a hole for their stands.

Danny Driscoll was not involved in this feud. 'He is an associate of low-class betting men,' ran one police report, 'but not constantly in the company of the other prisoners.' Driscoll, who had convictions for petty theft and using obscene language, was said to travel the country 'selling furs of doubtful quality, representing they have been smuggled from Russia.' Another member of 'the fur-selling gang' was said to be Harry Sedgwick, a Birmingham bookmaker who regularly attended Cardiff races. He was active in promoting a petition for Driscoll's reprieve.

According to the Birmingham City Police, 'Practically the whole of the persons who were out with the petition forms were men who frequent racecourses, bookmakers of the lowest class, clerks, tic-tacs, pickpockets and men who have been convicted of crimes of violence.' Sedgwick himself had been convicted of assaulting a policeman.

The New Appeal

The fact that Driscoll kept unsavoury company, and was a dubious character himself, does not mean that the jury were right to find him guilty of murder. The law, and court procedures, as well as society, have changed radically since 1927, and Bernard de Maid is convinced that the case will be returned to the Court of Appeal.

'Nowadays,' says de Maid, 'the conflicting eye-witness evidence alone would be sufficient to have the case thrown out. The definition of "joint intent" has also changed. Even if Driscoll was involved, he would not be deemed guilty unless he clearly knew that Rowlands intended to kill Lewis. Prejudice was stirred up by the prosecution counsel, and the judge failed to direct the jury properly.'

Driscoll's nephew will be awaiting developments eagerly, but Danny also had a daughter. Vera was born in 1915, two years before her mother, Alice, died, aged 22. Vera was brought up by her grandmother, and emigrated with her to the US. Vera will be 84 now, if she is still alive.

In November 1999, Bernard de Maid submitted his evidence to the Criminal Cases Review Commission. Three years later, the CCRC concluded that it could not pursue the case without transcripts of the trial, which have not been located and may no longer exist. De Maid argued that there was still sufficient evidence to justify referring the case to the Court of Appeal but the CCRC was not persuaded.

The racecourse gangs mentioned during the trial of Danny Driscoll plagued racecourse betting rings between the two World Wars and were famously highlighted in Graham Greene's classic 1938 novel, *Brighton Rock*. My search to find out more ended in Hove cemetery, at the grave of Darby Sabini.

THE REIGN OF THE RACECOURSE GANGS *Racing Post*,
29 June and 3 July 2006

The gang of about 30 men, all from London, all armed, first walked behind the row of bookmakers' pitches, then in front of them, scanning the bookmakers' faces. James Spinks, the gang's leader, finally spotted Alfred Solomon and Mark Frater,

Solomon's clerk. The gang rushed towards them. Solomon was struck on the head but managed to escape; Frater didn't. While Albert Blitz held his arms, Spinks hit Frater with a hatchet. When Frater fell to the ground, other gang members kicked and beat him. Then, mercifully, the police arrived. It was about 12.45pm on Monday 8 June 1936, at Lewes racecourse.

The gang fled, shedding weapons as they went, weapons that would soon be displayed at Lewes Assizes. Hammers, iron bars, jemmies, knuckledusters and broken billiard cues were scattered around the ring. Some of the gang escaped but 16 were arrested and, on 27 July, they appeared before Mr Justice Hilbery, charged with maliciously wounding Frater, assaulting Solomon, and riotous assembly.

Solomon did not give evidence and, while on bail, Spinks had a drink and a chat with Frater, after which Frater disappeared. The police retrieved him in time for the trial but his evidence was useless. Terrified, Frater copied the example set by many other victims of racecourse gangs, and lost his memory.

Detective Sergeant Collyer and Detective Constable Janes hadn't lost theirs and, although all 16 defendants denied having been involved, all 16 were found guilty. 'Crimes of gang violence in this country will meet with no mercy,' the judge told them. 'There is no case here for leniency. You will receive sentences which I hope will teach you once and for all that crimes of this sort don't pay.'

Spinks and Charles Spring were sent to prison for five years, Blitz for four, the rest of the gang for periods ranging from 18 months to three years. What Brighton's *Evening Argus* called the 'Lewes Racecourse Fracas' was one of the inspirations for Graham Greene's 1938 novel, *Brighton Rock*. The infamous affray effectively marked the end of gang warfare on Britain's racecourses.

The gang at Lewes were not racecourse regulars and William Bebbington, the Jockey Club's supervisor of racecourse detectives, believed that their arrival was linked to recent clashes between two men, one of whom was an associate of Solomon. When the gang couldn't find their intended victim, they turned on Solomon and his hapless clerk.

Another possible explanation involved Albert Blitz. During the trial, Blitz was asked about his relatives. He replied that he was illegitimate and that his real name was not Blitz, which made it easier for him to insist that he had never heard of Barnett Blitz. He didn't know, he said, that in 1924 Solomon had been sent to prison for three years for Barnett Blitz's manslaughter.

Solomon, a regularly violent man, had been lucky. Only the theatrical persuasiveness of defence barrister Sir Edward Marshall Hall had saved him from being convicted of murder, and the gallows. He had Hall to thank, and 'Darby' Sabini, the leader of the Sabini gang. At that time, Solomon was an associate of the gang, and Sabini arranged for Hall to represent him. Sabini could afford the best, but by 1936 his influence was waning. It was said that Alfred White, formerly Sabini's lieutenant, had sent the gang to Lewes, but Sabini had been tipped off, passed the tip to the police, and told his men to stay away. Perhaps.

*

Soldiers returning from the First World War, and the families they returned to, had money and were in a mood to spend it. During the brief post-war boom, racecourse attendances reached record levels.

Bookmakers' satchels bulged, and so did the eyes of the criminals who preyed on bookmakers and punters alike, at railway stations and racecourse car parks, on the racetrains and at the racetracks, where pickpockets, card sharps and three-card tricksters plied their cheating trade, and race gangs terrorised the ring, and each other.

On many racecourses, particularly in the cheaper rings and in open areas distant from the grandstands, pitches were allocated, not by right, but might. Bookmakers often had no choice but to share their profits with gangsters, and to pay for the services they offered – protection, lists of runners, chalk, sponges and buckets of water, wanted or not. Sometimes, bookmakers were asked to contribute to a charity. They were necessary contributions, as those who declined to make them could testify, although testifying against gang members was not advisable, if you wanted to remain in business, unscarred.

The Brummagem Boys, led by Billy Kimber, ruled the roost. An undisciplined gang, some from Birmingham but, according to a 1922 police report, 'mostly convicted London thieves of the worst type,' the gang charged bookmakers as much as 50 per cent of their profits for the privilege of conducting their business unmolested. Some layers were as amoral as the criminals who protected them, using the gang's services to dissuade winning punters from pressing their claims for payment.

Faced with the threats and demands of the Brummagem Boys, and related off-shoots, some southern bookmakers, many of them Jews from London's East End, welcomed the arrival of the Sabini gang.

Joseph or Octavia or Olavio or Charles Sabini – he gave different names in the 1891 and 1901 censuses and on various birth and marriage certificates – was born in Italy in about 1856, moved to the Little Italy area of Clerkenwell, married an English woman, Eliza Handley, and bred six sons and a daughter.

The sons had a sometimes deliberately confusing habit of varying and exchanging their names. The eldest, Frederick, was born in 1881, followed by Charles, Ollovia, Joseph, George and Harry, born in 1900.

Ollovia, born in 1888 or 1889, appeared as Thomas on the 1891 census form. Later, he was sometimes called Charles or Fred, although they were his brothers' names. On his death certificate, he appeared as Ollovia but the name on his gravestone, his nickname, was the name he was usually known by, Darby Sabini.

A modestly successful boxer, who later worked on the racecourse, Darby controlled a gang made up largely of Italians and Jews. When they challenged Kimber's Birmingham gang for control of southern racecourse pitches, the result was bloody warfare.

In March 1921, at a trotting meeting at Greenford, Darby Sabini was threatened by members of the Birmingham gang, led by George 'Brummy' Sage, Kimber's London-based ally. Sabini produced a revolver, and fired it. No one was hurt, and the court accepted Darby's claim of self-defence. He was fined £10 for possession of a firearm.

Four days later, encouraged by Walter Beresford, a respected bookmaker, Kimber visited Sabini with a peace plan. It involved the Sabinis abandoning their claims at Ascot and Epsom, the jewels in the southern crown. Sabini's counter-proposal called for Kimber's gang to retreat to the Midlands. The meeting ended abruptly when Kimber was shot by Solomon. Kimber stuck to the gangland rule book, and declined to cooperate with the police investigation. A jury subsequently accepted Solomon's claim that it was an accident.

A few weeks later, at Epsom's Derby meeting, Andrew Towie, an associate of Kimber's, was attacked with a mallet and bottle. It was small beer compared with what followed.

*

The light blue charabanc was parked at the top of the hill, near the Brick Kiln Inn at Ewell, on the London Road. A gun was pointed at driver Frank Lane's head, to discourage him from driving away. Nearby, Walter Giles sat at the wheel of a taxi, waiting. Another man stood peering through his binoculars, towards Epsom. 'Here they come,' he said.

A Crossley tender chugged up the hill, carrying a party of ten bookmakers and their assistants home from the final day of the 1921 Derby meeting. As they approached the brow of the hill, Giles drove the taxi into their path.

'Here come the Italian bastards,' one of the Birmingham gang yelled. 'Kill the bloody lot of them.' And 30 or more men, armed with hammers, iron bars, razors, spanners, hatchets and bricks surrounded the tender, and attacked its occupants. Only one of the victims, Charles Schwartz, a bookmaker's clerk with a string of convictions for theft, recognised any of his assailants, and Schwartz declined to testify. 'If I did,' he told the police, 'I would not be able to go racing again.'

The Birmingham gang put several men in hospital, but they were the wrong men. The Brummagem Boys had intended to ambush the Sabini gang. Instead, they had mistakenly attacked their own allies, from Leeds. Schwartz was the only victim from London.

The gang piled into the charabanc and ordered Lane to drive to Kingston Hill as fast as possible. The police were soon in pursuit, and Police Sergeant Joseph Dawson spotted the charabanc parked at the George and Dragon pub. He walked in, confronted them, pulled out a revolver and warned, 'I shall shoot the first man who tries to escape.'

Twenty-eight men, all from Birmingham, were arrested and, at the Surrey Assizes in Guildford, 17 were convicted of causing grievous bodily harm and given prison sentences ranging from nine months to three years. For the Birmingham gang, it was a spectacular own goal.

*

Bookmakers clearly needed to do something and, in August 1921, Walter Beresford became the first president of the Racecourse Bookmakers' and Backers' Protection Association. Its initial objective was to protect southern punters and layers from molestation but, with neither the racing authorities nor the police providing adequate assistance, the Association felt obliged to turn to the experts in protection, the Sabini gang. Beresford already employed Harry Sabini as his clerk.

The Association's vice-president was Edward Emmanuel, an eyebrow-raising choice. Emmanuel was a noted criminal. According to Arthur Harding, another underworld figure, he was 'the Jewish Al Capone,' with both the police and the Sabini gang allegedly on his payroll. When Solomon stabbed Barnett Blitz in the back of the head with a stiletto knife in the Eden Social Club in 1924, Emmanuel was with him.

Several stewards were appointed, at an attractive wage of £6 a week, to protect the Association's members. The stewards' identity was equally alarming. The police reported that they 'were mostly well known racecourse frequenters of a pugilistic tendency.' They included Darby Sabini, Alfred White, Fred Gilbert, a member of the Sabini gang later accused of betraying it, and Philip Emmanuel, a relative of the vice-president.

The new Association was in immediate danger of being tainted by its choice of representatives. In February 1922, White and Solomon were among those arrested for a razor attack on Michael Sullivan and Archie Douglas, both members of the Birmingham gang. A few weeks later, Solomon was again arrested after Gilbert was attacked with a razor. The victims declined to identify their attackers.

In July, at Brighton, the Sabini gang slashed John Phillips with razors and, at

Newmarket, they attacked JM Dick, the racing correspondent of the *Evening News*, who had condemned the gangs.

The following month, Joseph Sabini and White, described by the police as the Association's chief steward, were among those charged with shooting at Gilbert and Sage outside the Southampton Arms pub in Camden High Street. Despite the disappearance of a key witness, White and Sabini were convicted and sentenced to five years and three years in prison, respectively. Mr Justice Roche remarked that the sooner the Association was dissolved, the better.

By then, it had dispensed with the stewards' questionable services, partly because the stewards had started to levy unauthorised charges of their own. Meanwhile, the gang war took another twist, as elements in the Sabini ranks demanded a bigger share of the gang's racecourse takings. In November 1922, at the Fratellanza Club in Clerkenwell, Darby and Harry Sabini were attacked by the four Cortesi brothers, formerly their allies but now aligned with Gilbert, Sage and the Birmingham gang. Harry Sabini, recently charged with assaulting George Cortesi, was shot, while Darby's false teeth were broken. At the Old Bailey in January 1923, Enrico and Augustus Cortesi were both sent to prison for three years, and the Sabinis reasserted control.

White's conviction had been quashed on appeal, on a technicality, and he, George Drake and George Sabini were soon offering wardens at Maidstone prison £2 a week to act as go-betweens for one of their prisoners, Joseph Sabini. The wardens reported the approach to the governor and, in February, White and Drake appeared in court at Maidstone charged with conspiring to incite prison officers to contravene the Prisons Act.

The Racecourse Bookmakers' and Backers' Association may not have severed its links with the Sabini gang completely because it was their solicitor who applied for bail for the defendants, unsuccessfully. In June 1923, White and Drake were sentenced to 18 months and two years hard labour, respectively. Yet peace on Britain's racecourses was still a long way away.

*

The race gang war between the Brummagem Boys and the Sabini gang raged for over two years before the authorities took serious notice, and it was another two years before they were provoked into meaningful action.

The Jockey Club, as slow as a tortoise, stirred at its own pace. At the end of 1922, Sir Samuel Scott, the senior steward, suggested a conference with senior police officers following complaints 'respecting the increase of ruffianism in the rings at race meetings.'

While the Jockey Club stewards, chief constables and Home Office officials pondered, the ruffians continued their ruffianly conduct. Following the 1923 Derby, Darby and Harry Sabini appeared at Epsom Police Court charged with assaulting Maurice Fireman, alias Jack Levene, during a pitch dispute on the Downs. Darby had allegedly hit Fireman with a knuckleduster, while Harry threatened to take Fireman's eye out with a knife. There was some evidence that Fireman was the aggressor, and the case was dismissed.

By then, the Sabini gang had almost won the battle for southern supremacy, and settled into a lucrative routine of overcharging racecourse bookmakers for a peaceful pitch, lists of runners and other tools of the trade. Detective Chief Superintendent Edward Greeno later recalled, 'the obliging man with the large bucket and small sponge who ran up the lines wiping out the odds on the bookmakers' boards between races was not doing it for love. It cost half a crown a time, and it was no use the bookmaker trying to save his half-crown by doing it himself. Nor was it any good saying he had brought enough chalk for the day; he had to buy chalk from the man who offered it. For every race the bookmaker needed a printed list of runners. They were printed by a Mr Edward Emmanuel for maybe a farthing apiece. To the bookies they were half a crown a set. Sometimes a bookmaker with a mistaken idea of independence refused to pay, and there are still a few around with razor-scarred faces to show how foolhardy they were.'

One anonymous correspondent, writing in 1923, informed the Home Office that Emmanuel was still financing the Sabinis, was still often seen in the company of friendly police officers, and that 'nine racing men out of every ten live in absolute terror of them.'

There is no doubt that some, perhaps many, police were in the pay of the Sabinis, and gang leaders who controlled teams of violent thugs were sometimes referred to in surprisingly complimentary terms, even by senior officers. Former Chief Inspector Tom Divall, writing in 1929, described Billy Kimber, the leader of the Birmingham gang, as 'one of the best,' and some of his gang as 'really good fellows.' In Divall's eyes, the fact that Kimber and George Sage refused to give evidence after they had been shot by members of the Sabini gang showed 'what generous and brave fellows Sage and Kimber were.'

Many years later, in 1940, former Detective Superintendent F. Taylor, asked for information on Darby Sabini, who Taylor claimed to have known for 20 years, confined himself to observing, 'His livelihood has always been among the racing world. To me, Sabini appeared straightforward and one who would go a long way to prevent trouble.' Although it was true that Sabini preferred persuasion to violence, it was a remarkably indulgent assessment of the leader of a gang that owed its success to physical intimidation, a gang made up of violent crooks and villains.

Even Walter Beresford, president of the Racecourse Bookmakers' and Backers' Protection Association, once described Sabini as 'a prince of a fellow,' after Darby had escorted him to Doncaster for the St Leger meeting, in defiance of a warning from Kimber that southern bookmakers should stay away.

During 1924 and 1925, on the racecourse and off it, a variety of gangs engaged in what the press depicted, often exaggerating wildly, as full scale battles, until the government and Jockey Club finally responded.

In 1925, Sir William Joynson-Hicks, the Home Secretary, declared, 'It is a state of affairs that cannot be tolerated,' and pledged to break up the gangs. Under Chief Inspector 'Nutty' Sharpe, the Flying Squad began to target potentially troublesome race meetings, while the Jockey Club appointed a team of about 60 ring inspectors, mainly retired police officers, to patrol the courses.

The regionally based Bookmakers' Protection Associations, which would unite to form the National Bookmakers' Protection Association in 1932, set up pitch committees to make pitch allocation fairer, and racecourse officials became involved in pitch administration. Some of the rules that later acted as an obstacle to modernisation, including a prohibition on the buying and selling of pitches, were designed partly to protect the ring from criminal gangs. They were only partially successful.

In 1926, Darby Sabini denied a suggestion that he made £20,000 to £30,000 a year on racecourses but, two years later, an anonymous 'Londoner' informed the Home Secretary that, 'upon the racecourse, the Sabini gang reign supreme. The police never interfere with them. It is foolish to cry, "God save the King," one is safer if one shouts, "God save the Emperor, Darby Sabini," a far more powerful monarch.'

In 1929, 'Nutty' Sharpe, commenting on two recent assaults, observed, 'assaults of this kind by desperate racecourse-frequenting criminals are not infrequent but police have the greatest possible difficulty in obtaining evidence. Persons who obtain their living on racecourses shrink in fear from the thought of attending courts of justice to give evidence.'

As if to confirm Sharpe's assertion, when Darby Sabini appeared in court at Brighton later that year, charged with assaulting David Isaacs, a bookmaker, following a dispute at Hove Greyhound Stadium, there was the usual distinct shortage of witnesses. Asked for an explanation, Isaacs replied, 'How can I get witnesses against a man like this, when everyone goes in fear of their life of him?' Sabini was fined £5.

Darby had moved to Brighton in about 1926, while his brothers remained in London, although Harry Sabini later moved from Clerkenwell to a 'palatially furnished' house in Highbury. Brighton was a popular home for criminals, and the racetrack, like Epsom, was difficult to police because it was not fully enclosed.

With their racecourse operations increasingly curtailed by police and Jockey Club action, the Sabini brothers turned their attention to West End clubs and greyhound tracks. Fred, the eldest brother, operated a pitch at Harringay and the White City, trading under the name of Bob Wilson; Charles worked with Joseph Levy, supplying lists of runners at the West Ham greyhound stadium; Joseph stood as Harry Lake, at Harringay, while George supplied tissue prices at Harringay and the White City. The police regarded Charles's and George's businesses as 'rackets.'

Alfred Solomon, a former Sabini associate who had once shot Billy Kimber and killed Barnett Blitz, was also active. A 1930 police report suggested that he was now the leader of a gang that demanded money from bookmakers at greyhound tracks. When the track manager at Clapton threw Solomon out, the manager was later attacked by Solomon's men.

As the 1930s progressed, blatant intimidation of racecourse bookmakers became rare, and Darby Sabini, reaching his fifties, reduced his involvement. This left the way open for Alfred White, his former lieutenant, who was also active at point-to-point meetings, to challenge the Sabinis' control.

The fracas at Lewes in 1936 reflected the changing location of power, and whatever control Darby Sabini retained ended when Italy joined the war on Germany's side, in 1940. Darby and Harry Sabini, together with many other British citizens with Italian ancestors, were both interned, as 'persons of hostile origin.'

Darby, who was living in Hove under the name of Fred Handley, Handley being his mother's maiden name, was arrested at the greyhound stadium. Local inquiries about him produced a range of responses. Hove's chief constable reported that he knew Sabini as Fred, that he stood as a bookmaker at Hove dog meetings, collected money from racecourse bookmakers in return for protection and racecards, and that 'Sabini and his brother (Harry) are persons who were at one time feared among the lower type of bookmakers on horse and dog racing tracks.'

Detective Inspector E.Greens was more outspoken. 'He is a drunkard and a man of most violent temperament,' Greens wrote, 'with a heavy following and strong command of bullies of Italian origin and other undesirables. A dangerous gangster and a racketeer of the worst type.'

Darby appealed against his internment and, during his examination in December 1940, testified, 'It is like going to church today, on a racecourse. All that rough business is finished.' For the previous three years he had been standing as a bookmaker under the name of Dan Cope, and also worked for the Bookmakers' Protection Association, selling lists of horses on a commission basis.

During a court appearance in 1929, Sabini had described himself as a printer's agent and, in a statement he made shortly after his internment, he said that he worked as the representative of a printing company. The company was the Portsea Press, whose proprietor was Edward Smith, alias Edward Emmanuel, the 'Jewish Al Capone' reputed to have controlled the Sabini gang in its early days, now producing lists of runners and betting tickets for sale to bookmakers. Emmanuel and Darby Sabini were still working together.

In February 1941, the Home Office advisory committee dealing with Sabini's appeal recommended his release. The following month, a report sent to the Home Secretary by the Brighton police made it clear that they regarded Sabini's criminal activities as a thing of the past. 'There is little doubt,' the report continued, 'that Sabini was the head of a race gang and considerable trouble was experienced by police with this gang, and others running in opposition on various racecourses. These gangs were finally broken up and it is safe to say that gang warfare during the past few years has been practically negligible, owing to police action, whilst the Sabini gang can rightly be said to be non-existent.' Sabini was apt to be violent when drunk, but this was a rare occurrence. Contrary to Greens' opinion, he was not now regarded as a dangerous gangster or racketeer.

Harry Sabini also appealed against his internment, and claimed to have been a professional punter since 1932, but a police report described him as dangerous and violent, and remarked, 'he does not appear to have been engaged in any honest work,' although 'a fairly wealthy man,' wealthy enough to embark on an ill-advised legal action in an attempt to accelerate his release.

In January 1941, an application for a writ of *habeas corpus* was made in the High Court, on Harry's behalf, on the grounds that he may have been a victim of mistaken identity. The Lord Chief Justice, Viscount Caldecote, and two fellow judges, were wholly unpersuaded. Mr Justice Humphreys considered that Sabini, who used the alias of Harry Handley, had 'committed deliberate perjury and deceived this court.'

Although the internment order was revoked that March, Harry was soon back in custody, serving a nine-month sentence for perjury. Two years later, in 1943, it was Darby's turn, when he was sent to prison for three years for receiving stolen goods. While there, he received the news that his only son, Harry, who had joined the Royal Air Force, had been killed in action in Egypt, aged 21.

After the war, a new generation of London gangsters, led by Jack 'Spot' Comer and Billy Hill, took control. They concentrated on clubs rather than racecourses, and Hill recruited several former members of the Sabini gang, including Pasquala Poppa, alias Bert Marsh, and Alberto Dimeo, alias Albert Dimes.

Darby Sabini, for a while the criminal emperor of Britain's southern racecourses, lived on in a small terrace house on the Old Shoreham Road in Hove. He died, barely noticed, in 1950, aged 62, his death certificate giving his occupation as turf commission agent. It was a quiet end to an explosive life.

Crime and courts have featured regularly in the history of horseracing, sometimes as a result of rascals running a 'ringer,' a horse disguised as another. Francasal was an infamous ringer but when I told the tale in *Ringers and Rascals* I didn't know why the jury had failed to reach agreement on their verdict, resulting in a retrial. The answer lay in a Metropolitan Police file.

THE NOBBLED JURY *Racing Post*, 14 May 2006

On 2 February 1954, after a trial lasting three weeks, the jury at the Old Bailey retired to consider their verdicts. Five men, Harry Kateley, Maurice Williams, Gomer Charles, Victor Dill and William Rook, were accused of conspiring to commit fraud by running a 'ringer' in the name of Francasal at Bath the previous July.

Francasal, alias Santa Amaro, had duly won at 10-1, a price sustained by the helpful expedient of cutting the telephone wires to the racecourse, thereby preventing off-course bookmakers from using the 'blower' service to send money to the racecourse ring. The conspirators stood to win the equivalent of £1 million but were quickly exposed. Now they faced the prospect of prison.

When the 12 jurors were ushered into the jury room, most of them expected their deliberations to be short, with 'guilty' verdicts a formality. Not, perhaps, Grace Marriner. During the lunch interval on the final day, before the jury retired, another juror, Pat Beason, had told her that they would be sitting all night. In anticipation of a lengthy session, he had brought 60 Players' cigarettes with him.

Near unanimity was soon established but an immovable obstacle prevented the jury from reaching the unanimous verdict required by the court. The obstacle was James Louis Patrick Beason.

A 49-year-old storekeeper from Clapham, Beason was soon the only dissenter from the jury's shared view that all five defendants were guilty. Fellow juror Harry Nelson later told the police that, but for Beason, guilty verdicts would have been returned within half an hour.

His irritation was shared by other jurors. Dennis Bouffler and Norah Capito complained of Beason's 'obstinate attitude,' which 'disgusted' Marriner. Vivian Bode expressed 'extreme indignation' at Beason's refusal to accept that Williams was guilty, while Nelson and Jack Jay almost came to blows with Beason in the jury room.

The odd man out could not be persuaded. He maintained that the horses had been switched accidentally, and was resolute in his defence of Williams. After three and a half hours the judge was informed that the jury were unable to agree. Majority verdicts were not permitted until 1967. Mr Justice Sellers ordered a retrial.

The following day two anonymous phone calls were received at the offices of the Director of Public Prosecutions and prosecuting counsel. The caller stated that he had been one of the jurors at the Francasal trial. He was ringing to let them know that another juror had talked to men sitting at the back of the court and had been seen in a nearby café with some of the defendants. The caller said, 'the juryman's name was Pat and he sat behind the foreman.' The juror behind the foreman was Beason.

The police were asked to investigate and were authorised to interview all the jurors. Jay told them that he, his wife and son had received suspicious telephone calls during the trial. The police believed that Jay was probably the juror who had made contact after the trial.

Beason admitted having spoken to Williams, one of the defendants, in the nearby café during the trial. Initially, he told the police that he had remarked to Williams, 'You've not got much to worry about, have you?' although, in his written statement, Beason changed this to, 'You're not doing so bad.' Either way, if this contact had been brought to the judge's attention, Beason would, at the least, have been severely rebuked.

Further inquiries revealed that the men sitting at the back of the court included Kateley's father and Israel Edelstein, alias 'Bayswater Issy,' a criminal; that Williams had allegedly approached Beason on the final morning of the trial; and that, after the trial, Beason had allegedly been paid by Isaac 'Ike' Andrews, another criminal.

On 9 February, the prosecuting counsel received another anonymous telephone call. The caller said, 'Williams is bragging about how he got Pat, one of the jurymen, squared up. This was in the bar at Walthamstow dog track.' Williams was a professional gambler who regularly attended Walthamstow.

When the second trial opened at the Old Bailey, on 16 February, the result of the police investigation was presented to the judge, Mr Justice Byrne. The police believed that associates of Kateley, Williams and Charles, people 'of a dangerous and unscrupulous type,' would again attempt to contact jurors. As a result, the defendants were refused bail and a policeman was allocated to each member of the jury, to escort them to and from the court.

On 17 March, the jury found all the defendants except Rook guilty. The four convicted men were given prison sentences ranging from nine months to three years. The evidence against Beason was not considered strong enough to justify prosecution, and the suggestion that he had been 'nobbled' remained an unproven suspicion.

The court that Steve Donoghue and Michael Beary were obliged to attend was a very different one: the bankruptcy court.

CHAMPIONS AT THE BOTTOM *Racing Post*, 23 July 2006

Kieren Fallon is familiar with courtrooms but it is hard to imagine the six times champion jockey appearing in a bankruptcy court. Can you imagine Frankie Dettori, or Pat Eddery, or Lester Piggott, bankrupt? Yet it once happened to a ten times champion Flat jockey, who was soon followed into the bankruptcy court by a rider who won the Derby, the Oaks, two St Legers, and trained a Two Thousand Guineas winner. The bankruptcy files for Steve Donoghue and Michael Beary now sit in the Board of Trade's archives.

During the years following World War I, Donoghue, gregarious, popular, impulsively generous, financially careless and clueless, dominated the championship, the Derby, and the racing public's affections. 'Come on, Steve' was the famous cry. Champion from 1914 to 1922, and joint-champion in 1923, Donoghue won 14 British Classics, including six Derbys, four of them between 1921 and 1925. He had wonderful hands, and a mastery of Epsom.

Yet when Manna won the 1925 Derby, Donoghue estimated that he was already almost £8,000 in debt. In 1928, the year before he won the first of six consecutive Queen Alexandra Stakes on Brown Jack, 23 creditors lodged proof of debts totalling over £36,000. Donoghue had assets of £590.

How could it have happened? Part of the answer was that Donoghue received the standard riding fee of just three guineas per mount, five guineas per winner. There were presents from owners, sometimes big presents, but they were dwarfed by the demands of Donoghue's reckless gambling, generosity, and carefree lifestyle.

Donoghue blamed his problems partly on the shoulder injury he sustained when Aquatinte II was brought down during the 1925 Grand Prix de Paris, and partly on the need, in about 1926, to pay the Inland Revenue between £6,000 and £7,000, but his problems pre-dated both.

Some of the biggest presents Donoghue received were from Jimmy White, a forceful speculator and deal-maker who owned Foxhill Stables in Wiltshire, where Gordon Richards was first apprenticed. Donoghue claimed that, from 1920, White promised to pay him an annual retainer of £6,000 but that all he received was £3,000 of shares in the Beecham Trust, of which White was chairman.

In 1923, while champion jockey, Donoghue made his first approach to moneylenders, who offered the usual extortionate terms. Donoghue agreed to pay £5,000 in return for an advance of £3,000, over £2,000 of which went to a friend. He paid the debt by borrowing from other moneylenders.

At about the same time, White told Donoghue that 'times were very bad with him,' reminded the jockey of past generosities, and persuaded Donoghue to sign a promissory note for £21,000, despite the fact that Donoghue claimed not to owe White anything.

Donoghue was also borrowing money on behalf of an unnamed lady, probably Lady Torrington, a close friend. In 1923, he provided the National Provincial Bank with a guarantee for £10,000, to cover the lady's overdraft, secured with two life insurance policies.

Two years later, he borrowed more money from moneylenders, and shared the proceeds with the anonymous lady. In 1928, Donoghue still owed almost £8,000 in respect of these borrowings. Donoghue's generosity didn't save Lady Torrington. She was also the subject of a receiving order and in 1931, depressed by financial worries, committed suicide.

White, his business empire collapsing after a disastrous speculation in British Controlled Oil Field shares, had killed himself four years earlier. When the Beecham Trust's solicitors sorted through his papers, they found the promissory note signed by Donoghue.

The official receiver concluded that Donoghue had contracted debts 'without having at the time of contracting them any reasonable or probable ground of expectation of being able to pay them.' During his examination in the High Court in January 1929, Donoghue, then 44, testified that, for the previous three years, he had been earning about £2,000 a year, considerably less than in his heyday, and far less than he was spending.

The Inland Revenue claimed over £9,000 and a list of creditors revealed debts to tailors and hatters, bootmakers and saddlers, in London and Newmarket. White's executors agreed to accept £250 in settlement of the £21,000 promissory note; the Inland Revenue reduced its claim to £1,040; and unsecured creditors were offered five shillings in the pound. Donoghue, bloodied but largely unbowed, rode on. So did Michael Beary.

Shortly after Donoghue's appearance in court, Beary won the 1929 St Leger on Trigo and was retained by the Aga Khan. In 1932, he won the Oaks on the Aga Khan's Udaipur and finished second on the same owner's Dastur in both the Derby and St Leger, again finishing second in the St Leger in 1933, on Felicitation.

The Aga Khan, who had recently moved his horses from Richard Dawson's yard to Frank Butters, did not retain Beary for the 1934 season, although it was agreed that he would make himself available when required. Beary blamed Butters, eight times champion trainer, for his downfall, and for the damage done to his reputation.

In a statement made during bankruptcy proceedings, in 1936, Beary claimed, 'Mr Butters resented my riding so many gallops and he resented my becoming so thoroughly acquainted with the merits of the Aga Khan's horses. I both wrote and saw the Aga Khan and told him what a slur this had been on my reputation and that the fact that I had not ridden for him caused owners to be suspicious of me and to think that I had done something dishonest. The Aga Khan replied that he had written to Butters to give me rides.'

On 16 June 1934, Butters gave Beary the ride on the Aga Khan's Sindhi in the Gatwick Foal Plate. Sindhi finished fourth of six, at 5-2 on, and Beary claimed that Butters had deliberately given him the ride on a rogue. George Lambton, a distinguished trainer, told him, 'that was a nice swine you rode yesterday. I saw four men trying to get him on the gallops, and when they got him on, he bolted off.' Beary omitted to say that he had ridden Sindhi twice previously, in April and May, unplaced, before Billy Nevett finished second on the two-year-old at Doncaster.

Beary claimed that, after Sindhi's defeat at Gatwick, he lost most of his Royal Ascot rides, and that his bloodstock activities were also affected. He appealed, unavailingly, to the Aga Khan and complained to the official receiver, 'On the severance of my connection with the Aga Khan it was quite impossible for me to get any rides in first-class races and almost impossible to get rides at all. I have been compelled to ride gallops and take such part as I could in smaller races. Owing to the stigma which had attached to my name in consequence of my treatment by Mr Butters, I found it extremely difficult to obtain purchasers or good prices for my stock and this caused a serious loss.'

Beary, who had been made bankrupt before, in 1924, actually had more rides in 1934 than in 1933, although his tally of winners fell from 41 to 32. He stated that, between 1934 and 1936, his expenditure exceeded his earnings, with the Inland Revenue his largest creditor.

His split with the Aga Khan and Frank Butters may well have cost Beary dear, since the combination won the 1935 Two Thousand Guineas and Derby with Bahram, ridden by Fred Fox, and the 1936 Derby with Mahmoud, ridden by Charlie Smirke.

Bankrupt that year, aged 40, Beary won the 1937 Derby on Mid-day Sun, trained by Fred Butters, Frank's brother, won the St Leger for a second time in 1949, on Ridge Wood; and started his training career with a flourish when winning the 1951 Two Thousand Guineas with Ki Ming. It wasn't enough to cure

Beary's chronic financial problems and when he died, in 1956, he was a poor man.

Those unearthed stories were all interesting, but the most fascinating, and revealing, was buried in a Board of Inland Revenue file, a file on the tax affairs of trainer Stanley Wootton.

THE £10 MILLION TRAINER *Racing Post*, 23 May 2006

Early in 1954, the tax inspector for the Epsom district sent a memorandum to Mr Barford, the chief inspector of taxes, seeking his advice. The district inspector wasn't sure what to do. Stanley Wootton, one of Epsom's leading trainers, enjoyed 'a substantial standard of living, but has paid no taxes during or since the war.'

Wootton was the Australian-born son of champion trainer Richard Wootton, and brother of champion jockey Frank Wootton. Stanley took over from his father at Treadwell House stables in 1919 and quickly established a reputation as a shrewd gambler and outstanding tutor of young jockeys, including Charlie Smirke, Staff Ingham and Frenchie Nicholson.

Wootton paid no taxes because, according to his tax returns, his training and farming businesses made heavy losses. Yet he was a wealthy man. The explanation was that, since 1940, Wootton claimed to have made £375,000 from betting. Winnings from betting were not liable for tax.

The sum of £375,000 is a lot of money today and was a considerable fortune in wartime and post-war Britain. According to the Office for National Statistics, it is the equivalent of £9.6 million today. Since Wootton's reputation as a big and successful punter extended back to the 1920s, when he bought Epsom's Walton Downs, and forward to the 1960s, his total winnings were almost certainly considerably greater.

The chief inspector was understandably sceptical. 'It is understood that Wootton has the reputation of betting on a grand scale,' he wrote. 'Even so, the suggestion that he acquired £375,000 profit by betting is extremely unusual.' Perhaps Wootton had exaggerated his betting profits to give credence to his claim to have made a loss on his training and farming activities.

The district inspector had already considered that possibility. 'I agree that it is difficult to believe that betting profits of the order of magnitude shown in Wootton's accounts are possible,' he replied. 'Enquiries regarding these winnings have been made from time to time and on the most recent occasion [1952] the accountants said that betting receipts and payments were recorded in detail and that 80 per cent of the receipts and 75 per cent of the payments were thoroughly vouched.'

Barford examined Wootton's accounts himself and was satisfied that there were no serious grounds for suspicion. He then decided to make enquiries in other tax districts where trainers operated. Local inspectors reported that Tom Masson, in Sussex, and Frank Cundell, in Berkshire, both 'live on betting profits.'

The cases of a dozen Newmarket trainers were reviewed, only three of whom, Jack Jarvis, Jack Watts and Jack Waugh, consistently made a profit from their training businesses. The district inspector remarked, 'it was common for trainers not to make profits although they were able to live sumptuously out of betting winnings.'

The inspector suggested why trainers were able to do so well from betting. He had been told, 'the race meetings at Yarmouth are run mainly by Newmarket trained horses and the results of the races are decided amongst the Newmarket trainers before the dates of the meetings.'

Barford consulted Mr Swift, in the enquiry branch of the Inland Revenue, who had experience of cases involving betting. Swift confirmed that 'trainers do bet regularly, and are generally very successful,' yet bookmakers were 'willing and even anxious to keep open losing accounts with trainers.'

Swift had no doubt of the reason. 'The bigger bookmakers are ready to pay trainers for information whether their horses are running to win or to lose,' he said. 'The bookmaker is particularly interested to know if a horse is not intended to win, in racing parlance is "running dead".'

Barford reached the conclusion that 'many trainers make more out of betting than they do out of training. We suspect that there may be a tacit conspiracy between trainers and bookmakers under which the latter contribute, in effect, to the profits of the former and indirectly receive, in return, valuable information through the medium of the bets.'

Wootton was merely 'an extreme instance of a practice which has become common for trainers of racehorses, to make losses in that trade and live tax-free on large betting winnings.' The Epsom trainer 'could be considered primarily as a successful backer who carries on training and farming as sidelines.'

The Epsom district inspector wanted to know whether or not they should attempt to tax Wootton's betting profits, since his punting was arguably an integral part of his business. Over 40 years earlier, in 1912, the same question had been raised in relation to Wootton's father, Richard, also a successful gambler.

On that occasion, it had been decided not to proceed and, after considering the implications of attempting to tax Wootton's betting profits, including the possibility that trainers and other gamblers would seek tax relief in respect of betting losses, it was decided to let the matter rest.

At the end of 1954 RJ Lloyd, a solicitor, advised, 'I doubt very much whether tax assessments raised on Wootton in respect of betting winnings could be defended successfully.' Wootton was free to carry on making a living as a professional punter who also trained and farmed.

15
GREAT EXPECTATIONS

Charles Dickens, racegoer.

The oldest Classic race in the world, the St Leger has long provided Doncaster with its most exciting, and rowdiest, event, as Charles Dickens and Wilkie Collins were to discover.

Dickens related his experiences in *The Lazy Tour of Two Idle Apprentices*, which appeared in instalments in *Household Words* in October 1857. On the 150th anniversary of his visit, Dickens' account and that of contemporary newspapers was a reminder of the meeting's huge popularity, its importance to the town, and the fact that there was then no racing on the Saturday of St Leger week!

CHARLES DICKENS AND WILKIE COLLINS AT THE ST LEGER

Racing Post, 11 September 2007

On the morning of Monday 14 September 1857, two men caught a train from Leeds to Doncaster. The younger of the two, Wilkie Collins, was limping. A few days earlier his companion, Charles Dickens, had insisted that they climb Carrock Fell, in the Lake District. Collins slipped on a wet stone and twisted his ankle. He had to be helped down the mountain, but Dickens was determined to continue their tour, and reach Doncaster, where he had already booked rooms at the Angel Hotel.

Monday marked the start of St Leger week, the week when, according to *The Doncaster Chronicle*, 'Doncaster is the beau ideal of a sporting town, when the tocsin sounds for its autumnal revelries.'

The four-day race meeting started the following day but racegoers were already pouring into Doncaster. Dickens reported that, during their train journey, 'no other business than race-business any longer existed on the face of the earth. The talk was all of horses and John Scott' – Yorkshire's champion trainer, who had already won the St Leger 13 times.

When they reached Doncaster station, barriers had been erected to control the crowds. Dickens wrote, '40 extra porters were sent down for this present blessed race-week, and all of them making up their betting books in the lamp-room or somewhere else. All work but race-work was at a standstill.'

The celebrated author wanted his visit to pass unnoticed, which was unlikely. Collins, aged 33, had not yet written the first of his successful novels, *The Woman in White*, but Dickens, a youthful 45, had already produced popular classics such as *The Pickwick Papers*, *Oliver Twist*, *Nicholas Nickleby*, *David Copperfield* and *Bleak House*.

As they made their way to the hotel, Dickens found the town likeable enough, but its occupants repellent. He noted, 'all the mob-lunatics out, crowding the pavements of the one main street of pretty and pleasant Doncaster, crowding the road, particularly crowding the outside of the betting rooms, whooping and shouting loudly after all passing vehicles. All degrees of men, from peers to paupers, betting incessantly.'

The evening brought no respite. 'Town lighted up,' Dickens recorded, 'more lunatics out than ever; a complete choke and stoppage of the thoroughfare outside the betting rooms. A vague echoing roar of "t'horses" and "t'races" always rising in the air, until midnight, at about which period it dies away in occasional drunken songs and straggling yells. Tuesday morning, at daybreak. A sudden rising, as it were out of the earth, of all the obscene creatures who sell "correct cards of the races".'

Every day, when Dickens looked out of his hotel window, he saw 'the lunatics, horse-mad, betting-mad, drunken-mad, vice-mad.'

They had come for the racing and the revelry. Dickens had not. He was determined to be in Doncaster during race-week but the attraction was not the racecourse and the horses but the theatre and the actresses, in particular, Nelly Ternan.

Earlier that year, Dickens and Collins had collaborated to produce a successful play, *The Frozen Deep*. In August, when the play moved to Manchester, the cast included several members of the Ternan family, including Nelly, aged 18. Dickens, whose marriage was breaking down, quickly became obsessed with her. Nelly Ternan was to be an important but secret part of Dickens' life until his death in 1870. When he learnt that Nelly had been booked to appear at the Theatre Royal in Doncaster, he made his plans accordingly.

On their first evening in the town, Dickens and Collins went to the theatre, for a performance which ended with a dance by girls dressed as jockeys. The writers were spotted by *The Doncaster, Nottingham, and Lincoln Gazette*, which reported, 'The distinguished author of the *Pickwick Papers* – his greatest work – was evidently the lion of the evening.'

There were other visits to the theatre but Wednesday was St Leger Day, and Dickens went racing, almost certainly in the company of Nelly and her family. *The Doncaster Chronicle* reported that a 'great stream of humanity began to pour into the town at an early hour. The arrivals from all parts of the country were incessant, completely blocking up the main thoroughfares of the town.' The *Gazette* added that, at the racecourse, 'The attendance was immense, never on any former occasion so great. As for the grandstand and enclosure, they were literally "crammed to suffocation." The demand for admission exceeded all anticipation, not a single ticket was left.'

The *Gazette* put this down partly to the attraction of Blink Bonny, who had already won both the Derby and Oaks, and was favourite to add the St Leger. 'So famous had Blink Bonny become in the minds of the racing community,' claimed the *Gazette*, 'that the deepest interest was manifested in all parts of the country, as well as in Ireland, Scotland and elsewhere, even to get a look at so extraordinary an animal.'

Despite the crowds, Dickens found the racecourse 'a most beautiful sight, with its agreeable prospect, its quaint Red House, its green grass and fresh heath.' He backed three winners but also fell into 'a dreadful state concerning a pair of little lilac gloves and a little bonnet that he saw there,' a reference to Nelly Ternan.

Blink Bonny, the 5-4 favourite, finished a well beaten fourth behind Imperieuse, 100/6 despite having won the One Thousand Guineas and being trained by the great John Scott. The *Gazette* noted, 'When at length No. 9 went up as the winner, a funereal stillness almost prevailed.'

Blink Bonny's jockey, John Charlton, was believed to have been paid to lose and, two days later, when Blink Bonny won the Park Hill Stakes, the *Gazette* reported that 'an attempt was made to mob Mr I'Anson [the owner] and Charlton, on account of the time being less for this race than for the St Leger.'

Dickens was at the racecourse and, presumably referring to the losing jockey in the St Leger, wrote that, after Friday's big race, there was 'a violent scuffling, and a rushing at the losing jockey, and an emergence of the said jockey from a swaying and menacing crowd, protected by friends, and looking the worse for wear.'

On Saturday, when there was no racing, Dickens walked to the course. 'It is quite deserted,' he wrote. 'Heaps of broken crockery and bottles are raised to its memory, and "correct cards" and other fragments of paper are blowing about it.'

The following day, Dickens took Nelly on a trip into the country and visited the ruins of Roche Abbey. On Monday, while Nelly returned to the theatre, Dickens and Collins caught the 11.00am train to London, their eventful experience of Doncaster race-week over.

16
COURT 12

Jane Glass, alias The Legal Blonde.

On 7 October 2007, Kieren Fallon won the Prix de l'Arc de Triomphe on Dylan Thomas. The following morning, he was in the dock at the Old Bailey, charged with conspiracy to defraud Betfair customers. The six times champion jockey would be there for two months, in company with fellow defendants Miles Rodgers, Darren Williams, Fergal Lynch, Shaun Lynch and Philip Sherkle.

There was a large legal cast, led by the judge, Mr Justice Forbes, with Jonathan Caplan QC, counsel for the prosecution; Peter Kelson QC, for Rodgers; James Sturman QC, for Williams; George Carter-Stephenson QC, for Fergal Lynch; Christopher Sallon QC, for Shaun Lynch; Michael Hubbard QC, for Sherkle and, the dominant presence, John Kelsey-Fry QC, representing Fallon. Not forgetting Jane Glass, Fallon's solicitor.

It may have been misery for some of the participants but I don't think I have ever enjoyed going to work more.

DAY ONE *Racing Post*, 9 October 2007

Dylan Thomas already seems a long time ago. It is now *War and Peace* (war mainly) in Court 12 at the Old Bailey. Kieren Fallon, Miles Rodgers and Philip Sherkle are here, sitting in the glass-fronted dock, but Darren Williams and the Lynch brothers, Fergal and Shaun, are not, yet.

There is no hurry. There are legal submissions to be submitted. Mr Justice Forbes has a round, avuncular face and spectacles. Hopefully, he also has enormous stamina. There are 26 lawyers in the well of the modern courtroom, and 23 seats available to members of the public in the gallery above, not all of them occupied. Maybe they haven't got back from Longchamp yet.

At 11.27am, the jury appears. They sit on two benches, each with three display screens. The screens are more impressive than at some racecourses. One lady, perhaps with ambitions to work for the Tote, is wearing a lime green and black outfit. The clerk of the court reads the charges and, at 11.30am, the judge thanks the jurors for their patience and forbearance. 'I propose to give you short breaks both morning and afternoon,' he says, 'so that the concentration required of you isn't going to be required over too extended a period.' True to his word, at 11.32am he announces a ten-minute break. I think this trial may take quite a long time.

On their return, the jurors are introduced to the barristers. Peter Kelson QC, for Rodgers, smiles affably, Christopher Sallon QC, for Shaun Lynch, half rises and bows, then, at last, Jonathan Caplan QC rises to open the case for the prosecution.

Caplan is not a man with strikingly distinctive features or mannerisms. He does not have a large boil on his cheek, nor an eyepatch. He does not seize the lapels of his gown fiercely and proclaim loudly. He does not appear to have modelled himself on Rumpole, also of the Bailey. No, Caplan does not even scratch his nose, although he may do so later. Medium height, grey hair beneath a greyish wig, white shirt and collar, black gown, Caplan is a straightforward, untheatrical speaker. He talks in a slow, measured way, as if guiding the jury slowly into the realms of advanced physics. 'Flat racing,' he explains, 'is where horses do not go over the jumps.' Counsel for the defence do not object.

Caplan introduces the court to the evidence, and to the defendants. We learn that Rodgers owns a pub in Penistone, south Yorkshire, called the Bridge Inn, and an Italian restaurant, called the Tiamo; that Sherkle is a barman who once worked in a furniture shop in Dublin, and met Fallon through the owner of a pub in Newmarket.

The prosecution alleges that the 27 races it proposes to examine, run between December 2002 and August 2004, were fixed, and that Rodgers used a dozen people's Betfair accounts to lay the horses to lose a total of £2.12 million. One QC is tapping away at his laptop. Maybe he is contributing to the Betfair forum. One juror is leaning on her elbows; 11 jurors are not. Maybe she is an independent thinker.

At 12.17pm, a barrister strides into court bearing a large brown envelope marked 'urgent.' This is more like it, like a proper court drama on television. Disappointingly, she sits down, along with the envelope, and says nothing.

Fallon rode in 17 of the 27 races, winning five of them, victories which Caplan maintains cost the conspirators about £440,000, which he was expected to 'work' off. The prosecution homes in on three races, as examples of the way in which the conspiracy operated, each jockey – Fallon, Williams and Fergal Lynch – featuring in each race. The jury has its first, doubtless of many, encounters with details of mobile telephone and text exchanges, of betting activity, of covert recordings and secretly taken photographs.

At 12.50pm, the judge asks the jury, 'How do you find the temperature in court?' 'Cold' is the reply. The judge assures them that action will be taken, with the result that, after lunch, he observes, 'The temperature is rather too warm now. We are rapidly reaching the point where I will invite the barristers to doff their wigs.' Fortunately, that point is not reached.

After lunch, the defendants are allowed to leave the dock. Fallon sits next to a blonde woman, while his fellow defendants sit next to rather older men. There are 16 people in the public gallery, some of them journalists. Everyone strains to listen to recordings of a series of telephone conversations involving Miles Rodgers. The words are often indistinct but, if you swear a lot, you would recognise many of them.

DAY EIGHT *Racing Post*, 18 October 2007

The case of Regina v Miles Rodgers et al has claimed its first victim. Christiana Hayward Kourabas, a member of the team representing Shaun Lynch, slipped in her bathroom and broke her leg. She has gained a pair of crutches and several titanium screws but temporarily lost the ability to walk. Every time the court rises, Kourabas tries to.

Mr Justice Forbes has had problems of his own, thanks to a signal failure in the Raynes Park area and, one way and another, the kick-off is delayed until after 11.00am. At 11.26am, Darryll Holland [a jockey] is called.

Sporting a shock of slick black hair and a turquoise tie, Holland stands with his hands in his pockets and offers testimony that highlights the perils of paying for something before it is delivered, in this case, a taxi. The taxi that didn't arrive.

The absence of the taxi and the presence of Miles Rodgers and his Mercedes in the Leicester racecourse car park ultimately combined to see Holland, Kieren Fallon and Seb Sanders given a lift by the recently warned-off Rodgers, although Holland didn't know that it was Rodgers and, judging from his testimony, the corpse in a hearse would have had more to say than they did during the short journey to the airfield.

The legal blonde has changed earrings. The big gold rings have been replaced by smaller, more discreet ones. Jane Glass's ears have stayed the same. The temperature is holding steady at 75 degrees Fahrenheit. The weather problems in Court 12 seem to be behind us, although serious legal problems remain.

Christopher Sallon QC, for Shaun Lynch, tries to address them by asking Holland how tall he is, a subject that featured prominently yesterday. Holland testifies, under oath, that he is 5ft 4in, Sanders 5ft 3in, and Fallon 5ft 4in. Neither Sallon, nor any of the other counsel, challenge this, which is disappointing.

George Carter-Stephenson QC, for Fergal Lynch, has briefly abandoned his yellow marker pen in favour of a rather nice fountain pen. I wonder if he uses Quink ink. I wonder if you can still get it. Soon, he reverts to the marker pen and, soon after that, Kate Bex, his junior, wields one of her own. I hope it isn't an infectious compulsion.

Holland leaves, and PC Richard King (short hair, dark suit, standing with his hands clasped in front of him) arrives. The blonde with the different earrings plucks a blue file from the library of files in front of the dock. Most are blue, a few are yellow; maybe, in time, some will be red.

King is detained for just six minutes, then replaced by PC Colin Gibbs (short hair, dark suit, standing with his hands clasped in front of him), who barely stays long enough for his mobile phone to go off. A forgotten lunchtime appointment, perhaps.

Nicholas Griffin, for the Crown, suddenly says, 'My lord, we are now going back in time.' For some reason, I suddenly think of Futalognkosaurus dukei, the enormous dinosaur they've just unearthed in Argentina, but that was 88 million years ago, and Griffin has a more modest journey (three years) in mind. Pity.

Gibbs lasts just nine minutes, and is replaced by Vanessa Benton, a receptionist at the Bedford Lodge Hotel in Newmarket. We learn that, in May 2004, bed and breakfast cost £90, with a £50 deposit needed to cover extras. Mr Southall, who wasn't really Mr Southall, and Mr Walker, who wasn't really Mr Walker, were booked into rooms 10 and 123. And then something remarkable happens. Michael Hubbard QC, representing Philip Sherkle, finally stands up. It is, he says, in a proper barrister's voice, 'my baptism.' At once, Hubbard's characterful face and distinctive mannerisms put us in the land of Charles Dickens, only to be cruelly plucked away by lunch. I do hope that isn't the end of Hubbard.

It is for the time being. After lunch, Peter Kelson QC rises, while Kate Bex reveals a surprising choice of reading material. There are all sorts of things in Court 12, except witnesses. 'To be frank,' Mr Justice Forbes tells the returning jury, 'had I not heard you outside the door I would not have troubled you to come in.'

At 2.21pm, the court rises. Shortly afterwards, so does Christiana Hayward Kourabas.

DAY EIGHTEEN *Racing Post*, 1 November 2007

'Your name is Ray Murrihy, correct?' 'Look, according to the circumstances. I'm not saying there aren't times when my name's Ray Murrihy, because there are. I'm not denying that, but ... ' Sorry, my mistake, Murrihy didn't say that. The chairman of New South Wales's stipendiary stewards did say a lot of other things, although the words 'yes' and 'no' were rarely among them.

Murrihy formed one half of a gladiatorial contest that lasted all day; the other half being John Kelsey-Fry QC, counsel for Kieren Fallon. It was a fascinating encounter.

Questions are a barrister's tools, carefully shaped and employed. The words form the cutting edge, their effectiveness dictated partly by their delivery. Like an actor, a barrister has a bag of techniques, changing form to meet the occasion, now encouraging, now disapproving, now genial, now sharp. Kelsey-Fry's bag is bulging, full of different tones and volumes, pauses and stares, eyebrows ready to be raised high, silent sighs poised for deployment, sadness and anger, pleasure and dismay.

He starts off briskly, questioning the appropriateness of a steward unfamiliar with British racing, its rules and culture, passing judgement on riding performances at British racecourses. Weren't British stewards better placed to make such judgements? 'I have some difficulty with that proposition,' says Murrihy, who, time will tell, has considerable difficulty with most of Kelsey-Fry's many propositions, as Kelsey-Fry has with most of Murrihy's many responses. In Court 12, agreement is like the giant panda, rarely to be found and in grave danger of disappearing altogether.

The cold that has plagued Kelsey-Fry has almost gone, which is fortunate, as throats are vital to barristers. If they aren't speaking through their own, they are gripping somebody else's. At last I've remembered who Murrihy reminds me of, Woody Allen, but without the jokes.

Kelsey-Fry reminds Murrihy of the case of Barking Mad, where Murrihy would have called a stewards' inquiry, despite Fallon having won the race. Murrihy objected to Fallon having repeatedly looked round and eased down, practices frowned on in Australia. Kelsey-Fry shows Murrihy three other winning rides where Fallon did the same, and asks if he would have called a stewards' inquiry. The range of possible answers appears to be limited but, several minutes later, progress towards a 'yes' or 'no' remains poor, provoking Kelsey-Fry to ask, 'Would you answer my question, Mr Murrihy, please?'

'So,' says Kelsey-Fry, a little later, returning to the situation in respect of Barking Mad under British rules, 'no stewards' inquiry?' 'I don't disagree with that proposition,' replies Murrihy. 'The answer's yes, then,' ventures Kelsey-Fry. 'Yes.' Kelsey-Fry reaches into his bag and plucks out a heavy sigh.

The court's two stenographers are diligently stenographying. The legal blonde has taken off her light jacket, but replaced it with a dark one. Murrihy relates that he has seen jockeys, in a desperate panic at the prospect of winning, restrain their mounts in the final few yards, or jump off. 'I've given them 12 months for it,' he says. 'That's 12 months' suspension, I take it,' says Mr Justice Forbes.

As a prelude to re-examining the case of Ballinger Ridge, Kelsey-Fry shows the court eight other races in which jockeys have been caught near the finish after easing down. In every case, they were subjected to the mandatory ban for breaching Rule 156, having been found guilty of monumental blunders, unintended.

Kelsey-Fry is wearing a tone of exasperation, of the type commonly used with uncooperative dissenters or members of your family. He asks Murrihy to imagine that Ballinger Ridge is the only horse in the world and that there are no others. It's an interesting thought, although I can't help thinking that it would pose serious problems for horseracing. Kelsey-Fry suggests that his client was guilty of a reprehensible, horrendous error of judgement and, since Fallon doesn't jump up and shout, 'No, I wasn't, you're fired,' we are left to assume that Fallon doesn't disagree with that proposition.

'That's unfortunate,' says Kelsey-Fry, soon afterwards. 'The five-furlong marker has just obliterated Mr Fallon.' We have moved on to the case of Doctor Hilary, at Ayr, and a lengthy debate about the meaning of 'covered,' later followed by another on the meaning of the flashing tail attached to Daring Aim. They can't agree on that, either. I suspect that Kelsey-Fry will be bringing his bag with him again tomorrow.

DAY NINETEEN *Racing Post*, 2 November 2007

Good news. William Hibbert, representing Philip Sherkle, has found his wig. Evidently another barrister had taken it, perhaps mistaking his own head for

Hibbert's. Hibbert still doesn't stand up, though, leaving that to John Kelsey-Fry QC, who resumes crossing words with Ray Murrihy.

For Murrihy, it must be like boxing ten rounds with Lennox Lewis, then being asked to step back into the ring for the same again. No wonder New South Wales's senior steward seems rattled, first confusing Krynica with Daring Aim, then getting in a muddle over racehorses' birthdays, then mistaking his right hand for his left. In comparison, Sydney must seem wonderfully inviting and an electric shock quite pleasant.

Murrihy and Kelsey-Fry quickly relapse into persistent disagreement. Kelsey-Fry suggests that, when Lost Soldier Three was stepped up in distance from one mile two furlongs to over one mile five furlongs, the step up was 'significant.' Murrihy disagrees, regarding it as merely 'a reasonable step up.' Evidence of exasperation makes an early appearance, as the ground for disagreement shifts to the stretch of turf neighbouring the inside rails at Newbury, where Murrihy contends that Kieren Fallon should have gone and Kelsey-Fry contends that he should not.

There is a brief outbreak of coughing (non-equine) in Court 12, where very little is black and white, apart from the legal blonde's rather fetching outfit. She is wearing small pearl earrings, while Kate Bex, for Fergal Lynch, is wearing long dangly ones. Bex is wearing a wig but soon, in civil cases, barristers won't wear them anymore, which is surely a mistake. That will give the impression that they are normal human beings.

At 12.10pm, Kelsey-Fry asks Murrihy what he meant when he said, in relation to evidence of unsatisfactory riding by Fallon on Goodwood Spirit, 'no, it's not strong.' Kelsey-Fry keeps asking, as Jeremy Paxman once did with Michael Howard, and Murrihy keeps replying but, as with Howard, we never do discover the answer. It's lucky Kelsey-Fry and Murrihy aren't married. It would be hopeless. 'Here are your cornflakes, dear.' 'No, they're not.'

Maybe it would help if counsel rotated. Tomorrow, Kelsey-Fry could represent the Crown, while Jonathan Caplan QC took over Fallon's defence. Just an idea.

Kelsey-Fry (still representing Fallon) observes that Murrihy 'opined,' a word that, along with rostral and laccolith, you very rarely hear. And then we reach Beauvrai, one of the horses Fallon won on but not in a manner satisfactory to Murrihy, who objects, in particular, to Fallon's tardy removal of the hood and consequent loss of several lengths at the start.

We learn that, in Australia, trainers must inform stewards in advance if there is a departure from the instructions usually given to the rider of a particular horse. If the same applied in the UK, the rule might have been relevant in Beauvrai's case since, according to Kelsey-Fry, the instructions given by trainer Vince Smith to Fallon began, 'miss the break.'

Murrihy roundly condemns this instruction as unacceptable and ridiculous and suggests that Fallon should have ignored it. 'He should rip the instructions up and ignore them?' Kelsey-Fry asks. 'It happens every day,' replies Murrihy. Kelsey-Fry delves into his bag and pulls out a look of utter astonishment. 'Are you saying that you would criticise the jockey for doing what he was told?' 'It is simply not appropriate to deliberately miss the start,' Murrihy replies.

Kelsey-Fry's jaw drops and his eyebrows rise. 'If Mr Fallon was given those instructions by the trainer, are you saying you would criticise Mr Fallon for following the trainer's instructions. Yes or no?' 'Yes,' replies Murrihy. Upon which reply, Kelsey-Fry informs the court that he has no further questions, and sits down.

It is a rule of British justice that someone must be standing in court at all times, in conformity with which James Sturman QC, for Darren Williams, promptly pops up. His wig is conspicuously white, and it is hard not to notice that he is holding a long piece of pink ribbon, which he proceeds to wind around two of his fingers, which should be all right as long as he doesn't need them to point with.

'My lord,' says Sturman, 'there are some bundles.' In the case of Regina v Miles Rodgers et al, there invariably are. Sturman begins by asking Murrihy questions that elicit the information that several City of London policemen visited him in Australia, went to Bondi beach, and got sunburn. If Murrihy is concise with his answers, there is a good chance he will catch a flight back to Australia this evening.

He's missed it.

DAY TWENTY-TWO *Racing Post*, 7 November 2007

The question countless journalists have asked over the years is finally answered. The way to get Sir Michael Stoute to stand still and answer questions is to put him in the witness box at the Old Bailey and subject him to a barrage of barristers. Unfortunately, this may not always be possible.

Stoute still remains mute on occasions, his silence tending to be interpreted as a 'yes.' Portly, with a mop of greying hair and something of Peter Butterworth (it's not my fault if you're too young to remember) about him, Stoute is prone to startle the court with an unexpected chuckle. He has a chuckle all his own, sudden and abrupt. Sometimes, the chuckle is at his own expense (of Dubai Venture, 'It certainly looked as if the trainer didn't do a very good job teaching him anything'), sometimes it seems to appear from nowhere, as if Stoute is engaged in a conversation of his own, and laughing at that.

We learn that he is more likely to be found at Newbury or Newmarket than at

Thirsk or Pontefract, that he doesn't like the whip used on young horses, that Krynica was a filly with a dreadful action, that he has a high opinion of Kieren Fallon's riding skills and that, at the slightest tracheal evidence of bleeding, he will work horses on Salix (or Lasix as it used to be called), as he did Russian Rhythm three days before she won the 2004 Juddmonte Lockinge Stakes. It makes you wonder how many horses set off up Newmarket's gallops each morning on Salix.

Earlier, Edward Alexander Leeper Dunlop had lounged in the witness box; tall, thin, fair hair, light blue jacket, shirt and tie, at a dandyish, even foppish angle. 'The key at Lingfield, as you all know, is to get cover,' he says.

Although I have every confidence in the jury, whose attentiveness through thick and thin (thin, mainly) does them credit, they may not yet be familiar with the riding tactics required when drawn high over one and a half miles at Lingfield.

Later, David Loder, bald at the front of his head but not at the back, slanders Bonecrusher, who is unable to defend himself from the charge of being 'thoroughly unreliable' and a 'non-trier' (the horse, not the rider).

'Thank you for coming,' says Jonathan Caplan QC, for the prosecution. 'Not at all,' says Loder.

Where Dunlop lounges, and Loder sits, Michael Bell stands straightbacked, military in bearing and in his responses, which are brisk and crisp. All four trainers declare themselves somewhere between happy and elated at the rides Fallon gave the horses under examination. 'A tremendous ride' (Russian Rhythm), 'beautiful horsemanship' (Krynica), 'a brilliant ride' (Daring Aim), 'a copybook ride' (Barking Mad).

The legal blonde has abandoned her gold earrings in favour of the smaller pearl ones. Who knows why? Neither the prosecution nor the defence ask her. Kate Bex, on behalf of Fergal Lynch, is reading a law book. She's up to page 1,273, so she will soon be halfway. Detective Constable Richard Gordon appears in the witness box.

'He is in the public bundle,' Michael Hick, for the prosecution, explains, after which Gordon is ignored completely, while Peter Kelson QC, for Miles Rodgers, plays some recordings, which he warns are 'very poor quality, with some really irritating crackling on them.'

He is right. They are; it is. It reminds me of an old 78rpm record my Uncle Norman used to have, with Gracie Fields singing a song called the Isle of Capri. 'T'was on the Isle of Capri that I found her, beneath the shade of an old apple tree, I can still see the flowers blooming round her, the day we met on the Isle of Capri.' That was full of crackles, too. You'd think recordings would be better now.

Then, without fanfare, we are introduced to the transcripts of two police interviews with Fallon, the first at Bury St Edmunds police station on the day of his arrest, 1 September 2004, and the second at Bishopsgate police station on 14 June 2006. Detective Constable Matthew Hussey plays the part of the police while, more difficult to imagine, Hick pretends to be Fallon.

Fallon tells the police that he has never been asked to lose a race, that it wouldn't be possible to fix one, and that his knowledge of the practice of stopping or pulling horses is drawn from Dick Francis novels.

Mr Justice Forbes smiles, in avuncular fashion, at the jury when they return from their afternoon break, to hear Hick resume his impersonation of Fallon. Hick continued, but he had more room than me.

DAY TWENTY-SEVEN *Racing Post*, 14 November 2007

Jim McGrath of Timeform. Just bear it in mind for later. Meanwhile, the ten occupants of the public gallery include a courting couple. It's an unusual choice of venue for a date.

11.47am. Breaking news. The legal blonde returns to Court 12 carrying a yellow file. For a while, that seems likely to be the highlight of the day.

The matter of the £2 million lingers on, as does Acting Detective Inspector Mark Manning's and Peter Kelson QC's inability to reach agreement on the subject. Manning does not dispute that he was mistaken in believing that the £2m referred to Miles Rodgers' profit from laying horses, as opposed to his potential liability, nor that Rodgers' actual profit was less than £300,000, but he strongly disputes Kelson's assertion that it was 'a deliberate misrepresentation, that Manning had deliberately deceived the Chief Constable of South Yorkshire,' and that we are in the land of 'lies.'

Manning stands with his hands on either side of the witness box, leans forward, and bends his head towards the microphone. When he has almost reached it, he dismisses Kelson's allegations as 'grossly unfair, wholly inaccurate.' I can't remember what happened when Mohammed wanted to meet the mountain but, if they had been in Court 12, neither of them would have budged.

Kelson finally abandons the £2m and moves on to the subject of a statement signed by Manning on 26 June 2007, relating to applications made for authorisation of covert surveillance, and a statement on the same subject signed by Detective Constable Mark Horsfall a few days earlier. Kelson, for Rodgers, wants to know why Manning travelled to Sheffield to collect Horsfall's statement, which was composed when Manning was, for part of the time, in the same room.

Later, George Carter-Stephenson QC, for Fergal Lynch, wants to know the same thing. Why didn't Manning ask Horsfall to send his statement by email, or fax, or post? 'I can give no explanation,' replies Manning, then gives one. 'Let's be fair,' he says. 'From time to time, it's nice to get a day out of the office.'

Kelson and Carter-Stephenson want to know why the wording of three objectives cited in both statements is identical. 'You are lying to the jury about how those three objectives came to be written,' Kelson suggests. 'You simply won't tell the truth about it.' Kelson believes that there was collusion; Manning insists that there was not.

Ian Winter QC, for Kieren Fallon, is studying *Archbold*, the legal bible. Surely it's a bit late to be trying to understand the law now. The legal blonde is fiddling with a marker pen. The girl who forms half of the couple in the gallery looks bored. If I were him, I'd try something else, a lecture at the Institute of Civil Engineering, perhaps.

Throughout the afternoon, in relation to the testimony of police officer Manning, Carter-Stephenson maintains a consistently high level of disapproval. He disapproves of Manning's treatment of the information contained in Annexe E to the Jockey Club's March 2004 submission, detailing the results of Rodgers' betting activities. He disapproves of Manning's failure to investigate the truth of Rodgers' explanation for having Fergal Lynch's bank details in his briefcase. Above all, he disapproves of Manning's evidence in relation to Jim McGrath, of Timeform.

It's a pity the couple in the gallery have left (I expect she told him she needed to get home to wash her hair) because everyone in Court 12 fortunate enough to have ears now has them pricked up. On 28 March 2006, Manning and three other police officers held a meeting with McGrath; a meeting Carter-Stephenson suggests 'wasn't a particularly pleasant meeting' and that Manning concedes was 'an uncomfortable meeting for Mr McGrath.'

Carter-Stephenson suggests that the unpleasantness stemmed from the fact that McGrath expressed opinions about the rides given to horses featuring on the list of 27 allegedly fixed races that differed from those held by Ray Murrihy, the Australian steward and prosecution's expert witness. The police did not ask for a copy of the notes McGrath had at the meeting, and the notes Manning took, which included some of McGrath's contrary views, were not disclosed to the defence until recently.

In a telephone conversation the day after the meeting, Manning told McGrath his statement should not include his opinion on race-rides. Repeatedly pressed to acknowledge that McGrath was an expert on such matters, Manning declined to do so, insisting, 'I don't know whether in the eyes of the law he is deemed to be an expert.'

Interesting, isn't it?

DAY TWENTY-EIGHT *Racing Post*, 15 November 2007

At the Old Bailey, traditions are respected. Do you remember when Wednesday was half-day closing? Today, Court 12 sits at 11.30am and rises at 12.45pm, which seems fair enough. When it's all over, I hope the barristers club together, buy a racehorse and call it Court 12. It can be ridden by ... well, that can be decided later.

If Acting Detective Inspector Mark Manning spends many more days in the witness box, he's going to run out of clothes. If he leans any closer to the microphone, and slips, he's going to swallow it. I don't know what the legal position would be then, or the medical one.

George Carter-Stephenson QC, representing Fergal Lynch, picks up where he left off, in conflict with Manning. He returns to the meeting between Jim McGrath, of Timeform, and four police officers, including Manning, on 28 March 2006. Carter-Stephenson asks Manning what frame of mind he thought McGrath was in after the meeting. 'Was Mr McGrath a happy man or an unhappy one?' 'I believe he was a happy man,' replies Manning.

It's so difficult to know with happiness, isn't it? Personally, I found *The Happiness Hypothesis* by Jonathan Haidt helpful, even though it turns out that more than 50 per cent of our level of happiness is genetically determined.

C-S (I'm getting fed up with typing it all out) and Manning engage in a lengthy rally about the exclusion from McGrath's statement of his opinions on the rides given to the 27 horses that are Court 12's raison d'être. C-S asks what the problem was with including them? 'I don't think Mr McGrath is able to give evidence about something not necessarily in his field of knowledge,' Manning replies. The rally continues, even though C-S maintains that 'it's as plain as a pikestaff' that the reason McGrath was told not to include those opinions was because they conflicted with the opinions held by Ray Murrihy, the prosecution's expert witness. (Sorry if this is reminiscent of yesterday. There's a reason for that.)

The legal blonde is wearing a rather fetching jacket with grey squares and black stripes. She is also wearing high-heeled boots, unlike Kieren Fallon, who is wearing something but, whatever it is, it doesn't look as good.

Many of Manning's answers are very similar to many of his other answers although, to be fair, so are many of C-S's questions. We learn, for example, several times, that Manning believes he has conducted the investigation in an open, honest and ethical way, a belief that C-S has yet to embrace.

The prospect of a Paul Scotney–Mark Manning combination at the BHA or, as Manning tends to say, 'association,' moves closer [Scotney is the BHA's director of integrity sevices]. Having testified that he has been offered a job by the BHA but not accepted it, Manning now adds that he 'may well' accept the post in the future.

Yippee! Michael Hubbard QC, for Philip Sherkle, gets to his Dickensian feet, creating difficulties for Manning in deciding which way to turn, Hubbard and Mr Justice Forbes being in opposite directions. 'Don't worry about me,' says Hubbard. 'I'm just stuck in the corner.'

Hubbard is somehow different, from an older finger of the legal body. Slim, tanned face, his slightly rasping voice promising the unexpected. 'Three and a half years in the office and you chose to go to Sheffield for the day out!' he exclaims, reminding Manning of his controversial trip to collect officer Mark Horsfall's statement. 'Had you not thought of anywhere else?'

Hubbard leans across a set of box files, clasps his hands, a thumb waving, and sets off on a line of inquiry. Just as I am wondering where it is leading, he sits down.

C-S has a logistical problem, caused by his need to be in two courts at once. The possibility that he might consider splitting himself down the middle, between Carter and Stephenson, briefly arises but becomes redundant when a consensus is reached, endorsed by Mr Justice Forbes, that, with various legal matters to be discussed, it would be best to adjourn until tomorrow.

DAY THIRTY-SEVEN *Racing Post*, 28 November 2007

Please let me die.

To get a flavour of the scene in Court 12, ask a friend to put a wig on while you stand in a box. Then get the friend to read every entry in the telephone directory, while you keep saying, 'That is correct.'

At the Old Bailey, your part is taken by Daniel Jenkinson, a civilian analyst working for the police, while your friend is played by Christopher Sallon QC, for Shaun Lynch. If Jenkinson says 'that is correct' many more times, he may not be able to stop. 'Would you like a poached egg for breakfast, dear?' 'That is correct.' 'With mushrooms?' 'That is correct.' 'Do you like me in these suspenders, darling?' 'That is correct.'

Sallon, followed by George Carter-Stephenson QC, for Fergal Lynch, wishes to make it clear that it was not only on racedays featuring 'suspect' races that there were frequent telephone contacts between their clients and others, including Miles Rodgers. There was a similar pattern of telephone activity on non-racedays and racedays when no suspect races were run.

Jenkinson confines his answers almost exclusively to the 'that is correct' formula, possibly because he is anxious to catch a plane to join his family at an undisclosed holiday destination. I expect that is why he is carrying a beach ball and wearing flippers (okay, I made that bit up). A compassionate agreement between the prosecution and defence allows Jenkinson to jet off while Carter-Stephenson, followed by James Sturman QC, for Darren Williams, manage without him. We have to imagine that Jenkinson is still there, saying 'that is correct.'

Once again, Sturman's wig does not seem to be in complete harmony with his head. He really must change one of them.

Sturman does not have a stud through his tongue, unlike one of the female occupants of Court 12. She has asked me not to reveal her secret, which is safe as long as she doesn't stick her tongue out. Christiana Hayward Kourabas's broken leg, for Shaun Lynch, continues to make progress. Her legs are now encased in fishnet stockings, although the effect is spoilt slightly by her socks and sandals. Kieren Fallon's tie collection continues to impress, though less than the legal blonde. Peter Kelson QC, for Rodgers, briefly sits in Jonathan Caplan QC's seat, for the prosecution. It's a bit late to be changing sides now, isn't it? *Archbold* would be proud to know how often he is consulted, although I can't help thinking that if Delia Smith resorted to Mrs Beeton as often as these barristers resort to *Archbold*, we might wonder how much she really knows about cheese scones.

Carter-Stephenson leads us through another telephone schedule. It goes to show what different lives we lead. On the day in question, Fergal Lynch's phone was forever ringing. If it had been me, C-S would have said, 'We have a call at 10.30am. It was a wrong number.' 'That is correct.' 'And another call at 3.45pm, from the You Want A New Kitchen Company.' 'That is correct.'

Acting Detective Inspector Mark Manning is like a rubber duck in a bath. You push him down but he pops back up in the witness box again. Old ground is re-covered; Manning's trip to Sheffield, the £2 million tag placed on Rodgers' alleged fraud. Do you remember the Memory Man in *The 39 Steps*? He had the same initials as Manning but there the similarity ends.

C-S invites the jury to go behind tab three in the blue file although, to be honest, it was more exciting behind the bicycle shed. C-S reads out a lot of boring things, then reads out a lot more. The schedule he is dealing with does have some quite nice colours in it – yellow, green, red – which reminds me of the raspberry jam we used to put on the rice pudding at school. I keep telling myself, it's a lot worse in Baghdad.

Kelson accuses Manning of having deliberately lied. Manning denies lying, and invites us to join him on a shopping expedition to Sainsbury's, where his wife has sent him to get three things. He returns home with only two. Manning doesn't say what happened after that.

At 3.26pm, a barrister yawns. Another barrister appears to be asleep. Maybe they stayed up to watch the Steelers play the Dolphins. Peter Pimm, for Rodgers, stands up for the first time, his spectacles worn in the legal fashion, well down his nose. The proceedings continue but I honestly don't recall a thing. I'm beginning to feel like a witness.

FINAL DAY *Racing Post*, 8 December 2007

Do you remember those tokens they used to have on packets of cereals? When you'd collected four, you sent them to Kellogg's and they sent you a plastic submarine. You put bicarbonate of soda in it and put it in the bath, and it went up and down. When I was eight, it was fantastically exciting. That's what they should have done in Court 12. Every day you attended, you'd get a token (double tokens on deadly dull days) and, today, only those with at least 12 tokens would be allowed in for the exciting bit.

They haven't been issuing tokens, or submarines, and Court 12 is packed. The chatty intimacy has gone. There are unfamiliar faces. Everyone knows that today is the day. Those of us who have been here every day know the case is going to be thrown out; we think we know.

Kieren Fallon, as usual, is dressed in a smart suit and tie, a blue one, with spots. The legal blonde, sitting next to him, is wearing a black jacket, black skirt, black boots and white pearl earrings. Mr Justice Forbes, without any preliminaries, launches himself into his ruling. Will he accept the defence submissions, made at the close of the prosecution case, that there is no case to answer?

Speaking uncharacteristically quickly, the judge refers to the six strands that make up the prosecution's largely circumstantial case. On the prosecution's own admission, the strand composed of Ray Murrihy's expert evidence is crucial; if that strand snaps, the entire rope breaks. The allegation that Fallon, Fergal Lynch and Darren Williams were party to a race-fixing conspiracy can only be sustained if Murrihy's evidence is strong enough to sustain it.

Kate Bex, Fergal Lynch's junior counsel, is studying a map of the world. Perhaps she has worked out the financial merits of the case of Regina v Miles Rodgers et al, and decided that the Seychelles look particularly appealing, provided John Kelsey-Fry QC, Fallon's counsel, has not already bought them.

Murrihy's witness statement and written reports suggested he had expertise in the UK's rules of racing and that, in the 13 races over which he would have called a stewards' inquiry, there was a prima facie case that Rule 157, relating to intentionally not riding a horse on its merits, had been breached. But, in the witness box, Murrihy made no such claims. Instead, he made what the judge described as 'an extraordinary admission, tantamount to disqualifying himself as an expert witness,' namely, 'I have not said that I am an expert in UK racing.'

Furthermore, when Murrihy criticised the jockeys' rides, he was merely making an initial observation, with Australian rules in mind, that might lead to further investigation, which might or might not lead to a jockey being charged with a breach of the rules. 'It is abundantly clear,' says the judge, 'that his evidence fell far, far short of establishing a prima facie case for a breach of Rule 157 in any race.' Very little, if any, weight could be attached to Murrihy's evidence.

The result is clear, yet the tension remains. Fallon, chewing a mint, is bent forward, his hands on his knees, his legs crossed, one leg swinging. Bex is now studying a map of south-east England. Maybe she has decided to go to Eastbourne, instead. Evidently she rides a moped, evidently George Carter-Stephenson QC rides a Harley-Davidson. Tomorrow, I expect he will be riding two. Christiana Hayward Kourabas's broken leg, for Shaun Lynch, is almost walking again.

Mr Justice Forbes rules that the defence submissions of no case to answer 'must succeed.' A ripple of whispers runs around the court; the jury is called in. 'Let me explain what has happened,' Mr Justice Forbes says to them, in his kindly, avuncular manner. 'It is my duty to direct you to return verdicts of not guilty on all counts.' Then he explains why, and the tension leaks out of Court 12.

At 12.25pm, the defendants are told to stand. It is curious watching the six of them. The foreman of the jury, a grey-haired, bespectacled lady, also stands, while the court clerk asks for the jury's verdicts, on each defendant in turn. 'The defendants are discharged,' declares the judge. Then, rather movingly and fittingly, for their attentiveness has been commendable, Mr Justice Forbes pays tribute to the jury's care and patience. The legal blonde hugs Fallon.

'Very well,' says Mr Justice Forbes, 'I think that concludes the proceedings.' Forgive me, but I'll rather miss them.

The following day, Kieren Fallon's snakes-and-ladders life slid downwards again, as it emerged that he had failed a drugs test in France for a second time, and faced a worldwide 18-month ban.

17
THE DERBY

Emily Davison – 'Deeds not Words'.

The race closest to the heart of British Flat racing, the Derby is a thick story-book, its tales written on Epsom's unique, idiosyncratic stage. Every Derby has a special meaning, enlarged by the race's prestige and long, rich history, full of evocative names, of horses and riders, trainers and owners, memories of gripping moments, of triumph and despair.

More than any other race, the Derby is both an end and a beginning, the climax of an annual search stretching back to the juvenile promise and partial clues of the previous season, and forward to the fresh challenge faced by every

Derby winner, of confirming his status in competition with older horses. A Derby winner's name conjures up memories of the race itself but also of what the horse had been, and what it became.

My selection of Derby favourites was not based purely on racing ability, although all were exceptional racehorses, but on what they meant to me.

MY SIX FAVOURITE DERBY WINNERS Racing Post, 31 May to 5 June 2010

1968 Sir Ivor

My first Derby, and first trip to Epsom, on a schoolfriend's scooter. Everything was new, fascinating, strange, absorbing, exciting. Here, in the flesh, were names previously seen only in the pages of *The Sporting Life*, while on the crowded Downs there were dubious Gypsy Rose Lees and equally dubious bookmakers.

My enthusiasm wasn't matched by my knowledge of the runners but, like everyone else, I knew that Lester Piggott was riding Sir Ivor, that Sir Ivor was trained by Vincent O'Brien, and that he was the favourite, wearing Raymond Guest's chocolate and pale blue colours. Guest, the US ambassador to Ireland, had backed Sir Ivor at 500-1. I had £2 on Sir Ivor, at evens. It was enough to make me long for him to win.

We couldn't see the race, not really, however much we stood on our toes and darted to small, brief gaps between the deep, jostling rows of bodies and binoculars, heads and hats. We snatched glimpses of the horses, like frames from an old film, and words from a distant commentary, and tried to make sense of the crowd's responding shouts.

As they raced down the straight, there was Connaught and Sandy Barclay, and a stomach-sinking gap behind. Where was Sir Ivor? Where was Lester Piggott and the chocolate and pale blue hoops? It was too late, anyway, Connaught, galloping on strongly, was too far ahead, the winning post too near. Suddenly, the crowd roared, and there was Piggott's already familiar, demanding body, urging Sir Ivor forward. A flash of hope, answered by the realisation that the gap was still too large, there was still too much to do, and then Sir Ivor producing an amazing turn of foot that, impossibly, easily, raced him past Connaught, and Piggott relaxing to show that he knew all along. That it was no surprise, to him.

I followed Sir Ivor after that, beyond his defeat by Vaguely Noble in the Arc, and on to his final, transatlantic triumph in the Washington DC International at Laurel Park but it was the Derby that mattered, Sir Ivor's Derby. That's what I remember. Everybody there did.

1971 Mill Reef

The perfect racehorse, of two, in a unique year blessed with both Mill Reef and Brigadier Gerard. I went to Newmarket for the Two Thousand Guineas, to watch the anticipated duel between Mill Reef, the good little one, and My Swallow, the good big one, and saw Brigadier Gerard emerge, to scythe them down, instead.

Mill Reef had been extraordinary as a two-year-old, in a different world from his opponents in the Coventry Stakes, the Gimcrack, the Dewhurst but, after the Two Thousand Guineas, Ian Balding's champion was not immune from the questions annually asked of lesser Classic contenders. Was Mill Reef as good at three as he had been at two? Would he stay one and a half miles? As so often, the Derby provided the answers, and set the scene for the rest of Mill Reef's wonderful career.

There was always something special about owner Paul Mellon's black and gold colours, and the sheepskin nosebands that invariably accompanied them. They came into their own on Mill Reef.

There were 21 runners that year but, if it was a concern, it didn't show. Mill Reef wasn't a big horse but a compact one, who moved perfectly. Geoff Lewis coasted along handily on him, cruised towards the pace-setting Linden Tree, winner of the Observer Gold Cup and Chester Vase, then quickened to take the lead, and take the Derby. It was straightforward, and amazing. As Balding said, 'Horses that win races like he did as two-year-olds don't go on to be one-and-a-half-mile horses, and win the Derby. That was the phenomenon. The further he went, the faster he went. It was quite extraordinary.'

The question soon became, and would long remain, would Mill Reef and Brigadier Gerard meet again and, if they did, which of them would win? While speculation and debate fuelled anticipation, each went their separate, mighty ways, Brigadier Gerard outstanding at one mile, Mill Reef at middle distances.

Mill Reef's Derby became the trigger for memories of what lay ahead that season, trouncing the older Caro in the Eclipse, winning the King George by six lengths and, a fitting climax, adding the Arc, in course record time. No one from that era forgets Mill Reef.

1981 Shergar

The Derby creates lasting images, captured in Epsom's unique frame. Few compare with the image of Shergar, deep-girthed, athletic, his big white blaze unmistakably proclaiming his name as he drew imperiously clear of his rivals, with Walter Swinburn, just 19 years old, perched happily on top in the Aga Khan's famous green silks with red epaulets. It was a moment to savour.

There was not the grip of uncertainty that often fills the Derby's final furlong but there was space and time simply to admire, for Shergar could be named the winner from as far away as the naked eye could see, always well placed, always moving easily, quickly asserting his authority. 'He pulled me to the front,' Swinburn related, 'and just got stronger as the race went on. I could feel him building underneath me. He was the complete racehorse. Nothing I have ridden ever came close to him.' The winning distance was ten lengths, a record for the Derby, and could have been more if Swinburn had desired for, as with Eclipse, it was a case of Shergar first and the rest nowhere.

Only the extent of his superiority was a slight surprise, for Shergar, exceptional in his homework for Michael Stoute, had already won Sandown's Classic Trial by ten lengths and the Chester Vase by 12, scuttling his quick, short-strided way to odds-on favouritism for Epsom. Although the Derby field was weak, Shergar's victory confirmed that everything said of him was true; he was, truly, a marvel. Stoute, winning the Derby for the first time, later reflected, 'On Derby Day, Shergar was very special. He was so dynamic. I haven't had a middle-distance machine like him.'

Having duly won the Irish Derby and beaten older rivals in the King George, when Shergar ran disappointingly in the St Leger, the Arc was ruled out, but thoughts quickly, happily reverted to earlier triumphs. Those could not be washed away.

The Derby offers a lasting image of Shergar but, uniquely, there was to be another, an image, not recorded on camera but imagined by many horsemen and racefans, of Shergar, 20 months later, being kidnapped from Ballymany Stud, to an uncertain but bloody end. One glorious image, one infamous one.

1989 Nashwan

There is always the engaging question of what will win but, sometimes, there is also the nervous anticipation of greatness. Nashwan approached the Derby already firmly entrenched in racing's thoughts. A striking chestnut with one white ankle and a fluent, raking stride, veering between athleticism and leanness, it was enough that the unbeaten colt had won the Two Thousand Guineas in brilliant style but there were other elements to Nashwan's picture.

There was the tale, quickly part of racing's folklore, of the spring day when Willie Carson partnered Nashwan in a gallop with Misbah, a decent four-year-old ridden by the experienced Brian Procter. Procter watched in disbelieving awe as Nashwan disappeared into the distance, while other watchers hurried to back him for the Guineas, from 33-1 to 3-1 favourite.

Then there was the position of trainer Major Dick Hern, a distant figure to the racing public yet fondly regarded and respected, confined to a wheelchair since a hunting accident five years earlier, who had undergone heart surgery in 1988 and promptly been informed by the Earl of Carnarvon, the Queen's racing manager, that his services were no longer required. Sheikh Hamdan stepped in with a new stable, and with Nashwan. The roar that erupted when Hern welcomed Nashwan into the winner's enclosure after his Guineas success was a very public expression of opinion about the trainer's shabby treatment. Carson, a public favourite, now 46, shared the celebration, and the Derby rounded it all off.

It was not a strong Derby field but Nashwan, the 5-4 favourite, had style and speed and opened up with his long, smooth stride to dismiss his only serious market rival, Cacoethes, winner of the Lingfield Derby Trial, leaving Terimon, at 500-1, to be closest at the finish, five lengths behind. An acknowledged star, and a crowd pleaser, Nashwan won the Eclipse Stakes and King George but a lot was asked of him in the Eclipse, and it showed at Ascot, where Nashwan struggled to fight off Cacoethes. After a disappointing run in the Prix Niel, Nashwan was retired. It didn't alter the impression he made on Derby Day, and before and after it. On his great days, Nashwan was king.

1995 Lammtarra

There is the race, and there is the story behind it. Lammtarra's race and story were both remarkable.

By a Derby winner, Nijinsky, out of an Oaks winner, Snow Bride, Lammtarra had won his only race as a two-year-old, when trained by Alex Scott, who promptly had £1,000 on him at 33-1 for the Derby. Less than two months later, Scott was murdered by a disaffected former employee and Lammtarra was sent to Dubai, to join the new Godolphin and its even newer trainer, Saeed bin Suroor.

In January, Lammtarra had a fever; in February, he became the first inmate of Dubai's new equine hospital. Lammtarra slowly recovered but did not do his first serious piece of work, at Al Quoz, until 11 April, under Sheikh Mohammed's personal supervision, for Lammtarra was the apple of Sheikh Mohammed's eye.

Godolphin, which would race just 23 horses in Britain in 1995, when almost 200 carried Sheikh Mohammed's maroon and white colours, was still a puzzle to British racefans, compounded by the fact that Godolphin's subsequently familiar royal blue colours were not yet carried by every horse. Lammtarra bore the green and white colours of Sheikh Saeed Maktoum Al Maktoum, Sheikh Maktoum's son.

Lammtarra went into the Derby having raced only once in his life, and with a rushed preparation. He was 14-1, with Sheikh Mohammed's Pennekamp, the Two Thousand Guineas winner, the 11-8 favourite and Tamure, also owned by Sheikh Mohammed, 9-1. Leaving the starting stalls, Lammtarra lost a shoe. As they raced up the hill, he was bumped, then trapped on the rail. When the leaders set sail up the straight, Walter Swinburn switched towards the outside and, once balanced, Lammtarra started to make ground but, two furlongs out, he was still hopelessly adrift, with seemingly no chance of being involved in the finish. Then Lammtarra flew; extraordinary.

Lammtarra beat the course record set by Bustino in the Coronation Cup 20 years earlier, and was the first horse since Grand Parade in 1919 to have won a 20th-century Derby on his seasonal reappearance.

Sheikh Mohammed, his Tamure second, was delighted. A Godolphin horse, trained in Dubai, had won the Derby.

Raced just twice more, Lammtarra won the King George and the Arc, the first horse to complete the treble since Mill Reef in 1971. In both races, he needed, and showed, great battling qualities.

2009 Sea The Stars

We are always looking for a champion to follow, to hold our breath for, to cheer on, to celebrate. When Sea The Stars came along, it was as if we only truly appreciated his greatness towards the end of his racing career, and then tried to make up for it with paeans of praise.

Asked to nominate the highlight of the year, trainer John Oxx replied, 'The Derby is the Derby.' That said more about the thrill and importance of winning the Derby than about the merit of his champion's performance in it, for his Epsom triumph was not the pinnacle of Sea The Stars' career but a stepping stone to greatness, appreciated more in hindsight.

Sea The Stars had not been expected to win the Two Thousand Guineas, if the betting was to be believed, and when he did, his pedigree, by Cape Cross out of Urban Sea, the 1993 Arc winner, sent inconclusive signals. It made him a half-brother to Galileo, the 2001 Derby winner, but Galileo was by Sadler's Wells whereas Sea The Stars was by Cape Cross, whose progeny generally stayed less well.

Aidan O'Brien, who trained half the Derby field, seemed certain to arrange a pace to suit the more stoutly bred Fame And Glory, the favourite, and test Sea The Stars' stamina, yet it took a while for the pace to pick up, which was likely to suit stablemate Rip Van Winkle more than Fame And Glory. Pulling a bit early on but always well placed and travelling strongly, Sea The Stars quickened to take the lead from the tiring Golden Sword a furlong out and won looking as if there was more in reserve if required, a feature of Sea The Stars' performances. He was dominant without being spectacular, which was partly why the acclaim took time to grow.

Sea The Stars was the first Two Thousand Guineas winner since Nashwan, 20 years earlier, to complete the Guineas–Derby double, and there would be other record book entries to come, including being the only horse to win the Two Thousand Guineas, Derby and Arc, for the Derby formed part of a greater whole, which also embraced the Eclipse and Juddmonte International. If Sea The Stars did not put a foot wrong, neither did Oxx, whose management of a great champion was impeccable. Perfection is elusive in racing; Sea The Stars rubbed shoulders with it.

Long before Sir Ivor, the Derby already boasted a long list of dramatic incidents. None matched that of the 1913 Derby, when the story of Emily Davison was planted, one foot in the history of the Derby, the other in that of the suffragette movement. For all the incident's familiarity, I discovered that there was more light to be cast on the shocking occasion, hidden away in the archives.

THE TRUE STORY OF EMILY DAVISON AND THE 1913
DERBY *Racing Post*, 25 May 2006

Emily Davison was a militant suffragette who committed suicide by throwing herself under the King's horse in the 1913 Derby. That is the story that has passed into Derby history but the truth is less straightforward, with its own small mysteries.

Emily Wilding Davison was certainly a militant suffragette, prepared to sacrifice her life for a cause she believed in with a fierce, consuming passion, but suicide was not Davison's intention when she slipped beneath the rails at Tattenham Corner.

She was 40 years old, a graduate of London University who joined the Women's Social and Political Union in 1906 and, three years later, abandoned her teaching career to devote herself fully to the campaign for votes for women, and women's rights. The WSPU, led by Emmeline Pankhurst, believed that direct action was the only way to make the Liberal government address the issue of women's suffrage. When suffragettes disrupted political meetings and threw stones through the windows of government buildings, Davison was an enthusiastic participant. With many others, she began a round of repeated imprisonment, hunger strikes, and force feeding, which was very painful.

In 1911, Davison refused to complete a census form, declaring, 'As I am a woman and women do not count in the State, I refuse to be counted.' Later that year, she soaked a piece of cloth in paraffin, lit it, and pushed it into a pillar box, an initiative soon followed by other suffragettes.

Sent to Holloway prison for six months, Davison threw herself down a stairwell in protest at the treatment of fellow prisoners, many of whom were repeatedly force fed, even if they were not on hunger strike. In 1913, the government passed an Act nicknamed 'The Cat and Mouse Act,' under which suffragettes who went on hunger strike were released from prison then, after recovering, rearrested, to face more force feeding.

Davison felt a burning sense of injustice, not only at the denial of political and social rights for women but also at the treatment of fellow suffragettes. The WSPU's leaders regarded her as dangerously independent and unpredictable and, when she caught a train from Victoria station to Epsom on Wednesday 4 June 1913, it was without their knowledge or approval.

That morning, Davison called in at the WSPU's headquarters and borrowed two flags in the organisation's colours, purple, white and green. She bought a return train ticket and, at Epsom, on a bright if cloudy day, joined the huge crowds gathered on the Downs. King George V and Queen Mary also travelled to Epsom by train, and then by carriage.

Newsreels were an exciting recent development, and Topical Budget, Pathe Gazette, and Gaumont Graphic all had their cameras rolling. Later, Gaumont Graphic claimed that it 'alone secured the thrilling incident at Tattenham Corner, resulting in the death of Miss Davison.' That was not true but their newsreel, which I have studied at the British Film Institute, provided the clearest, if still indistinct, pictures of the tragedy.

In the National Archives, at Kew, there is a Metropolitan Police file on the incident. A report written the day after the Derby states, 'in consequence of a telegram sent to the Jockey Club, intimating that suffragettes would make an attempt to interfere with the race by placing nails on the course, the whole of the police on duty were instructed to keep a sharp look-out.'

Fifty policemen were spread along the course, among them, at Tattenham Corner, Sergeant Frank Bunn and Constable Samuel Eady. The crowds were dense, pressed against the rails, as the field of 15, led by Aboyeur, rounded the turn and came into view. The first nine horses were fairly well bunched. There was then a gap. It was into that gap that Emily Davison stepped.

With the horses coming into view so suddenly, and moving so fast, and with no racecourse commentary, it is hard to believe that Davison could have singled out one horse, the King's horse, Anmer. *The Times* reported, 'The general impression of those who saw the incident at close quarters seemed to be that the woman had seized hold of the first horse she could reach, which happened to be the King's. That the horse was the King's was doubtless an accident.'

At the inquest into Davison's death, held at Epsom Crown Court on 10 June, eye-witnesses gave conflicting accounts of whether or not she had deliberately targeted the King's horse. Gilbert White, the coroner, expressed the opinion that she had not done so.

Perhaps not, but Davison would have seen Anmer, either when he led the parade or on his way to the start, with jockey Herbert Jones wearing the King's purple, scarlet and gold colours. After she stepped onto the track, the first horse to reach her was Agadir, ridden by Walter Earl. Earl told *The Daily Telegraph*'s reporter, 'she dashed right under the head of Agadir with her eyes fixed on Anmer.'

Earl may have seen her eyes fixed on a spot behind him but he could not have known where they were fixed; Anmer was three horses back. The newsreel confirms that Davison deliberately avoided Agadir and the next two horses, after which there was another gap to Anmer, and two stragglers. It is impossible to be certain that she knew the horse's identity but, whether she did or not, that was the horse Davison deliberately stood in front of.

Witnesses said that her arms were raised, and some reports state that she was holding a flag, with another wrapped around her waist. The evidence of the newsreel is inconclusive, which is unfortunate, because Davison took the suffragette flags to Epsom for a purpose, and a possible purpose was to attach one to the King's horse, and wave the other.

Most accounts suggest that, when Davison walked onto the track, she was either holding a tightly furled flag, or about to produce one from her coat sleeve. Yet the reports by Sergeant Bunn and Constable Eady, who saw the incident, both refer to her arms being raised but make no mention of a flag. Crucially, Bunn's report, written on Derby Day, states, 'On her jacket being removed I found two suffragette flags, one and a half yards long by three-quarters of a yard wide, each consisting of green, white and purple stripes, folded up and pinned to the back of her jacket on the inside.'

A week later, police inspector G. Whitebread reported, 'The suffragette colours were not tied round the woman's waist but were pinned to the inside of her jacket, apparently to act as a pad for her back. The flags were completely hidden in the back of her jacket. The flags were not seen until the woman's jacket was removed at the Cottage Hospital. No one in the vicinity had any idea that the woman was a militant suffragette until the flags were found.' The following day, Bunn and Eady produced further reports supporting this statement.

The police may have been anxious to avoid any suggestion that they did not react quickly enough to a suffragette with a flag but Bunn's account of finding the flags was written at the time and rings true, and Whitebread's later statement was written the day after the inquest, at which there was no criticism of the police. It would have been surprising if there had been, since Davison acted so quickly.

Did Davison expect to die, and made sure that the insignia of her cause would be found? Or was she hoping to stop the King's horse, however doomed the attempt, and then recover the flags, and display them? If she intended suicide, would she have attempted to catch hold of the horse's reins?

She snatched at the reins and was violently bowled over, while Anmer crashed to the ground, sliding on his side, with Jones propelled to the turf. Davison's hat rolled away, the horse stood up, the bodies lay dreadfully still.

Then the crowds rushed onto the track. Jones, unconscious, was attended by Dr Percy John Spencer, later joined by Dr Coulthard, the racecourse surgeon. Jones was suffering from 'abrasions of the left side of the face, over the left eye and shoulder, contusion of the left elbow joint and shock.' He recovered sufficiently to be taken back to the grandstand in a police ambulance and spent the night in a London hotel before returning to Newmarket the next day.

Davison was also unconscious. Writing that evening, Dr Jasper Vale-Lane proudly recalled, 'I was the first to render medical assistance to the woman. I took charge of the case. I found her suffering from concussion of the brain and heart failure and her life ebbing fast.'

When whisky failed to revive her, Vale-Lane requisitioned a thermos flask of hot tea, poured it onto a handkerchief, 'and applied it to the left wrist. The second application had the desired effect by restoring the heart action.' A Mr Faber of the Manor House, Ewell, offered his car to move Davison to Epsom Cottage Hospital, with some of the crowd jeering as she was taken away.

When Sergeant Bunn emptied Davison's pockets, the contents included the return half of a railway ticket, a helper's pass for that day's WSPU summer festival in Kensington, a racecard – 'Dorling's List of Epsom Races,' including two selling races – and a handkerchief bearing Davison's name, which was how she was identified.

Two of Davison's closest friends and fellow campaigners, Mary Leigh and Rose Lamartine Yates, were among those who visited the hospital but refused to give their names. They draped WSPU flags over the bed and screen.

On 6 June some newspapers, including *The Times* and *Daily Express*, reported that Davison had recovered consciousness and taken some nourishment but they were mistaken. That day, Charles Mansell-Moullin, a London surgeon who was a member of the Men's League for Women's Suffrage, operated to relieve the pressure on Davison's brain but she died on Sunday 8 June, never having regained consciousness.

The inquest delivered a verdict of death by misadventure, her death certificate stating that Davison died from a 'fracture of the base of the skull caused by being accidentally knocked down by a horse through wilfully rushing on to the racecourse at Epsom Downs.'

It seems likely that Davison's intention was not to commit suicide but to stop the King's horse and display the suffragette flag, as a dramatic way of sending a message to the King, and his government. She knew that she might die in the attempt and, if necessary, she was prepared to die.

It was the reckless act of an extremist and was widely condemned. According to *The Times*, Davison's action stirred 'an intense indignation among those who saw it,' and the public were 'gradually coming to the conclusion that many of the militant suffragists are not altogether responsible for their acts.'

The Daily Telegraph described it as 'a daring and dastardly suffragist outrage, a mad act' which, among onlookers, provoked 'a feeling of fierce resentment with the miserable woman.' Davison's action, in the view of the *Daily Mail*, 'could only be explained by madness.' She was 'a notorious militant with a thirst for martyrdom.'

Under a headline in *The Daily Mirror* reading, 'Woman's mad attack on the King's Derby horse,' it was reported that, 'but for her obviously serious injuries, she would have undoubtedly fared badly at the hands of the crowd,' who displayed an 'evident desire to lynch her.'

Several newspapers gave greater prominence to the controversial disqualification of the favourite, Craganour, and promotion of Aboyeur, at 100-1, than to Davison. *The Sporting Life* was dismissive to the point of callousness. When its editorial finally moved on from the Craganour incident to 'The Anmer Incident,' the paper complained, 'If it were not enough to have the disqualification of the winner, we were not allowed to see anything to indicate the class of the King's horse, Anmer, for the reason that some wild woman broke from the crowd and stepped right in front of the royal representative.' The royal representative, at 50-1, was already well beaten.

It was a very different story in *The Suffragette*, the WSPU's weekly paper. Its front page portrayed an angel, with the caption, 'In honour and in loving, reverent memory of Emily Wilding Davison. She died for women.'

Christabel Pankhurst, Emmeline's daughter, described Davison's action as 'a tremendous imaginative and spiritual achievement! A wonderful act of faith! So greatly did she care for freedom that she died for it. So dearly did she love women that she offered her life as their ransom.'

In the eyes of *The Suffragette*, Davison had 'taught the world that there are women who care so passionately for the vote and all it means that they are willing to die for it.' Davison was presented as a martyr in a noble cause, and the WSPU intended to make maximum political capital from her death. The funeral arrangements were detailed and impressive. At 1.00pm on Saturday 14 June, marchers gathered in Buckingham Palace Road to accompany Davison's coffin from Victoria station to St

George's Church, Bloomsbury, and then on to King's Cross, en route to Newcastle and Morpeth, where she was to be buried.

Over 6,000 suffragettes, some wearing black and carrying purple irises, others in white, with white lilies, joined the long procession, watched by tens of thousands. When Emmeline Pankhurst attempted to join them, she was arrested but the mourners included Herbert Jones's wife. Another 30,000 attended the funeral at Morpeth, where Davison's gravestone, appropriately, bears the WSPU's motto, 'Deeds not words.'

It took the contribution women made during the First World War to persuade the government, in 1918, to give the vote to most women aged 30 and over. In 1928, the qualifying age was reduced to 21, the same as for men.

When Emmeline Pankhurst died, that year, Jones attended the funeral, bringing a wreath bearing the forgiving inscription, 'To do honour to the memory of Mrs Pankhurst and Miss Emily Davison.'

The flags found in Davison's coat were taken by Mary Leigh, a similarly firebrand suffragette, who produced them during later demonstrations, including the first Aldermaston march by the Campaign for Nuclear Disarmament, in 1958. Today the flags, and other items, are held at the Women's Library in London.

Less seriously:

YOUR DERBY QUESTIONS ANSWERED *Racing Post*, 6 June 2009

Derby day can be a puzzling time. Whether you are a dedicated racefan or a once-a-year flutterer, this is where you will find the answers to your Derby day questions.

Dear Sir

I wore pink socks on Oaks day and, today, I will be wearing blue socks. Pink for the girls and blue for the boys! What a silly sausage I am, aren't I.

Rupert

Dear Rupert

Aren't you just! What will you think of next?

*

Dear Sir

I have been studying past Derby results carefully and have noticed that three-year-olds have an exceptionally good record. Can you suggest a reason?

Baffled

Dear Baffled

I think you will find that this is not always the case. You may have overlooked the 1844 Derby, won by the four-year-old, Maccabeus. Nevertheless, it is an interesting theory. Well done! [Maccabeus was a ringer for Running Rein. He was subsequently disqualified.]

*

Dear Sir

My father always used to say that Lester Piggott shot through the Derby field like a dose of Epsom salts. How we used to laugh! Have you ever heard anything as funny?

Gerald

Dear Gerald

Yes, when Bob Monkhouse said, 'They laughed when I said I was going to be a comedian. They're not laughing now.'

*

Dear Sir

What is the admission charge for the best seat at Epsom, and how much can I expect to spend while I am there, including a few bottles of bubbly and a few decent bets on the Derby? I need to know for an expenses form I am filling out.

Anon MP

Dear Anon MP

About £4,000 should cover it. Don't forget the limousine home.

*

Dear Sir

Is Gypsy Rose Lee still telling fortunes on the Downs? I only ask because, in 1998, she told me that I would meet a tall, dark stranger and last week, in Tesco, I did, serving on the check-out. Now I want to ask her if I should speak to the stranger.

Wondering

Dear Wondering

When I saw her last year, Gypsy Rose predicted that she would be back again this year. On the other hand, she was wrong about my ante-post bet.

*

Dear Sir

I remember when Crepello won the 1957 Derby. Nothing's the same, is it?

Arthur Longbottom (94)

Dear Arthur

The Queen? (83)

*

Dear Sir

There'll never be another Lester Piggott, will there?

Frank

Dear Frank

I wouldn't think so, no.

*

Dear Sir

I am absolutely sick to death.

Appalled, Home Counties

Dear Appalled

We all are, eventually.

*

Dear Sir

I have not missed a Derby since 1933 but I will not be going this year. I died early last week.

Yours, posthumously, Sid.

Dear Sid

It will probably rain, anyway.

Actors and actresses have often been involved in horseracing but only one has trained a Derby winner.

THE WEST END DERBY *Racing Post*, 2 June 2003

Tom Kirby Walls, a smartly dressed, naturally good-humoured man with a manicured moustache and what the *Tatler* called 'a salacious eye,' was a most unlikely, and long-forgotten, trainer of a Derby winner. Yet in 1932 it was reported, 'No owner of a Derby winner has ever had a greater ovation than that given to Mr Tom Walls, the owner-trainer of April The Fifth.'

Ridden by Freddie Lane at 100-6, April The Fifth owed his name partly to the date on which he was foaled and partly to the fact that it was a name with 13 letters. Thirteen was Walls's lucky number. There were 13 letters in his own name, 13 in that of fellow actor Robertson Hare, and *Tons Of Money* had opened at the Shaftesbury Theatre on 13 April 1922, starring both Walls and Hare.

For Tom Walls was a famous and successful comic actor and producer, who at one time combined acting with riding in flapping races, and both with being a London policeman, PC251, C Division. No wonder that, when he died, one obituarist remarked, 'Tom Walls lived the lives of five men and spent the income of ten.'

Walls graduated to the Shaftesbury Theatre via selling programmes at the Prince's Theatre in Manchester and playing Aladdin in Australia. When *Tons Of Money* proved a roaring success, transferring to the Aldwych and boasting 737 performances, Walls bought a Rolls Royce and followed up with a string of Ben Travers plays, which became known as the Aldwych farces. *It Pays To Advertise*, in 1924, was followed by *A Cuckoo in the Nest*, *Rookery Nook*, *Thark*, *Plunder*, *A Cup of Kindness*, *A Night Like This*, *Marry the Girl*, *Turkey Time* and, finally, in 1932, *Dirty Work*. Walls, who produced the plays as well as performing in them, forged a celebrated acting partnership with Ralph Lynn.

He boasted, 'In my time as actor-manager in the theatre, I doubt if there were any others of the same period making as much money as I was.' He used some of it to buy oysters and some to set up as a trainer in Epsom, where he and his Staffordshire bull terriers, led by Buller, looked after a small string of horses from stables behind Walls's house, The Looe, at Ewell.

After an evening performance in the West End, Walls was prone to order celebratory oysters by the scores of dozen before making an early morning appearance on Epsom Downs, followed by breakfast, with sherry for the first course and whisky for the last. There may have been a boiled egg in between.

The actor-trainer bought April The Fifth as a yearling for 200gns, and though the colt finished sixth in the Two Thousand Guineas, he did not win a race until mid-May, at Gatwick, following up with a more promising victory in the inaugural Lingfield Derby Trial.

By this time, Walls had turned his attention from the theatre to the cinema, successfully transferring several Aldwych farces from floorboards to film. At Elstree studios, where Walls was filming *Thark*, the staff all backed April The Fifth, as they did at the Aldwych, where owner Mr C Sharpe declared, 'The whole theatre had something on that grand horse. Everybody here put money on April The Fifth for sentimental reasons.'

West End theatreland was said to have been in a frenzy of excitement and the barman at the Savoy marked the occasion with an April The Fifth cocktail, based on Walls's black and pink racing colours. 'Pinkish in hue, it contained grenadine, vermouth and gin, and a large black olive.'

The winning trainer declared himself 'wonderfully proud' and asked, 'Who says they cannot train a Derby winner at Epsom?' Having lost a lot of money betting in the past, Walls corrected the balance slightly by winning a reputed £10,000. He certainly needed it because, later in the 1930s, Walls's fortunes went into sharp decline. His son, Tom Kenneth Walls, shared his father's interest in racing and won the Grand Military Gold Cup at Sandown on Crafty Alice in 1934, but Walls senior lost a lot of money in an ill-fated investment in the inappropriately named Fortune Theatre.

During the filming of *Turkey Time*, late the previous year, Walls was accused of bad time-keeping. His reputation was not helped by a letter he wrote to the film's director, at the Gaumont-British Picture Corporation, which read, 'I should be very grateful if you could arrange for us to shut down for the two days, 14 August and 15. I will be perfectly frank in stating the reason. I want to go up to Cumberland and shoot grouse on those two days.' The director was not amused, and Walls's explanation, that his late appearances in the morning were the result of a heavy bag of fan mail, does not seem to have been regarded as acceptable.

Walls was a hard worker but he realised that, now in his mid-50s, he was no longer suited to the role of suave seducer, with which he had made his comic name. Although he returned to the theatre in 1939, he never achieved the same success.

Nor as a trainer. Financial problems forced Walls to give up training in 1948 and he died, bankrupt, the following year, aged 66. He had added his own, unique contribution to the Derby's rich history and his ashes were scattered at the scene of his great racing triumph.

There is the Derby seen from the grandstands and the Derby experienced on Epsom Downs, traditionally the temporary home of London's East End.

DERBY DAY ON THE HILL *Racing Post*, 8 June 2008

The drive towards healthy living seems to have faltered on the Hill at Epsom Downs, where burgers and beer reign supreme, and there is not a low-fat natural yoghurt in sight. A woman is buying sweets from a sweet stall, which is strange, because she looks as if she has already eaten all of them. There are a lot of large bosoms accompanied by a similar number of small blouses.

The Hill is the pram capital of Britain. Single prams, double prams, prams making bawling noises, prams pushed by girls who look as if it's not long since they were in one themselves. There is one 18-year-old without a pram, but she looks as if she will need one next week. There don't seem to be any stalls selling prams but there are stalls selling almost everything else, although, if my Aunt Beth was here, she'd be saying, 'Look at that. I wouldn't give it house room.'

There's an electric massaging chair, for a fiver, and doggy duvets, for the same price. For £1.50, you can buy a baby bib with a message reading, tastefully, 'Stand clear. Screaming shit machine.' Then there is Harriet Lee and Betsy Lee, clairvoyants, Betsy 'as visited by Pat Phoenix and Tommy Cooper.' I wonder if all her customers are dead.

It's possible that Betsy Lee ('My powers are great! I have the knowledge to remove bad influences!') hasn't moved with the times, although there is evidence that she has heeded the new consumer protection regulations, as evidenced by a small sign in the window of her caravan, reading 'For entertainment purposes only.' That should stave off the trading standards officer. I want to ask Betsy Lee for her prediction about the impact of the regulations but she must be busy palm reading or foretelling that, next year, she'll still be in the same bloody caravan.

The best buy is something called 'splattoid yucky sticky tomato with maggots' for £1. You hurl it against a flat surface, in this case the side of a white van, and it looks as you'd expect a real tomato to look if that's what you did with it, but you can scrape it off, and it's an artificial red tomato again. If that doesn't appeal, and you are huge, there's a stall specialising in clothes ranging from sizes 2XL to 8XL. I don't know what 8XL looks like, but I don't suppose it moves very quickly.

There are plenty of bookmakers, Jack Johnson from Hull, Charlie Miller from Luton, George Cooper from who knows where, but none of them has Maidstone Mixture at more than 250-1 for the Derby, although they may have left a nought off the end, by mistake. It must be difficult to concentrate with the pitiless thumping of the fairground music. It's mildly comforting to see Ivor the Engine chugging round in gentle circles, albeit devoid of passengers, who have been seduced away by Body Count, which spins you round and round and up and down until you are sick, or possibly dead. There's also a game with a spinning wheel with jockeys' names on it, although, like Betsy Lee, it seems to be looking towards the past rather than the future, with Ray Cochrane, Mark Birch, Jason Weaver and John Reid restored to the saddle.

A number 159 bus to Marble Arch drives in, which must be a surprise for anyone who had planned a shopping expedition to Oxford Street. The best buses are in the Lonsdale enclosure, where corporate passengers disembark to the sound of their own jazz band, champagne, and lobster.

And there's Jeremy Paxman, not looking at home as he leads an entourage of cameramen and microphonemen to an unknown destination, probably not *The Sun*'s bus, with 'We love it' emblazoned on the side, and two page-three girls nearby. It's easy to see the attraction.

A man asks me for a tip, which is like asking Gordon Brown for a joke. Shortly afterwards, Frankie Dettori kisses Willie Carson, which shows that Frankie's lost none of his courage.

In the parade ring, Aidan O'Brien grips each of his jockeys' arms and, intense, impresses unheard words upon them. On the other side of the grandstand, there is the unique sight that Epsom provides and, soon, the unique excitement this idiosyncratic racetrack presents. Kevin Manning gives New Approach a fine ride to provide another Derby story.

18
HORSES I HAVE LOVED

Ile De Chypre declines to win at Royal Ascot in 1988.

Ah, the horses. There are the champions and stars, Arkle and Desert Orchid, Brigadier Gerard and Frankel, Red Rum and Dawn Run, Nijinsky and Nashwan, and beyond; horses that lift the spirits and thrill nervous, expectant, praying crowds. Then there are other horses, idiosyncratic, infuriating yet, in their way, irresistibly engaging. At least, they engaged me.

This was the first article I wrote for *The Sporting Life*. The excitement!

EQUINE ENIGMAS AND ECCENTRICS *The Sporting Life,*
10 August 1988

So you still think Ile De Chypre was unlucky? After the horse had thrown away both Greville Starkey and Royal Ascot's King George V Handicap, racegoers who had hurled themselves off the stand after Royal Gait's Gold Cup disqualification were seen fighting their way back up the stairs to hurl themselves off again.

Personally, I don't know what all the fuss was about. When Ile De Chypre suddenly took it into his head to dispense with the formality of passing the winning post, and headed straight for Royal Ascot's presentation, his behaviour was strictly par for the course. Go to any British racecourse and you will find they are littered with small, semi-conscious figures staring, bemused, from the hallowed turf upon which their erstwhile mounts have just deposited them. Jockeys are coming off all over the place. It's part of the tradition.

And it's not even unique to Britain. Only last year, Glittering Halo was poised to capture Longchamp's Prix du Bois when, suddenly unpoised, he collapsed in an undignified heap with Tony Cruz playing the part of the rag doll. The fact is that racehorses don't need fences to encourage them to fall over or to floor their riders. They can do it perfectly well on their own.

Not all, it is true, display the aplomb of Ile De Chypre or Jellaby who, ten years ago, established his claim to be the undisputed winner of the Lockinge Stakes, then put his foot in the only hole on Newbury racecourse, leaving Brian Taylor to walk the final 100 yards to the winning post. Unfortunately, it doesn't count if you're on your own.

More recently, Tony Charlton had a much shorter but no less embarrassing walk when coming off Amantiss a good 18 inches from the finishing line at Devon and Exeter. At the time, he had what is known as an unassailable lead.

What makes the likes of Ile De Chypre a bit special is their eye for publicity and the acute sense of timing possessed by all great sports personalities. It's not just dumping the jockey that counts – any Evichstar or Sparky Lad can do that – it's knowing exactly when and where to dump him. For maximum effect the best place, as Geoff Baxter and his 1982 Epsom mount I'll See You will tell you, is about half a furlong out with the race in the bag.

It isn't really a laughing matter, as Willie Carson knows only too well. He managed to stay on Chilibang when the quirky roan went onto the course at Newmarket this season and promptly attempted to exit via the far rail. Willie wasn't so lucky in 1979, when Mystificateur insisted that seven furlong races at Haydock were run on the straight course, ignored the bend, jumped the rails and fell.

Nothing unusual about that. Horses are always ignoring bends and jumping rails. It was after Lyphard's idiosyncratic treatment of Tattenham Corner in the 1972 Derby that crueller observers suggested that the 'F' in F Head stood for 'Fat.'

Nelson Guest's Bedwell Boy showed a premature inclination to switch codes. At Ripon in 1983, facing only one opponent and with a mere six furlongs to negotiate, Taffy Thomas's mount behaved himself for three furlongs before trying to leap the rails. He failed. This season, at Downpatrick, Brown Pearl was more successful. He finished third in a Flat race only to be disqualified for having jumped a fence on the way round.

The truth is that some horses will do anything to avoid winning. Grundy's brother Centurius perfected the art of appearing to have a race utterly at his mercy and then contriving to lose it. The expression 'found nothing' was made for him.

Lobbing along on the bridle with the opposition dead on their hooves, the hapless Walter Swinburn would press the accelerator and Centurius would slam on the brakes.

Petrizzo, on the other hand, was prepared to win the occasional race but only on the understanding that he was disqualified – twice in the case of the Doncaster Cup. Petrizzo was lucky not to have had to pay a price for his errant behaviour. Others were less fortunate.

Given his name, it was perhaps no surprise that Jimmy Fitzgerald's Hardknockin did not have the energy to run into a place on any of his five outings in 1984 and that he was then gelded. Before long, Hardknockin had three wins under his belt but precious little else.

In the case of some equine delinquents, the problem is not how to get them to race properly but how to get them to race at all. In this respect, Mount Irvine took some beating, but it didn't make any difference. By the time this incorrigible rogue had been dishonourably discharged from the point-to-point field, he had moved well beyond run-of-the-mill antics, such as running out or refusing to start. Mount Irvine's speciality was to fling himself to the ground, from where it was extremely difficult to ride a start, let alone a finish.

Those who were at Warwick's late May meeting saw a potential successor to Mount Irvine. The selling race was so bad that students of form were offering 3-1 against there being a winner at all. While two of the runners went down early to give themselves time to recover their breath for the slow gallop back, Jack Berry's well named Not Too Far stopped ominously dead when the action moved from the undemanding confines of the parade ring to the course itself.

Irritated beyond measure by John Carroll's polite suggestions that he might like to move forward, Not Too Far threw himself turfward and had a very fair stab at crippling John for life. Limping but uncowed, although presumably suffering from severe concussion, John remounted. Eventually, against all the odds, Not Too Far arrived at the start and, later, was goaded into the stalls.

There was no way on earth he was going to run any sort of race after a display like that. You couldn't have backed him with Albanian money. The result? He battled on gamely all the way up the straight for a neck win.

Even that was less surprising than some of Knockroe's performances [for which, see below for a whole article devoted to the infuriating subject].

In 1976, in the Ascot Stakes, it was Tudor Crown's turn to send the form books flying out of the window. Acting as pacemaker for his stablemate, Coed Cochrion, the favourite, Tudor Crown set out to make the running and was still making it, at 66-1, when the field passed the winning post for the final time.

Perhaps it would have been better if some horses had never started at all. Dakota won the Ebor and the St Simon Stakes in 1975 but he didn't score many marks out of ten for good manners. At Epsom, in a virtuoso display of malevolence, he unshipped Geoff Lewis, attacked two other runners and rounded things off by biting one of the stalls handlers.

No one, however, even among those who backed Ile De Chypre, could have taken defeat quite as badly as Steve Nesbitt's useful sprinter Ubedizzy. After finishing second to Boldboy in the Abernant Stakes at Newmarket in 1978, Ubedizzy bit off a stable lad's finger. Ubedizzy was banned from Britain and taken to Ireland. It wasn't a success; he refused to let the handlers fit his blinkers. Of course, we shouldn't blame horses for jockeys' injuries. Already this season Kevin Hodgson has been savaged by a Jack Russell and Jimmy Bleasdale by a garage door.

As for Ile De Chypre having been unlucky, well, he's just a beginner. Now, if you backed Pinehurst Park in the Valley Gardens Handicap Hurdle at Ascot back in 1970, that was unlucky. John Jenkins rode him to victory, fair and square. He didn't carry the wrong weight, like Ray Cochrane on Crimson Court in 1981, or forget to weigh in, like Jimmy Carter on Harbour Bazaar in 1986 or Walter Swinburn on Ajdal in 1987, or unavoidably take the wrong course, like Mtoto at Goodwood this season.

No, the Jockey Club's senior starter sent them on their way. Unfortunately, he did it three minutes early and the race was declared void. Now that was a suitable case for suicide.

PRINCE CARLTON *The Sporting Life*, 16 December 1988

Forget about tomorrow's SGB Handicap Chase at Ascot and don't even spare a thought for the King George at Kempton on Boxing Day. What really matters is Major Eldred William O'Flaherty Wilson DSO, Mrs Beryl Bloom, Prince Carlton, and the Waveney Handicap Chase, the 1.15pm at Fakenham this afternoon.

To begin at the beginning. Sixty years ago, Major Wilson set a record when he made his first appearance at Fakenham as an amateur rider. From three rides, he managed to register four falls. He made the mistake of remounting one horse.

Luckily, the Major was well prepared, having practised falling by diving over a tennis net. (This is all perfectly true. They did things differently in those days, when anything dangerous seemed pretty tame compared to trench warfare.) Undaunted, Major Wilson went on to compete in the Liverpool Foxhunters' Chase twice, at a time when it was run over the full Grand National course.

In 1961, at the age of 55, he made his final ride a winning one when partnering his own Essandem to victory at Fakenham. That brings us to today, for Major Wilson's Essandem and Mrs Bloom's Prince Carlton share the course record, with nine Fakenham victories apiece. At 1.15pm, Prince Carlton will be trying for a tenth course win, to make the record his own.

Fakenham is a unique course, just a mile around. Alterations have changed the sharp corners into sharp bends but you still need a special kind of horse at Fakenham, the one described by Caroline Saunders – 'A very handy horse, a quick jumper who goes round bends well.' She is talking about Prince Carlton, and she should know.

In April 1982, Simon Sherwood, then simply Mr S Sherwood (7), won on Prince Carlton but was injured just before he was due to ride the horse again. It was the May bank holiday and Mrs Bloom couldn't find a replacement jockey so she rang her son, Michael, once the leading rider at Fakenham, for help. By chance, Caroline Saunders happened to be there and she was offered the ride. She won on Prince Carlton that day and went on to win on him another seven times, including five at Fakenham.

Caroline describes the 13-year-old gelding as 'a lovely little horse, narrow but with a big heart. He's an easy ride who doesn't pull and jumps particularly well.' Above all, Prince Carlton is a real family horse and a tremendous favourite at a course which loves its local favourites.

Mrs Bloom bred Prince Carlton, his dam and grandam, at the family farm at Wymondham in Norfolk. 'He'll never leave us,' says Mrs Bloom. 'He's the family pet. He's a very normal horse and not a very big horse. Although he has won with 12st 2lb, big weights are definitely against him.'

Mrs Bloom's son, Michael, partnered Prince Carlton when he first appeared on a racecourse in 1979, and in 1986 it was her grandaughter Caroline Bloom's turn to ride him and to win on him twice. 'He didn't make a mistake all season,' she says. 'He's a superb jumper and, at Fakenham, he's very good at the fence in front of the stands. He knows that you can't put in a big jump there and he often picks up a length or two round the following bend. He really scuttles round the corner. I adore him. He doesn't need a pilot there. He goes round like clockwork.'

Unfortunately, Prince Carlton struck into himself at Plumpton in May 1987 and missed the whole of last season. His third at Fakenham in October, when ridden by yet another Bloom, Mrs Bloom's grandson, Nigel, gave hope that there may still be another Fakenham victory in the old horse.

What is certain is that, if he wins today, there will be the most tremendous cheer. If he fails, there are four more meetings and four more chances this season. And, if time has caught up with Prince Carlton, then there will be at least one spectator ready to argue that a tie with Essandem is a fair and honourable result, for one of the directors of Fakenham is Major Eldred William O'Flaherty Wilson.

Prince Carlton finished second that day but in 1990, aged 15, he won at
Fakenham for a tenth and final time.

A repeated tale, I know. I just can't stop myself. Mad, bad and dangerous to
know, and yet, somehow, loveable. Knockroe was my favourite horse, in a way.

KNOCKROE *The Sporting Life*, 8 June 1989

'I'll never have a horse like him again. He was a once in a lifetime. If he had been
an entire and eligible to run, he would have won eight Derbys out of ten.' Is that
wishful thinking on the part of Knockroe's owner, Major Victor McCalmont?

Over to the gelding's trainer, Major Peter Nelson. 'He had supreme natural
ability. Snow Knight, who won the Derby in 1974, was a good, genuine horse but
Knockroe was better. If he had given his all, he would have been unbeatable, but
the horse had a peculiar temperament.'

That is one way of putting it. Major McCalmont is less reticent. 'He was always
a bastard,' he says. 'When he had his injections as a foal, he was like a bomb. We
had him with his bum stuck out of the door of the loose box. The vet had to run
past and jab the needle in him as he went by, the next time the syringe and, the
next time, press it. He was quite impossible. People were always telling me how
intelligent he was but he wasn't, he was a bloody fool.'

As for training him, that, as they say, was something else again. 'At home,' says
Nelson, 'he was unpredictable. You had to make special arrangements for him but
you could never find the key. Sometimes we'd drive the car up to the gallops, bang
on the roof and give a toot to set him off and then he'd work upsides the car. He
had great natural speed. We clocked him at 44mph up a severe incline. Not bad for
a stayer!'

Major McCalmont has a vivid memory of just what Knockroe was capable of
when he put his eccentric mind to it. 'As a three-year-old, we galloped him with
Apollo Nine, the 1971 Stewards' Cup winner, at level weights over six furlongs.
Knockroe beat him out of sight.'

Unraced as a two-year-old, Knockroe won five of his ten outings as a three-year-
old, including the Group 3 Cumberland Lodge Stakes at Ascot. For his final run,
Knockroe travelled to Longchamp for the Prix du Conseil Municipal. The stalls
handlers took exception to his awkward behaviour, Knockroe took exception to
their vigorous response and that, McCalmont suspects, was 'the beginning of his
impossibility. He never forgave the human race.'

Even so, Knockroe had a tremendous season as a four-year-old. It wasn't just
that he won four Group races (the Jockey Club Stakes, Yorkshire Cup, Cumberland

Lodge Stakes and St Simon Stakes), it was the way he did it.

Knockroe would come wide and from behind, well behind, late and very fast. There was an anticipation about watching Knockroe that few other horses have ever generated. On his day, you could almost spot the moment when the decision, and it was Knockroe's decision alone, hung in the balance and then, if he decided 'yes,' he would go. He'd use that scything turn of foot to cut down the opposition and take the breath away for, when Knockroe was good, he was very good, even though, when he was bad, he was bloody awful.

When Eric Eldin took over from Lester Piggott for Knockroe's last race as a four-year-old, in the 1972 St Simon Stakes, he experienced Knockroe at his knife-edge best. 'If you moved a muscle,' Eldin remembers only too clearly, 'he wouldn't go. To try and lay up was hopeless but you didn't wait with him, he waited with you.'

In the St Simon, Knockroe kept Eldin waiting and waiting until finally, when all seemed lost, patience was rewarded. With under two furlongs to go, Knockroe decided to join the race. A furlong out he had reached the front, lost interest as quickly as he had found it, and hung on by a short-head from Sol'Argent.

1972 had also seen Knockroe refuse to race in the Princess of Wales's Stakes and the infuriating grey opened his five-year-old season by being beaten five lengths by Rheingold in the John Porter Stakes after having given the Derby runner-up half a furlong start, as well as 4lb.

Worse was to come. On his next three outings, Knockroe declined to take an active part and, at Kempton, Frankie Durr lost patience with him. He experimented with a backhander. On reflection, this was a mistake. 'You couldn't lose your temper,' says Eldin, 'because if he was extra miserable, you were in trouble.' One second after the experiment started, horse and rider were 30 yards apart.

'I got fed up with the horse,' McCalmont admits. He was not alone. So had Knockroe's one-time regular partner, Lester Piggott, and so had every punter the right side of a padded cell door.

Nelson persuaded McCalmont to suffer just one more time, in the Weetabix Wildlife Handicap at Epsom, where it was hoped that a course almost as eccentric as the horse might provoke Knockroe's interest.

The owner dug himself into the bar, in preparation for further humiliation, while the starter invited Eldin to make an early attempt on the stalls. 'I said, "Leave him today",' Eldin recounts. 'So the other horses went behind and (glory of glories), Knockroe followed them. That day, he was always going to be all right. He didn't tail himself off, although he was with those at the tail. I took him over to the outside, to race by himself, and he won on the bridle. It couldn't have been easier.'

Since Mahmoud's victory in the 1936 Derby, there had been countless attempts on his course record. Nearly 40 years later, it was Knockroe who broke it, easing down.

'After the race, the vet came up to me,' Nelson remembers, 'and said, "I'm sorry, Major Nelson, but I'm going to have to check your horse again." He couldn't believe that Knockroe's heartbeat could be so slow. I knew the reason, though. Knockroe hadn't really exerted himself.'

Switched to another switchback track, Knockroe followed up by winning a Brighton handicap under 10st 4lb but was injured in the process and went back to Major McCalmont's in Ireland. Connections had a brief stab at turning Knockroe into a hurdler but, as McCalmont puts it, 'We never got him inside the wings.'

Having recruited a rider with a stunted instinct for self-preservation, a tempting life insurance policy and a pressing desire to test the theory of life after death, Knockroe was unleashed into the hunting field. It is not unusual for a horse to terrify its rider but it takes a Knockroe to terrify an entire hunt.

'Hunting was fun for him,' says McCalmont, 'but not for anyone else. He spent most of the time up on his hind legs or attacking the person on the back of the next horse.' They gave Knockroe two tries but decided to give the hat-trick a miss.

Following an outing at Limerick Junction, as an eight-year-old in 1976, Knockroe returned to what was now John Nelson's yard, still wearing heavy hunting shoes, for the Irish farrier hadn't been able to get near him to take them off. A couple of unpromising runs later, Knockroe was retired to McCalmont's stud and it was there, a few years later, that he died suddenly from a heart attack or, perhaps, from a brain tumour.

That would certainly explain a lot. For once, a cliché is true. There really never will be another Knockroe. He gave us all some great moments.

A more conventional favourite:

TINGLE CREEK *The Sporting Life*, 1 December 1990

There is a star on display at Sandown today. You will see him on the way to the start of the Tingle Creek Chase. Watch him carefully, because you will never see a more exciting jumper of fences.

You can't miss him. He's not grey, he's a chestnut with a white face and four white legs. 'All the things,' says his trainer, Tom Jones, 'that you are meant not to like.' He is 24 years old now and his name is Tingle Creek.

In 1972 Tingle Creek won four jump races in America and was then brought over to Tom Jones's Newmarket yard. 'He was very, very quick,' Jones remembers. 'The question was, would he jump British fences?'

Stan Mellor was sent out on to the Links to find out. 'He doesn't need any schooling,' said Stan when he came back, 'he's brilliant.' Jones never schooled Tingle Creek again.

After two warm-up races over hurdles, the six-year-old was sent to Newbury for the two-mile Oxfordshire Chase. Carrying top weight, Tingle Creek made all, unchallenged, to win by 15 lengths, with Game Spirit and the dual Scottish National winner Barona among those galloped off the map.

'Made all, unchallenged,' became a feature of Tingle Creek's entries in the Form Book, for that was always how the two-mile specialist did it. 'His forte was to kill horses off in the first mile,' says ex-jockey David Mould, 'and then to freewheel the rest of the way. He paralysed his opponents.'

Mould was Peter Cazalet's jockey and he was used to riding top-class horses but he says, unhesitatingly, 'Tingle Creek was the most exciting and the bravest horse that I have ever ridden. He was absolutely wonderful.' Many horses can jump fences and many can jump them well but few, very few, have ever jumped like Tingle Creek. 'He was extremely athletic,' says Jones, 'a great gymnast, made of elastic.'

When you took Tingle Creek to a fence he became something special. Ian Watkinson, who succeeded Mould as Tingle Creek's regular rider, explains. 'He wasn't difficult to hold until there was a fence in front of him. Then you had no choice. He would gallop into the fence and jump it flat out. That was what made him so brilliant.'

'He was the fastest jumper of a fence I've ever sat on,' says Steve Smith Eccles, who rode Tingle Creek in his last eight races. 'He always accelerated into his fences and he took them either on a long stride or an even longer one, with his feet up round his ears. I couldn't ride him now. I'd be trying to organise him and you couldn't do that; you had to be brave and sit up his neck.'

The horse was as brave as his riders. 'If you had asked him a mile off a fence he would have tried to reach it for you,' says Mould. 'When he was just beaten by Pendil at Sandown in 1974 he never gave in. It was such a brave performance. He got beaten but he showed so much guts and courage. I can't tell you what a joy he was to ride.'

Above all, it was Tingle Creek's jumping that took people's breath away. When Watkinson rode the American-bred star for the last time, at Fontwell in 1977, there were more people by the first two fences than there were in the stands. By the time Tingle Creek had reached the third fence, his opponents were still considering the second.

Sandown was made for him, just as it is made for Desert Orchid. The first time Tingle Creek ran there, in 1973, he broke the course record and, on his last appearance, in the same race five years later, Tingle Creek broke the course record again. 'It was as if he knew that it was his last race,' says Smith Eccles. 'I have never seen Tom Jones reduced to tears but there were tears in his eyes that day, and the only reception I have ever seen like it was when Dawn Run won the Cheltenham Gold Cup.'

That was Tingle Creek's 23rd victory from 49 chases, and the racy chestnut won 15 of them with over 12st on his back. Not many horses can give 16lb and a six-length beating to a dual winner of Cheltenham's Champion Chase, with a horse that had finished second in the Gold Cup 20 lengths further adrift, but that is what Tingle Creek did to Skymas and Leap Frog at Punchestown in 1974.

Tingle Creek was special, all right, and when his owner died, she left him to Tom Jones. He has been with him ever since, ridden out three times a week and clipped last Tuesday by Ian Watkinson, ready for Sandown today. 'He's bright as a button,' says Watkinson. He always was.

19
GRAB-A-GRAND 2010

Salvation in the guise of Camps Bay and Barry McHugh.

Another year, another humiliation in waiting, another chance for readers to laugh and for me to cry. Or, of course, I might win a grand, except that, in a fit of overconfidence, I had changed the target to two grand. Fat chance.

DAY ONE *Racing Post*, 15 December 2010

Personally, I think it's a bad sign when the jockey starts hitting the one you've backed with a circuit still to go. It's known as 'giving a reminder.' At Catterick, Mr O Garner reminds Railway Park, several times, that he is supposed to be moving towards the front of the field rather than dropping towards the rear. Sadly, Railway Park ignores him. One way (Betfair) and another (Sporting Index) it means that, before Folkestone has even started, I'm £145 down. To look on the bright side, I almost laid the winner, Sambelucky, on the ground that, although he had a fair chance on form, it appeared to be Mr R Lindsay's first ride under rules. Luckily, I didn't.

To get the bad news out of the way quickly, in the hope that no one will notice, the first race at Folkestone proves to be the last for my Placepot. To look on the bright side, again (I hope there isn't too much looking on the bright side), Alcalde jumped well and ran a promising race for John Berry and The Alhambra Partnership, possibly named after the theatre in Bradford where I once parked my car and came back to find that all that remained of it was a door handle. So things could be worse. I'm praying they won't be.

Trainer Warren Greatrex, trying to be helpful, expresses confidence in Strategic Approach's prospects of triumphing in the Beginners' Chase but Strategic Approach jumps big and slow and doesn't seem to care that I've had £80 on him, as well as £20 on Misstree Dancer, who runs well but not quite as well as Triggerman. To look on the bright side, the bookmaker at Albion Racing's pitch will be pleased, during a difficult time in the economic cycle.

Time to take stock. No, on second thoughts, better leave that until later. And to think that Folkestone might have been abandoned. At least the goldfish in the fish pond are fine. If I have to look on the bright side much more, I might be joining them.

A different approach is clearly needed. Instead of asking trainers and jockeys what they think, I'm going to play pretend, which seemed to work perfectly well when we were kids. Oliver Sherwood says, 'Yes, you're right, at nine on Sporting Index's 50-30-20-10 index, Global Power's a definite buy.' Mark Bradstock says, 'Is Super Villan 9? Really. Buy some for me,' and Greatrex says, 'Oddjob, 8! I can't believe it.' So I've bought all three, for £10 each and am about to see whether the trainers were right.

They were. Global Power wins and Super Villan's second, for a £540 profit, which means that I'm £199 ahead. Yippee! I was beginning to think I was a mug punter but it turns out that I'm not, at least until the next race, where the word 'moderate' barely seems adequate to describe the runners. Somebody loves them; Ladbrokes, probably. I 'invest' £55 on Jack's Lad at about 7-2. I expect Tim Vaughan will have the 11-year-old at his best and no one takes any notice of a 575 day break any more. With Watergate disrespectful of some fences, and Richard Johnson giving Jack's Lad a typically fine ride, his best is good enough. I'm enjoying it now.

How on earth has the handicapper managed to handicap Roi De Rose, fresh from Switzerland? He was running well at Aarau last year, possibly on a glacier, and Tom Scudamore, a friendly face, seems, well, if not encouraging, then not discouraging. He's hoping that Roi De Rose will take account of the fact that these are British fences, not Swiss ones. Anyway, I'm encouraged, and would like to think that Roi De Rose is thrown in on 114 and that the Pipe family have put Pond House on it.

With the benefit of hindsight, I hope they haven't, although Roi De Rose ran a promising race. As so often, 'promising' translates into a loss, in this case of £66.

Then I do something rather stupid, a match bet. Then I do something else stupid, a place bet on Kiltimoney. Suffice to say that neither were good ideas and, when I start to type out all my bets, it takes rather a long time. Although I've made a profit, the word 'selective,' so important for successful betting, does not spring to mind, while the word 'scattergun' does. Still, I've only been betting for 44 years. I'm sure I'll learn, in time.

To look on the bright side, it's Newbury tomorrow. Must be professional, must be selective, must ask Nicky Henderson if he knows one. Must make £1,900.

Total – profit £100.

DAY TWO *Racing Post*, 16 December 2010

What a splendid fellow Nigel Twiston-Davies is, and what a wonderful trainer. I certainly can't think of a better man, nor a better trainer. And what a fine jockey Paddy Brennan is, and what wonderful owners Baker Dodd & Cooke are. If there are better owners, I'd be surprised. And Major Malarkey! Of course he rattled a few fences, to make it more of a challenge, but it was a performance reminiscent of Kauto Star at his best, except that Major Malarkey hasn't won as many King Georges, yet.

I'd like to be able to report that my investment (I like that word) was the result of a brilliant analysis of the form book and video recordings but it was actually the result of Twiston-Davies saying hello while I was standing doing nothing. Still, it's important to be in the right place at the right time, a bit like those old-fashioned centre forwards who used to hang around the goal, occasionally sticking a foot out to score from one yard. Anyway, clutching Major Malarkey's saddle (what a splendid saddle it is), Twiston-Davies told me that he thought Major Malarkey's last run at Bangor had come a bit quickly after his previous winning one at Chepstow, and that he was confident of an improved, quite likely winning, run. So why (you may sometimes have asked yourself a similar question), why, why, why, oh why, did I only have £33 on it? Cowardice, I suppose. If there's an afterlife, I'm going to stick £222 on it.

Even so, that's made the day. Newbury (what a splendid track it is) and everyone here suddenly seem much better. Thank you. Earlier, in the juvenile hurdle, I backed Wild Geese at over 100-1, which turned out to be an accurate reflection of his performance, but also laid the favourite, Empire Levant, to win £107, after Betfair's commission. Things were going swimmingly until Encore View was unplaced in the maiden fillies' race at Lingfield (don't ask) and ditto Cotillion and

According (went out like the proverbial light) in the maiden hurdle at Newbury.

Wayne Hutchinson is one of my favourite jockeys and has an interesting collection of rides but when I ask about them, instead of saying 'I'm sure I'll have at least two winners and I might well have four. I'd do a yankee, if I was you,' he says that they have chances of sorts but nothing outstanding. He thinks Tante Sissi might be his best chance of a winner, in the bumper. At least it's given me someone to blame if things go wrong.

Back to Lingfield (I'm not proud), where Kingscroft's runner-up spot is worth £104. I quite like short-priced place bets, sometimes. Now it's time for a tot up. I don't mind an interim tot up when I know I'm ahead. When I'm not, I prefer to leave it until later, in the hope that things will look up. I'm £313 up. Good. After Major Malarkey's success, *The Independent*'s Chris McGrath suggested, 'Don't bet any more.' It was sound advice but I was taken aback because, rather worryingly, it was something that hadn't crossed my mind. Not bet? What, you mean – stop? I think I must have missed the last bit and what Chris actually said was, 'Don't bet any more today after half past three,' and I'm determined not to. Professional, selective, they are my watchwords. What's running in the next?

Why, why, why did I only have £22 on West End Rocker? Because I didn't know he was going to win, I suppose. He jumped brilliantly, and cleverly, and my advice to trainer Alan King (curiously, he has never asked for my advice, so I'll just have to give him it uninvited) is to target the Grand National. He's got Aintree written all over him, although in invisible ink.

While I was writing that, I missed the start of the novices' hurdle, in which I wouldn't have backed Pride In Battle, even though Hutchinson was riding it, so that's all right. Instead, I've gone, with some confidence, for Sonic Anthem and Present Your Case in the conditional jockeys' race at Bangor. One of them will win, surely? Hang on and I'll let you know whether one of them does. It just goes to show how wrong you (I'm reluctant to say I) can be. Twice, actually, because my banker of the day was Albertus Pictor in the apprentice race at Lingfield. The snail's pace heralded doom but I expect Archie Rice would have won anyway.

McGrath was right. I should have stopped. You just can't help some people. Now I feel a bit deflated. Must reflate myself overnight and come out bold and selective. Fat chance.

Daily total – profit £241. Running total – profit £341.

DAY THREE *Racing Post*, 17 December 2010

Yippee! (See below, if you can be bothered). I've always liked it at Towcester, and Noah would have liked it here today, with Captain Scott of the Antarctic taking over at half-time. I wonder if he'd have survived.

De Forgotten Man likes it, too, in the opening novices' hurdle, which is very nice for trainer Martin Keighley, owner Mrs Peter Andrews and jockey Robert Thornton, but not so nice for those of us who backed Skipper Robin (fourth) and Aeronautica (eighth). Why didn't they run faster? Never mind, I'll soon be celebrating the winner of the next, the novices' chase, which will, of course, be Dromore Hill, who will plod his way to victory under Jimmy McCarthy.

In the weighing room, Jonjo O'Neill is optimistic about Aztec Treasure's chance, if he copes with the ground, which is like sticky toffee pudding. For some reason, whenever I bump into Jonjo, it makes me feel better, but I can't back Aztec Treasure because I've already set my heart on Dromore Hill. McCarthy, as you won't remember, rode Cetti's Warbler to a memorable 100-1 success here seven years ago. Dromore Hill isn't quite that price. I've backed him at 7-2.

We reminisce a bit about Cetti's Warbler and then McCarthy says, 'The trip will suit Dromore Hill and the ground will suit him, and he's got a good chance.' And the jockey, what's he like? 'The jockey's all right,' says McCarthy, 'don't worry, he's good enough if the horse is good enough.' Which turns out to be the problem. Dromore Hill isn't quite good enough. He keeps plodding away but needs another half mile to plod his way into the winner's enclosure, rather than into the space reserved for the third. A steeper finishing hill, perhaps.

Never mind (I hope there aren't too many 'never minds' this afternoon), Mac Aeda's going to get the ball rolling in the right direction, even though Graham Lee, an excellent jockey, is apprehensive about the ground. 'I thought he would tighten up for his previous run,' he says, 'but they either go on this ground, which is very dead, or they don't, and I don't know whether he will or not.' Nothing's straightforward, is it? Why don't jockeys ever say, 'If this doesn't win, I'll eat my own mother, and my father?' Despite the absence of confidence in Mac Aeda's chance, I still back him – why? He jumps a bit 'novicey' and gets tired, and doesn't set the ball rolling, which leaves the heavy responsibility of doing that in the hooves of Stadium Of Light in the maiden race at Southwell (no, it's not desperation). Barring adverse miracles, Stadium Of Light has to be in the first three, so I stick on almost £1,400 for a place at 1.24 on Betfair, and buy £10 at 28 on a spread index, which does make me a bit nervous. It's not risking the money. Well, yes it is, but it's also the thought of how stupid I'll feel if it's unplaced. Silly, really. Somehow, I've got to win two grand.

Being placed was not in doubt but Stadium Of Light wasn't desperately keen to reach the winning post before Fascination did, but finally condescended to. Maybe he didn't want to disappoint the Queen, who owns Fascination. With apologies to

Her Majesty, good, that's better. From £399 down to £132 up. That's more like it. What's a spot of rain, snow and blizzard when you're on a winning run?

If you remember (why should you?), Cetti's Warbler was trained by Mrs Renee Robeson, who specialises in stout stayers, which is my way of saying that, buoyed up by a change of fortune, I back Bobby Gee. In he goes, generally jumping well, with the odd nervous flutter. Well done Renee, well done Tom O'Brien, well done The Oakley Partnership, and well done me. When things are going badly, punting's impossible. When it's going well, it seems easy, like stealing oranges from a monkey after he's been given a general anaesthetic.

So why did I follow up by having a coward's place only bet on Upthemsteps? Who knows? Still, that's another £100 profit. The first grand is in touching distance, and I've got a small blob next to Riddleofthesands in the next. Maybe he's named after that novel by Erskine Childers. Sam Twiston-Davies doesn't say but, helpfully, he tells me that, although Riddleofthesands jumps well, he tends to be keen, which might be his downfall on the testing ground. So I don't back him and think of laying him, instead, but that would be a bit unseemly, so I don't. In fact I don't have another bet, but shut up shop and wallow in my success.

Professional, selective, disciplined. If only I was. Now I'm looking forward to Uttoxeter, or Ascot, or Southwell, or Wolverhampton, or Monmore dogs.

Daily total – profit £585. Running total – profit £926.

DAY FOUR *Racing Post*, 18 December 2010

Uttoxeter and Ascot having cried off, it's down to Southwell, where they built a workhouse in 1824, in readiness for the poor from the racecourse. I quite like Southwell, where there's a community spirit founded on shared adversity, hot pies, and the unlikelihood of being able to work out which horse in each race is least awful.

Actually, they're not bad today and I half fancy one in the first, a claimer. The field is made up of horses no longer able to run to their handicap rating (Hard Rock City and Masked Dance), horses with lots of wins on Polytrack but not on Fibresand (Abbondanza and Ebraam), and horses who aren't good enough (Baby Judge, Bertbrand, Dancing Wave and Takajan). As Sherlock Holmes once said, 'When you have eliminated the impossible, whatever remains, however improbable, must be the truth.' Not impossible, admittedly, but the truth, I submit, is Punching, who ran well here on Sunday after a lengthy break. Yes, he's the one. Must find trainer Conor Dore to tell me that he'll be amazed if Punching doesn't win easily.

Tall, slightly stooped, with a woolly hat, Dore is encouraging. 'He's got a good chance and I'll be disappointed if he's not in the first three, and he may win,' he says. 'There aren't as many question marks about him as there are about some of the others and he might come on a bit for his last run.' Right, that's it then, £44 win and £243 for a place, which I'm pretty confident he'll achieve. Punching breaks well, travels well, is ridden well, by Hayley Turner, and holds on well. This is a doddle. I don't know why I didn't think of it before.

After a spot of wallowing and feeling pleased with myself, I bump into Paul Dixon, owner of Even Stevens and leader of the Racehorse Owners' Association. He's going for the biggest prize on offer here today, just over £3,000. Dixon thinks Even Stevens will win, and so do I, and so does Even Stevens, who proves it by romping home, carrying 7st 5lb. That will do something awful to his handicap mark. Dixon, wearing a smile and a flat cap, confesses to having had 'a fairly hefty' bet. Perhaps a house or two, to cover the Christmas presents.

That's two out of two, and all is well with the world, apart from Iraq, Afghanistan, the Ivory Coast, the Gaza Strip and that sodding barking dog over the road. Earlier, my heart had sunk when Uttoxeter was abandoned but now it's, if not soaring, then not sinking, and I celebrate with a very nice cottage pie at The Pantry. What a great sport horseracing is. I love it.

My third winner will be Loyalty, stepping up in trip and on Fibresand for the first time (warning bells failed to sound) but, as trainer Derek Shaw tells me, he's progressive and 'there's more for him than against him.' Despite having two people to guide him around the parade ring, and various things stuck on his head, Loyalty settles well, the pace is suitably modest, and all looks fairly well until stamina is called for in the closing stages, when it fails to appear. Never mind. I'm still £524 up.

And then I do an amazingly silly thing. Stupid, very stupid, and embarrassing. A novice's blunder. Hopefully, no one is still reading this. If you are, it would be a kindness to stop. Least said, soonest forgotten. The fact is, I'm not £524 up today, I'm £142 down, because of THAT THING.

The weather's not bad here now, how is it where you are? How's your car going? Doing anything nice for Christmas? Family keeping well? Ever considered suicide? Also, can I have my money back, please? Idiot, idiot, idiot.

Moving quickly on, Antony Brisbourne, brother of trainer Mark, whose horses are in fantastic form, told me earlier that he thought Itsthursdayalready had a good chance but, unfortunately, possibly because the balance of my mind has been disturbed by THAT THING, I forgot and latched on to Sir Louis (will he stay the extra furlong? no he won't), who sends another pile of banknotes flying into the betting industry's ever-open mouth, while Itsthursdayalready finishes a creditable second. That reminds me, I must remember to take an anti-depressant pill.

I'm going to stop now; stop punting, stop writing, get some sweeties from the sweetie stall, to cheer me up, and look forward to an evening in the Saracens Head, where I thought I might indulge in a spot of moaning. Hopefully, there'll be a bar stool for me and nowhere to escape for the barman. What a silly sport racing is, isn't it? I hate it. What's running tomorrow?

Daily total – loss £423. Running total – profit £503.

THAT THING was Zeavola. She never ran again, unless it was in Mongolia. Too ashamed, I suppose.

FINAL DAY *Racing Post*, 19 December 2010

Help! Have you seen the card at Southwell? It's impossible, but the impossible is merely a gauntlet to be picked up, an imposter to be exposed, an ant in the path of a giant anteater. Who am I kidding? I'm doomed. In desperation, I've looked at Navan, and found no salvation. I've thought of pretending to be stuck in a snowdrift. No, I must gird my loins (how do you do that?) and knuckle down to the task.

Right. I've found one. You do if you stare at the form long enough. It's Camps Bay, in the claimer. It's been over three years and 23 runs since the six-year-old's last win, he's not as good as he was and he has never run on Fibresand but he has been running respectably in handicaps at Wolverhampton off a mark that gives him an excellent chance today. Diggeratt, the favourite, likes the surface and recently stepped up in distance successfully, to one mile three furlongs, but might disapprove of the extra furlong. That's the theory. So my fate is in Barry McHugh's hands, with a saver on Yossi, in Sean Palmer (7)'s hands. It's a desperate state of affairs, although Sporting Index have generously offered to match my winnings with them over the week. At the moment, I'm £370 up with them. Better try not to convert that to £370 down.

Meanwhile, at Crayford, the dogs are being led across the snow for the 11.23am. The poor hare must be cold. Should I back trap 6, at 3-1? No, I shouldn't. Trap 1 wins, trap 6 finishes last, so that's a minor victory for self-discipline.

Having backed Camps Bay, I ask McHugh for his opinion (the other way around might have been a better idea), and McHugh, a likeable man, boosts my fragile confidence. 'I think he's got a great chance,' he says. 'He's probably my best ride, my nap of the day. I'm really hopeful.' Excellent. Then I bump into trainer Brian Ellison, who is equally confident, reporting that Camps Bay is 'spot on' and should probably have won one of his races at Wolverhampton, although there is a rather worrying proviso – 'if he goes on the surface.' Camps Bay is going to be my make or break bet, but not my only one.

Ed Thompson, betting in the ring under the name of Ed Thompson, thinks that Je Suis Unrockstar will struggle to get the extra, sixth furlong in the opening nursery, particularly from his inside draw, so I've laid him, at odds on. If Je Suis Unrockstar wins, remember that name, Ed Thompson. He's to blame. Now I'll just rest on my laurels, or my backside, and wait for hope to be overtaken by reality. Will Je Suis Unrockstar go out like a light in the first? Will Camps Bay do the decent thing in the third? Will fate kick me in the balls?

Je Suis Unrockstar doesn't quite stay (well done, Ed) and George Chaloner (7), whose progress will be interesting to watch, rides Dunmore Boy nicely to make me £106. Goodee. Thank you, Ed.

Time passes, as it tends to, until it arrives at the moment of truth. McHugh holds Camps Bay up and, as they turn into the home straight and McHugh switches Camps Bay to the outside, away from the kickback, he immediately moves more sweetly, sweeps into the lead and draws clear, winning by a staggering 21 lengths. It's one of those lovely moments when all you have to do through the final furlong is savour it. Sadly, Camps Bay is claimed, which seems a cruel end to the celebration.

Now, there's a tricky decision to make, because I'm just over a grand up and it would be nice to look after the four-figure total. On the other hand, it would be nice to have a bit on Yankee Storm in the 2.05pm. Needless to say, I succumb to the temptation (a difficult thing not to succumb to, I find). Fortunately, Yankee Storm hangs on to third, which counts on Betfair.

Oh, dear, another temptation, in the form of Sioux Rising. There are ten runners, and Sioux Rising finishes tenth, which doesn't count on Betfair. Now I'm £996 up, and need to win £4. It's up to Bel Cantor and Andrea Atzeni to be placed in the last, and they are, for a profit of £8. And that's it, the end of a really enjoyable week. Thank you to everyone who has helped, or tried to. It's been great fun.

The £1,004, plus £610 from Sporting Index, will be divided equally between Racing Welfare and The House That Jack Built, Jack Berry's charity to fund a facility in the north, similar to Oaksey House in Lambourn.

Daily total – profit £501. Running total – profit £1,004.

That took my Grab-a-Grand grand total profit to a rather impressive £5,985. Unfortunately, in 2011, lured out of retirement by Victor Chandler's generous offer to underwrite the enterprise for £5,000, I put up a pitiful display, and lost £995. No one has approached me to start a tipping service.

20
ROYAL ASCOT

The royal in Royal Ascot.

For some, Royal Ascot is the highlight of racing's social calendar, to be followed by Glorious Goodwood; for others, it is a highlight of racing's racing calendar. I have mixed feelings about the meeting, although my views have changed over the years. The ageing process, probably.

MY VIEW OF ROYAL ASCOT *Racing Post (supplement),*
14 June 2009

Royal Ascot coming up, goodee. Of course, standards have slipped. Until 1955, divorcees were not allowed into the Royal Enclosure, a rule which threatened to leave the Queen with no one to talk to. The Duke of Norfolk, Her Majesty's Representative, did his aristocratic best to preserve the past, stepping in to keep hot pants out in 1971 and staving off porn star Linda Lovelace three years later. Linda arrived in a silver Rolls-Royce bearing the number plate PEN15 and presented herself at the royal portals in a see-through blouse. A gentleman in a bowler hat refused to admit her, leaving Lovelace to pose for photographers on the bonnet of her car. They seemed to enjoy it.

For a long time, the meeting wasn't a favourite of mine. Watching Gertrude Shilling in her annually ridiculous hat (Gertrude was particularly fond of vegetable gardens) didn't appeal, and Royal Ascot suffered from a surfeit of aristocrats who had temporarily abandoned their estates for the express purpose of getting in the lower orders' way. Royal Ascot was full of people in the way and generally ripe for assassination.

The Queen's arrival on the racecourse made things worse, triggering the erection of a barrier of ropes and royalists designed to prevent punters from reaching the rails, and Victor Chandler. Having snatched a glimpse of the Queen, the landed aristocracy reassembled around the parade ring, to prevent serious racefans from catching more than a glimpse of the horses. Meanwhile, bowler-hatted gatemen deployed their full vocabulary ('No, sir') to prevent people from going where they wanted to (the betting ring), to do what they wanted to (bet). I don't suppose the late Queen Mother had that problem, and I expect she had a bit on her daughter's Colour Sergeant when it won the Royal Hunt Cup in 1992, at 20-1. A small castle, perhaps, followed by a large gin and tonic.

During that era, my fondest memory of Royal Ascot is backing Gildoran to win the 1984 Gold Cup, at 10-1. I wasn't there, of course. I rarely went to Royal Ascot, for fear of killing someone. I preferred Brighton, which had more selling races and fewer rules. Later, older, more tolerant, and more appreciative of high-class racing, I found that I could go to Royal Ascot without wanting to shoot too many people and could cope with the need for ironed shirts by buying four (now five) new ones. It's a good system, and I recommend it. The alternative is staff. Jeeves, sadly, is not available.

Having mellowed, nowadays it's even rather nice to see the also mellowed bowler-hatted brigade, who remind me of the days when commuters to the City, similarly hatted, lined suburban station platforms clutching *The Daily Telegraph*. John Betjeman probably wrote a poem about them, although what I always remember about Betjeman was his answer, in old age, when asked if there was anything he regretted. The venerable poet pondered for a while, then said, in his gentle way, 'Yes, I wish I'd had more sex.'

Today at Ascot, there's a new regime, and a new grandstand, opened in 2006, and reopened in 2007, with viewing added. It has the most colossal escalators, reaching up towards the remnants of the class system, and a wind tunnel on the ground floor. Like semolina pudding at school, we must try to love it (a dollop of jam in the middle helped). My favourite spot is where the paddock used to be. Happily, the beautiful trees are still there and this year, as every year, I'll be asking people what kind of trees they are. So far, I haven't managed to find anyone who knows. Royal Ascot doesn't seem to attract arborists and, rather than study the trees, or the horses, most people concentrate on studying each other. It starts with hats, and moves down; first a furtive glance, then a barely concealed stare, graduating to an unabashed gawp and ending, several bottles of champagne later, with a shameless leer. By then, it's pretty much a classless society.

There is wonderful racing as well, with seven Group Ones, including the Ascot Gold Cup, which is always won by either Brown Jack, Sagaro or Yeats. Lunch features prominently on many visitors' agendas but, for serious racegoers, it is out of the question. There's far too much form to study. The best thing to do is to ask what you can have for a fiver, then sit down and enjoy your cup of coffee and Kit-Kat while continuing to try to work out the Wokingham.

My favourite races are the Ascot Stakes and Queen Alexandra Stakes, which offer good opportunities to go to the toilet without queuing. When the Queen Alexandra is over (it takes quite a long time), people gather around the bandstand for the traditional sing song and jingoism. It always reminds me of 'Oh! What a Lovely War.' I'm looking forward to it.

I seem to have had a thing about royalty and the aristocracy, and their annual gathering. In 2004, they gathered for the final time before work started on knocking down most of the old Ascot and building a new one. In 2005, the royal meeting was temporarily moved to York.

LADY BUTTER ON PARADE *Racing Post*, June 16 2004

The trees near the parade ring look lovely. I expect they'll be chopping them down soon, to move to York.

By two o'clock, the crowds are lining up to watch the royal procession, which features the splendidly named Lady Butter (I expect she puts on a good spread etc.), the Countess of Euston (known to her friends as 'Buffers') and Major James Duckworth-Chad, which is the sort of name people in royal carriages should have. I'm not much of a monarchist. The Queen's okay, but that Prince Philip says some silly things, doesn't he?

Thierry's trying to sell Ascot radios for £5 a listen. She says the men in top hats are polite and the women in short skirts aren't, and so far she's sold 12, and she finishes at three o'clock, which she's rather looking forward to. She's rather nice, Thierry (as in Henry, but without the bald head).

Pink's popular this year, with high heels. It must be murder being a transvestite. Men have had their usual agonising decision to make. Should the top hat be black, or grey? Black is definitely the colour of 2004, which means that there are a lot of men wandering around looking like undertakers from a Charles Dickens' novel. To look good in a morning suit (black or grey), it's best to be tall. Short men look like Groucho in a Marx Brothers film.

I find myself standing near an entrance with a sign that reads, 'Royal Enclosure Badgeholders Only,' which makes me want to stand at the entrance and say, 'Lend us a castle.' Before I can, a tall man called Claude suddenly announces, loudly, 'I've lost my wife.' At least he's hung on to his umbrella. I expect she'll come back if it rains.

They announce a delay to the first, the Coventry Stakes. There's a technical problem. Either they can't open the gate on to the track or the judge has forgotten his tie and they won't let him in.

Someone must have lent him one, because they're off. For a while it looks as if Frankie Dettori's going to win on Council Member, prompting people near me to shout, 'Go on, Frankie,' then it looks as if Kieren Fallon's going to win on Iceman, prompting other people near me to shout, 'Go on, Kieren.' The second lot are more pleased than the first lot. I don't suppose Frankie's that pleased, but you have to feel sorry for the third, Capable Guest. Two years ago, Kawagino finished third in the Coventry and, later today, he's got a bit of a squeak in the novices' hurdle at Newton Abbot. It might be best to sell Capable Guest now.

There are some beautiful women. Unfortunately, most of them are about the age my daughter would be if I had one. Never mind, I'm going to have an ice-cream. That usually makes everything seem all right again. You can't beat vanilla ice-cream. Well, you can, but it doesn't do it any good.

In the booth for broadcasters, Clare Balding's back is wearing a pale dress, with a zip down it. I don't know what her front's wearing.

Eventually, they move on to the King's Stand Stakes. I'm hoping Cape Of Good Hope will win, for the good of international racing, and he almost does, but The Tatling wins, instead, for the good of Dab Hand Racing and Milton Bradley, who's rather good with sprinters.

My banker of the day is Azamour but, having turned my back on betting, on the grounds that I might enjoy it, I try to wallow in the aesthetic pleasure of John Oxx's training achievement, and the satisfaction of a successful analysis, unsullied by the, well, sulliedness, of a bet. I fail. Sod it. Excuse me while I go out and have another ice-cream. I've half a mind to have a chocolate flake in it.

LADY BUTTER SLIDES OFF *Racing Post*, 18 June 2004

As I feared, Lady Butter's slipped out of contention; and on Ladies' Day, too. Royal carriage Tuesday, detached motor car Wednesday, nowhere in the royal procession at all yesterday. Surely she could have sat on the Duke of Gloucester's knee. Maybe she was worried she'd slip off. (Enough butter – Ed).

Evidently there have been complaints that standards in the Royal Enclosure have fallen. They haven't fallen far enough for me to be allowed in, nor the woman with a football pitch on her head, although, to be fair, there may not be room for her.

There's a very attractive lady with a dress full of holes, although the holes aren't quite where you'd like them to be. I venture a smile but she gives me a look that says, 'not even if the only alternative was my grandfather.' I might try another smile later, in case, like the Royal Enclosure, her standards have slipped.

Good heavens. There's a girl with dimples. I haven't seen a pair of those for years. I thought they'd gone out of fashion and been filled in with Botox.

I'm supposed to be keeping an eye out for celebrities, but I'm not very good at recognising celebrities. There's no sign of Sara Palmer-Tomkinson, or Tara Palmer-Tomkinson, or ... whoever. There's Clare Balding in a lime-green dress, next to an older lady with a pink gyroscope on her head. She's very affable and natural, Clare. People come up and ask her to pose for photographs with them and she does, several times. It's rather nice.

In the parade ring after the Norfolk Stakes, all the jockeys who weren't placed explain why they weren't placed. It goes something like this, 'I always thought it was bloody stupid running him here. He could have won at Nottingham. I expect he's buggered now. I think his suspensory's gone.'

Lord Huntingdon strides up, gives a woman in a pink dress a big kiss, then dashes off, probably on his way to cycle round Surinam. He's already done Borneo. Henry Cecil's wearing turquoise socks (both feet) and Mrs Stephen Lussier (funny name for a woman, Stephen) or it might be Mrs Oppenheimer, or it might be someone else who partly owns Hidden Hope, has a mauve satellite dish stuck on her forehead, possibly so she can watch At The Races.

For those who swear by the system, Modesta's first into the parade ring for the Ribblesdale and Ted Durcan's last – 'Sorry, forgot I had a ride.' I can report that Richard Hughes doesn't get any shorter and Willie Carson doesn't get any taller and that it was a Dubai finish, with Godolphin's Punctilious getting the better of a tussle with Sheikh Hamdan's Sahool, but you probably know that already.

In the Gold Cup, the Japanese jockey, N (Norman?) Yokoyama, is wearing striped silks, like those peppermints you can get at Woolworths. The first circuit provides the perfect opportunity for an ice-cream, nothing much happening on the track and no queue. It turns out that spagnola flavour is cherries and vanilla, no spaghetti at all. Next time, I think I'll just have a Magnum.

After they've gone round a few times, Westerner is still pulling a bit, Ingrandire, all the way from Japan, is about to declare that he thinks he's gone far enough, and several women are screaming, no, shrieking, 'Come on Frankie!' in my ear. It's a triumph for Godolphin, with Papineau being by Sheikh Mohammed's Singspiel.

Godolphin are doing rather well. If Dubai Destination wins the next, grown men will be crying in the betting ring. He looks as if he might win, but doesn't. England will be playing Switzerland soon. If Switzerland's football is anything like their cheese it shouldn't be hard to find a way through their defence. Meanwhile, I tell someone what's going to win the Britannia. He bursts out laughing. No, I'm not going to tell you now. You'll have to work it out.

THE FINAL DAY *Racing Post*, 19 June 2004

Get up, set off for the newsagent, meet Mrs Fred Honour walking the greyhounds, pat one on the head, ask how business is (not too bad), ask how Fred is (ditto), asked how I am (give long medical history), have a chat with Mr Dhariwal, the newsagent, about Godolphin, get a *Racing Post*. Go home.

Make a cup of tea, stick some Crunchy Nut cornflakes in a bowl. Read the *Post*, cleaning off the tea and cornflakes as necessary. Turn on Sky. Watch New Zealand rub England's face in the Auckland mud, start to watch Scotland get massacred by Australia, leave for Ascot before South Africa beat Ireland, again.

Arrive at Ascot, put on tie (resentfully), have a Pimm's, tell anyone who's listening that my Auntie Beth called her wire-haired fox terrier Pimm's, because it was her favourite drink. Think about doing a Placepot, decide I can't be bothered. Gawp at a few women. Moan about being 55.

Look at the Chesham, decide it's too difficult. Wander round to see if the rugby's on any of the televisions. It isn't. Moan a bit more. Have a look at Ayr, Newmarket and Redcar, just in case. Wonder if The Bonus King will ever win again, wonder if Say What You See will take George Duffield a bit closer to however many more winners it is he needs to get to however many it is he wants to get to before he retires. Have a chat with someone I don't really want to talk to about next year's Ascot being at York. Complain about being hot. Have an ice-cream. Feel better.

Stare at the horses in the parade ring. Try to look as if I know what I'm looking at. Worry about how thin their legs are. Look down. Wish I'd cleaned my shoes. And ironed my shirt. Think about having an enormous punt on Doyen in the Hardwicke. Picture Basil Fawlty in that scene where Sybil asks if he's been betting and Basil replies, 'No, dearest, that little pleasure has been denied me.' Watch Doyen win Hardwicke, unbacked. Think what a nice colour royal blue is. Watch Frankie do a flying dismount.

Stroll through subway to grandstand. Wonder if they're going to preserve the tunnel as a heritage site for nostalgic racegoers to wander through. Imagine guide pointing and saying, 'And that's where the mile course used to be. And that's where the Queen Mother tripped up after she'd just had her maximum on Gildoran. And here's one of the bowler hats the gatemen used to wear. And that's where the gate was where they threw you out.'

Look at the card for the Wokingham, or most of it. It's difficult to look at all of it. Keep staring at it on the basis that, if you stare at any field for long enough, eventually you fancy something and, soon after that, you can't bear the thought that it might win and you haven't backed it.

Wander aimlessly over to the Champagne Bar. Think about the US Open and wonder if the wind's blowing at Shinnecock. Hope it is. Wish they'd build golf courses with deeper rough and deeper bunkers, to make it more fun for television viewers. Look forward to watching Phil Mickelson with that dopey look on his face, if it isn't rained off.

Suddenly remember that the Queen Alexandra Stakes is coming up and stop complaining for a while. I like the Queen Alexandra, even now that they've made it more difficult for staying chasers to win by persuading Flat horses to run in it.

Ask bookmakers how they've got on. They've lost again. Watch them troop despondently across to their Mercedes. Notice that Germany are a goal up against Latvia. Say, 'See you at York next year.' Say 'yes' when people say, 'See you at York next year.' Get back in car. Take tie off. Wonder what's going to win the amateurs' race at Warwick.

For some, Royal Ascot couldn't be the same when it was at York. There were a lot of complaining letters on the subject. The person staying at the Old Swan Hotel in Harrogate was me.

I REALLY MUST COMPLAIN *Racing Post*, 16 June 2005

Dear Sir

I did not become a member at Ascot in order to go racing at York. If I had wanted to go racing at York, I would have been born in Yorkshire. That Douglas Erskine-Crum [Ascot's chief executive] is a disgrace to all those fine men (and the odd fine woman) with double-barrelled surnames. He doesn't deserve to have one. In future I, for one, will call him Crum. I suggest that your newspaper does the same.

Yours irately, Lord Berkshire-Surrey-Hants-Bawders.

Dear Sir

The thing's a complete disgrace and a nonsense. If my father hadn't been cremated, he'd be turning in his grave. My mother's still alive, and she's spinning like a top.

Dear Sir

I told you no good would come of it (Letters, 10 April) and now we've had two French horses win and we've only had one day of so-called Royal Ascot. I didn't serve in the Home Guard for this to happen. It's gone to the dogs, and so will I. PS Damn it all, there was even a German runner.

Dear Sir

If one more southerner comes up and says, 'Ee bye gum, luv, get us a Yorkshire puddin, an't mushie peas,' I won't be responsible for my actions, or their injuries.
Yours on the sausage and pie stand, Gladys Longbottom.

Dear Sir

I am staying in the Old Swan Hotel in Harrogate, which is where Agatha Christie stayed when she had a funny turn and went missing for a while in 1926. If any readers bump into her, could they please ask her to send Miss Marple along to see if she can find any hot water, because I can't.
Yours, cold, wet, and pissed off, room 229.
PS According to a sign next to the lift, they are about to launch a £4.2 million refurbishment. I don't think it will be enough.

Dear Sir

I feel sorry for the Queen, having to go all that way in that old carriage. Why couldn't they have held it at Windsor?

Dear Sir

On behalf of Arena Leisure, we would be happy to stage next year's Royal Ascot at Windsor (let's face it, there's no chance of Ascot being ready), and will guarantee minimum prize-money of £3,000 a race, maybe more.
PS If Windsor's no good, there's plenty of parking at Southwell.

Dear Sir

I really must complain.
Yours, Tunbridge Wells

ROYAL ASCOT AT YORK *Racing Post*, 16 June 2005

Thank God. I've finally met a Lady, possibly in both senses of the word. According to her badge, she's The Lady Caroline Warren (to distinguish her from any old Lady Caroline Warren). I don't know what aristocratic ladies normally look like, but she looks absolutely gorgeous. I can't believe Robespierre would have chopped her head off, although Madame Robespierre may have forced him to, for her hat.

Sara Cumani looks fantastic too, although, according to her badge, she's no Lady. Next year, I might overturn a lifetime of worst-turned-out awards and wear morning dress. In the meantime, I might iron a shirt. You've got to start somewhere.

Some of the raindrops are quite big, and some are quite small. All of them are wet and most of them seem to be bouncing off my bald head. According to the illuminated sign, it's still good to firm (the track, not my head).

Any minute now, the Queen's going to arrive. I do hope she's remembered her umbrella. In the royal procession, they always split up the husbands and wives; Earl of Wessex in the first carriage, Countess of Wessex in the second; the Hon. Harry Herbert in the second carriage, the Hon. Mrs Harry Herbert in the third. I think it's to stop them arguing.

Samantha Labadie and her sister Joanne Labadie-Parkin (what are you to do if you marry a Parkin?) explain the art of keeping enormous hats on your head while avoiding putting a high heel in one of the cracks in the wooden walkway. Even when one of Joanne's heels disappears, she doesn't fall over and doesn't even swear. I expect she went to finishing school. She can probably balance Bibles on her head and make soufflés rise, but possibly not after another glass of champagne.

According to Compton Hellyer, late of Sporting Index, the first race is going to be won by Camacho and the last by Quickfire. 'Cecil's horse could improve a lot and I always like Stoute's horses in handicaps,' says Hellyer. In case his tips turn out to be hopeless, Mitchell Platts, who was *The Times*'s golf correspondent for ten years, has some of his own for the US Open today. What you have to do is back Sergio Garcia at 25-1, Justin Leonard at 50-1 and David Howell at 150-1. Then you back Leonard to be top American player, Howell to be top European player, and Angel Cabrera to be top rest of the world player. Don't say I didn't tell you (unless they all blow out, in which case don't forget Mitchell Platts told you.) I've laid Eden Rock in the Hunt Cup, on the grounds that the ground may be wrong and he's too short a price for his draw, even with Sir Michael Stoute and Kieren Fallon on his side.

Have you ever listened to the noise made by thousands of people chattering? You could try the Knavesmire Stand. Excuse me a minute, while I go and watch the Jersey Stakes. In case you missed it, Camacho ran very well but Proclamation ran even better. Everything's better today. There are lots more people, mainly men and women. There's more of a buzz, and the women seem to look better, although that may be the champagne. The men look the same as usual.

On the big screen, Clare and Willie are chattering away. Willie's the one who gets everything wrong and drives you mad and Clare's the other one, in black with white spots. I bump into Saeed Bin Suroor, one of the nicest people in racing. Saeed reminds me that Sundrop is about to run in the Windsor Forest Stakes but I forget to ask him whether she's going to win or not. For a long time it looks as if she is going to win, then Peeress wins instead.

I don't know about you, but my feet are beginning to hurt. Still, it was just the same at Ascot.

The Duke of Devonshire was the Queen's representative at Royal Ascot but the imaginary Duke portrayed here bears no relationship to that contrastingly progressive aristocrat.

When the royal meeting returned to a very different, redeveloped Ascot, in 2006, serious problems had emerged requiring expensive corrective action.

2007: A DUKE ANSWERS YOUR GOLD CUP DAY QUESTIONS *Racing Post*, 21 June 2007

Dear Duke

Will I be able to see the races? Call me a moaning Minnie but, when I came last year, although I saw some lovely hats and bookmakers' umbrellas, I couldn't actually see any horses racing. I'd rather hoped to.

Dear Minnie

Thank you for your whining complaint. You don't say how tall you are but I'd bet one of my castles to your miserable terrace in Stoke-on-Trent that you're about as tall as Napoleon. There is nothing wrong with being short, I've employed some very short jockeys myself, but you shouldn't expect to be able to see properly. I myself am very tall. If you are unable to be tall, stilts are available for hire this year. Otherwise, you could stand on a stool at home and watch on television.

Dear Duke

May I say how much I liked your father, the 11th Duke. He was an excellent fellow and, unlike his son, didn't devote his life to destroying the Royal Enclosure which had provided generations of the over-privileged with harmless pleasure, unsullied by contact with the sweating masses. If there is one thing worse than a liberal, it is a liberal Duke. At least, after last year's debacle, you have had the sense to realise that those in the Royal Enclosure and the mob simply do not mix – remember Marie Antoinette? I don't really have a question. I just wanted to say that.

Dear Sir Henry

I think you will find things more to your liking this year. We hope to give the Klu Klux Klan a run for their money when it comes to segregation! We are also training a new generation of men in bowlers to chant, 'No, you can't come in, neither can you.'

Dear M'Lord

Sorry to mention it, but in the Silver Ring last year, I spent two hours queuing for a toilet. Will it be better this year?

Dear Bert

If you are that bothered about toilets, you should pay to get into a decent enclosure. I've never been to the Silver Ring myself but I understand that it is full of people who drink too much. If you drink pint after pint of that horrid beer, you are bound to need toilets, aren't you? Judging from your handwriting, which is that of an old man, you should stay at home instead of cluttering up our toilets. Although you don't deserve it, this year we have turned the wretched Silver Ring into one giant lavatory. I hope you are satisfied, but I don't suppose you will be, your kind never are.

Dear Sir

I understand that you are close to the Queen and wondered if you could get Her Majesty's autograph for my mother. She is 98 and in poor health and it would be such a lift for her.

Dear Mrs Wilkins

Her Majesty has more important things to do than pander to your mother. I suggest she tries to hang on for another two years, when she will get one of those telegrams someone in the office sends out although, with so many people living to 100 nowadays, I don't suppose that will last much longer. It must cost a fortune in stamps.

Dear Lord

What should I wear?

Dear Social Inadequate

If you have any sense of decency, morning dress. Otherwise, it doesn't really matter because no one will be paying any attention to you, but at least wear a jacket and tie. If your wife has decent legs, get her to show as much of them as possible! My wife has tremendous legs, and is always showing them off. I think a Duke's wife should.

Dear Duke

Why is the Gold Cup regarded as the highlight of Royal Ascot?

Dear Mr Evans

If you weren't a commoner, you wouldn't need to ask. It is to do with history, tradition, and breeding. Also, it gives people a bit of time to try to find a seat and have a cup of tea before the race is over.

2008: CLEAVAGE AND KNICKERS *Racing Post*, 20 June 2008

At Royal Ascot, it's always tricky knowing what to do before the Queen turns up and racing finally starts. Wandering around aimlessly is quite popular, as are cleavages. This year, I've discovered a new option. You stand inside the entrance and watch people come in. It's fascinating. A man, a woman, a man, a woman, a not-quite-sure.

A very tall, slim blonde walks through the entrance in a pink dress, then suddenly stands still and beams at a gaggle of photographers, provoking a frenzy of clicking. I ask her who she is and she says, 'I'm Kaja Wunder. I'm Estonian. I used to be a model and a Bond girl. Now I do events. Who do you photograph for?' When I say, 'No one, I've never had a camera,' she seems to lose interest.

Nearby, a lady with a microphone is interviewing another new arrival, who is called Anneka Svenska and has a set of theatrical masks piled up on her head in a shaky edifice that will be what milliners call 'completely buggered' if the wind gets up, which it periodically threatens to. Anyway, the lady with the microphone suddenly asks Svenska, 'Are you wearing knickers?' To which she replies, 'You'll never find out.' I ask the interviewer why she asked about the status of Anneka's knickers and she explains that it's something to do with the dress code.

The experience inspires me to take more interest in the fashion side of things, especially as it's Ladies' Day. I've already noticed that shoes are very popular this year, there's barely a foot without one.

At 2.05pm, the royal procession can be seen making its way down the straight mile. Intriguingly, the first carriage, containing the Queen, the Duke of Edinburgh and the Duke of York, also contains the Marquis of Cholmondeley who, as you probably already know, is a descendant of former prime minister Sir Robert Walpole. The second carriage contains the Earl of Portarlington, who was born George Lionel Yuill Seymour Dawson-Damer in 1938. I'm not sure what happened after that, if anything.

I am hoping that either Elegant Cad or Flashmans Papers will win the Norfolk Stakes, but they don't. I think I'll go and see if I can find some celebrities, although I'm not sure I'll recognise them if I see them.

Princess Anne enters the pre-parade ring carrying a black handbag; Princess Haya enters carrying a cream handbag; Sir Michael Stoute enters not carrying a handbag at all. A pretty young lady enters carrying Sir Robert Ogden.

The Ascot Gold Cup is an excellent opportunity for afternoon tea. The order doesn't change for the first ten furlongs, then Yeats wins. No wonder you never see Johnny Murtagh or Aidan O'Brien misspelt nowadays.

The packet of Maltesers I've just eaten contains E440, E442 and E492, but they don't taste as good as the Es in that white Magnum ice-cream. Perhaps they should try adding E471 and E407. Hold on while I watch the Hampton Court Stakes. Good, Collection won, which was what I hoped he'd do.

Returning to the fashions, white is popular, as is black. A lot of women look exotic, while a lot of men don't, although their long trousers may conceal a daring choice of socks. At the exit, Paddy Power are giving away free flip-flops, so we'll just have to see what the Queen is wearing tomorrow.

2009: LADIES' DAY *Racing Post*, 19 June 2009

Yeats is important, granted, but may I draw your attention to the teabags? Where are you supposed to put them? There it is, the latest teabag, sitting stewing in my cup, and there's nowhere to put it. I submit that those who supply cups of tea at Royal Ascot should be obliged to supply receptacles for the teabags. A small point, perhaps, but important, I think. A royal edict wouldn't come amiss.

It's Ladies' Day, and there are ladies all over the place, many elegant, many beautiful, some straining dangerously, but rather excitingly, at the seams. Every lady sports a head and every head bears a hat, many of them rather splendid. It's amazing how long some people (they're on the telly) can twitter on about hats although, to be fair, over the years I've been in some very long discussions about the Ladies' Derby, which is being run at Ripon today. An each-way bet on Mister Pete might prove rewarding. Put your hat on it.

I wonder how many steps there are in that big escalator in the grandstand? The obvious answer is to buy a packet of Wrigley's Sugarfree Gum (no sugar but plenty of sorbitol and maltitol) for 50p from the Tobacco Kiosk (alias the sweetie stall) and stick a piece on one of the steps. All you have to do then is stand by the side of the escalator, wait for the Wrigley step to come around, and count the steps until the one with the chewing gum stuck to it appears again. There is, as I have just discovered, a slight flaw in this approach; the chewing gum is prone to getting caught in the prongs at the top of the escalator. There's always something, isn't there? Maybe bubble gum would be better.

As well as Ladies' Day, today is Gold Cup day. The first Gold Cup was run in 1807, almost 100 years before teabags were invented. That was in 1903, the year, as you will remember, when Maximum II won the Gold Cup. I've had a coward's place only bet on Patkai, on Betfair. It's out of my hands now, and in those of Sir Michael Stoute and Ryan Moore. Please don't cock it up.

My confidence has already taken a bit of a nosedive since bookmaker Adrian Pariser expressed the opinion that Patkai isn't a Group 1 horse. Hopefully, he will be soon. Pariser's pitch, bearing the name Sam Harris (bookmakers never seem to be who you think they are), is quite busy. I've noticed that every time Linda, his assistant, bends forward, a punter comes up and has a bet.

2.30pm. Will Yogaroo continue the sensational run of Wesley Ward's US two-year-olds and win the Norfolk Stakes? 2.40pm. No, he won't.

Someone who looks just like W C Fields, nose included, walks by. He's looking remarkably well for a man who died in 1946. It was Fields who said, 'Horse sense is the thing a horse has that keeps it from betting on people.' And look, there's the Earl of Huntingdon who, if Wikipedia's to be believed, doesn't seem to have said anything. There's still time.

It's good to see Godolphin have a winner with Flying Cloud, after which the also-rans gather in the unsaddling area for a round of post-mortems until vacating it for the next batch of losers. Buckets of water are already waiting for them, to drown their sorrows. Time flies. The Gold Cup has started. Patkai's pulling a bit. I wish he wouldn't because, in my experience, horses that pull early tend not to pull late. It's a typical Gold Cup. They lob around for a while, then Yeats goes quicker than the others, and wins. Patkai, mercifully, comes second.

Yeats's memorable achievement is barely over before the Ladies' Derby hoves into view, at Ripon. Dimashq scoots clear, at 25-1, while Mister Pete (rated 58) conspicuously lacks Yeats's (rated 122) turn of foot, and finishes ninth. Life's full of disappointments. I'll just wait to give you the result of the last at Ascot. It was won by Cosmic Sun, at 66-1. Ffos Las soon.

2010: GUTTED FOR LADY VESTEY *Racing Post*, 17 June 2010

The sun is out, the sky is blue, but enough about that, Safina's going to win the Sandringham Handicap, isn't she?

Meanwhile, an interesting discovery. According to Richard Warren, of Warrens of Warwick, purveyors of tobacco (lung cancer etc.) and sweeties (obesity etc.) at Royal Ascot, Scottish racegoers have stopped buying Mars bars. It's because the new World Cup wrappers have got England and a George Cross on them. Personally, I've gone for a traditional Bounty, which contains 21 per cent desiccated coconut and a smattering of E471, one of my favourites.

Strange to think that everyone about to watch the Jersey Stakes will be dead in 100 years. It makes it all seem a bit pointless. And that's not the only thing to worry about. There's the wind, too. It's blowing across the track, which might give horses drawn low an advantage, because they'll be shielded from the wind by the horses drawn high. (It just goes to show how wrong you can be.) I hope it doesn't spoil Balcarce Nov's chance in the Royal Hunt Cup. Balcarce Nov is drawn 33, which is quite an achievement when there are only 30 runners.

I may as well tell you now, I've backed Balcarce Nov and Mull Of Killough and Tryst in the Hunt Cup, and Safina and Pollenator in the last. Hope springs eternal or, at least, until about 5.40pm.

The Royal Procession is cutting it fine. Maybe there's been an argument, possibly linked to the fact that, while Lord Vestey is in the second carriage, Lady Vestey is bringing up the almost rear, in detached motor car number six. One can only feel gutted for Lady Vestey.

Oh, no – and you may have heard this before – I almost backed that. That being Rainfall, winner of the Jersey Stakes. At least I didn't back anything else, and there's a stroll in the sunshine to enjoy, to the Silver Ring. If you're thinking of making the same journey, better check your feet first. Mine ache by the time they arrive. On the way, it's hard not to notice the striking effect created when very long legs combine with very short skirts, especially on women.

Beyond the three-furlong marker, at the end of a long row of bookmakers, stands Jolly Joe. 'It was miserable yesterday,' says Jolly, 'I wouldn't miss it for the world.' Jolly, small and neat, in a cardigan and tie, is 84, and keeps turning up for the fun of it. When I ask if Jolly ever bets to his opinions, he thinks for a moment then says, 'I've got the greatest respect for somebody else's money.' Like almost all bookmakers nowadays, he bets to figures, not opinions. Jolly tells me that he introduced John McCririck to bookmaking. Never mind, we all make mistakes.

I go to the parade ring to see the runners for the Windsor Forest Stakes. There are several rows of watchers in front of me. So far I've seen a big red hat, a big blue hat, and a big bald head, but only the occasional glimpse of a horse. I knew I should have worn high heels, and make a point of getting to the pre-parade ring early for the Prince of Wales's Stakes. An aristocratic sounding couple behind me are discussing the reasons for getting married. 'Raw sex and money,' suggests the man, who is prone to saying 'yaa' and 'darling' and knows a lot less about horses than the lady with him, who is impressed by Byword, Glass Harmonium and Mawatheeq.

There's Lord Huntingdon, who used to train and then went bicycling in Borneo, and there's Sir Michael Stoute, who still trains and now mops his brow. Bicycling in Borneo probably isn't on the agenda. On the steps of the grandstand, a buzz of human conversation rises up, soon to be followed by raucous cheers as Byword strides towards the line. 'Let's get some drinks in,' shouts a man who looks as if he already has.

In South Africa, Switzerland take the lead against Spain. So much for Swiss neutrality. At Ascot, Invisible Man takes the lead against everything else in the Royal Hunt Cup, to give Frankie Dettori his statutory Ascot winner, and the crowd gets its Frankie fix. At least Tryst has the decency to finish fourth.

Time, and the Queen Mary Stakes, pass, the latter taking up less than a minute of the former, a tribute to the power of the sun and drying properties of the wind. All that remains is for Pollenator (drawn 2) and Safina (drawn 6) to defy the evidence of the previous two races, draw-wise. Hold on a minute and I'll tell you what happened. Safina almost did it. If Timepiece and Blue Maiden hadn't run, she'd have won.

21
GAMBLING AND GAMBLERS

My friend John Mort Green - The Butterfly.

There are two sides to every betting counter. The most interesting characters tend to be on the gambling side, where people really care what wins the 3.40pm at Southwell, while the most financially successful ones occupy the other side.

I've always liked gamblers. They don't engage you in conversations about pension arrangements or keep their money anxiously in a purse, and they know they are full of flaws. Some of my best friends have some cracking ones; so do I.

To be fair, there are some very nice bookmakers. Fred, for instance.

In case you were wondering, yes, this is true.

MEET MY BOOKMAKER *The Sporting Life*, 2 September 1995

Let me introduce you to my bookmaker. He's called Fred Honour, after the sign outside. Fred wanders between the living room and the shop in a blue and white striped dressing gown, coughing. I don't know why Fred always wears a dressing gown. Possibly, he has just got out of bed, or is just about to get in to bed, or is on his way to Folkestone.

One of the regulars is a parrot called Toby. It's a girl. She's a proper parrot with big feet and a big beak and real wings, which she sometimes uses to fly into a tree where she sits and does nothing for a couple of days, until there's a decent race on. Then she flies down, knocks on the door, waddles across the floor, jumps on to the counter and looks at the television screen.

There are two greyhounds, as well, hiding behind the counter. One of them used to be called Big Choice but is now called Herman, and the other one used to be Mystery Leader and is now just Leader. I suppose they must have solved the mystery. They like their dogs at Fred's. They've got a promising young one called Friends Galore. Keep it to yourself.

Fred also has a horse, which is called Wilkins and is trained by Roland O'Sullivan, which means that, sooner or later, it will be the subject of the most tremendous gamble. I must ask Fred when.

When Fred isn't there, which is most of the time, Val looks after the shop. When Val isn't there, the customers put their bets on themselves. Fred bets on the racecourse, but he doesn't wear his dressing gown to do that. Sometimes, Val makes cups of tea for her customers. She would probably make one for me if I wasn't such a miserable bugger.

They have got Tote Direct, which is more than you can say for Ladbrokes, and I've been in there some days when there are six, maybe even seven punters. There would be more, but there's nowhere to put them, unless you let them into the living room, but you can't do that, because the dogs might eat them.

I like it in Fred's. Fred doesn't go in for company colours and logos and uniforms like the Big Three, unless you count his blue and white sign and blue and white dressing gown. There are no drink dispensers or special offers and there's no point turning up on a Sunday, because the door's closed. Come to think of it, it's closed in the evenings, too. It still seems to be open in the afternoons.

I don't think Fred's got any rules, apart from the one written across the top of the board which says that the maximum payout is £10,000. I don't think we need worry about that.

I called in there last Wednesday, before going to Ascot with Mort. Mort gave me a tape of Blossom Dearie playing at Ronnie Scott's. 'Now I'm deep into Zen meditation and macrobiotics and, as soon as I can, I intend to get into narcotics.' Dear old Blossom. Dear old Fred.

A few years later, some bastard stole the parrot, although they left Fred.

KATH REMEMBERED *Racing Post*, 23 November 2006

Does it have to be 2006? Can it be 1975, instead? If it can, then I'd like to nominate Kath for Betting Shop Manager of the Year.

I can't remember Kath's surname but I can picture her, a small, busy, bespectacled, half-bird, half-terrier woman, empress of the tiny, smoky Ladbrokes corner shop in Lidget Green, in Bradford.

When I arrived in the mornings, Kath had already put *The Sporting Life* on the walls, settled the betting slips that needed settling, put them in their various piles, either in the rack of pigeon holes, sorted like letters in a sorting office, or deftly wrapped in a rubber band. She was ready, waiting, and eager. Kath loved her job; she didn't always love Ladbrokes, but she loved her job. She was dedicated to it. I think it gave shape and purpose to her days.

The small counter had a glass screen and there were two tills, one for Kath and one for Doris, the nervous and slightly hopeless cashier. Doris was always asking Kath what she should do, and Kath was always telling her.

It was cramped behind the counter, with a raised platform for the boardman, me. At one end of the platform was a stool, with a bucket beneath it, full of bleached water and cleaning rags. At that time, I was learning to ride. I'd stand on the metal bar linking the legs of the stool, and put my weight down into my heels, thinking it might help. There was an extractor fan but it never worked and the shop was as smoky as betting shops were in those days, horribly smoky, so that even a short visit made your clothes stink.

Kath liked her customers. She greeted the first ones of the day with an energetic smile and breezy words of welcome. 'Oh, kid,' she'd say, to one of the daily pensioners, putting on his 10p doubles and trebles.

We rarely took a big bet and any bet that took out more than £250 had to be reported, but occasionally a yankee or accumulator would threaten the shop's nervous calm. Kath would prop the offending slip up on the till and stare at it, pace up and down, then pick it up and study it again, as if it unable to believe the cheek of it, affronted, and anxious. Every now and then, she'd turn to me and say, 'Oh, kid,' as if the shop and life as she knew it could be about to end, skewered by a thoughtless 10p Heinz.

It was the only time Kath was intimidated. Belligerent drunks, a rarity, didn't worry her. She was like a terrier, undeterred by the size of her opponent. It was her shop, and she was in charge. If someone misbehaved, Kath told them and, if they didn't like it, they went. I can't remember anyone getting the better of Kath. The shop was her territory, everyone else was merely a visitor, including the district manager.

Every now and again, smart and thrusting, he would call in with the latest promotion, leaving posters and instructions and, after he'd left, Kath would say, 'Oh, kid, bugger that for a game of soldiers.' But she'd do it.

On Saturday mornings there were the Hackney dogs and, at lunchtime – there was a lunchtime but not a lunch break – Doris would go next door to the fish and chip shop. Haddock, mushy peas, lovely.

On the white board, the marker sheets held up by Sellotape, I'd diligently put up the going, and jockey changes, and overweights; otherwise, punters wouldn't know, because there was no television.

Imagination took its place, mental pictures of what might be happening, informed, or misinformed, by the Extel commentary. No television, no FOBTs, no evening or Sunday opening, a world dominated by the horses and the dogs. And Kath.

When I went back, years later, the shop was gone. I hope Kath had retired by then.

BETTING SHOP SURVEY *Racing Post*, 19 June 1999

We are proud to present the first survey to be carried out by my mate Mart on the pavement outside Ladbrokes, just after the last at Royal Ascot.

1. Back any winners? (Mart explained that this was a 'warm-up question' to win participants' confidence.)

2. You are involved in three successive photofinishes. Do you come out best in (a) one of them (b) two of them (c) all three of them (d) yes, that's right. What a game, eh?

3. What is your view of the following statement? Bookmakers' computer forecasts are an excellent product, regularly modernised for the benefit of customers. Studying the formulae can provide hours of entertainment. I am looking forward eagerly to the next improvement. (a) agree (b) strongly agree.

4. You have backed a particular horse on its last four runs but have been rewarded only with disappointment. Your patience is finally exhausted; this time you abandon it. Does the horse (a) win at 6-4 favourite (b) win at 6-1 (c) win at 25-1 (d) what do you think?

5. As a punter, how would you describe yourself? (a) unlucky (b) very unlucky (c) you wouldn't believe it if I told you.

6. What lessons have you learnt from Royal Ascot? (a) If you are bald, don't stand in the sun (b) Never expect a bookmaker to say, 'Yes, stuffed the punters something rotten. I shouldn't think they've got a tenner left between them. That Michael Tabor won't be back for a while.'

7. It's two minutes to the off. You are standing outside a telephone kiosk, waiting to ring your bookmaker. Sharon is in the kiosk, giggling at her boyfriend. She leaves, but they were off right on time. Does the horse you would have backed (a) win by five lengths at 20-1 (b) win by three lengths at 16-1?

8. It's two minutes to the off. You are standing outside a telephone kiosk, waiting to ring your bookmaker. Sharon leaves and, luckily, they are late off. Does the horse you back (a) lose by a short head (b) lose by a head (c) lose by a neck after stumbling ten yards from the line (d) never get a mention?

9. How many of Ladbrokes' pens did you nick last year?

10. It is a truth universally acknowledged, and probably enshrined in the constitution, that if you back a couple of winners to small stakes, as soon as you increase your stakes, all selections will get stuffed. True or false?

11. Which expression is more irritating? (a) your money is only lent (b) you backed it each-way, didn't you?

12. Why does that bloke in the blue pullover always stick his pen through the newspaper?

13. This year's Classic form is the worst there has ever been. True or false? (The answer is true. There have already been two Derby winners rated 34 and 58,

May King Mayhem and Mr Fortywinks, in the Ladies' Derbys at Newmarket and Ripon, respectively. According to Mart, this question was designed to weed out the know-alls.)

14. What betting shops need is (a) more racing, especially in the mornings and on Christmas Day (b) noisier machines, and more of them (c) more pens that work.

15. You couldn't lend us a few quid, could you?

TERRY RAMSDEN *Racing Post*, 23 November 1999

The dark, shoulder-length hair, just the same. Still the black polo-neck shirt. Ten years on and more, the chirpy cockiness hasn't died. 'I'm not from Essex,' says Terry Ramsden, 'I'm from Enfield.' People were always getting that wrong.

Wayne, the big minder, has gone, but Ramsden, 47 now, is much the same; only the bank balance is different. He is working on it, in the Berkeley Hotel, mobile phone ring, ring, ringing.

'I am the ultimate resilient man,' says Ramsden. 'I've been stripped to the bone, lost my money, lost my reputation, lost my marriage. I've been in prison, bankrupted, but it takes a very hard shot to stop Terry Ramsden. I'm a very bright person. I'm entrepreneurial. I make money. That's what I do. A lot of people respect my ability, some in this country who aren't bigots, some in the US. We will see what Terry Ramsden can do. Life is not quite over yet.'

It came close. Racing has seen many rockets rise and fall, but few have risen as fast or fallen as hard as Ramsden. During the mid-1980s, he shot across racing's sky, burning with a fierce, firefly light, then disappeared, leaving barely a trace.

Ramsden's father, Alfred, was a telephone engineer. His mother, Florence, was a cleaner in a factory. When Terry was 16, he left school and got a job as a clerk at a City stockbroker's. When he realised that he was making a lot more for the firm than they were paying him, Terry set up on his own.

He specialised in the Japanese market, gambling on a rising market. In the mid-1980s, the market of the Rising Sun kept on rising. In 1984, Ramsden bought Glen International and, in three years, increased its turnover from £18,000 to £3.5 billion. The money poured in, and the money poured out. Ferraris and Rolls-Royces, jet planes and Walsall Football Club, strings of houses and strings of racehorses.

Ramsden says he was too busy to enjoy them. 'Everyone who worked for me had a nice time enjoying my money. I was too busy, always first in, last out, still am. I still work 15 or 16 hours a day.'

Ramsden registered as a racehorse owner in 1981 but his fearsome spell stretched from a few days before the 1984 Irish One Thousand Guineas to a day at Redcar in October 1988, when Up The Kop carried his royal blue and white hoops for the last time.

In May 1984, Jack Fisher and Benny Schmidt-Bodner were asked if they would sell Katies. Their filly had won a small race at Leicester before finishing third in the Group 3 Princess Elizabeth Stakes at Epsom. Fisher and Schmidt-Bodner would gleefully have accepted £200,000. Ramsden brought £500,000 round on a scooter.

That Saturday, at the Curragh, Katies won the Irish One Thousand Guineas at 20-1 and, less than a month later, beat Pebbles to land the Coronation Stakes at Royal Ascot, at 11-2. 'I'm a stockbroker from Enfield,' said Mick Ryan's new owner. 'I've got long hair and I like a bet.' Ramsden liked a bet so much that Katies was said to have won him £1 million. 'It wasn't £1 million,' says Ramsden, 'it was £2 million. That was one of my three biggest wins. Katies at Royal Ascot, Motivator at Cheltenham, and Cry For The Clown at Ripon.'

Motivator's win in the 1986 Coral Golden Hurdle Final won Ramsden a small fortune, but he says it would have been a larger one, £6 million, if Brunico had finished first instead of second in the following day's Triumph Hurdle.

As well as Ryan, Ramsden sent his horses to Alan Bailey, Rod Simpson and Jenny Pitman. Stearsby won the 1986 Welsh National, Not So Silly the 1987 Ayr Gold Cup. Yet Ramsden's string was more about quantity, 75 or more horses at its peak, than quality, and it was his punting that got him noticed. A fortnight before the 1986 Grand National, he bought Mick Easterby's Aintree hope, Mr Snugfit. Carrying Ramsden's reputed £50,000 each-way, the 13-2 favourite finished fourth to West Tip.

Ramsden's bets were too big for most bookmakers to handle. If you took Ramsden on, you couldn't make a balanced book. It was him or you. Usually, it was him.

'My betting was based on what trainers told me,' he says. 'I betted too emotionally.' His biggest single losing bet was £1 million, on Below Zero. Ramsden believes that jockeys on other horses were bribed to hamper his runner. 'I was told about a man called George,' he says. 'If he couldn't bribe the jockey to stop one, he'd bribe the other jockeys to stop it.'

For a spell in the mid-1980s, Ladbrokes' profit-and-loss account was shaped by Ramsden's betting. Their shareholders had a lot to thank him for. According to an affidavit filed by the City of London Police, in 1985-86 Ramsden's gambling losses totalled £26 million; the following year, £23 million; in 1987-88, a mere £9 million. By then, the game was over £58 million in three years.

Ramsden says it isn't true. 'If Ladbrokes were running a confidential credit operation, what were they doing releasing the figures? Even if it was £30 million over five or six years, so what? Those sums for a man of my capabilities are no big deal, are they? You have to put it in perspective. At that time Glen International would take regular, daily, £20 million to £30 million punts on the stock market. Was gambling a problem? An annoyance, and that's about it.'

Ramsden is convinced that he didn't always get a run for his money. 'Could anyone,' he asks, 'gamble as badly as I am supposed to have done?'

At the beginning of 1988 Ramsden still had 50 horses in training, 29 of them with Bailey, but the glossy cover concealed an empty barrel. The previous year, Glen International had collapsed and, in August 1987, Ladbrokes took Ramsden to Tattersalls Committee, where he agreed to repay debts of £2 million in instalments. By the end of the year, he had announced his withdrawal from race sponsorship and the sale of most of his bloodstock. In October 1988, Ramsden was back in front of Tattersalls Committee after failing to keep up with his payments to Ladbrokes. The Jockey Club warned him off, bringing Ramsden's colourful but painful experience of the Turf to an abrupt end.

His opinion of Ladbrokes isn't a high one and, at the time, many punters felt that chasing a man who had done so much to boost Ladbrokes' profits was like demanding Ramsden's limbs when they had already had his body. 'What sort of company is it that takes a cash bet in one of its shops, on Point Of Light to win the 1989 Abernant Stakes, £32,000 to come, pays out £7,000 in cash and a cheque for the rest, then stops the cheque?' he asks.

'I still think well of Mick Ryan, Alan Bailey, Celia Radband [an amateur rider], Mick Miller and Geoff Lewis. And Clive Brittain is the nicest man in racing, no side to him. I was always very well received in Ireland, and at Ayr, but in England it was "Oh, God, it's him again," despite my giving maybe £2 million to charity and in sponsorship.'

In 1988, Ramsden was still billed, mistakenly, as the 57th richest person in Britain. Three years later, he was prisoner No. 95899 in a Los Angeles jail, trying to give the gang leaders who shared his floor a reason for not killing him. Massively in debt, Ramsden had fled to the US, and the Serious Fraud Office was trying to extradite him.

'The violence was a nightmare,' recalls Ramsden. 'It was a madhouse. They were all in gangs, they all wanted to kill each other.' On New Year's Eve, 1991, a pipe burst and the floor was flooded. Two Mexicans, Silva and Valencia, were wrongly accused of causing the damage and taken to 'the hole.' No one came out of 'the hole.' Ramsden prepared their defence, persuaded all the warring inmates to sign it, and the men were released. 'I was carried round the floor like an FA Cup winner. That's how I survived, by doing legal work for inmates. Otherwise I'd have come back in a body bag.'

Early in 1992, Ramsden agreed to return to Britain. Arriving at Heathrow, he was asked if he had anything to say. 'Yes,' he replied, 'never fly BA World Traveller Class.' Soon after his return, he was declared bankrupt, with the Inland Revenue claiming £21.5 million.

In 1993, Ramsden was convicted of having fraudulently induced finance houses to invest in Glen International, but Judge Henry Pownall was satisfied that it was a case of criminal recklessness rather than deliberate dishonesty, and gave him a two-year suspended sentence. Ramsden still insists that, if Glen International's credit lines hadn't been shut down overnight, all would have been well. 'I didn't hide behind the corporate veil. I am an honourable man. I used my own money to try and protect the company. I shouldn't have done.'

Bankrupt, separated from his wife and said to be reliant on help from friends, Ramsden was soon under fresh investigation, for alleged breaches of the conditions of his bankruptcy. In 1998, Ramsden was sentenced to 21 months in prison for having concealed assets from bankruptcy officials, including the £77,000 he had won from William Hill during York's May meeting in 1992. Between August 1992 and December 1993, Ramsden was said to have received over £300,000 from a trust set up in New York in 1982, including sums paid to his family.

Ramsden served just over ten months, mainly at Stanford Hill prison in Kent, leaving just after this year's Cheltenham Festival, to make way for Jonathan Aitken [a former Cabinet minister jailed for perjury].

His father died during the investigation and his mother died, in Ramsden's arms, on Mother's Day last year. 'The worst thing of all was coming out of prison, having my mum and dad dead, and having nowhere to live. I don't pretend it's only affected me,' Ramsden says, showing me a photograph of his son, Jake. 'I don't have the same friends as before. I've reclassified people who like to call themselves my friends as acquaintances, apart from one or two close ones.'

Ramsden is critical of the lack of help provided for prisoners on their release. 'The probation service's rehabilitation plan for Terry Ramsden was just to make him check in as often as possible. Lesser men reoffend because they have no money, nowhere to live and no one cares. Today I am running programmes of assistance for offenders. My personal financial circumstances are not what they were, but I am doing my best to change things, and still helping people I believe need helping. That's the real Terry Ramsden.'

Ramsden has been busy on the internet, buying websites, making deals. 'I am involved with Netdive, which is part-owned by Juniper, a Nasdaq-quoted company. Its technology is two generations ahead of its competitors. In a year or two, it will be a leading internet company.' Then there is cyberbookie.com and wannapunt. com, vehicles for Ramsden's protégé, Gary Calder. 'I will put up £10,000,' says Ramsden. 'Gary against anyone. That's how much I rate him.'

And there is talk of a book and a film, *True Brit, True Grit*. 'It's not the money,' says Ramsden, 'my life's never been about money. The buzz is to do it, to see a company become huge from nothing, and Netdive will become huge. I'd like to own horses again but I don't want to beat my head against a brick wall. I offered a compromise to Ladbrokes, with me making a substantial donation to charity, but they refused. Mike Dillon said, "I couldn't sit in the same room as Terry Ramsden and face my board of directors". I'm still involved. I still follow the horses. I still have a bet. I miss going to the races but, is it going to break my heart? No".'

Ramsden picks up his mobile phone. 'Whatever else you say about Terry Ramsden, he was good for racing.'

Terry Ramsden's racehorse owning days were not quite over. Between 2003 and 2005, Jake The Snake, Royal Atalza and Banjo Patterson won five Flat races between them in Ramsden's new colours, but he was soon embroiled in further financial and legal battles. In 2012, Ramsden returned to the winner's enclosure, when Jake The Snake won for him, again, at Goodwood.

JOHN MORT GREEN, ALIAS 'THE BUTTERFLY'

Racing Post, 30 August 2011

He was called the Butterfly because he flitted around the betting ring, from pitch to pitch, chasing the odds, watching who was betting, on what, for how much, ears open. Either that, or it was the incident with the Japanese girl in a cocktail bar in Tokyo. She became upset when John Mort Green spoke to another girl. 'You no good, you butterfly,' she said.

The Butterfly flitted around the world, full of colour and life, stories and sayings, and poems. 'Inflate my ego gently, tell them heaven sent me. I'm not in racing for the bread, I'm in it for the gravy.' And the champagne, the girls, the Rolls Royces.

Mort, rather than John or Green, was born in Brisbane in 1929, the son of bookmaker Thomas Mort Green. Mort worked for his father, listening, watching, learning. 'Never refuse cash,' said his father, who gave Mort £1 a day betting money. Mort did well, and decided to make gambling his life and living. 'Son,' said his father, 'if you are going to back horses, prepare yourself for a life of poverty.' Poverty was not on Mort's agenda, and he preferred his own saying, 'One thing you learn about being broke is that you don't want to be broke for long. Tenacity of purpose and the will to win. That's what saw me through.'

In 1960, Mort visited England, and watched St Paddy win the Derby. In Queensland, they raced only two days a week; in Britain, they raced six and, on Sundays, there was racing in Paris. In 1963, Mort moved to London, set himself up in an apartment in the White House, near Regent's Park, and set to work.

He worked hard, studying the form from 8.00am each day. 'I pray every night,' said Mort, 'and all my prayers start with, "Please God, save me from tomorrow's good thing." Systems don't work, but methods do.' There was the form, and the people. Mort knew about horses – in Australia he competed in trotting races – and was good with people. 'Horses don't talk but jockeys do,' was a creed with the Butterfly, who had watched a bookmaker in Australia and noticed that, when he pushed out the odds on a particular jockey's mount, the horse always lost. It made Mort think, for racing in the 1960s was a world away from racing today. Much more often, a punter's money was lost before the race had started.

Mort, charismatic and willing to pay for information, established a network of contacts. 'I pride myself on one thing,' he said, in 1965, 'I'm never on dead meat. I might bet ten horses a year that are being stopped. The average punter might back 300 and never know that his horses were dead from the beginning. You have to know your jockeys.' Mort did know his jockeys, and the ones he knew best were from Australia.

The 1960s were years when several top Australian jockeys were based in Europe; Bill Williamson and Bill Pyers, George Moore and Russ Maddock, Scobie Breasley, Ron Hutchinson, Garnie Bougoure and Pat Glennon. Mort was a friendly face in a sometimes hostile world and was often told things that others were not. 'Those who know do not say, those who say do not know,' was one of Mort's mottos, but those who knew did sometimes tell Mort, and Mort listened. 'If they operated on me,' he said, 'they'd find a stomach full of ears.' Exiting the parade ring, a jockey would sometimes quickly rub a finger across his upper lip, to signify that he was trying. If he rubbed it on his silks, he wasn't.

Average earnings in the mid-1960s were £28 a week. One way and another, Mort reckoned to make £200, equivalent to about £3,000 today. A chauffeur drove him to the races in a Rolls Royce, from which Mort emerged wearing expensive suits, hand-made shoes and Pierre Cardin hats, with a butterfly on the back, shipped from Paris. 'I'm full of money,' he'd declare. When asked the time, he'd look at his watch and reply, '15 diamonds past two rubies.' His binoculars were Zeiss 850s. 'They're so powerful,' said Mort, 'that you can see the jockeys changing their minds.'

Mort was interested in who was backing what, and other gamblers were interested in what Mort was going to back. 'Do you want a tip?' he'd ask the curious. 'Don't eat sausages.' Some days, he'd reach an agreement with a bookmaker. The agreement was that, whatever bet Mort put on, was void. Those watching and listening thought Mort was backing one horse, when he, or his helpers, had already backed another.

In 1965, *Sports Illustrated* devoted a double page spread to the Butterfly, who told an incredulous American journalist, 'Racecourses during the day for business, Mayfair at night for pleasure.' 1965 was a pleasurable year for Mort, the best.

Etienne Pollet had a star in his Chantilly stable, Sea Bird II. He was ridden by Pat Glennon, who told Mort that the horse was too fractious to be shipped to Epsom. Instead, the target was the French Derby. That's what everyone thought. Then, less than two weeks before the Epsom Derby, Glennon phoned Mort again. There had been a change of plan, Sea Bird II would run at Epsom. Racing news from France travelled slowly in those days. Sir Peter O'Sullevan was the first with the news but by then, the Butterfly had flown.

Bookmakers, seeking mug money, quoted Sea Bird II at 20-1, or longer, expecting him to be a non-runner. Mort borrowed some overalls and travelled around London, from betting shop to betting shop, never putting on more than £8. At the end of a tiring day, he had laid out £860. The average price of a house was less than £4,000. The Butterfly stood to win five houses. On Derby Day, he stood in the grandstand and, as the field rounded Tattenham Corner, turned to his neighbour and said, in his Australian way, 'time and margin.' The result was already obvious, it was just a matter of how far, and how fast.

Shortly afterwards, the Butterfly booked a six-month luxury cruise on the Queen Mary, to America and Japan, Bombay and Beirut. Money was for living, and Mort knew how he wanted to live, flying to Paris on Sundays, enjoying the company of bubbly champagne and bubbly women. Champagne sometimes, always beer. 'I'm a bar-room brawler,' said Mort, his boldness defying his slim build, which explained his Australian nickname of Soupbones. He was certainly a bar-room talker.

In 1969, he wrote a book, *Come Fly with the Butterfly*, revealing his ten secrets of successful punting, and describing himself as 'a professional punter with good looks and good sense and a damned good bank balance.'

In 1974, Mort returned to Australia, where he was known as the 'Voice of Racing.' Ten years later, he was briefly banned in connection with the Fine Cotton 'ring-in,' when Bold Personality won a race at Eagle Farm in the guise of Fine Cotton. Mort, tipped off about the ring-in, had backed the horse heavily. He spent much of his enforced absence in California, preaching the word of the Lord from 'The Glory

Bus.' 'They loved the way I said Calvary,' Mort recalled. 'I had their eyes rolling in their sockets. Myself, I don't believe in God.'

It was fitting that, in the early 1990s, Mort arrived at Royal Ascot dressed as an archdeacon, with a purple shirt and gold cross. Another year, he played the part of chef, complete with the traditional headwear. At the time, he was living in a Belgravia apartment owned by a Saudi Arabian prince, who lent Mort his Rolls Royce and chauffeur, who drove him to Maxwell's fish and chip restaurant in Belsize Park. He was always welcome at restaurants, for the Butterfly believed in tipping generously, before dinner, during dinner and after dinner.

Mort returned to Britain permanently in 1994. Now 82, his gambling days behind him, he lives a quiet life in Kent with his lovely wife, Rosemary. 'My wings are closed now,' he says. 'My race is run. I'm out of the money and in the departure lounge.' He says he has lost his panache but remains a unique character. 'Fame is fleeting,' says the Butterfly, 'memories last forever.' And a favourite, 'Laugh often, it is life's lubricant.'

22
COURT 73

Rod Fabricius, High Court undertaker.

In 2008, racing was back in the Royal Courts of Justice, its home from home, for another expensive legal battle.

For over 20 years, Satellite Information Services, with major bookmakers the major shareholders, had been the sole suppliers of live pictures of horseracing into betting shops. In 2007, the monopoly was broken when TurfTV, operated by Amrac, a joint-venture between Alphameric and 30 Racing UK racecourses, signed exclusive media rights deals with those racecourses, as well as with Ascot, leaving SIS to supply pictures from the other 29 courses, also on an exclusive basis.

Bookmakers complained that, with two picture suppliers, they were being asked to pay more for an inferior service. They claimed that Amrac's exclusive deals breached UK and EU competition law and constituted illegal price fixing. Amrac counter-claimed that the major bookmakers had colluded to resist TurfTV's entry into the market. Mr Justice Morgan was asked to give his opinion, but that was very much later. It seemed longer.

CALL THE ... ER... DOCTOR *Racing Post*, 20 May 2008

I do hope they paint Court 73 later, to give us the excitement of watching the paint dry. Unfortunately, Court 73 doesn't need painting. It's one of those modern, functional courtrooms that makes you wish that the extraordinarily tedious hearing of Bookmakers' Afternoon Greyhound Services Ltd & ors versus Amalgamated Racing Ltd & ors was moved to one of the proper, Gothic courtrooms that are in another part of the High Court.

I expect they've put racing and betting in Court 73 because they've already been in all the others. Nowadays, courtrooms are where these industries conduct their business, occasionally breaking off for a trip to the Old Bailey, by way of a change.

Chris Bell and Alan Ross (Messrs Big at Ladbrokes) are here, along with Ian Spearing and David Hood (Messrs Big at Hills), Tom Kelly (Mr Big at Bags), Terry Ellis (Mr Big at SIS), and Simon Bazalgette (Mr Big at TurfTV). David Harding (formerly Mr Big at Hills) is sitting on his own, in the witness box.

There are a lot of bookmakers, but even more lawyers. They love racing and betting, which many of them rely on for a living. Today, there seem to be 21 members of the legal profession in attendance, including a dozen wearing wigs and one wearing a turban. They must cost a few Group 1 races every day. Let's hope it's worth it.

Peter Roth QC, for Amrac, stands up and says nothing that merits reporting. Bespectacled, Roth has a thin face, featuring a forehead with pronounced frown marks, and a voice that does not boom. I'm glad my mother isn't here. She wouldn't be able to hear a word.

Harding is wearing a grey suit, reddish tie, greyish hair and spectacles, which he takes off to read. They are not, I submit, reading glasses. Brian Doctor QC, also for Amrac, is in charge of asking Harding questions that Harding would rather he didn't ask him.

Doctor's approach is slow and hesitant and frequently features the word 'er,' occasionally followed by the word 'um.' Reports of the proceedings are unlikely to contain the words 'electric,' 'breathtaking,' or 'sprinted.' Doctor clearly does not believe that the end of the world is nigh, although, after a few more hours of this, it may seem desirable.

Doctor, one way and another, suggests that the big three bookmakers had an agreement, or at least an understanding, that they would not sign up to TurfTV, whose unwelcome arrival they worked together to repulse. Harding denies the existence of any such agreement or understanding.

What does soporific mean? As time passes (I'm guessing), Harding reveals the hint of a sore throat. Do they still make those TCP lozenges? They don't really help but they make you feel as if you're doing something. No one offers Harding a lozenge. He will have to wait for lunchtime, thoughts of which creep up with increasing insistence.

At 1.00pm, we are allowed out on parole. At 2.00pm, parole ends, and Harding explains that he and Neil Goulden, Gala Coral's managing director, had 'a strong banter relationship.' When Hills reported higher average profits per shop than Ladbrokes, Goulden sent Harding a text message reading, 'Well done, that's stuffed them.' Harding's relationship with Bell was 'a bit more acrimonious.' They didn't have a banter relationship, or exchange texts.

Later, Harding explains that Hills had considered changing their strategy towards TurfTV when they discovered that, if Ladbrokes signed up, they were equipped to begin broadcasting pictures immediately, whereas Hills would require several months to install all the necessary equipment. Ladbrokes, says Harding, were 'likely to stab us in the back.' Doctor suggests that this expression hints at an alliance between Hills and Ladbrokes. Harding disagrees.

The afternoon drifts away, as do my thoughts. I wonder how Ofarel D'Airy got on at Newton Abbot?

UM ... ERM *Racing Post,* 21 May 2008

Today, it's Ian Spearing's turn to sit in the witness box in Court 73. If he was Cherie Blair (he isn't), Spearing would probably enjoy the attention. Like Cherie, Ian has just had his hair done.

In less than three hours, we learn that Spearing's middle name is John, that his birthday is on 11 September, that he didn't get a Blackberry until March 2007, and that, only a week ago, he became William Hill's corporate affairs director. Yes, I think that just about covers it.

Not everyone who was here yesterday is here today (they're probably pretending to be dead), but Chris Bell and Alan Ross of Ladbrokes are manfully sitting through it, which makes you wonder who is running Ladbrokes. Maybe they've brought back Cyril Stein.

Brian Doctor QC is here, asking most of the questions. I hope his feet are sturdy, because he stands on them a lot. I expect he's wearing sensible shoes which, when I was a child, used to be associated with Clarks. Their shoe shops used to have

X-ray machines you stood on to see the bones in your feet. Everyone who grew up wearing sensible shoes will probably die of foot cancer.

Since Doctor is slightly older than yesterday, and some of us feel a lot older, it's no surprise that he hasn't speeded up. I don't know what the most popular word in the world is but, in Court 73, Doctor is a great advocate of the word 'er.' Here an er, there an er, everywhere an er-er. Or an er-um.

Finally, at 12.22pm, I decide to count the number of times that Doctor says 'er,' as well as 'um.' I soon discover that Amrac's barrister has developed a strong affection for the closely related word 'erm,' possibly because it combines the best of both 'er' and 'um.' It is, a barrister might argue, a way of saving the court's time. Anyway, during the seven minutes between 12.23pm and 12.30pm, several of them occupied by Spearing's answers, Doctor says 'um' five times, 'er' 19 times and 'erm' 15 times.

Between the ers, ums and erms, Doctor asks a lot of questions all seeking the answer, 'Yes, I admit it, Hills colluded with Ladbrokes and Coral to throttle TurfTV at, or shortly after, its unwelcome birth.' Spearing doesn't say that. Instead, wearing a dark blue suit, light blue shirt and blue tie, he denies there is any truth in any of Doctor's allegations.

Doctor invites Spearing to consider various communications, then places an interpretation upon them that Spearing resolutely rejects. Spearing considers it natural that the big bookmakers, thinking independently, should have reached the same, implacably hostile, position in regard to TurfTV. 'It doesn't take a rocket scientist to work out that we were all in the same boat,' says Spearing. 'It's blindingly obvious.'

If they turned Court 73 into a transatlantic aircraft (unlikely, admittedly), passengers would arrive at Chicago having enjoyed a decent flight's sleep. It's difficult not to let your mind wander. I find myself considering which occupant of Court 73 I fancy most. It's not creditable but it is human and, I submit, under the circumstances, forgivable.

I wonder what jokes Doctor's surname provoked at school. 'I'm a Doctor. Take all your clothes off. Now, what seems to be the trouble?' At times, I think Doctor may be from South Africa, or Australia. I expect he comes from mid-Sussex. There's something about Mr Justice Morgan's accent, too. Is he Irish, or Scottish, or Welsh? Or English?

Now and again he intervenes with questions of his own. Unusually for a judge, Morgan does not wear spectacles and looks remarkably normal. He does not have enormously bushy eyebrows, nor a large growth on his nose. I, for one, have every confidence in him.

The gentleman in front of me is doing quite well with his Sudoku. Later, he does quite well with his crossword. I wonder how Bell will do. It's his turn tomorrow.

ANYONE FOR A GUILLOTINE? *Racing Post*, 22 May 2008

The day opens with shocking news. The case of Bags & ors v Amrac & ors may not finish until after 20 June.

The judge may as well have put his black cap on. Please hide any ropes, barbiturates and tall buildings, just to be on the safe side. Even Mr Justice Morgan is desperate. 'No one's asking for a guillotine?' he asks, possibly praying for the answer, 'Yes, please, m'lud, me first.' Peter Roth QC, for Amrac, declares himself in favour of the guillotine under certain circumstances, possibly when a neck belonging to Bags's legal team becomes available.

At 10.50am, Christopher Bell, Ladbrokes' chief executive, blows his nose, promises to tell the truth, and sits down in the witness box. It will be a long time before he stands up again, unlike Mr Roth. Roth, his spectacles perched on the end of his legal nose, is difficult to hear. We'll just have to hope that he doesn't say anything important. It's a pity it's not his brother, the one who wrote *Portnoy's Complaint*.

Bell quickly slips into the language of the witness box, where 'yes' is rarely heard but 'that is correct, my lord,' is commonplace as, in Bell's case, is 'to be quite frank.'

Certain things soon become clear. Bell believes that, 'if there is an initiative, it's usually the bookmakers who end up paying for it,' and he is not an admirer of TurfTV, which he believes, passionately, offers bookmakers a worse service at a much higher price.

The subject of price occupies Court 73 for some time. Roth presses Bell to acknowledge that it was misleading to cite a price of £6,500 a year for TurfTV's service, since Ladbrokes had been offered the service for £3,500. 'It was still too expensive,' Bell insists, several times. 'We wanted a much lower price than any of the ones being offered. I had been paying £1,600 and I was being asked to pay considerably more for a retrograde service.'

It would be nice to judge for ourselves. There are plenty of screens scattered around the courtroom. They could show Goodwood and Ayr this afternoon, with the sound off. It might attract a few more customers, who seem to have been lured away by the relative excitement of Bath Plug Supplies Ltd v Ceramic Tiles (Salford).

Suddenly, high drama grips Court 73. 'I put it to you,' says Roth, thumping his fist on one of the 375 lever arch files on which his case depends, 'you have lied, and lied, and lied again, to save the company you love.'

I'm sorry, Bell's right, you can't believe everything you read in the press. Roth didn't say that at all, although I wish he had. Instead, he puts it to Bell that Ladbrokes had an understanding with Hills and Coral not to take TurfTV. Bell denies the allegation, in conformity with a now well-established pattern.

It's a bit like 'The Archers'. You feel you could miss a few hours and hardly notice. It's 12.47pm. It has been for some time. Please, please, please say it's lunchtime. But Roth is relentless.

Bell plays him like Geoffrey Boycott. If all else fails (it has) there's always daydreaming. Give me a few minutes and I'll be working out what to do with the £5 million I've just won on the Scoop6. Oh, and my horse has just won the Derby.

After lunch, Roth steps down, and Helen Davies QC, for SIS, steps up. Davies's hair (long and gingerish) is more interesting than Roth's (scant) but her script is no more gripping. Roth returns, and Alan Spencer Ross, a director of all sorts of things, including Ladbrokes, takes Bell's place. Ross has been in court virtually throughout – 'I've enjoyed every minute of it,' he says.

Ross wears several hats and Roth explores which hats Ross wore on which occasions. Finally, just as I'm about to feign a coronary, Mr Justice Morgan grants a reprieve. Oh, thank you, m'lud.

BUILDING VALUE *Racing Post*, 23 May 2008

What colour is that outfit? It's not brown, yet not quite red. For a moment, I thought it was rust, but now I'm not sure. Whatever colour it is, Janet Sheila Walker is wearing it in the witness box. I keep hoping that one of the barristers will ask her, 'Miss Walker, I put it to you that you are a scarlet woman, are you not?' 'No, I'm dark red.'

Walker, Ascot's financial and commercial director, immediately reaches for the gin, or possibly the water, and answers questions put to her by Nicholas Green QC, for Bags. My bet is that Green is a wine connoisseur. He's a wine connoisseur, while Peter Roth QC, for the other side, is a cyclist, as well as a character in a Charles Dickens' novel, possibly *Bleak House*, involved in the case of Jarndyce and Jarndyce. It's just a hunch. Anyway, Walker comes later, after another protracted dose of Roth versus Alan Ross, of Ladbrokes.

We discover that, on 6 March 2007, at the RAC Club, Ross beat Andrew Gould, Jockey Club Racecourses' finance director, at snooker, and that Ross and Alan Morcombe, Alphameric's chief executive, are friends. They dine together, lunch together, and go to the races together. Nowadays, they probably watch Turf TV together.

Proceedings seem a little perkier today, and when Roth says, 'Something did happen, Mr Ross, didn't it?' I thought he was going to show us that he was a proper barrister, one who would have continued, 'Because you took a hammer and clubbed the fish and chip shop manager to death, did you not, Mr Ross? And why? Because the mushy peas were not to your liking.' But Roth didn't say that. Pity.

Of the dozen barristers wearing wigs, eight are men and four are women. Is this evidence of the progress women have made, or of the distance still to travel? Does the fact that more than a quarter of the occupants of Court 73 are wearing spectacles suggest the law is blind? Will that machine in the corridor be working today, so I can buy a Twix?

No one answers questions with a 'yes.' Where Ladbrokes' Chris Bell favoured 'that is correct,' Ascot's Walker favours 'it is.' 'Is it true you are the only person in this courtroom who is not dressed for a funeral?' 'It is.'

Walker is articulate, measured, calm and, at 2.30pm, she completes her testimony and leaves, possibly to dash to the Hills' shop round the corner to see how Sixties Icon gets on at Goodwood (TurfTV), a pleasure denied the rest of us.

Next up (there are rumoured to be more than 20 more witnesses, heaven help us) is William Derby, York's chief executive. Derby is not wearing a dark-red skirt. He's wearing a bright pink one. Sorry, that's a lie. He's wearing a dark suit and bright purplish tie and soon makes it clear he is not a lover of Bags, who held York's media rights until York sold them to Amrac.

Bags fees were 'a source of considerable dissatisfaction.' They weren't high enough, and had a horrible habit of shrinking as the years went by. Bags didn't pay anything for the races shown on terrestrial television and showed no enthusiasm for working as partners to 'build value.' Derby is a great believer in growing value or, as Green puts it, 'making money.' York had 'endured' Bags, which offered 'no channel of communication or dialogue' and no opportunity to work together to grow value. Amrac's arrival offered the prospect of having to endure Bags no longer.

When Tom Kelly, Bags' chief executive, wrote to Derby in 2006, it was a standard 'Dear Sir' letter, the wording of which Derby found 'odd. It didn't feel right.' He did not reply, and Kelly didn't follow up the letter. Unlike Ross and Morcombe, Derby and Kelly do not dine together, lunch together, or go to the races together, although they do occupy Court 73 together.

That's it for today. Good. I think I may go to that Hills' shop and see if I can grow value.

CALL THE UNDERTAKER *Racing Post*, 4 June 2008

Court 73 is considering several cases of asbestosis, possibly even more deadly than the case of Bags & ors versus Amrac & ors, which has been moved upstairs, to Court 76, perhaps to prevent the walls becoming permeated with tedium.

Neither Nicholas Green QC nor any of the other QCs who litter Court 76 inform his lordship, Mr Justice Morgan, that a settlement has been reached. Sadly, a settlement has not been reached, and we carry on where we left off, with the testimony of Roderick Norwood Fabricius, Goodwood's managing director.

Fabricius would make an excellent undertaker. Everything about him smacks of burials. Tall, thin and melancholy, he has the doleful expression of a man forever talking to someone with a freshly deceased relative. At the moment, he would dearly like to bury Bags and SIS, two organisations he regards as different heads of the same monster.

Helen Davies QC (the one with ginger hair) asks most of the questions, on behalf of SIS. Her face reminds me of Auntie Olive, although Olive wasn't a barrister, but a housewife. Every Monday, she washed the family's clothes in a tub with a corrugated washboard. I don't suppose Davies does that. I'm not sure they have housewives any more, or washboards.

Davies is crisp, businesslike. Fabricius is slow and careful, slowly and carefully assuring the court of his low and declining regard for SIS. 'The experience we'd had with SIS was not a happy one, or one that conveyed any sense of partnership,' he testifies. 'One's past experience had been that negotiations proved disappointing, if not futile, in terms of achieving value for the rights we were selling.'

Encouragingly, there is a brisk flow of witnesses, with Fabricius soon followed by Andrew Gould, Gould by John Smee, Smee by Nick Rust. Gould, finance director of Racecourse Investments Limited, a subsidiary of Jockey Club Racecourses, has a grey suit and blue handkerchief but little in the way of hair. The combination of his mouth and the witness box's microphone offers the promise of being able to hear what he has to say. Unfortunately, neither mouth nor microphone are powerful, and they are a long way apart. If my mother were here, she would be telling Gould to speak up, sit up straight and pull his shoulders back. Unfortunately, she isn't. Now he's fiddling with his chin; now with his throat. I suppose it's all right, as long as he doesn't strangle himself.

Briefly, Brian Doctor QC is on his feet, in the cause of Amrac. Three ums, three ers and three erms in just over one minute. He advises Gould, 'That's the page that begins with the word ... um.'

Doctor sits down and Pushpinder Saini QC, for Bags, stands up, to question Smee, group racing director of Jockey Club Racecourses. Smee's tie is enormous, although Smee is not. Saini, clear, straightforward, asks Smee about his relationship with Tom Kelly, Bags chief executive. It is not what it was, a deterioration Smee ascribes to the arrival of an unwelcome challenge to SIS's monopoly. Smee is on the small side, but Rust is not.

Coral's new managing director has a large striped suit (necessary to accommodate his body) and a yellow-and-black tie. Later, it emerges that he also has a blue umbrella. Rust, formerly of BSkyB, does not look like a conventional bookmaker. So there is hope, after all.

This time, it is Peter Roth QC's turn to conduct the interrogation. Evidently I was mistaken in my surmise that Roth is a cyclist. He isn't. Maybe, like George Carter-Stephenson QC, in the Miles Rodgers et al trial, he rides a Harley-Davidson.

Rust is soon removed, to be replaced by Simon Louis Bazalgette, executive chairman of Racing UK and a director of Amrac. He has bushy eyebrows that remind me of an actor – oh, what is his name? I wish Green would ask him. After all, by the time we finish, he's asked him everything else. Well, apart from everything he will ask him tomorrow.

PHYLLOSAN? *Racing Post*, 5 June 2008

Death, where is thy sting? Not in Court 76, where, after 17 days of Bags & ors versus Amrac & ors, it would seem the merest pinprick. Anyway, since time stands still, Court 76's occupants may have become immortal.

At 10.30am, battle resumes between Nicholas Green QC for Bags, tall, patrician, bespectacled, and Simon Bazalgette, for TurfTV, also bespectacled, hunched over the witness box, still sporting flyaway eyebrows.

Like the Somme, it is an enormously long battle in which positions become entrenched, although, so far, there have been fewer deaths. A pattern is established. Green invites Bazalgette to confirm that Green's reading of the document being discussed is correct. Bazalgette declines to do so and presents an alternative interpretation. Green, polite yet persistent, declares that Bazalgette's interpretation flies in the face of the evidence, and invites him to reconsider. Bazalgette, having done so, repeats what he said before. Perhaps it would be helpful if they found some common ground; whether the earth is flat, for instance. You have to start somewhere.

Mr Justice Morgan has a hand over his mouth. The evidence that it is there to stifle a yawn is inconclusive. It has not been established beyond reasonable doubt but, on the balance of probabilities . . .

At 10.45am, the judge declares himself reluctant to interrupt Mr Green's cross-examination, then does so, in an attempt to ensure that time is not absorbed in asking unnecessary questions. Necessary or not, the questions flow on, rather like the Danube, but longer.

Soon, we enter the world of 'exclusive' and 'non-exclusive' rights. Like quicksand, once you have stepped into it, it is very difficult to get out. In a dramatic outburst (all things being relative), Green puts it to Bazalgette that Amrac had been in 'a heightened readiness for war,' with 'litigation uppermost in your mind.' I leave it to you to guess whether Bazalgette replied along the lines of, 'yes, that is correct,' or 'no, that is complete b******s.'

A member of Amrac's legal team passes a note (yellow) to Messrs Peter Roth QC and Brian Doctor QC. It reads, 'Do you want a tuna or prawn mayonnaise sandwich for lunch?' Just guessing.

Those yellow notes, along with pink marker pens, are the lifeblood of the English judicial system. Several decorate the borders of the document Green is studying; several paragraphs highlighted in shocking pink.

I do wish Bazalgette would sit up properly, instead of slouching, and mumbling. Posture isn't what it was. When did you last see a young lady walking across the room with a Bible balanced on her head? Quite. My case rests, m'lud.

Court 76 remains devoted to the subject of exclusivity. Countless files are ordered and studied in its pursuit. The decision by Northern Racing and Arena Leisure to license their rights on an exclusive basis to Bags was, it is suggested, a key moment in the history, if not of the world, then of the part of it that Amrac was seeking to enter.

After lunch, we have more (and more, and more) of the same. No one in Court 76 dies, although several people consider the possibility. I wonder if they still sell Phyllosan, famous years ago for fortifying the over-40s? We could do with some. I've started playing games. I look round the courtroom and try to decide who is likely to die first. I think it could be me.

As I look, I realise that Roth is missing. Where is he? I hope he hasn't had an accident on his Harley-Davidson. Good heavens! Green sits down. I expect his feet are killing him.

Charles Hollander QC, for SIS, stands up – slim, dark eyebrows, large right ear (I can't see his left one) – and takes up the exclusivity baton. As he settles into a question-asking rhythm, he clasps and unclasps his hands, and sways and rocks slightly, without raising serious concerns for his perpendicularity. Finally, at 4.00pm, Bazalgette is released from the witness box. I bet he's pleased. I know I am.

Mr Justice Morgan found against Bags & ors in respect of their claim that Amrac's agreements were in breach of competition rules, a ruling confirmed upon appeal. He found for Bags & ors in respect of Amrac's counter-claim alleging collusion.

GLOSSARY OF RACING AND BETTING TERMS

These appeared at various times in the *Racing Post* between 1999 and 2008.

A bit on the leg. Tall blonde.

Accumulator. Bet requiring punter to make additional selections until one loses.

Ante-post. Arrangement under which punters can continue to bet after their death. Facility for losing six months before a race takes place.

Apprentice race. A race in which small animals who are learning to ride sit on large ones who have no idea who they are, travelling at 30mph.

Auctioneer. Madman armed with a hammer.

Auction races. Races introduced to prove to owners that, however little their horse cost, it was too much.

Backward. Give me a ring in a couple of years and we'll see how he's getting on then.

Betting shop. A bank specialising in deposits.

Betting slips. Weapons of mass destruction.

Blinkers. The first act of desperation.

Bloodstock agent. Person who charges for persuading you to buy a horse for 10 times more than it will soon be worth.

Bookmaker. Wealthy victim of repeated misfortune.

Blunder. A brief incident rendering hours of study redundant.

Bumper. A race for horses that are unsuitable for running on the Flat but can't jump either.

Catch right. Select the one day in the year when the horse feels like trying.

Change legs. Undergo major surgery.

Change of scenery. To remove a horse from one box and place it in another, 300 miles away, in the hope that it might run faster.

Cheekpieces. Another act of desperation (*see also* blinkers, visor, hood, tongue-strap).

Chester Cup. Race for horses whose left legs are shorter than their right ones.

Claiming race. A race in which horses that no one wants to buy can be bought.

Clerk of the course. Official in charge of mistakes.

Computer Straight Forecast. An impenetrable construction designed to remove a punter's shirt from his body.

Court. Place where British horseracing authorities conduct their business.

Depression. Small dip in racing surface. Chronic condition contracted in Ladbrokes.

Dewhurst Stakes. Race staged to decide which horse ante-post punters will lose most money on during the following six months.

Distances. In spread betting, things you should almost always sell but for some reason you keep buying.

Each-way. Opportunity to lose twice in one bet.

Fall. The sudden replacement of hope by despair.

Fire. Attempt to cure a horse by committing arson on it.

First past the post. About to be disqualified.

Foot. Part of leg used for stepping on nails or stones.

Form book. Historical work, useful for predicting what will happen in the past.

Getting out stakes. The final race of the day, offering punters the chance to leap from the frying pan into the fire.

Going. Good to soft, according to the clerk of the course.

Going meter. Mythical device said to indicate the firmness of the ground.

Gone in the wind. Sequel to film starring Clark Gable and Olivia de Havilland.

Good doer. He can't run to save his life but you should see him eat!

Got a leg. Encouraging piece of news passed on to owners by trainers.

Group race. A race in which all the horses are triers. Such races make up only a small proportion of the racing programme.

Handicap. A race in which horses of different abilities are given an equal chance of winning, to the delight of Betfred and the despair of their customers.

Heavy. A description of the going, sometimes at racecourses, more often in William Hill's.

Hold up. Keep a horse at the back of the field until a suitable pocket can be found for it.

Horsebox. A vehicle that does five miles to the gallon, specialising in trips to Hamilton.

House. As in, 'to lose your house.' (*See* spread betting).

Jackpot. A bet in which you select five winners, the requirement being six. (*See also* Scoop6.)

Jockey. Person employed to ruin your day.

Judge. Official with no legal training or sense of justice, about to sentence you.

Jump from fence to fence. Take the most enormous leap between fences.

Keen. A horse that wants to go faster, but only for a while.

Lent. As in, 'your money is only lent.' Lost.

Lucky 15. An argument for strengthening the Trades Descriptions Act.

Maiden handicap. Race for maidens not good enough to win a maiden race.

Maiden race. Race for horses unlikely to win one.

Median auction maiden. Race for horses that were never likely to be much good, and aren't.

Nose. Distance by which you have been beaten.

Off. Term used to describe a horse's sixth run of the season.

Over-reach. Bet too much.

Over the top. Ran badly in the autumn.

Overweight. Excess fat carried by jockey.

Pen. Item stolen from betting shop in order to make you feel that at least you've won something.

Photofinish camera. Equipment employed to prolong the agony.

Prayer. Act of desperation, invariably treated with contempt.

Pull. Run very hard at the start of a race in preparation for running very slowly at the end.

Punter. Noble individual dedicated to hope in defiance of experience.

Queen Alexandra Stakes. Race for sprightly jump horses.

Queue. What is in front of you when you are about to be just too late to back a 16-1 winner.

Recapture. As in, 'if he can recapture his old form.' Used to be good but is hopeless now.

Replay. Watch it go horribly wrong, again.

Sales race. A surcharge entitling racehorse owners to a ticket in a lottery.

Saver. Bet placed by punter in the belief that two bets will be less expensive than one.

Seller. A race in which the winner is offered for sale to people who don't want it. A race in which horses that have no value are allotted one.

Setback. Common disorder in which a racehorse retains the ability to generate bills but loses the ability to race.

Short-head. Narrow defeat.

Sore shins. The result of a young racehorse putting one leg in front of another.

Spread betting. An exciting introduction to the official receiver.

Starter. Official who waits until the one you have backed is facing the wrong way, then pulls a lever.

Stayer. A slow horse.

Steward. Official employed to disabuse you of the belief that you have just backed your first winner for three months.

Talking horse. A horse that runs fast on the Newmarket gallops but slowly on the Rowley Mile course.

Trainer. Person employed to explain that your horse ran a lot better than it appeared to, despite finishing last, again.

200,000 gns yearling. 2,000gns two-year-old.

Unlucky. Horse that took part in a race but did not win it.

Vet (*noun*). Creature renowned for its enormous bill.

Vet (*verb*). To examine a horse with a view to discovering why you should not have bought it.

Win. A spot of absent-mindedness by God.

Winning post. White stick with a red circle on it situated in the wrong place.

Wintered well. It's almost April and he's still alive.

Worked well. Visited the gallops.

Zetland, Lord. Aristocrat named after the Zetland Gold Cup at Redcar.

AU REVOIR

I hope you enjoyed that dip into the wide-rippling pool of horseracing: an exciting sport, sometimes infuriating, constantly engaging, a teasing crossword puzzle, a testing big dipper.

Racing is rich in history, with its heroes and villains, human and equine, playing their parts at a wonderful array of racecourses and racing stables. It has everything: drama and suspense, unbridled joy and desperate disappointment, fine horses and skilful horsemen. Brave, modest riders, too. It is difficult to be a prima donna when the next obstacle may send you sprawling in the mud, clutching another broken collarbone.

I love it – the racing, the gambling, the people, the fun, and the writing, too. Sometimes I reflect on what Arthur Jones told me. To adapt it, racing is what I've spent much of my adult life doing, and I would do it again, because you meet so many nice people. Obviously, you meet a few complete shits, too.

So, in the word of that horrible expression: Enjoy!